Garden Glory

Garden Glory

An Oral History of the New York Knicks

Dennis D'Agostino

TRIUMPH
BOOKS
CHICAGO

Library of Congress Cataloging-in-Publication Data

D'Agostino, Dennis.
  Garden glory : an oral history of the New York Knicks / Dennis D'Agostino.
     p. cm.
  ISBN 1-57243-541-0 (hc)
    1. New York Knickerbockers (Basketball team)–History. 2. Basketball players–New York (State)–New York–Interviews.   I. Title.

GV885.52.N4D34 2003
796.323'64'097471–dc22

2003058164

This book is available in quantity at special discounts for your group or organization. For further information, contact:
Triumph Books
601 South LaSalle Street
Suite 500
Chicago, Illinois 60605
(312) 939-3330
Fax (312) 663-3557

Printed in U.S.A.
ISBN 1-57243-541-0
Design by Eileen Wagner, Wagner/Donovan Design
All photos courtesy of AP/Wide World Photos unless otherwise indicated.

For my family: for Helene, and Mom and Dad,

and Jeanne and Freddie and Emilie and Charlotte . . .

. . . and to the memories of Red Holzman, Dave DeBusschere, and Leonard Koppett.

–D.D.

Contents

Foreword by Walt Frazier ix

Preface xi

Acknowledgments .xiii

Introduction: The Starting Lineup xv

Chapter 1: One Game, One Town 1

Chapter 2: Beginnings 8

Chapter 3: The Drought 38

Chapter 4: Heaven on 49th Street 58

Chapter 5: Step by Step 68

Chapter 6: Clyde and the Cap'n 86

Chapter 7: Red 98

Chapter 8: Camelot 108

Chapter 9: Hangover 152

Chapter 10: Hubie and B 170

Chapter 11: MSGU 192

Chapter 12: The Big Fella 214

Chapter 13: It's All About Soul 222

Chapter 14: Jeff's Time 246

Chapter 15: To Be Continued 278

Foreword

Late one afternoon during my rookie season with the Knicks, I was walking up Eighth Avenue to the Old Garden on 49th Street. We were playing the Lakers that night; I soon realized that Lakers star Elgin Baylor was walking just ahead of me. I recognized him instantly–whether playing basketball or walking down the street, Baylor carried himself with a regal bearing.

As a youngster, I was in awe of Elgin. He had those marvelous moves as well as a touch of serendipity in his game that made him a court magician. So I just stayed behind Elgin and followed him, with a mixture of awe and respect, for several blocks all the way up to the Garden. I was literally walking in that great man's footsteps.

On that day, at that moment in my life, I could only imagine what the future held in store for me. What kind of example would my teammates and I set for future generations? Would the basketball players of tomorrow feel the same sense of awe and respect toward us that I felt toward Elgin Baylor that day? What kind of footprints would we leave behind?

More than 30 years later, I know the answer.

I am constantly amazed at how much our championship teams of the seventies still mean to the people of New York. Every day, I'm reminded of just how much we've meant to the city, how much we touched people's lives, and of the great impact we had. Kids who weren't even born when we won the championships come up to me and recite statistics and game details as if they had been there. Older people tell me stories of where they were–in a restaurant, or at a friend's house, or listening to the radio–during those magical nights.

That's one kind of footprint. There's also another, more personal kind. It's forged by the memories. The memories that we not only leave the fans with, but also the memories that we, ourselves, have as participants. Decades later, I still imagine myself dueling my arch-nemesis Earl Monroe, who would later become my teammate and backcourt partner. I can still remember how we were all inspired by an injured Willis Reed, or enlightened by Red Holzman's wisdom, or galvanized by the challenge of having to win a deciding playoff game at the hallowed Boston Garden.

All of those great memories are here in this book. But there are also memories of a much more personal nature, things my teammates and I hadn't thought of in years until Dennis D'Agostino jolted our collective psyches. Look through these pages and you'll find me chasing Dancing Harry from our locker room in Baltimore or walking the streets of mid-sixties San Francisco with my first roommate, Phil Jackson. You'll see me in a Rolls Royce showroom in Manhattan, putting a down payment on the Clydemobile. You'll share my closet-sized room at the New Yorker Hotel and my memories of coming home to find my agent on my apartment steps, almost in tears, telling me I'd been traded.

The continuity of memory is a wonderful thing. It can close the generation gap, providing a bridge between what has happened and what is yet to be. The memories gathered here link the entire history of the Knicks, from the beginning in 1946 right up to the present day.

Enjoy the journey that follows. Speaking not only for myself but for all of us who have worn a Knicks uniform, I hope we've left the same kind of footprints for you that Elgin Baylor left for me all those years ago on Eighth Avenue.

–Walt Frazier

The taxi barreled down Seventh Avenue that springtime Sunday morning in 1994, and the Big Apple already had its game face on.

You noticed it in the logoed T-shirts worn by the morning joggers. You noticed it in the jerseys on the kids' backs, jerseys bearing names like Ewing and Starks and Oakley and Mason. You noticed it in the game highlights flashing on the giant video screen in Times Square. And as you got closer and closer to where all the magic came from, you noticed it in the blizzard of orange-and-blue giveaway signs that wall-papered every office window, every storefront, every gin mill, every coffee shop . . . right down to the sides of the hot dog wagon on the corner of 33rd Street. The signs that bore the staccato battle cry of the world's greatest basketball city: "Go NY, Go NY, *Go!*"

The roots of the New York Knickerbockers, the elements that make them not so much a basketball team as an ongoing passion play, lay in the black-tops, gyms, and schoolyards that dot the city's landscape. If you grew up in New York, you played basketball. It's that simple. You might not have been good enough to hit a curveball, or big enough to play full field tackle. But every New Yorker, at some point, has shot a pockmarked Spalding toward a dented, netless hoop.

The Knicks are New York's Team. Period.

For me, that simple fact was driven home every single day of the 12 years I spent with the team's front office, but never more vividly than during that Sunday morning taxi ride in 1994, when the Knicks came within a game—within a single shot—of an NBA Championship.

I was very, very lucky. I had the best seat in the house during the longest sustained run of success the Knicks have ever enjoyed: a total of 14 consecutive postseason appearances, four trips to the Eastern Conference Finals, and two to the NBA Finals. It was

a time, and a team, that seized a city's emotions. When I arrived in 1987 we were thrilled to get fifteen thousand people into the Garden for MetLife Cap Night. A decade later we were in the midst of a nine-year span during which each and every regular-season and playoff home game—433 in all—was sold out.

Through my time with the Knicks, I knew that a detailed, text-driven history of the team had never been written. There had been a wave of books, of course, following the championships of 1970 and 1973, and later works that centered on the eventful nineties. But the entire history of the team hadn't been brought together in one volume. So I often found myself wondering if—and how—I could ever tell the Knicks' story.

I had the advantage of working with every Knicks player and coach during my fulltime tenure (1987 through 1999), and I also got to know many of the team's past stars. Then, when I left the Knicks to relocate to California in 1999, I realized that I now had the gifts of time and flexibility that I didn't have in New York.

I was impressed with the oral history book for-mat that blossomed during the nineties. The words and emotions of those who had made history, to me, were far preferable to the seemingly endless proces-sion of sports histories written by "scholars," "ana-lysts," college professors, self-proclaimed "historians," and talking head know-it-alls who claim to have the inside story on events they only saw on television. I knew that if I ever had the opportunity, I would much prefer to seek out as many former Knicks as I could and simply say, "Tell me what it was like . . ."

During the course of the interviewing process, I was surprised and flattered that so many former Knicks would suddenly blurt out, "It's about damn time somebody is finally doing this . . ." Hopefully, those will be your sentiments as well.

Now for a few ground rules . . .

With one exception, I conducted all of the interviews. I decided against following the recent spate of team oral histories that use lifted quotes from decades-old books and articles. I felt it vital to maintain a present-day perspective throughout the book, and that's why you won't find, for example, recycled Joe Lapchick quotes from 1948.

I originally interviewed the late Red Holzman, Dick Schaap, and Phil Berger during the nineties. Leonard Koppett died suddenly three months after being interviewed in the spring of 2003. I felt I did have to make one, and only one, exception to the "first hand" rule—Fred Podesta, Ned Irish's longtime assistant who presided over the birth of the Knicks in 1946. Podesta, who died in 1999, was originally interviewed by Leonard Lewin for the Knicks in 1994. Due to Podesta's unique perspective and vivid memories of the franchise's beginnings, excerpts from Lewin's 1994 interview are presented here.

About half of the interviews were done over the phone; the others were conducted face-to-face. Over the course of eight months, I found myself at the corner table of a noisy Westchester diner (with Jeff Van Gundy), at a cliffside resort overlooking the Pacific Ocean (Al Bianchi), at a kitchen table in New Jersey (Willis Reed), on the visitors bench at Staples Center (Kiki Vandeweghe, Maurice Cheeks, John MacLeod, and others), pedaling a stationary bicycle (alongside Charles Oakley), and inside the Garden press room, where Dean Meminger told me to get on my feet and then demonstrated his defensive stance as if I were Jo Jo White. Some interviewees were cautious and conservative, while others were candid, emotional, and critical. Each played a key role in telling the Knicks' story, whether he was interviewed for 10 minutes or two hours.

I elected to confine the interview subjects to Knicks players, coaches, and executives, as well as selected fans and media members who have had a direct and longtime connection with the team. The interview subjects are "Knicks only," although those who were also noted opponents—such as Phil

Jackson, Pat Riley, Earl Monroe, Richie Guerin, and Don Chaney—spoke freely about facing the Knicks from the other side.

I regret that, due to deadline commitments, I wasn't able to talk to everyone I had originally targeted. Doubtless, there are more stories to tell than those presented here. If I've left out your particular favorite Knick player or memory, my deepest apologies.

By its very nature, an oral history is more a series of recollections and anecdotes than a structured recitation of historic facts, key dates, and important games. Therefore, this book isn't meant to be an all-encompassing Knicks encyclopedia. Don't go looking for a lot of statistics, graphs, pie charts, or all-time records, because you won't find them. That's what the *NBA Guide* is for. Here, stories take precedence over statistics.

Naturally, widely differing and sometimes conflicting viewpoints may exist concerning the same event, and you'll find several examples throughout the book. Please keep in mind that the words and opinions expressed belong to the interview subjects, not me. My job was to set the stage, then get out of the way and let the cast of characters take over.

As in any oral history, specific dates, game details, and scores may be incorrect in the original telling. Whenever possible, I have corrected these errors, without, of course, changing or editing any other part of the interview.

Admittedly, you won't find too much on the ownership machinations of Madison Square Garden, from the days of Graham-Paige to Gulf + Western to Viacom to Cablevision. As anyone familiar with the Garden can tell you, that subject alone is worth a book in itself.

As complete as I hope this book is, there is nonetheless a painful, gaping hole. Dave DeBusschere was on board with this project from the start, and we spent the better part of the winter and spring of 2003 trying to hook up as he commuted between Florida and New York. We had one date set to talk, then another, then another. I left my final voice mail message with Dave about 12 hours before getting the phone call that he had passed away.

Acknowledgments

The only peril to acknowledging those who assisted me on this book is that I know I'm going to forget somebody.

The most important of all, of course, are the 82 individuals who were gracious enough to share their time and memories.

Also, my sincerest thanks to . . .

The Knicks' public relations staff, who assisted in so many aspects of this book: Joe Favorito, Jonathan Supranowitz, Dan Schoenberg, Sammy Steinlight, KeJuan Wilkins, and Pat Hazelton. Also, my former Knicks colleagues: Chris Weiller, Lori Hamamoto, Josh Rosenfeld, Chris Brienza, and Brian Flinn, all of whom tolerated that guy who talked to himself just a little too much.

John Monteleone, an agent who never stopped trying, never stopped working, never stopped believing.

The staff of Triumph Books, especially Mitch Rogatz, Mike Emmerich, Linc Wonham, and Scott Rowan.

Eddie Oliva and the NBA's Zelda Spoelstra, both of whom provided many leads and opened many doors during the interview process. I'm not exaggerating in the least by saying there's no way this book could have been done without their help.

Tommy Sheppard of the Denver Nuggets, Jeff Twiss of the Boston Celtics, Brian McIntyre of the NBA, and especially Tim Donovan of the Miami Heat: four of the most supportive friends a person could want.

From Madison Square Garden: Barry Watkins, Eric Gelfand, Rebecca Taylor, Sarah Miller, Josephine Traina, and the immortal Frank Murphy.

Each and every one of my NBA PR brethren with whom I've had the honor of working for nearly two decades. Those who went above and beyond the call of duty as I hounded them throughout the 2002–03 season were: Arthur Triche of the Atlanta Hawks; Tim Hallam of the Chicago Bulls; Gregg Elkin of the Dallas Mavericks; Matt Dobek and Kevin Grigg of the Detroit Pistons; Raymond Ridder of the Golden State Warriors; David Benner of the Indiana Pacers; Stacey Mitch of the Memphis Grizzlies; Kent Wipf of the Minnesota Timberwolves; Cheri Hanson and Bill Evans of the Milwaukee Bucks; Gary Sussman of the New Jersey Nets; Joel Glass of the Orlando Magic; Julie Fie of the Phoenix Suns; Mike Hanson and Brian Facchini of the Portland Trail Blazers; Jim LaBumbard of the Toronto Raptors; Kim Turner of the Utah Jazz; Nicole Hawkins of the Washington Wizards; and Terry Lyons, Mark Broussard, Tim Frank, and Jeanne Tang of the NBA. And from my (new) hometown: John Black, Mike Uhlenkamp, Alison Bogli, and Josh Rupprecht of the Lakers and Joe Safety, Rob Raichlen, Rob Brown, Steven Esparza, and Ta'Nisha Cooper of the Clippers, all of whom probably said at one point, "Why is he *always* here?"

Special thanks as well to Ken Albert, Betsy Becker, Beth Montgomery, Marita Green, Billy Diamond, Charlie and Gail Papelian, John Eisenberg of the *Baltimore Sun*, Joel Siegel of the *New York Daily News*, and not one but two David Halberstams (the writer *and* the announcer). For vintage Knicks video and audio tapes, thanks to Jarad Franzreb of NBA Entertainment and collectors Aaron Mintz and Tom Kleinschmidt.

And most of all, to Helene. Yes, honey, we can go to Disneyland now.

The Starting Lineup

The following list represents the complete lineup of individuals interviewed for Garden Glory. *The beginning of each chapter also lists all the people interviewed in that chapter, in the order in which they appear.*

Al Albert, the middle of the three announcing Albert brothers, is the television voice of the Indiana Pacers.

Marv Albert has been the definitive "Voice of the Knicks," on either radio or television, since 1967. He was inducted into the announcers' wing of the Basketball Hall of Fame in 1997.

Steve Albert, the youngest of the three Albert brothers, is the voice of boxing on the Showtime cable network.

John Andariese has been an analyst on Knicks radio and television broadcasts for a quarter of a century, following a standout playing career at Fordham University.

Harvey Araton is a columnist for *The New York Times*; his early career included a stint as Knicks beat reporter for the *New York Post* during the tumultuous late seventies.

Phil Berger was a noted sportswriter whose *Miracle on 33rd Street* remains the most enduring and penetrating look at the 1970 championship team. Berger died in 2001.

Al Bianchi served as Knicks general manager from 1987 to 1991, during which New York began its run of 14 consecutive postseason appearances. A perennial NBA figure as both player and coach, the native New Yorker is currently a scout for the Phoenix Suns.

Rolando Blackman is a four-time NBA All-Star who played the final two seasons of his 13-year career with the Knicks, including the 1994 Eastern Conference Championship campaign.

He is now a player development coach for the Dallas Mavericks.

Vince Boryla was a Knicks mainstay throughout the fifties as a key member of the three-time Eastern Division Champions and then as both head coach and general manager. Now retired after a successful business career, Boryla lives in Englewood, Colorado.

Bill Bradley has become a renowned author and lecturer following an 18-year tenure as a United States Senator that included a bid for the 2000 Democratic presidential nomination. "Dollar Bill" played 10 memorable seasons as a Knick, was a key member of two championship teams, and was elected to the Basketball Hall of Fame in 1982.

Hubie Brown coached the Knicks to back-to-back playoff berths in 1983 and 1984 during the franchise's most successful run since the championship era. After a 15-year career as the game's premier broadcast analyst, Brown returned to coaching in 2002 to take over the Memphis Grizzlies.

Marcus Camby played four seasons as a Knick and was a key member of the 1999 Eastern Conference Championship team. He now plays for the Denver Nuggets.

Don Chaney is the head coach of the Knickerbockers, having taken over on December 8, 2001, after originally joining the team in 1995 as an assistant coach. A two-time NBA Champion during his playing career with the Boston Celtics, he played a major role in the fabled Knicks-Celtics wars of the early seventies.

Dave Checketts presided over the longest sustained period of success in Knicks history. He joined the Knicks as club president in 1991, then was promoted to president and CEO of Madison Square Garden in 1994, and remained in that position until 2001.

Maurice Cheeks played just two seasons in New York, but etched his name in club history as the main cog in the famed 1990 playoff triumph over Boston. A five-time All-Defensive selection during a brilliant 15-year playing career, "Mo" is now the head coach of the Portland Trail Blazers.

Marvin Cooper (also known as **Dancing Harry**) is a skycap at Baltimore-Washington International Airport.

Hubert Davis became one of the NBA's top three-point shooters during four years as a Knick, including the 1994 Eastern Conference Championship season. Today he plays for the Detroit Pistons.

Mel Davis is the executive director of the NBA Retired Players Association. New York's top pick in the 1973 NBA Draft, he played four seasons as a Knick.

Patrick Ewing is an 11-time NBA All-Star, one of the 50 greatest players in league history, holder of virtually every Knicks career record, and arguably the greatest player to wear the orange and blue. Following a spectacular 17-year playing career (15 of which were spent with the Knicks), the future Hall of Famer is now an assistant coach with the Houston Rockets.

Walt Frazier became the Knicks television analyst on MSG Network following a legendary playing career during which he was a seven-time NBA All-Star and the floor leader of both Knicks championship teams. One of the 50 greatest players in NBA history, "Clyde" was elected to the Basketball Hall of Fame in 1987.

Harry Gallatin was elected to the Basketball Hall of Fame in 1991 on the strength of a brilliant nine-year Knicks career during which he was a seven-time NBA All-Star and played in a club record 610 consecutive games. A star of the three-in-a-row Eastern Division winners of the fifties, "Harry the Horse" later served as Knicks head coach. Today he lives in Edwardsville, Illinois.

Mike Glenn is the longtime television analyst for the Atlanta Hawks. "The Stinger" played three seasons with the Knicks and was the 1981 winner of the NBA's J. Walter Kennedy Citizenship Award.

Sam Goldaper was the Knicks beat reporter for *The New York Times* for nearly two decades as part of a career in journalism that began with the *Brooklyn Eagle* in 1940. He was elected to the writers' wing of the Basketball Hall of Fame in 1992.

Johnny Green was one of the most popular players in Knicks history, and a three-time All-Star during a seven-year tenure in New York that began in 1959–60. Following a 14-year NBA career, "Jumpin' Johnny" lives in New York.

Ernie Grunfeld authored a two-decade Knicks success story as player, coach, broadcaster, and finally as the architect of two Eastern Conference Championship teams (1994 and 1999). He served as general manager for six seasons and as club president for four. Following four years as general manager of the Milwaukee Bucks, Grunfeld was named president of basketball operations for the Washington Wizards in 2003.

Richie Guerin was a six-time NBA All-Star as a Knick, and the team's brightest star as they struggled through the late fifties and early sixties. Retired after a long career with the Bear Stearns investment firm, the native New Yorker now lives in Florida.

Derek Harper played three seasons in New York, and his acquisition in 1994 was a key factor in the Knicks' run to the Eastern Conference Championship. Following a standout 16-year playing career, "Harp" is now a television analyst for the Dallas Mavericks.

Pam Harris, who headed the Knicks' marketing department throughout the nineties, is the founder and chief executive of Skilo Brand, a Manhattan-based sports marketing firm.

Sonny Hertzberg was the leading scorer (8.7) of the original 1946–47 Knicks, and later served as a scout and broadcaster. Retiring in 2003 following a 29-year career with Bear Stearns, Sonny lives on Long Island.

Red Holzman was the legendary coach who piloted the Knicks to NBA Championships in 1970 and 1973, and his 613 wins as Knicks headmaster are by far the most in club history. Elected to the Basketball Hall of Fame in 1985, Red served as the Knicks' basketball consultant until his death in 1998.

Allan Houston has been a two-time NBA All-Star since joining the Knicks in 1996, helping to lead New York to the 1999 Eastern Conference Championship. In 2002–03 the Knicks' captain scored a career-high 22.5 points per game and became the first Knick ever to lead the NBA in free throw percentage (.919).

Mark Jackson was the NBA's Rookie of the Year in 1988, an NBA All-Star the following season, and a key player in the Knicks' resurgence during the late eighties. Nine years after he was traded away Jackson returned to the Knicks in 2001 and played two more seasons in New York. The third-leading assist artist in NBA history–behind only John Stockton and Magic Johnson–Mark played for the Utah Jazz in 2002-03, his 16th NBA season.

Phil Jackson is the head coach of the Los Angeles Lakers, and the winner of a record-tying nine NBA Championships as coach of the Lakers and the Chicago Bulls. During a 10-year playing career with the Knicks the future Hall of Famer was a member of the 1968 NBA All-Rookie Team and, after missing the 1969–70 season due to injury, was a main contributor to the 1973 NBA Championship team.

Stu Jackson is the NBA's senior vice president of basketball operations. Originally joining the Knicks as an assistant coach in 1987, he later served as head coach for two seasons and led the club to its fabled come-from-behind 1990 playoff victory over Boston.

George Kalinsky has been the award-winning staff photographer for the Knicks and Madison Square Garden for nearly four decades.

Ralph Kaplowitz played for both the original 1946–47 Knicks and the NBA's first champions, the 1946–47 Philadelphia Warriors. The native New Yorker is semiretired after a long and distinguished career with the Equitable Financial Companies.

Les Keiter was the colorful radio voice of the Knicks during the late fifties and early sixties. Still going strong in a broadcasting career that spans seven decades, Les lives in Hawaii.

Bernard King is the only Knick ever to lead the NBA in scoring (32.9 in 1984–85). One of the most electrifying and dominant players in franchise history, the four-time NBA All-Star now heads several businesses in Atlanta.

Freddie Klein and **Stan Asofsky** are perhaps the Knicks' two most celebrated "superfans," holding court under the Garden basket since the early sixties.

Leonard Koppett was a brilliant sportswriter who chronicled the Knicks and the NBA from their beginnings. A member of the writers' wings of both the Baseball and Basketball Halls of Fame, "The Erudite One" died suddenly in 2003.

Dr. Richard Lapchick, son of Hall of Fame Knicks coach Joe Lapchick, heads the University of Central Florida's Institute for Diversity and Ethics in Sport.

Scott Layden is the president and general manager of the Knickerbockers. Following a successful front-office career with the Utah Jazz, he joined the Knicks in 1999.

Fuzzy Levane coached the Knicks for two seasons in the late fifties. A member of the New York City Basketball Hall of Fame, Levane returned to the Knicks as a scout in 1976 and has remained with the team ever since.

Leonard Lewin was the Knicks' beat writer for the *Daily Mirror* and the *New York Post* for nearly half a century. He was elected to the writers' wing of the Basketball Hall of Fame in 1993.

Jerry Lucas capped his Hall of Fame career with three seasons as a Knick, and was a key member of the 1973 World Champion team. A longtime educator and memory expert, Lucas is based in Templeton, California. One of the NBA's 50 greatest players, "Luke" is reachable through his website: www.doctormemory.com.

Ray Lumpp played five seasons as a Knick and was a member of the NBA Finalists of 1951 and 1952. The native New Yorker has been a longtime official of the New York Athletic Club.

John MacLeod was the Knicks' head coach for the bulk of the 1990–91 season, succeeding Stu Jackson. One of the 15 winningest coaches in NBA history, he's now an assistant coach for the Denver Nuggets.

Anthony Mason displayed a brand of toughness and passion that personified the Knicks during the Pat Riley era. His five seasons as a Knick were highlighted when he was named the NBA's Sixth Man of the Year in 1995.

Bob McAdoo averaged 26.7 points per game over three seasons as a Knick, still the franchise's all-time career best. He was a three-time NBA scoring champion, a five-time All-Star, the League's MVP in 1975, and a 2000 inductee into the Basketball Hall of Fame. McAdoo is currently an assistant coach for the Miami Heat.

Dick McGuire has been synonymous with Knicks basketball for virtually the entire history of the franchise, as player, head coach, scout, and currently as director of scouting services, a title he has held since 1987. The Big Apple hoop legend was inducted into the Basketball Hall of Fame in 1993.

Dean Meminger played four seasons over two tenures as a Knick, and as a sophomore was a main contributor to the 1973 NBA Championship team. Dean "the Dream" still lives in his native New York.

Steve Mills is the president of sports team operations for Madison Square Garden. Following a standout playing career at Princeton and a 16-year tenure at the NBA, he originally joined the Knicks as executive vice president of franchise operations in 1999.

Earl Monroe joined the Knicks in 1971 and climaxed his fabled career as a key member of the 1973 NBA Championship team. A four-time All-Star and one of the 50 greatest players in NBA history, "The Pearl" was elected to the Basketball Hall of Fame in 1990. He is currently president of the New Jersey–based Earl Monroe Group and works occasionally as a Knicks radio color analyst.

Charles Oakley was "The Chairman of the Boards" for 10 memorable seasons in New York; his rugged, no-holds-barred style symbolized the Knicks of the nineties. A two-time All-Defensive selection and a 1994 All-Star as a Knick, "Oak"

played for the Washington Wizards in 2002–03, his 18th NBA season.

Phil Pepe was the Knicks' beat reporter for the *New York Daily News* during the 1969–70 championship season, and has been one of New York's most popular sports journalists for nearly 40 years.

Fred Podesta was a Madison Square Garden executive for over three decades and presided over the birth and growth of the Knicks as Ned Irish's top assistant. Podesta passed away in 1999.

Cal Ramsey is the longtime community relations representative for the Knicks and Madison Square Garden. A Knick briefly in 1959–60, he later teamed with Bob Wolff to form one of the most beloved duos in New York sportscasting history.

Willis Reed was the undisputed leader of the Knicks during their greatest era. A seven-time NBA All-Star, he is the only Knick to be named NBA MVP (1970), and was cited as NBA Finals MVP in both 1970 and 1973. He also served as the Knicks' head coach for two years in the late seventies. One of the 50 greatest players in NBA history, "The Cap'n" returned to the Knicks in 2003 as special basketball advisor.

Micheal Ray Richardson was a two-time All-Defensive selection during his meteoric four-year Knicks career. Banned from the NBA in 1986 for violating the league's substance abuse policy, he played professionally in Europe for 14 years. Clean and sober for more than a decade, "Sugar" returned to America and the NBA in 2003, when he joined his hometown Denver Nuggets as community relations representative.

Pat Riley coached the Knicks to four consecutive 50-plus win seasons, two Atlantic Division titles, and the 1994 Eastern Conference Championship. A four-time championship coach with the Los Angeles Lakers, the future Hall of Famer is the president and head coach of the Miami Heat.

Spencer Ross has been one of New York's most popular sportscasters for more than three decades. One of a score of Marty Glickman protégés, Spencer currently hosts the Knicks radio pre- and postgame shows.

Bob Salmi was a Knicks assistant coach for seven years in the nineties, and was one of the pioneers in the use of computer generated and edited coaching video.

Mike Saunders is the longest-tenured athletic trainer in Knicks history, and celebrated his silver anniversary with the team in 2002–03.

Dick Schaap was a celebrated writer and commentator who coauthored Dave DeBusschere's 1970 book *The Open Man*. Schaap passed away in 2001.

Dr. Norman Scott has been the Knicks' team physician since 1978, and is the founder and chairman of the Association of Professional Team Physicians.

Mike Shatzkin is an author as well as the founder of The Idea Logical Company, a Manhattan-based publishing consulting firm. His first book, *The View from Section 111*, was a fan's diary of the 1969–70 championship season.

Charles Smith became a successful New Jersey–based businessman and entrepreneur following a nine-year NBA career. He spent four seasons with the Knicks, including the 1994 Eastern Conference Championship campaign. Charles also heads the Charles E. Smith Education Center in Bridgeport, Connecticut, which celebrated its 15th anniversary in 2003.

Rory Sparrow was a tenacious defensive specialist during six Knicks seasons, including the Hubie Brown era. Today he's the NBA's manager of player programs.

Latrell Sprewell is a four-time NBA All-Star whose five-year tenure as one of the most exciting and explosive players in Knicks history ended when he was traded to Minnesota following the 2002–03 season in a four-way deal that brought Keith Van Horn from Philadelphia to the Knicks.

John Starks went from unheralded free agent to Knicks mainstay; his unique blend of emotion, explosiveness, and unpredictability stamped him as one of the most popular Knicks ever. His eight-year career in New York was highlighted by All-Defensive honors in 1993, an All-Star citation in 1994, and the NBA's Sixth Man of the Year award in 1997.

Tom Thibodeau was a Knicks assistant coach for seven seasons prior to joining the Houston Rockets in 2003.

Kurt Thomas joined the Knicks as a free agent just before the 1998–99 season and became the team's starting center upon the departures of Patrick Ewing and Marcus Camby.

Trent Tucker enjoyed a nine-year Knicks career as one of the most prolific long-range shooters in club history. The leader of the 1988–89 "Bomb Squad" and later a member of the 1993 World Champion Chicago Bulls, Tucker is now a radio host and analyst in Minnesota.

Dick Van Arsdale is the senior vice president of player personnel for the Phoenix Suns. He began his 12-year playing career with three seasons as a Knick, and was named to the NBA's All-Rookie team in 1966.

Kiki Vandeweghe is the general manager of the Denver Nuggets and the son of fifties Knick Dr. Ernie Vandeweghe. A two-time NBA All-Star, he played four seasons as a Knick following his acquisition in 1989.

Jeff Van Gundy is the third-winningest coach in Knicks franchise history–trailing only Hall of Famers Red Holzman and Joe Lapchick–and piloted the Knicks to the 1999 Eastern Conference title. Following two years as a television analyst, Van Gundy is now head coach of the Houston Rockets.

Peter Vecsey is the longtime, outspoken basketball columnist for the *New York Post*.

Tim Walsh became the head athletic trainer of the New Jersey Nets following 13 years as an assistant trainer with the Knicks.

Charlie Ward became the senior member of the Knicks in 2000 following the Patrick Ewing trade. As he completed his ninth season with New York in 2002–03, only seven players in franchise history had enjoyed longer Knicks careers.

Herb Williams became an assistant coach for the Knicks following an 18-year playing career that included seven seasons as one of the most popular players in Knicks annals. Williams was a member of the Knicks' Eastern Conference Championship teams of 1994 and 1999.

Bob Wolff is the Hall of Fame sportscaster who served as the Knicks' television voice for nearly 20 years, including during the championship era of the seventies.

Garden Glory

Bob Cousy (with ball) and Dick McGuire were among the millions who learned basketball in New York.

THE LINEUP: John Andariese; Dick McGuire; Freddie Klein; Stan Asofsky; Ernie Grunfeld; Dean Meminger; Cal Ramsey; Ralph Kaplowitz; Phil Pepe; Walt Frazier; Mike Glenn; Rolando Blackman; Scott Layden; Harry Gallatin; Spencer Ross; Al Albert; Steve Mills; Earl Monroe; John Starks; Al Bianchi; Charles Oakley; Trent Tucker.

Whether on the playground, in city leagues, or at the high school, college, or professional level, basketball is an integral part of the fabric of New York City. And everyone has stories.

John Andariese: It goes back to when I got a gift of a basketball from my sister. I think I was in the 10th grade. That, to me, was the beginning. That's when I got married to basketball.

Dick McGuire: I really don't know how it developed. I didn't start playing basketball until I was a senior in high school. I never bounced a basketball until I was a junior, because they built a court down in Rockaway and that was the only reason I ever started playing basketball. I scored 18 points my whole senior year in high school. I didn't start; I came off the bench. And then my brother John went down to St. John's. They didn't scout as much in those days, so John went and lied to Father Brown that I was a talent. Nobody checked it out, and they gave me a scholarship to St. John's.

Freddie Klein: We were playing basketball at the 92nd Street Y, and somebody said, "There's a crazy guy playing named Stan. If he guards you, he's going to hit you because he hits everyone else." So he was guarding me and they called a foul, and I took a swing at him. And we became best friends.

Stan Asofsky: Freddie had a habit of holding on to the ball. He had very strong hands. And what I did was, I let him back up to me, and I just walked away from him. He fell on the floor and he said, "Hi, I'm Freddie Klein."

Ernie Grunfeld: As a kid, it really made it a lot easier for me to be accepted in the community, to be accepted on the playground, to make friends at an early age, because I really couldn't speak the language. Being a good athlete, you tended to make friends a lot easier.

John Andariese: What appealed to me about it was that you could do it all by yourself. I could just go off by myself and shoot. I was very impressed with guys who were older, and better, like Ed Conlin, who was an All-American at Fordham. He was a big-name guy and probably to this day the best player Fordham has ever had.

Dean Meminger: I played in the Rucker League. Today they call it the Entertainers League, but that's different from the Rucker League. It's played at Rucker Park, but it's not the Rucker League. Rucker was ballplayers playing. These guys are entertainers.

John Andariese: I can actually remember getting my first tip-in, down at the school yard. I know exactly where it happened. And that feeling of tipping a ball into the basket . . . It's so funny [that] I still remember that.

Dick McGuire: Bob Cousy and I played an awful lot against each other in the church leagues. The church leagues were big, big, big in those days. He'd play for a team on Long Island, I'd play for a team in Rockaway. I've known Bob all my life and I think he's a great, great player and extremely talented.

Basketball was played everywhere in New York. The Garden, however, was where the best played, and where every kid dreamed of playing. But almost any court would do for those with a love of the game–and New York had plenty of both.

Cal Ramsey: In 1952 I started high school at Commerce. And during those days they had the Public School Championships at the Garden. That was the borough championships as well as the finals. And the big goal for all of the kids in my neighborhood who played basketball was to try to get to the Garden. And every year we worked hard to try to get there. And luckily, in two of my three years, we played PSAL games in the Garden. It was exciting. Big crowds and some great high school basketball players in those days.

Ralph Kaplowitz: At that time, we didn't know anything about a one-handed shot. It was basically all two-handed shooting. And with two-handed shooting, you really can't get in too close to shoot because it's easy to be blocked. You'd have to shoot from what today would be the three-point line. That way the defensive player gave you a little room. We didn't have a point guard. We had a guy that brought up the ball, and then everybody circulated, everybody moved. If you gave the ball to somebody on the right side, you cut to the basket and went around. By that time, somebody else came around and got the ball. You tried to look for an opening. So all five people were moving all the time, trying to find an opening. You would try to help one another by picking off for one another, trying to block for one another, so that your teammate could get a shot off.

John Andariese: We had a park in Bay Ridge, on 83rd Street right behind Fort Hamilton High School. On Tuesday and Thursday nights in the summer, there was always action. Guys came from all over the city to play. I was a bystander. To me, that was the Garden. I'd get on that court and play with guys who were early college guys–you really looked up to them. I didn't belong in that crowd, but I'd go and watch. And when those hotshot guys left the scene, that location was still a hotbed of local guys who would play. I used to get on

my bike, go down there, and work my way in against these older guys. There was one guy, Tom Burns, who I'll always remember. He was a rough guy who was probably 10 years older than anyone on the court, and he was tough. He liked to push guys around and teach guys the rough part of basketball. I remember working my way into a game and encountering him and getting a taste of a guy who's a bully. It was good training, because either you stood up to him or you wimped out. So you got used to pushing somebody back.

Phil Pepe: The first game I ever saw was the Knicks against the Baltimore Bullets, and Buddy Jeannette played. Now, that's going way back. Certain things stick out. The Knicks had a player named Paul Noel, and because it was around Christmastime, I guess that's why I remember that name. Bud Palmer played, so that had to have been around 1948.

Walt Frazier: Growing up in Atlanta, you'd pick up the newspapers and there wouldn't be hardly anything on basketball. Here [in New York] there were 5 or 10 pages every day, just on basketball. And with the way all the fans reacted at the games, I was going, "Man, this would be some place to play." But I never thought it would happen, because the Knicks had so many backcourt players.

Mike Glenn: I had come to New York with Southern Illinois for the NIT [National Invitation Tournament] in my sophomore year, kind of following in Walt Frazier's footsteps. Walt had always been such a huge hero of mine. It was almost like destiny. We both came from Georgia; we both went to Southern Illinois. In all my fantasies, I was a guard playing for the New York Knicks in Madison Square Garden.

Rolando Blackman: When I was growing up, I patterned my game after Dollar Bill Bradley coming off the [Dave] DeBusschere and [Willis] Reed screens without shooting the ball. I remember everybody in the neighborhood in East Flatbush pretending to be Earl Monroe, grabbing the ball and doing the spin to the basket. And then when you got fouled, to be cool like Walt Frazier, not to show your emotions and be cool like Clyde. That was a big deal for me, growing up with a New York basketball team. They lived within all of us as kids.

Scott Layden: I remember when I was a young boy, I went to the first camp that Lou [Carnesecca]

Walt Frazier witnessed the adulation New Yorkers had for their basketball heroes early on—and then later experienced it for himself.

and Red Sarachek had together, up in the Pocono Mountains. It was unique because there were 19 campers. I was one of the 19. But there were more counselors than campers, because the thing was just getting off the ground. But that's the way basketball was: I'm the head coach here, you're the head coach there, and we're competing, but we'll still go out and have pizza afterward. I'm not sure it's the same way anymore, with the big conferences and the schools with high profiles. Something has been lost, and that's unfortunate. So if being with my dad in the gym when he was coaching Seton Hall High School, or Niagara . . . if that's a gym rat, then I plead guilty. Sometimes the term *gym rat* can have a negative connotation, and it shouldn't because it was a way of life, a passion, and one that we're very fortunate to be part of.

Harry Gallatin: We did a lot of clinics in New York, with the PSAL, to stimulate interest in the league in the early fifties. It's something that maybe some of the modern players should think about, because it was important for us to go out and catch the interest of the youngsters. We used to play three-on-three at a lot of the high schools. One event that I remember very well was playing a three-on-three game at Lafayette High School in Brooklyn. Some kid went up on me and dunked the ball, which at that time was something we didn't do. But this one kid from Lafayette, all of a sudden he jumped up and dunked the ball. Of course, all of us went, "Who was that kid?" Well, that kid happened to be Sandy Koufax.

John Andariese: I played in the Eastern League for one year with the Allentown Jets. Brendan McCann was the coach as well as a player. I wasn't a star by any means. I remember guarding Paul Arizin in a workout one day. Paul, of course, was one of the greatest of all time. He had retired from the NBA and went to work for IBM, and also played in the Eastern League on weekends for Philadelphia. I'll never forget: Paul went up for a jump shot, and here I am trying to impress everybody. I put my hand up and I thought to myself, "If I even try to block his shot, I'm gonna be officially a jerk." So I went straight up instead of trying to block it.

Some of the CCNY guys played in the Eastern League: Ed Warner, Floyd Layne. They were great players. Those guys were tough. And they'd all be playing in the NBA today, with 29 teams.

Scott Layden: So many of us whose fathers were coaches were really fortunate. I always considered myself fortunate because I was surrounded by a sport that we all loved. And the characters who were in the sport just added to the whole atmosphere. For example, when my dad was a high school coach, he was friends with Lou Carnesecca; he was friends with these guys who were great college coaches. Some of the all-time great men, but also characters in their field.

What the late author Pete Axthelm dubbed "the city game" continues to generate warm memories among fans, former players, and former coaches.

Spencer Ross: The first game my father ever took me to at the Old Garden was on a Saturday afternoon, and Dolph Schayes hit a basket at the buzzer to beat the Knicks. I was 10 years old, and I cried. Fast-forward now to my oldest boy, who's now 31. When he was about 10 or 11, I did a game here at the Garden on television. It was a Home Box Office game, the Knicks against the Philadelphia 76ers. And I took my son to see the game. Julius Erving drove the lane and hit a shot at the end to beat the Knicks, and my son cried. I tried to make him understand.

Al Albert: Our parents were great in letting us go out. We used to go to the Garden all the time. The Knicks were Tuesday and Saturday nights, the Rangers were Wednesdays and Sundays. We went on the subway from Brooklyn into Manhattan. No problems. Maybe back then there was nothing to worry about. Either that or they just wanted to get us out of the house and get rid of us. "You've got a game? Good!" You'd go with friends, get on the subway, and crush up a cup and play hockey on the subway. Then you'd have a Nedick's, smell the cigar smoke, and go inside. The whole atmosphere . . . John Condon on the PA . . . that just hooked us.

Walt Frazier: Early in my rookie season, Willis Reed took me to Harlem, up to Small's Paradise, Wilt's place. They introduced me and people cheered, but Willis got a standing ovation. I was like, "Man, I hope I can be a success in this city."

Dean Meminger: I came to the Knicks with ambivalent feelings. But after getting here, I fell in love. It was a love affair. Coming home, playing at home, I couldn't have been in a better situation.

Scott Layden: When my dad was coaching the Jazz, the staffs were very small. He was the head coach and general manager. Jerry Sloan was the full-time assistant on the bench, and I was an assistant coach/scout, so I would go out and look at opponents and college players, then come back periodically and be with the team. So I'd be all over the place. And my dad let me make my own schedule; I could come and go whenever I wanted. But the only request he had in regard to my schedule–the only, *only* request he had–was that I be on the bench with him in New York when we came to the Garden. It was very simple. He said, "Son, this is something special, to be in New York, to be in the Garden. I want to be with you during that time." And I understood that, the whole atmosphere and nature of being in the Garden.

Mike Glenn: At that time, we were the only team in the NBA who chartered [took a chartered plane] on back-to-back games. The other teams had to have these 5:30 and 6:00 A.M. wake-up calls to catch planes early the next morning. That was something that was distinctly New York. Another thing we did was have our game-day shoot-arounds at the Garden. Then we'd all check into the Statler-Hilton across the street, grab something to eat, and take a nap until it was time for the game. It was so wonderful, rather than taking the Long Island Rail Road back and forth from home. On other teams, guys would be driving back and forth, back and forth, all day. And guys on other teams knew that New York took care of its players better than anywhere else. That was representative of the Knicks. There were a lot of teams then that tried to lowball you and abuse you in some way. The Boston guys would tell us how Red Auerbach would try to sell them on all that Celtic Pride stuff and would wind up paying them far less than what they were worth. But the Knicks had the luxury of charter flights and such, and that set them a cut above.

John Andariese: Playing in college and in the rec leagues fed my love for the game and my understanding of how much talent NBA guys have. That's what feeds me to this day, that I realize the gift, and I love to share the understanding of that gift with people.

Freddie Klein: I was sitting in the Carnegie Deli once with Hubie Brown and Howie Garfinkel.

We sat there for three or four hours talking basketball. Peter Falk was on the other side of the room, and finally he walked over to us and said, "Don't you guys want to talk to me?"

Steve Mills: I think I was the one class [at Princeton] between at least four or five years before me and four or five years after me, that didn't play at the Garden. Back then it was something where the guys who had played before me would talk to me about what it was like to play at Madison Square Garden. And after I had graduated, they played in a tournament here, and I talked with the guys I was still friends with about playing in the Garden. So, clearly, it was something I missed. And I think about it a lot. Whenever I'm actually in the arena, I always think about the fact that I never got a chance to play here.

Scott Layden: It's hard to articulate. It's a feeling we all have. And I can't tell you how many people I talk to who say, "Wow, I saw a great game at the Garden" or "I want to bring my son to the Garden." It's a special, special thing.

Dean Meminger: I never had a car in New York. Why would I need a car in New York? I had a relationship with people. I was an All-American in high school; I was an All-American in college. So the same people that saw me play, I have a relationship with them. So why am I hiding? What do I have to hide from? They would think I'm crazy if I did that. And my relationship with New York was a little different from Clyde's and Earl's. They were out-of-towners.

Earl Monroe: Just walking down the streets, in restaurants, people let you know. It's a good feeling. It lets you know that people appreciate the things you did. I've kind of felt, even with all this, like a person without a place. I was in Baltimore, left there, came to New York. But this is Clyde's place. Baltimore was my place. There's still that kind of feeling even today. I think the most die-hard Knicks fans still feel that way. But at the same time, I've had such a great relationship with fans in general that it really doesn't matter.

Steve Mills: You don't come to play here if you don't want a lot of media pressure, if you don't want fans that expect a lot from you. Then you go someplace else; you don't play in New York and you don't play at the Garden. I'm not going to name anyone, but there have been times when we've had free agents visit with us, and they would say, "You know, I'm really nervous about the media scrutiny. I'm gonna come in here and take this player's place, and I wonder how the media's going to react to that." And you know what? This isn't the place for guys who think like that. There are huge opportunities playing in this market, for this team in this building. And if you're not up to it, it's a huge liability.

John Starks: Some players can't play in that atmosphere. I relished it. I relished every moment I played in the Big Apple. Some people don't like dealing with the truth, but I do. I like people to be honest with me. And one thing about New Yorkers, if you're playing well they'll tell you. And if you're playing bad, they're gonna get on top of you. When I was playing bad, they did that. And I respected that because that meant I wasn't doing the things I was supposed to be doing. That just motivated me to play even harder.

Al Bianchi: I had so much fun. There were stressful times, with people all over you. But I always look at it this way: What other city can you go in, after you've been there for one year, where you're standing there on a summer day waiting to cross the street, and there's a guy there with a jackhammer, and he looks up and stops the jackhammer and he goes, "Hey, Al!" Everybody stops and looks around, and the guy says, "I like that trade!" Or another time, a guy will say, "Hey, why don't you get rid of that so-and-so?" I would just crack up. And I learned that, in New York, whether it was by the Garden or on Fifth Avenue or where I lived up in the Sixties, people would come up to me. A guy would run up all upset and start in with me, and I would just stand there with a big smile on my face. I'd defuse it right away. And the guy would get it off his chest, and then I'd put my hand on his shoulder and say, "You know what? That's a hell of an idea. When I go back, I'm gonna talk to my bosses and tell them what you said." Now the guy has a smile on his face. It took me a little while to learn that.

John Andariese: I think there's a legitimate understanding of the game. If the Knicks never won a game, there'd still be eight to ten thousand people there every night. That's the feeling I've always had. The love of the game is so intense that there are so many people—mostly men in the earlier years—who love the game. The sport is fed by the enthusiasm of so many fans in New York. You'll get young players noticing the reaction when a guy blocks a shot or when a guy throws a great pass. They're not cheering for the guy who put the ball in the basket, they're cheering the pass. That's the difference in New York. And I don't even think it's an arguable point among basketball people. The New York fan is on another level of sophistication, knowledge, and feel. I also think the New York fans are very kind, despite what some people may think. I think they know the truth. And if they're booing, it's like they're running right onto the court and saying to the players, "If you were in the stands, wouldn't you be booing, too?" And I think the players would agree.

Charles Oakley: I hear it all out of town. Being in New York 10 years, then being traded, when you walk around it's like this team won a championship because of the way they treat you. It doesn't matter where: Miami, L.A., big cities. When I travel, I check into a hotel and they say, "Man, we miss you." That's like love.

Scott Layden: In New York, we know that our fans are passionate and knowledgeable. They're equally as passionate as they are aware of what the team is, what it's about, and the history. Because of the intense media, the fans are so knowledgeable as to what's going on. And that makes for a great franchise. There's a real vibrant feel whenever you're talking about the Knicks, whenever you're in the arena. And those things we never take lightly. Ask someone if they were at the game when Willis came out of the tunnel. It's inside of us all, and it's an incredible history. We know how New Yorkers are about all their teams. We love the Knicks, we love the sport, and that's why we all work hard at trying to make this team better. For the city, this great city that we live in. It's something special.

Trent Tucker: That's what I am: I'm a New York Knick. Even though I won a championship in Chicago, everywhere I go I'm identified as a Knick. New York prepared me for a lot of things, and prepared me for the life I'm living today. The maturation process of going to New York as a young person is always tough. But if you can survive in New York City, you can survive anywhere.

Dick McGuire: The only place, even today, in my life where I feel comfortable is on the basketball court. I know I'm not a good speaker. I don't enjoy speaking, and I've shied away from so many places where they want me to speak. I'm not comfortable with it. The only time I've ever been sure of myself was on a basketball court.

The always passionate and knowledgeable—and sometimes critical—Knicks fans motivate players like John Starks to play harder.

The founding father: Ned Irish in his Madison Square Garden office in the mid-forties.

THE LINEUP: Leonard Koppett; Fred Podesta; Leonard Lewin; Ray Lumpp; Fuzzy Levane; Ralph Kaplowitz; Vince Boryla; Dick McGuire; Bob Wolff; Johnny Green; Dr. Richard Lapchick; Spencer Ross; Harry Gallatin; John Andariese; Cal Ramsey; Kiki Vandeweghe; Les Keiter; Marv Albert; Steve Albert; Sonny Hertzberg.

The story of New York's Team begins on June 6, 1946, against the backdrop of a booming postwar economy, a group of arena owners with a calendar full of empty dates, a rotund commissioner named Maurice Podoloff, and an organization called the Basketball Association of America.

Leonard Koppett: When the idea of a pro league started up, right about the time the war ended in the spring of 1945, the arenas had an association they had formed based on the fact that the Sonja Henie ice shows were coming to all the arenas, along with things like the rodeo and the circus. When Ned Irish started the college doubleheaders in the late thirties, they spilled out to the other arenas. Evidently, they had an agreement among them that if they ever went into a pro basketball league, as many of them would go as possible.

Fred Podesta: [Irish] told me that a new professional basketball league was being formed and they wanted New York in it. He didn't want professional basketball at that time. For one thing, it was going to be a loss situation for an indeterminate number of years. More important, we had no Garden dates for it. We were booked 100 percent and were in the middle of what was to be the most productive season the building ever had.

Boston, Chicago, Detroit, Toronto, Cleveland, and the other places were ready to go. They had to have a New York franchise to make it mean something, but we didn't have a building to speak of. We had the Garden, but no dates to handle a 60-game season.

Leonard Lewin: They made it very obvious that New York was very important to the operation, because New York was the capital of the basketball world.

Irish and the Garden people were disenchanted because they couldn't give them any dates in the Garden. College basketball was so hot. So they were talked into it by Podoloff. They said, "We need New York." Irish relented, but he was reluctant to do it even then. But he did it for them. He didn't need it, since the Garden was a sellout every night for college basketball.

Fred Podesta: We were not going to be able to play a lot of games in our building. On the other hand, all the other owners, who were primarily hockey people, were looking to fill open dates in their buildings, which is why they decided on pro basketball.

It was a natural to cash in on the publicity and excitement that the college players were creating. AAU [Amateur Athletic Union] ball signed up some of the college players, as well as some Industrial

League ball. Otherwise, the highly publicized players had no place to go once their college careers ended.

There were other people who had similar ideas, no doubt. There was a National League at that time, which operated primarily in the Midwest and later merged some teams with the Basketball Association of America to form the NBA. But no one ever did it on this scale with so many major buildings, and, especially, with a New York team.

Leonard Koppett: Max Kase was the sports editor of the *Journal-American* and was familiar with the pro basketball of that time. He went to Walter Brown with the idea for a pro basketball league. It seemed like a great idea. The colleges were getting so much attention, producing All-Americans and Olympic teams and so forth. And the minute these guys graduated, they became worthless. If you had a pro league, you could cash in on their reputations, which the old National League, with its small cities and small arenas, couldn't really do.

Leonard Lewin: He [Max Kase] was involved because of the *Journal-American*. He was the sports editor, and he was going to get involved with the New York operation. I don't know what commitment they made to him, but he wanted it. It never turned out.

Leonard Koppett: So all of the arena people wanted to go into it, except Irish. First of all, he didn't have the dates. The Garden was booked all the time, so he didn't want it. Kase came along with a request to have a New York team and rent the Garden for a few open dates, and play somewhere else the rest of the time. Irish couldn't see letting someone else in New York come in as a rival with a pro team. So they bought Max out, and the Garden had the New York franchise. Clearly there was a financial settlement, although I don't know the details of it. And Kase never held it against Irish; he became one of the greatest supporters of the Knicks.

The upstart pro league instituted a sprinkling of new rules to distinguish it from the college game. The New York entrant needed a name, a coach, and, of course, a roster of players.

Fred Podesta: College basketball was our competition, so we had to devise some things that were unique to our pro game. That's how we came up with 12-minute quarters. We had to give the fans something more for their money, and the college game was two 20-minute halves. So we gave the pro fans eight more minutes of basketball when we started. I think that came from hockey's three distinct periods, as these were all hockey people.

We signed more than 40 players that first season and had so many, we couldn't tell our players *with* a scorecard.

Leonard Koppett: Having been dragged into the BAA, Irish's ideas about how to operate a big-league operation were completely at odds with all the other mom-and-pop arena owners. So the conflict was there from the beginning. Nevertheless, they all needed him completely to give them credibility. Some of the things he insisted on, he got. And a lot he didn't get.

Fred Podesta: The name came out of a hat. We were sitting in the office one day–Irish, [publicity man] Lester Scott, and a few others on the staff. We each put a name in the hat. And when we pulled them out, most of them were "Knickerbockers," after Father Knickerbocker, the symbol of New York City. It soon was shortened to Knicks.

Leonard Lewin: They hired Neil Cohalan because Joe Lapchick wasn't available. In fact, at the end of the first season when we went to the playoffs, Lapchick went with us. Although Cohalan was the coach, Lapchick went too. Cohalan knew he was there only because Lapchick couldn't take the job for the first year.

Ralph Kaplowitz: From what I know, the job as coach was originally offered to Joe Lapchick of St. John's. But since it was a new league, he wasn't sure that it would survive. As a result, Neil Cohalan filled in the first year. Cohalan knew that it would only be a one-year job. Cohalan coached at Manhattan College and I guess was considered a good coach, but as players we weren't impressed with him. We felt he wasn't much interested in ballplayers; he was there to fill out the year and do what he had to do. I didn't think his player selections were all that good or that he knew much about basketball. Talking with the other players, they felt the same way.

Fred Podesta: We had a salary cap, or call it a budget, at the time. The league decided no player would be paid more than $5,000, and that was our policy. We never deviated and paid some players under the table, though we realize others might have.

Ray Lumpp: There was a salary limit at one time of $5,000 and that's why we didn't get Dolph Schayes. He went to Syracuse for $500 more. All the Knicks players should have taken the money out of our pockets and given it to him. Then we would have won some rings, with Schayes in New York.

Ralph Kaplowitz: I spent four and a half years in the service, and I was discharged in February of 1946. Earlier, in December, Eddie Gottlieb, who was the owner and coach of the Philadelphia SPHAs [South Philadelphia Hebrew Association] of the American League, contacted me. In the American League, players had regular jobs and played on weekends. Gottlieb had heard about me, and he invited me to see a game between the SPHAs and the New York Gothams, in New York. When I got there, he signed me up to play with his team for the balance of the year.

So I played for the SPHAs, and we wound up winning the championship. At that time, there were rumors of a new league starting. And sure enough, the rumor came true, because in July of 1946, I got a telegram from Ned Irish saying that he was interested in having me play professional basketball, and to call him. That started it going.

Sonny Hertzberg: I always considered basketball to be a sideline. I played in the American League before the BAA started, and I was an optician by trade. I had gotten out of the service and then I got the telegram from Ned. I thought it was a chance for a league to get started, but I never thought it would mushroom to the extent that it did. I said, Why not give it a chance? It was just a sideline, and I could always quit if I didn't like it.

Ralph Kaplowitz: I really didn't have any plans. I was married and had a child who was almost three years old. I went ahead with it because it was

where I was at. It was a great thing. When I called Irish, I spoke to Fred Podesta, who was Ned's right-hand man. He offered me $4,000. What's funny about that is we had no agents and knew nothing about making deals.

Sonny Hertzberg: They sent me a contract, and I thought it was very nice. The contract was for something like $4,500. They said I could spend time in the optical business during the off days, but as it happened with the schedule, I couldn't. At the end of that first season, I was the high scorer of the Knicks and I got a $1,500 bonus.

Ralph Kaplowitz: They signed up about 25 players, and we all went up to training camp at the Nevele Country Club in the Catskills. I knew of some of the guys, and I was quite friendly with them, like Sonny Hertzberg, Ossie Schectman, and Leo Gottlieb, who I played with in high school. I knew guys like Stan Stutz, Dick Murphy, and Tommy Byrnes. We were all New York guys. That's how it was. In Philadelphia, they had guys from Philadelphia. In Cleveland, the same thing. It turned out that when the final Knicks team was selected, we had six Jewish ballplayers and four or five Gentiles.

I had worked at the Nevele on the athletic staff when I was still in high school. I knew the place, and I was familiar with playing basketball on the cement court. The court was big enough, but it was very tough to play on because you're running on cement.

The management was really nice to us. After a week or so, they invited our families up to keep us company. We were there about three weeks in training camp, and we had our families with us. It worked out very nicely, and it was very enjoyable.

Sonny Hertzberg: I had never gone to training camp with the American League. We were on our own, and we'd meet the night of the game. I don't think we ever had a practice session. Some of the fellows were working in the garment center; some were out of school doing other things. But here was a chance to get into good condition, whereas a lot of fellows in the American League weren't in very good shape. Bear Mountain was exciting. The courts were outdoors and our meals were taken care of. It was something that was a complete surprise.

The Knicks and the Toronto Huskies opened the inaugural BAA season one night ahead of the rest of the league: Friday night, November 1, 1946, at Maple Leaf Gardens. Final score: Knicks 68, Huskies 66.

Ralph Kaplowitz: Everybody started on that Saturday night, and we were also supposed to. However, they had a hockey game on Saturday night and couldn't change it. So as a result, we played the night before. What I remember about that first game was that it was the first time we felt there was a little anti-Semitism around. Most of the fans in Toronto were pretty nice, but some of them kept yelling, "Abe! Abe! Abe! Throw the ball to Abe!" You know, sort of mimicking the Jewish people. Of course, we ignored it. But you can't help remembering that this is what went on.

Fred Podesta: We had to make up attendance figures in those days, in the Armory and at the Garden. Sometimes the crowds were so small, we even gave out home addresses.

Sonny Hertzberg: I had played for Nat Holman, of course, at City College. All my basic basketball was good; there wasn't much Neil [Cohalan] could teach me. Being a professional coach, whether in 1946 or in 2003, he has to know balance. He has to know when to put the big men in, or the fast guys, or the scorers, or the defensive men. In Toronto, in the first game, I don't think I played more than three minutes. He did not recognize the talent. He didn't know me from the American League, where I was one of the top scorers and we had a lot of great talent. Subsequently, I won my way in.

Ralph Kaplowitz: There was no style. I don't remember him [Cohalan] setting up any plays. You just went out there and played. And if a guy looked like he was working hard and knocking his brains out, he figured that was a good ballplayer. That's how I felt about it. And even though I was the second-highest scorer on the team when I got traded, I didn't play that much. The guys were really unhappy, but as kids, what did we know? He was the coach and you don't question the coach.

We played a game at the Garden, and I was playing very well. I scored about 8 or 10 points within the first quarter. Then he takes me out and I'm sitting on the bench. And now we're beginning to lose. People are starting to yell, "Put Kaplowitz in! Put Kaplowitz in!" I didn't play for the rest of the game. So how can you respect a coach like that?

Sonny Hertzberg: Neil did very little coaching. When he was in the service, he had one or two players that he saw and brought them onto the Knicks. He thought they would be outstanding, but they didn't last the full year. I guess he didn't know the talent that was around in the League. He had coached at Manhattan College for many years, and Manhattan was able to get a great many of the high school players from the Catholic schools. He had some very nice material there.

Sonny Hertzberg: We were playing Cleveland in the [1947] quarterfinals. Well, Cleveland's floor wasn't the best to play on. There were nails and splinters and whatnot. I ripped my leg up, and somebody else got cut. Every call went to Cleveland; I don't know whether the crowd influenced them or if it was just poor judgment. At any rate, we went into the locker room and we were hosed. There's no question about it. We should have won easily. We were waiting for words of wisdom from the coach, and the first thing Neil said to us was, "Fellows, I hope there's beer on the train." That was very important to him. So that gives you an idea. I wouldn't want to knock him, but that was what he was thinking of.

Ralph Kaplowitz: I used to say to the guys, "What are we going to do about making a living after basketball?" We didn't think that the league would really prosper the way it ultimately did. In fact, the first year I think four teams went bankrupt: Toronto, Pittsburgh, Cleveland, and Detroit. So we didn't know; we just went along. But I was very concerned about what would happen when basketball was over. You can't play basketball all your life.

Sonny Hertzberg: We lost [to Philadelphia] in the semifinals of the playoffs, and the playoff money was huge. I'm not sure, but maybe it was $700 or $900 per share.

Edward S. "Ned" Irish, the founding father of the Knickerbockers and the man who would control their destiny for the better part of three decades, had already left a lasting imprint on the game a decade before the BAA was founded.

As a young sportswriter for the New York World-Telegram, *Irish conceived and promoted the concept of holding college doubleheaders in major arenas rather than in the cramped gyms of the era. The first Garden doubleheader, on December 29, 1934 (NYU–Notre Dame, St. John's–Westminster), was a rousing success and firmly established the college game in New York. Irish parlayed his success as the "Boy Promoter" into an executive vice presidency at the Garden, becoming the single most powerful figure in the sport.*

In 1946, Irish, and the Garden, would turn to the pro game. Alternately loved and loathed until his retirement in 1974, Irish would leave behind the franchise he founded as his enduring legacy.

Leonard Koppett: Irish was a very good businessman, to a degree. A good businessman in terms of setting up an organization and a system for the colleges where none had existed before. He was very arrogant. He came from rather modest beginnings and became very powerful, very rich, and made the most of it.

Leonard Lewin: His strength was that he was the head of Madison Square Garden basketball. That was his strength. That's it, period. He was in a great position. That's why everybody went after him to get him in the league.

Leonard Koppett: He had the brains and the forcefulness to organize the college doubleheader system, which revolutionized the game. And it coincided with the abandoning of the center jump and making it a much better spectator game.

Ray Lumpp: Ned was tough, but I always liked him. I always got along with Ned. He was the one who brought basketball to New York, first with the college game and then with the pros. He, Walter Brown in Boston, Eddie Gottlieb in Philadelphia, and Arthur Wirtz in Chicago really started the NBA.

Leonard Koppett: Irish knew no more about basketball than somebody's wolfhound. He knew the basketball *business.* He knew nothing about basketball, the game.

His whole complaint with the National League teams coming in–Rochester, Syracuse, and Minneapolis–was that they were minor league cities. That led to the famous marquee: "George Mikan vs. Knicks." It wasn't, as the players often took it, a put-down of other players. It was a refusal to put the word *Minneapolis* on the marquee, which had complete minor league connotations at that time.

Leonard Lewin: He didn't know anything about pro basketball. Even his moves were crazy. He didn't know what to do. He wasn't into pro basketball at all. What he did was, he took advantage of the fact that college basketball was so big in New York, and he loaded up the roster with New York guys.

Ralph Kaplowitz: I didn't deal with Ned Irish at all. When I played for New York University, I remember that Ned had been quoted in the papers as saying, "Ralph Kaplowitz is the best player I've ever seen." So I guess they wanted me.

Like many sports team owners of his era, Ned Irish tightly controlled the purse strings, which undoubtedly helped the fledgling league survive during those shaky early years.

Harry Gallatin: Ned wasn't giving away anything to anyone. You had to establish yourself with Ned. He was pretty close to the vest with his money, not like some of the owners today, that's for sure. I think he made a handsome profit for Madison Square Garden. And when the former players think about what our contracts were, we just wonder about how much they did make.

Leonard Lewin: He was tough with a dollar, very tough. Very careful.

Vince Boryla: I negotiated personally with Ned Irish. Ned called me and said that he had obtained my rights, so we had a couple of conversations. He sent Bud Palmer out to see me, and when I got through talking to him I said, "Bud, I know you've played for the Knicks, but I don't want to negotiate or talk with you." However I handled it, he knew we weren't making any headway. So the next thing I know, Ned calls me and says that he's on his way out to San Francisco and he'd like to stop by Denver. So he came here and we made our deal.

Harry Gallatin: We didn't have agents at the time. I negotiated all of my contracts with either Fred Podesta or Ned Irish. In most cases, Fred would say pretty much what the limitations were, and they were a lot. My first contract was for $4,500 in 1948. Never been to New York. It was the first plane ride for me as well, from St. Louis to New York. I was like a little country bumpkin in the big city.

Vince Boryla: At that time, Ned was by far the sharpest and most astute businessman I had ever met. I kind of knew that I was in a very enviable position because of the fact that however he had obtained my rights, I knew they weren't through normal channels, so to speak. Plus, I always had the ability to go back to school for my senior year. That put me in an excellent negotiating position. Somehow, the Good Lord has always blessed me with being able to negotiate very well. So I negotiated a contract for three years, at a total of $49,500– $16,500 per year–and it was a no-cut contract. And I had it paid out over four lump sums, $12,000 when I signed and one payment at the first of every year.

Dick McGuire: I didn't deal much with Ned. My brother John was my agent. He's the one that got me five thousand bucks my first year. It wasn't a lot, and he took half of it, I think. We probably dealt more with Podesta than with Ned. And I guess in those years they had a limit of five thousand or something. But after it was all over you heard that other guys did get paid a little bit more under the table or something.

Ralph Kaplowitz: After I left, Ossie Schectman got hurt in one of the games. He was seemingly OK, and then they went to Chicago. Ossie and Sonny Hertzberg roomed together. Sonny told me later that while they were in the room, Ossie was having trouble, and Sonny called for an ambulance. They got him to a hospital right away; otherwise, he would have died. Apparently, something was ruptured inside, either his spleen or something else. Fortunately, they got him to the hospital in time.

The Knicks management had Ossie's wife, Evelyn, come to Chicago to spend time with him. Ned Irish was very good that way.

Irish understood the importance of the media, and kept close tabs on what was written and said about his team.

Bob Wolff: I never saw Ned Irish. He hired somebody to review my shows all the time, all the telecasts. And I always got a copy of the reviews, which I was going to frame: "Superlative job as usual. . . . Great appeal. . . ." I don't know if Ned ever heard me, but these were glowing reviews. Which was fine with me. My only contact with Ned, really, was to say hello and good-bye.

Fuzzy Levane: Not that he was aloof, but he was very hard to get to know. And he knew enough about basketball to be dangerous, like most owners. There was one time when a kid from Utah [Wat Misaka] played against Kentucky at the Garden, and he did a heck of a job on Ralph Beard, held him to a couple of baskets. When the draft comes around, Ned takes Wat Misaka as the number one draft choice. Now, I'm not going to tell you how long Wat Misaka lasted, but if you look it up . . .

Leonard Lewin: He didn't like my uncle, Murray Lewin, who was a boxing writer with the *Mirror*. So he didn't like me when I started out, either.

Johnny Green: Ned was always a distant type of guy. Sometimes he'd come to practice and sit in the stands. If you happened to walk past him you'd speak a little to him, but other than that, we had very little contact with him.

Fuzzy Levane: Tom Meany was an old sportswriter who was a great friend of Ned's. After I came back from a road trip, Ned invited me to sit with Wellington Mara at one of the Giants' playoff games and to bring a couple of my friends. And Meany said, "Boy, you're really in good with Ned now." So that's when I knew I was accepted by Ned.

Bob Wolff: One day I did have a little skirmish with Ned. This is later on, after I'd been there for six or seven years. After a game, I said to him, "Hi, Ned."

He pointed his finger at me and said, "You're the reason we lost–and you know it!" "Well, no, I don't know it. What happened?" Ned said, "You went on the air at the beginning and said that we had a 10-game win streak at home, and that if we got one more it would be our longest home win streak in five years. That jinxed the game from that point on, and it was your fault." I apologized and told Ned that I had taken that from the Garden press release, so I assumed it was OK to use on the air. He almost threw me out of the room. He was serious.

Leonard Koppett: Irish himself was a very uncongenial person. Nobody enjoyed talking to Irish or going to dinner with him or anything like that. But he had a very good sense of what was important in public relations, and that's why he made Lapchick the coach. He was willing to wait a year to get him.

Leonard Lewin: Ned always thought the media was important. You know why? He not only was a sportswriter but also the publicity man for the football Giants before he hooked up with the Garden. He was there with Jim Wergeles' father, Chick.

Vince Boryla: He and I always got along very well. I admired him. I looked to him like my dad.

Leonard Lewin: Never was a fan of his. Never was. I treated him like he treated me: indifferently.

One year later than expected, Joe Lapchick finally took over as head coach, in 1947. Both as a player with the fabled Original Celtics and as coach at St. John's University, "the Big Indian" had already secured his place in the game's history. His Knicks tenure was such that, more than three decades after his death, he is still spoken of in reverent tones.

Fred Podesta: Joe was getting $3,500 from St. John's to coach basketball and $500 more for baseball, so we doubled that. We also promised him that no Knicks player would ever make more than the coach, and no one ever did.

Dr. Richard Lapchick: He did some things prior to taking the Knicks job that left an impression on me later, an impression of always striving to do the right thing. In 1946, he wrote a letter to one of his St. John's players, talking about the fact that he

had been offered the coaching job of the Knicks in this new league and that they were offering him double his salary. But he told the Knicks that he owed it to his seniors at St. John's to stay there until they finished; therefore, he turned down the job. With all the movement that goes on with college coaches today, my father showed a loyalty both to St. John's and to his players that you don't see much today.

Leonard Lewin: I knew him from the Original Celtics, with Nat Holman and those guys. We used to talk a lot about the Original Celtics.

Leonard Koppett: Lapchick was the most gregarious person in the world. He was a real publicity man for the Knicks. Ned had a very capable publicity man in Lester Scott, who did the work of releases and stuff like that. But the real public relations face of the Knicks and for the league as a whole was Lapchick. Lapchick was *the* great former pro star, *the* very successful St. John's coach. So all of the after-game sitting around at Leone's and other places, the luncheons and news conferences, were really opportunities for Lapchick to be friends with everybody. For the first few years, that was the key.

Bob Wolff: He was a high-energy coach. He'd come up to you and greet you, "Hello, Bob! How are you!" and all that. Tall, slender, domineering-type person. He loved to talk. Loved it. He loved to go to Leone's after the game and just talk basketball.

Ray Lumpp: We used to call him "the Tall One." He kept to himself. He had his own way of coaching.

Dick McGuire: Just a great, great person. He treated you like a man. He treated you very nice and you just went out and played hard. He wasn't a ranter or a yeller. He got very nervous at times, but he was a great, great person. I was fortunate to play for a lot of guys. But you'd be happy to have him as a father.

Leonard Koppett: Players who played for Lapchick really related to him. He had a way of inspiring a person's pride, which is what he talked about all the time. He wasn't a great *X*s and *O*s technician the way Clair Bee was, for example. But he was a leader. He could get people to want to do better than they were doing.

Spencer Ross: Lapchick had a theory when the game started that nobody could take a shot until everybody touched the ball. Can you imagine that? Obviously, if you're on a fast break it's different. But off the opening tip, that's what it was.

Dick McGuire: He got you in shape. He made us run a lot. We ran an awful lot with the fast break all the time.

Harry Gallatin: Joe was probably one of the nicest persons that I had met in pro ball, throughout the years that I had played. He was a gentleman. He wasn't someone who was an expert with the *X*s and *O*s and that kind of thing, or an intricate kind of system. He just wasn't that type. He wanted you to give your best effort, and he stressed that more than anything else. Just give me your best, and we'll take that.

Leonard Koppett: Lapchick preached all the concepts of a five-man game, and he operated that way. He was the only coach in the first years of the league to not even try to have a five-man unit. He had an eight-man unit, with guys like [Ernie] Vandeweghe coming off the bench.

Dr. Richard Lapchick: There was a famous Knicks-Celtics game at the Boston Garden. Bob Cousy had scored a basket, but one of the Knicks, it may have been Carl Braun, knocked it out of the basket before it could pass through, so the referees didn't think it was good, although it was. Now the play comes down to the other end of the court, and the Boston Garden fans are all screaming their heads off because of this missed call. My father called timeout and pointed out to the officials that the basket was good. I hear that story a lot, and it just shows my father's integrity and his sense of right and wrong.

Leonard Koppett: There was a certain warmth about him. He played cards with everybody, and he wasn't the greatest card player in the world.

Leonard Lewin: When I started traveling, Lapchick would keep me up all night. I couldn't go to bed until he told me to. He'd say, "Len, you can go to bed now." Stayed up all night talking about basketball.

Leonard Koppett: We're coming back from Syracuse on the train, playing cards. It's like 9:00 in the morning and we're entering New York City, to wind up at Grand Central. Everyone is playing poker in the dining car. For whatever reason, the train comes into the railroad yards in the Bronx, just before you come over the bridge into Manhattan, and stops and just sits there. Now, everybody thinks they're gonna get off in 10 minutes. But the train sits in the yards for over an hour. And in that hour, Lapchick gets wiped out!

The people who didn't like Lapchick and thought he was a phony—and that was totally wrong—said that he was unexpectedly ahead and wanted to wind up behind the writers, so he arranged for the train to stop.

Harry Gallatin: He was the kind of fellow that you'd go through a brick wall for. He was just that nice of a guy, and he didn't put too much pressure on you at all. The only time he might say something would be if you didn't hustle. Then you'd sit on the bench. He always had that prerogative.

Dr. Richard Lapchick: I saw my father cry twice, and both times made a lasting impression on me. Once was after he had gone back to St. John's. Usually, when my father came home at night, the first thing he would do was go upstairs and change. Then he'd come back downstairs, read the *Yonkers Herald-Statesman,* have a drink or a cup of coffee or whatever. But this time he didn't come down. When I went upstairs I found my father in his bedroom, sobbing. What had happened was he had found out that some of his players were hardly showing up in class, getting credit for work they hadn't done. And it shook him. First of all, he was crushed that a Catholic institution could let this happen. Then he realized that in all the years he'd coached, he never took an interest in his players' academic lives. He'd ask about their girlfriends and their families or whatever, but he never took an active role in their schoolwork. And he knew that had to change. So the next day, he went in and instituted the mandatory study halls for all athletes at St. John's.

Leonard Koppett: One of the things Lapchick did when the [college betting] scandals broke was that he put together a scrapbook, which he would show at the beginning of the year to the team,

Joe Lapchick in 1945, two years before he took over the Knicks.

and also when he went back to St. John's [as a warning to his players about the perils of gambling]. He'd make sure everyone went through it and signed it.

Bob Wolff: In his last year of coaching, at St. John's, he won both the Holiday Festival and the NIT, and I did both of those games, in the old building. That was some way to leave.

Dr. Richard Lapchick: Every once in a while someone will tell me a story about my father that reinforces for me what kind of person he was. It tells me that people will remember you if you don't go around talking about yourself, if you carry the important values of life. In his later years, my father got very involved with the Police Athletic League, and he tried to give of himself as much as he could.

Bob Wolff: In his later years, when he was out of coaching, he would send me sketches that he had made and pictures with funny captions. I don't know if I've saved any. It was an unusual hobby that he had. He'd cut a picture out of the paper, write a couple of funny lines on it, and send it.

Dr. Richard Lapchick: After he retired from St. John's, he did a lot of work up at Kutsher's Country Club, which was the site of the Maurice Stokes Game each summer. This happened the year [1969] in which Kareem Abdul-Jabbar played against Wilt Chamberlain. Kareem is a great friend of mine; in fact, he once told my father that if he had still been coaching at St. John's, Kareem would have gone there instead of to UCLA. So my father went to the arena for the game, and he's waiting in line outside with the rest of the crowd. Obviously, at 6'5", he's towering over most of the people there. The guy at the door knew my father and tried to wave him ahead, but my father refused. He didn't think he should jump ahead of anyone in line. And because of that, he missed the game. He never saw it.

[About the game today] I think he'd probably say, "Man, I wish I had had players with all these skills." But I think he'd be disappointed by the lack of teamwork and all the emphasis on individualism.

John Andariese: The first interview I ever did as a broadcaster was with Joe Lapchick, in the gondola of the New Garden at the 1970 NIT. At that time, he was looked upon the way John Wooden is today, a completely respected and revered man.

Dr. Richard Lapchick: A few years ago, I went to Louisiana to work with [legendary football coach] Eddie Robinson on his autobiography. The first night I met with him at Grambling State was the same night they celebrated the 50th anniversary of Jackie Robinson breaking the color barrier in major league baseball. I was with Eddie very, very late that night; he got very emotional. Then I came back to my little motel room and at about 2:30 in the morning I called my wife, as I always do when I'm on the road but rarely as late as 2:30. And I said, "I'll always regret that you and our children never met my father. But if you ever meet Eddie Robinson, that may be the closest you ever come."

"If I were pinned down and had to make a choice," wrote Daily News *columnist Jimmy Powers in 1954, "I'd say that the Knickerbockers, as a whole, are the best-liked group of athletes in our town."*

These were the Lapchick Knicks, the Knicks of Carl Braun and Vince Boryla . . . of the McGuire brothers . . . of Harry Gallatin, whose ironman streak of 610 consecutive games was still a club record a half century later . . . of Ray Lumpp and Connie Simmons and Max Zaslofsky and Ernie Vandeweghe . . .

Vince Boryla: I would compare our old Knicks team with minestrone soup. You put a little bit of this and a little bit of that, this and that and so on, and all of a sudden . . .

John Andariese: Dickie and Al McGuire. Vince Boryla bouncing the ball eight or nine times before shooting a foul shot. The presence of Sweetwater Clifton and Harry Gallatin. Ernie Vandeweghe going through medical school while he was a pro.

Cal Ramsey: I remember watching Carl Braun and Bud Palmer. My mom was a big fan of Bud Palmer's. Sweetwater Clifton and Harry Gallatin. I recall one of the All-Star Games [1954] when Dick McGuire and Bob Cousy played backcourt together. The game got down to the final seconds, and it was a two-point deficit for the West. And they got the ball to [George] Mikan and he got fouled with no time left on the clock, and he just went to the free throw line, just all cool and calm and collected, and hit two free throws underhanded to send it into overtime.

Kiki Vandeweghe: That was a dream ever since I was a little kid. I'd go with my dad to Madison Square Garden, and he'd tell me stories of his days playing with the Knicks: riding the subway down from Columbia and getting there in the middle of the first quarter and dressing [for the game], then going on road trips with the likes of Carl Braun and Sweetwater Clifton and Dick McGuire. So I had a real sense of history, ever since I was little, besides being a Knicks fan for a very long time.

John Andariese: Carl Braun is a Knicks legend that a lot of people have forgotten about. Great shooter, great style. Terrific competitor.

Vince Boryla: He [Braun] was probably one of the most outstanding shooters in the league at that time. He was a super teammate, a great guy to play with, and an outstanding scorer.

Ray Lumpp: I'm surprised his number hasn't been retired. He's very disenchanted about that; he thought he should have gotten more recognition. Carl carried us. He was one of the great scorers, one of the greatest of the early-day players. Carl could shoot. Man, could he shoot. And then he became a playmaker. As he got older, and then went to Boston, his overall game got better. But in his early days, could he shoot!

Fuzzy Levane: Carl Braun changed his game when I coached him. When he first came, he was a pure scorer and Dickie was the playmaker. But Braun was my playmaker, my point guard. He didn't shoot as much as he did when he had someone to handle the ball.

Dick McGuire: A very, very good shooter who changed his whole game around for us and became a very good passer. Scoring was his strength coming out of college. He was a big scorer. But he came here, and we passed the ball, and he became a more than adequate passer. He changed his game along the way. We backdoored guys an awful lot, me and Carl. He was such a good shooter that he'd fake to come to me on a back door, and it was easy just to throw the pass right through there. And he got to where he could do that with other people.

Harry Gallatin: Carl was a real scorer, even more than Vince [Boryla]. He was a natural outside shooter. He had a two-handed overhead shot that no one could block. Carl had tremendous range and was really a competitor. Carl wanted to win badly and would go out of his way to do whatever he could. He had great offensive ability and worked at it a lot.

Leonard Lewin: Carl Braun was a very quiet guy. And the Knicks have insulted him by never honoring him, never retiring his number.

John Andariese: In the Downtown AC League, I played against Carl Braun. He was playing for Eastman-Dillon. I probably had the greatest game of my life with Carl Braun guarding me, 40-something points. And being a great competitor, he wasn't happy. For me at that time, it was a thrill and a half. But I would be embarrassed if Carl knew that I was talking about that today.

Harry Gallatin: From time to time I used to go down to Rockaway Beach. Of course, that's where Dick and Al lived and where their family owned a bar. One time I went down there and asked Mrs. McGuire, who was just as nice an Irish lady as you can imagine, "Mrs. McGuire, are you sure that somebody didn't leave Al on your doorstep? Your two boys are so different. One doesn't say a word, and you can't get the other one to shut up!" She said, "No, Harry, they're both mine. But they *are* different, aren't they?"

Leonard Lewin: Dickie was the basketball player, not Al. Al was a two-minute player who'd foul out. Dickie was a great passer, not a shooter. In fact, somebody once said that Ned Irish offered Dickie 10 dollars for every shot he took. And he still didn't shoot.

Vince Boryla: Put it this way: if Al, at that time, had told me something was white, I'd figure it had turned gray or black. And Dickie . . . I've often said I would give him my power of attorney. That was the difference.

Dick McGuire: For some reason Lapchick liked my game and whatever I did out there, and the rest was easy. As far as passing and shooting, I haven't the slightest idea why I did not shoot. I didn't look to shoot that much; I really didn't know why. It was not by design at all. And people started making me out to be a nonscorer. Hey, the guy who led us in scoring was Carl Braun, and he averaged about 12, 14 points a game. I averaged about eight. We're not talking big scoring–there's not a big difference there. I was happier making the play, I guess. It was easier than making the basket.

Vince Boryla: I love Dickie. We called him Mumbles. He was a great individual. He always had a roll of money on him. If you ever ran short, you could always borrow money from him. He was a great player, a great teammate, and above all, just a premier, super individual.

Harry Gallatin: The more I see Jason Kidd play, the more I think about Dick. To me, he and [John] Stockton remind me an awful lot of Dick. Except Dick wouldn't shoot! But all you had to do was go without the ball and try to find some room, and you got the ball just where you wanted it. There were times I felt I should have given half my paycheck to Dick, but I needed it for my family. He was a great playmaker and ahead of his time when it came to making the play.

Dick McGuire: I wouldn't know how to tell anybody how to become the middleman on a fast break. If I could have, I would have tried. I just knew that when the ball went up there, for some reason, I didn't give a damn what, I'd be in the middle. I don't know how the hell I got there or why I got there, but that's where I ended up. And I don't know if you can teach that. I just think it's something you have. It's not that easy to do, if guys aren't used to doing it.

Leonard Lewin: Al was the outgoing guy, a big talker. Always a lot of energy. Dick was casual.

Ray Lumpp: Al was very loud, and Dick was Mumbles, very quiet. Dick was a tremendous ballplayer, Al was a great competitor, and they both eventually made the Hall of Fame. When we started the [1951–52] season, Al was a rookie, and he carried the balls.

Vince Boryla: Al was Al. Most of us could shoot better blindfolded than he could with his

eyes open. He had the touch of a blacksmith. But he hustled, played great defense, and was an excellent card player.

Leonard Lewin: Al got into a fight one night at the Armory. John, his brother, who was a detective, came out of the stands to help out. They grabbed John and threw him out.

Dick McGuire: [Al was a] very good talker [laughs]. He hustled like hell. A guy who was a very poor shooter but a very good runner. He could finish on the fast break. That was his strength. And he was quick. He wasn't a bad defensive player. He wasn't afraid to hold you or foul you and all that. A great player? No. But he might have been a real good player.

Leonard Lewin: Once they were playing down at the Armory. There was a timeout, and Lapchick started chewing out Al McGuire for some reason. After a few moments, after the crowd had quieted down, suddenly somebody shouted out, "Bullshit!" It was Al.

Harry Gallatin: Dick and Bob Cousy were similar in the way they played, except that Bob liked to score quite a bit.

Dick McGuire: [Bob Cousy was] very, very tough. Extremely tough. And the weird thing about it is that my brother Al covered him over the years more than I did. Al played him more than I did. But he didn't own him. I played Bill Sharman more than Cousy.

Leonard Lewin: We're playing in Boston, and the game is over. There was a writer up there named Clif Keane who was a great Cousy fan. So Al sees Clif walk in the door, and he jumps on the table, turns to Dickie, and yells, "You don't know how to play Cousy! I own him!" So Clif Keane wrote the story, and the next game we came up there, the place was jammed.

Dickie once came to one of my son's birthday parties. What do you think he brought him? A bow and arrow. Metal tipped! My son never saw it. It went right in the incinerator. Otherwise I'd be walking around with an arrow in my head.

Vince Boryla: Harry Gallatin was a real strong, tough guy. Tough as a horse. He was a great

Carl Braun denies Boston's Bob Cousy as Sweetwater Clifton (No. 8) and Dick McGuire (No. 15) back up the play.

rebounder for his size and not a bad shooter. A very strong defensive ballplayer and a very fine person.

Dick McGuire: In his time, he was so good. When he slashed to the basket . . . if I was going left, he'd come slashing to the basket. It made it very easy for me to feed him with my left hand. Or if he was going the other way, I'd feed him off my right hand. He had a great knack for getting a guy off his back, and I was just able to get him the ball in the right spot at the right time. He'd come to play all the time. He's a really, really good guy.

Harry Gallatin: There were times when my wife told me I really shouldn't play. I did have the flu a few times. Something that was unusual–and I think it may have been true not only for me but for other people–was that when you may not be feeling well, you have a chance to relax and maybe you don't push yourself the way you otherwise do. And so I always had some pretty doggone good games when I wasn't feeling that well. I don't know what there is to that, but there must be something there.

Leonard Lewin: We had a funny thing happen in Syracuse one night. Under the basket they had a mat on the floor. It was depressed, you know, because the basket had to stand on iron legs. So they put the mat under the basket where the iron legs were so that no one would get hurt. One night Gallatin drove down the lane and slid, and his head went under the mat. They thought he'd lost his head.

Harry Gallatin: The thing I'm most proud of whenever people talk about consecutive streaks is this: My mother isn't alive now, but she probably could have told you that I didn't miss a game or a practice in grade school, in junior high school, in high school . . . didn't miss a game or a practice all the way through my basketball career, and that includes the playoffs. So when I say my prayers, I thank God for the health that I've enjoyed. I don't know of anybody else who hadn't missed a practice or a game in their entire basketball career. I really feel proud about that.

Leonard Lewin: Gallatin and his family lived next to Ernie Vandeweghe in Oceanside. And one day his kids took a paintbrush and painted over Ernie's brand new Cadillac.

Spencer Ross: We used to kid Vince Boryla that if he played in the church league we played in Brooklyn, every one of his shots would hit the ceiling. He took a set shot that was called the Boryla Bomb. It was the highest-arching set shot I've ever seen.

Leonard Lewin: Vince Boryla was a hard-nosed Notre Dame player. Hard-nosed. Rough rebounder. Fair shooter. A rugged player who'd knock you down all the time. Boryla was the muscle man. He didn't care; he just knocked bodies around.

Ray Lumpp: Vince and I were on the Olympic team in '48. After the Olympics, Vince didn't go back to South Bend. He got married and moved to Denver and went to Denver University. After he got through, Ned Irish sent Bud Palmer out to recruit Vinnie, because Vinnie had another year of eligibility but the Knicks were gonna draft him. Bud went out and made the arrangements for Vince to join the Knicks.

Vince Boryla: I signed with the Knicks in 1949. Somehow, the Knicks had gotten my rights. At that time, I had a year of college eligibility left at the University of Denver; I had transferred from Notre Dame after my second year. I came to Denver and played on an AAU team, the original Denver Nuggets, and so I decided to stay here in Denver. There was another pro league, the National League, and I had been negotiating with a club there. But I had another year of ball at the University of Denver. The Knicks, somehow, had obtained my rights. To be completely truthful, to this day I still don't know how. That's really the truth. The only one who would know would be Ned Irish, who's upstairs in a better place.

Ray Lumpp: Vinnie had been a center in college. He was 6'6". Now, 6'6" isn't usually a center, but Vinnie developed an outside shot, and he became the best outside shooter on the team. He had that high, two-hand set. Vince was never a great rebounder, but he could put that ball in the hoop. And he had a great hook shot, going across the middle. He converted his game from a center, playing in the keyhole, and moved outside where he could shoot with the best of them. He'd beat everybody in

H-O-R-S-E. He could outshoot anybody. And a good, tough competitor.

Vince Boryla: I really didn't know anything about the pro league. Being here in Denver, we didn't have TV or this and that. I really didn't know what to expect.

Leonard Koppett: There's a lot to say about Boryla. He was an outstanding player and also a very good businessman. Irish liked him. They hit it off very well. Big outside shooter and rough inside.

Harry Gallatin: Vince liked to score. He had a really good outside shot. He wasn't a great defensive player, somebody that would get in there and mix it up all the time. That's what I was. But he had a lot of intelligence as a player. Vince was successful because he thought about the game a lot and knew the inside. He got himself open a lot of times and got himself into a position where he could score. He wasn't extremely fast or anything like that, but he was a smart player.

Les Keiter: Vince Boryla was a great basketball figure. He was the first man to be an All-American on two different college teams: at Denver University first, and then at Notre Dame. He was already coaching the Knicks for a year or so before I became the voice of the Knicks. We traveled together and got to be very good friends.

Vince Boryla: Connie Simmons was a very, very underrated ballplayer. Connie played well. He was a nice person and very, very funny. He and Al were always cutting up.

Dick McGuire: Connie wasn't a big rebounder. Connie was one of the first big centers that could go outside and shoot the ball and handle the ball very well. But he wasn't very physical.

Vince Boryla: Connie was a great road ballplayer; he picked up the slack for us when Sweets [Sweetwater Clifton] didn't play well on the road. But when we came back to New York, Sweets played like hell and Connie took a back seat.

Harry Gallatin: Connie was one of the centers in the league who could play against George Mikan, because he could shoot outside, from 15 feet and out. He was a pretty good shooter with a nice touch from out there. He could get up and down the court

really well. We always thought we had an advantage with Connie playing against George, especially on offense. He could draw George out far enough where we could possibly penetrate and sneak in to the basket.

Ray Lumpp: Ernie Vandeweghe was a great competitor. He came to play. While he was in med school, he was playing games on weekends and going to school during the week. He was a helluva player. He'd come in and fire us up.

Leonard Lewin: Ernie was doing double duty, trying to get his degree in medicine and play with the Knicks. He'd get in just in time for the games. He was ready to play all the time. Very good shooter, good offensive man, good team player. He'd sacrifice for the team.

Ray Lumpp: After I played in the [1948] Olympics, I had been drafted by Indianapolis. Bruce Hale, Rick Barry's father-in-law, was the coach. That first year, I was the leading rookie scorer in the league, with 777 points. In January [1949], the Knicks traded Tommy Byrnes and money to Indianapolis for me. It was a strange situation. My wife and family were all in New York. I was living in a rooming house in Indianapolis with Lionel Malamed, who played at City College. I got a call one morning from the owner, Paul Walk, who owned the Ford agency out there. And he said to me, "Ray, how would you like to play for the Knickerbockers?" I told him I damn well would, you know, being that I was from New York. He said, "I'll put you in a Knicks uniform tonight." He said that since he owed me two weeks' pay, he'd pay for my plane ticket to Philadelphia, where the Knicks were playing, and that would square everything. I said, "Gee, since it's only a month or so into the season, I don't know if I want to lose that pay." So I walked out and called my wife. She said, "Honey, where have you been? Ned Irish has been looking for you. You were traded to the Knicks last night." So here was the guy trying to steal from me, and the deal was already made.

Spencer Ross: When the Chicago Stags disbanded, there were three players available. Everybody wanted Max Zaslofsky. Second choice was Andy Phillip, and the third choice was a guy named Bob Cousy. Well, there was the Celtics, the Philadelphia Warriors, and the Knicks. The Knicks picked first out of the hat and selected Max. Philly went second and took Andy Phillip, and the Celtics had to settle for Bob Cousy. That's like when Sam Bowie was drafted ahead of Michael Jordan.

Leonard Koppett: They were getting better and better. And in 1950, they picked up Max Zaslofsky, who was an All-League scorer. The Knicks were delighted. Zaslofsky made them a great team and a running team.

Spencer Ross: Max had a very interesting shot. He had a two-handed set shot, and people might say that there's no way he could have gotten that shot off today. Well, Max could have gotten his shot off at any time. Because what Max did was, he'd get the ball and take this little minidribble, either to his left or his right. He'd look for a pick, bounce the ball, and shoot fast. And that's how he was able to get the ball away quickly.

Fred Podesta: One of the great things then was the way the players cooperated in the clinics we staged. We rotated the summer camps around the area, and the players carried a projector and motion pictures with them. They were paid, I think, $500 for about two months, and there wasn't a player who refused or complained. They wanted to do it, and money wasn't a part of it.

Ray Lumpp: My biggest salary was $7,000. Today, my pension's more than that, so does that tell you something? But that's the way it was.

Vince Boryla: It was probably the first time I ever heard the word *chemistry* used to describe a team. As I reflect on the definition of the word *chemistry* in sports, I think our team was an outstanding example of that. Individually, we weren't that good. Collectively, we had a better-than-average ballclub.

Perhaps the best-loved Knick of the era carried the heaviest burden.

Born Clifton Nathaniel in Chicago, Nat "Sweetwater" Clifton had been a minor league first baseman for the Cleveland Indians and a much-publicized member of the Harlem Globetrotters prior to signing with the Knicks. With Boston's Chuck Cooper and

Washington's Earl Lloyd, the trio would break the NBA's color barrier at the start of the 1950–51 season.

New York would welcome Sweetwater with open arms. On the road, it was sometimes a different story.

Ray Lumpp: Sweets had been a Globetrotter, and during that time we always said to him, "Sweets, don't you want to join the Knicks?" Finally, Ned Irish made the deal with Abe Saperstein and got him to come to the NBA.

Leonard Koppett: It wasn't a revolutionary thing in Clifton's case for the following reasons: First, Jackie Robinson had done what he had done in 1947. The color line had been broken in baseball, and baseball was so much more important than anything else. Jackie in baseball, a few players in the All-America Conference, which was challenging the NFL . . . The issue of a black person in major league sports had pretty much been settled in '47 and '48. Clifton, after all, had been very prominent himself as a Globetrotter. And the Globetrotters weren't nobodies; they were bigger than the NBA at that point. So when he came in, it wasn't an issue of breaking a color line in New York at that time.

Ray Lumpp: I remember the first time Sweetwater came to practice. He was older than most of the players; you never knew exactly what his age was. We were practicing at NYU at the time. Ned had signed him to the contract, but he didn't come to practice for a while, for some reason. Then as training season was winding down, he showed up at NYU one day. Joe blew the whistle and said, "OK, let's pair up." Then he went to Sweets and said, "Sweets, where do you want to play?" Joe never asked any of us that, he *told* us. You were this, you were that. But with Sweets, he said, "Where do you want to play?"

Dr. Richard Lapchick: My father's views on racial injustice were formed very early on, when he played for the Original Celtics. They'd play the New York Rens, the famous all-black team, and after the game my father and the Celtics would get on this big luxury bus to go to dinner or to the next town. And he'd see the Rens bringing their food on their bus because no restaurant would serve them. That stayed with him.

The Rens had a great player named Tarzan Cooper. Whenever my father played against him, he wouldn't shake Cooper's hand before the center jump. Instead, he embraced him. It showed everyone where he stood on the racial issue.

Clifton was willful and tough on the court, but gentle off it.

Ray Lumpp: When Sweets first came, he couldn't shoot a lick. But I'll tell you what, he could rebound and play defense. But then his shot came a long way, and he could put the ball in the basket.

Dick McGuire: Not a real good shooter. He'd shoot a knuckleball from out there. But he had great hands and was very, very physical. He had huge hands, and it probably affected his shooting.

Harry Gallatin: He was only about 6'5". A lot of the publicity surrounding Sweets had him much taller. He wasn't really that tall, but he had good positioning underneath the basket. Once he got his hands on the ball, it was his. We really liked Sweets a lot, and he blended right in with our team.

Leonard Lewin: Big hands. Lapchick would say to the other players, "Don't touch him," because he was a tough fighter. I once said to him, "Hey, Sweets, what are you playing basketball for? Let me manage you as a fighter. I'll bring you along very carefully. I'll give you a fight with [Bob] Satterfield, the light heavyweight champ. You can start with him." Sweets said, "You wanna know something? When I was a kid, I used to kick the shit out of Satterfield."

Harry Gallatin: He used to meet up with Satterfield on the corner and have at it once in a while, growing up in Chicago. Sweets could handle himself.

Ray Lumpp: We loved Sweets. Loved him. My kids used to call him "Sweet Wah-Wah." Sweets was a loveable guy. He always had candy in his pocket, and my kids would come up and ask Sweet Wah-Wah for candy. Sweets was the best.

Leonard Lewin: One time Sweetwater was late for practice up at West Point. Lapchick asked him, "Where were you?" Sweets said, "I was getting a haircut." At West Point?

Harry Gallatin: The sweetest guy you'd ever want to know. Not very aggressive as a player, unless you challenged him. You'd never meet a nicer guy than Sweetwater. In fact, there were times when we thought he might have been a little too nice. He had a lot of talent, especially around the basket. Hands that were like suitcases. He could really handle the ball, and he was a much better defensive player than most people gave him credit for.

Vince Boryla: Sweets was probably one of the worst card players we had. When Sweets dropped out of a pot, it was like the roof was gonna come down. He just played every hand. He was a great guy to be with.

Harry Gallatin: Red Auerbach, we always felt, liked to have one player on his team who would take our best forward or center and get his measure of fouls, so to speak. We always called them hackers. Jim Loscutoff, Bob Brannum, and those guys were in that category, as was Bob Harris. From time to time, they'd get a little too aggressive in fouling.

Les Keiter: We were playing the Celtics, and they had a big guy named Bob Brannum. He and Clifton tangled in the middle of the game, and Brannum said, "I want a piece of you." And I can still hear Clifton saying, "You're not gonna have a piece of me. You're gonna have *all* of me."

Leonard Lewin: Bob Harris tested Clifton once, and Clifton flattened him. The Celtics started to come off the bench, then pulled up short. And Lapchick said, "You could smell the rubber burn." From there on, they left him alone.

Harry Gallatin: Sweets didn't like one of the fouls that Harris gave him, and he showed his prowess as a boxer, and from that time on we didn't have very much of a problem with Red Auerbach and his grizzly guys.

Vince Boryla: His ballplaying at home was about 40 or 50 percent better than it was on the road. When he played in front of a home crowd, in New York, he played outstanding ball. On the road, he didn't play like I thought maybe he was capable of. Every now and then, when we needed a win, everybody would go by Sweets during the warm-ups and pat him on the butt and say,

Lapchick was sitting pretty when he welcomed Clifton in 1950.

"Sweets, we need you tonight, baby." And Sweets usually delivered.

Harry Gallatin: When we went on the road, we would all be in Sweets' corner if there was any problem.

Leonard Koppett: For us, it wasn't a color issue. It was for Sweets, obviously, and for Ray Felix later on, because they had to live it. But in the context of the Knicks operation, to the public, it wasn't a big issue at the time. The issue had been settled.

Ray Lumpp: There were two cities where we felt very bad for Sweets. When we went to Indianapolis, we used to stay at the Claypool Hotel. Sweets wasn't allowed to stay there; he'd stay in the black area. When we went to Baltimore, we stayed at the Lord Baltimore Hotel. He wasn't allowed to stay there, either. He had to go to the other end of town. We felt very bad when we'd get off a plane and then take a cab or bus into town, and he couldn't stay with us. "I'll see you at the game," he'd always say. It never bothered him; it was just a fact of life back then. But all the guys felt bad that we could all play together on the court, but we couldn't sleep together. That was wrong. It had to be righted, and it eventually was.

Vince Boryla: You know what? I think if Sweets had had his druthers, he would have preferred to have stayed at the places he stayed. Because, I'm telling you, he was king of the hill at those places. When he walked in, it was almost like God walked in. He had the whole place to himself. They catered to him and so on. Had he been with us, he might have gotten pushed around. Even toward the end, where there were several places he could have stayed with us, he didn't want to stay with us. I think Sweets loved the life that he lived.

Leonard Koppett: The white world wasn't educated or attuned to it yet. Most of the hardships they went through were visible to their teammates, but not as visible to the press.

John Andariese: One of my greatest disappointments came several years ago, when I found out that Sweetwater Clifton was driving a cab in Chicago. One of my goals was to go to Chicago and capture him for an interview, to meet him, shake his hand, and tell New York where he is and what he's all about today. And he died! He died before I could get it done. I felt so bad about that.

For a city, and perhaps for an entire nation, the voice that described the Knicks' exploits during their formative years was the voice of basketball itself.

Spencer Ross: Marty Glickman was kind of like the Louis Armstrong or the Charlie Parker of broadcasting. He invented something. Like all the great musicians, he had people along the way who helped him. But Marty created the notes, he created the music, he created the rhythm of what basketball play-by-play was.

Leonard Koppett: Marty got into broadcasting just before the war, on WHN with Bert Lee and Dick Fishell. Marty was doing the college games, and he really created the style of how to broadcast a basketball game.

Marv Albert: Marty was the model of what a radio game should sound like, be it Knicks basketball, Giants football, whatever. His pre- and postgame shows were great. He was someone whose style I got to admire, and he was such a wonderful person, particularly with young people who were interested in getting into broadcasting. He took an interest in me during my days as a ballboy.

Spencer Ross: He invented the idea of geographically describing how a game was played. I used to kid Marty, "Do you realize there are young people today who still talk about the top of the key when describing the court?" And sometimes I'll say to someone very young, "What looks like a key or a keyhole on that basketball court?" But it's something that has lasted from Marty. He invented the term because at that time, when the lane was only six feet wide, it looked like a keyhole.

Leonard Koppett: He could talk fast enough to follow every pass, every play, every shot, every rebound. He had the talent to make it all make sense. He didn't just say, "Joe Blow passes to Joe Schmo who passes to . . . " He gave you the play: "So-and-so comes down the left side, passes in the middle to so-and-so, hook shot–good, like Nedick's!"

And nobody else was doing basketball in those days. All the big shots–the Ted Husings, Mel Allens, and Red Barbers–were doing football and baseball. And once the betting became more prevalent, everybody's listening.

Les Keiter: Marty had that great expression, and I admired it. One of the sponsors was Nedick's, the orange drink place in the lobby of the Garden. And with every good shot by the Knicks, he'd go, "It's good, like Nedick's." I thought that was a very clever line.

Al Albert: Not only was he incredible to listen to, he was always available with his time, and he loved to coach aspiring announcers. Any question about the business, he was always there. He was a walking textbook. If you were searching for something, he'd have the answer.

Spencer Ross: Marty's first analyst on the Knicks was a female tennis star, Sarah Palfrey Cooke. In her first game, Marty started off. Through about four minutes of the game, she didn't say a word. Then one of the Knicks hit a basket, made the score 17 to 14 or whatever, and Marty said, "Well, Sarah, what do you think of that?" She said, "Well, that was beautiful, Marty." And that's all she said for the rest of the first half. And Marty, who would develop a lot of female broadcasters later on, knew this wasn't going to work. She lasted about five games.

Leonard Koppett: When the Knicks started up, Marty was already a radio presence who added prestige to the Knicks broadcasts. So at the same time, he was one of us, and he's also an ex-athlete. He was the centerpiece of both the team and the coverage. He was a great person, an incredibly talented and original broadcaster. Both the players and Lapchick appreciated what he was, which hasn't always been the case with broadcasters.

Glickman had distinct ideas about how a game should be called, and he never wavered from them.

Spencer Ross: Marty had a problem with being the home team's announcer. Some guys call their teams "we." He didn't believe in that. But he did believe that you're doing the games for a particular team in a particular city. You lean to them. If you don't think you lean to them, that's the stupidest thing in the world. You know those people, they're your team. And the people who are listening to the game, who are they leaning to? They don't want to know that the Boston Celtics, with six seconds to go, have the ball and need a basket to win the game. They want to know what the Knicks have to do to stop the Celtics from getting that basket. That's the type of lean that Marty understood and felt was the only way to go.

Marv Albert: There were certain things he expected, and I believed very strongly in the same philosophy. You never wanted to let him down in any way. He was so giving in advice. What amazed me about Marty was that he would do a Giants football game or a Knicks game on the road, and I'd always listen. And then he'd ask me afterward, "What did you think?" And I'm like 20 years old, and he's asking me what I think! But there were certain things I would point out to him, and he'd listen, and it would affect his work, which was amazing to me.

Steve Albert: He was so close to Marv, it influenced me to a great degree because I saw the respect level between Marv and Marty. I would listen to Marty, and I thought that he was the greatest.

Al Albert: He was the guy. He drew us all into the profession. He was a star, just at an awesome level. When you listened to him, wherever you were, you felt like you were at the game. And he had just the right combination of excitement with information, and I think that became the guide for how we all processed what we did. Marty started all three of us [Al, Marv, and Steve]. He got me my first break in getting the Nets job. He got me to New York on WHN; he was close to Roy Boe, and everything kind of came together.

Spencer Ross: Marty liked numbers a lot on radio. I'd say, "But you can't see numbers on the radio." He'd say, "Yes, but you remember No. 10 is Walt Frazier, and No. 19 is Willis Reed." That becomes another identifying figure as you're imagining who these people are.

Marv Albert: When he did the High School Game of the Week, I was listed as producer. I'd go ahead to the schools and do all the research for him. The actual coproducers were David Garth, who became the great political analyst, and Peter Engel, who's a very successful Hollywood producer. He did *Saved by the Bell* and a lot of other shows.

Spencer Ross: Marty understood the difference between radio and television, and what to say and what not to say. You never had to say on television that the shot was good from the left baseline. All you had to say was, "Frazier . . . And the Knicks lead 10 to 6." It still makes me nuts to hear a lot of TV guys tell me the basket is good, that it was an 18-footer along the baseline. What do you have, a measuring rod?

Marv Albert: I'd be walking around where I'd constantly, in my own head, think of the terminology. I'd make lists up and review it. I'd see a game in the schoolyard and I'd be doing it to myself: "So-and-so along the right sideline, into the right corner, along the baseline . . . " All that stuff came very naturally.

Les Keiter: I'm not sensitive about it [the rivalry with Glickman] at all. I was an admirer of Marty Glickman before I ever left the West Coast to come to New York. I thought, with Harry Wismer, Ted Husing, and Bill Stern, he was a guy doing a lot of the major events. That's been built up as an ongoing, long-lasting feud, and it never was. I had complete respect for him, and as far as I could remember, he had respect for my ability. But he felt that I was a carpetbagger, because of our station coming in and getting the rights to all the things he'd been doing. But there was no feud at all. There were a few unpleasant moments, but he and I were rivals. It was a competitive situation, and it continued the whole time I was in New York.

Spencer Ross: Marty was my severest critic, and he was my biggest champion. I'm a very fortunate guy. I have three children, two of them twin boys who were three months premature. They're very fortunate to be alive. They were born in June of 1974. John was given no chance to live and David was given a 50-50 chance. They were in the hospital for about 60 days. During that time, I was doing a lot of work for Home Box Office, and Marty was an

official there. My mind really wasn't on my work at the time. I had a World Football League game in Philadelphia down at the old JFK Stadium. And I was about as unprepared as I've ever been for an event in my life. One thing about preparation is that when you prepare for an event, it's a piece of cake. It's easy. It's not rocket science. Marty taught me that. But this was the longest three hours I've ever spent in my life, because I wasn't prepared. And when I got back to New York, Marty yelled at me. And I said, "Don't you understand my situation?" And Marty said, "Yes, I do. But you had an option, and that was not to do it. Always remember that. If you're not prepared, don't ever go on the air." I never forgot that. And many years later, right before he died, we talked about that. And he said, "I have to tell you the truth. That happened to me once, too." I'm sure it happened to Marty Glickman only once.

Marv Albert: When I started doing games, he was so supportive. He would point things out and see things that no one else would be able to see. During one game I constantly had players driving "straight down the lane." He said, "You get into bad habits sometimes." He knew that players didn't just go *straight* down the lane, they went across the lane sometimes. Who else would think of that?

Spencer Ross: Marty used to spend the winters in St. Petersburg, and whenever I was in Florida I'd make sure I'd see him. This was about a year before he passed away. I didn't realize how much he had slowed down, and it was a very melancholy thing. We had lunch right on the beach. It was a fish place with these great fried fish sandwiches. I was starting to get very emotional, and he said, "Spencer, I know it's coming to an end. I know what I've lost, and I ain't getting it back. But you know something? What a great ride I had. Can anybody think of a better life than I've had? Life is a short trip, and this has been a great trip for me. Don't feel bad for me. Nobody could have had a better life than I had."

With their home arena perennially booked for other, better-drawing events, the Knicks would not play a complete home schedule at Madison Square Garden until 1960–61. Until then, their alternate home–and the site of

Cousy and Sweets chase down a loose ball at the Old Garden in 1955.

some of their most memorable games–would be the gray, high-walled fortress that still stands on Lexington Avenue and 26th Street, a century after its opening.

Fred Podesta: We just had to find a place in the city, somewhat in the vicinity of the Garden. It came down to the armories. We found most of them unsuitable for what we needed. They didn't have the right configuration for basketball. The only one that fit the basic needs was the 69th Regiment Armory. It was the best of nothing, but it had a balcony and a high ceiling. We used to run boxing matches at Yankee Stadium in those days, and we kept four to five thousand portable seats there. We not only had to move and store them at the Armory, we had to keep breaking down the setup according to Armory requirements, such as drills for the National Guard and other events covered by state regulations.

Spencer Ross: I loved the Armory. The first time I ever saw the Armory was on television. And to light it, apparently, they had to use these really harsh lights, and it made the floor look like a jewel. It was a beautiful floor.

Dick McGuire: The Armory floor was much, much better [than the Garden's]. The ball bounced much more truly. The Garden had a lot of dead spots where the ball could go down on you. It had a lot of dead spots where the Armory didn't. I enjoyed playing in the Armory, except that we didn't have as many fans there, not as much yelling.

Ray Lumpp: The floor was great: it was a solid floor. But it was still an armory. It didn't have the flair of the Garden, or the buildup. You didn't have the same feeling you had playing in the Garden.

Marv Albert: The Armory was almost like being in a theater watching a game. You had very low seats in the mezzanine area. The elevation of the seating areas wasn't much. You just didn't get the feeling you were in a basketball arena. It was just a big armory where they set up a basketball court. And there were some very big games played there in the early years. Good hot dogs, too.

Vince Boryla: We almost looked at the Armory as an away-from-home court, like we were on the road. It was easy to get to. We used to practice a lot there; that's where most of our practices were.

John Andariese: I played at the Armory for Fordham against St. John's, probably the only televised game I ever played in. It had linoleum floors and the weirdest clock in the world, a round clock with a dozen dials on it.

Phil Pepe: The Armory was an unusual place to play, and I clearly remember the doubleheaders. The Knicks would play in the second game, and more people would be there for the first game to see the Celtics, for instance, against whoever.

Marv Albert: The Armory was a unique place because the access that fans had to the players was very unusual. I recall working as a ballboy and being in the dressing room with the Syracuse Nats. Some of the players–I think Dolph Schayes was one–were using the urinals, and suddenly a couple of fans just walk in. So they're all lined up against the wall, and Dolph gave them a look. They said, "Hey, Dolph. How you doin'?"–walked in and walked out, and that was it. That would happen all the time, even though there were cops outside the door. It was pretty loose. You wouldn't see it today.

As an upstart team in the most demanding sports city in the nation, the Knicks needed an assist or two from the media to gain attention among New Yorkers during those early years.

Leonard Lewin: Everybody hung out at Leone's. That was the basketball hangout. Everybody went there after the games. Lapchick, even Ned Irish. Gene Leone was a big fan.

Fuzzy Levane: We used to go over to Leone's with our beat writers. I don't know if that's how it is today. It's a whole different ballgame today. It's a corporate thing. Our old office at the Garden was ridiculous; it was a couple of rooms. Now you've got a whole floor in a skyscraper.

Leonard Lewin: One day Podoloff came to one of our weekly lunches at Leone's. We put a 24-second clock on the balcony in back of him. And 24 seconds into his speech, the thing went off.

Les Keiter: Those luncheons were fabulous. When I first got to New York, there was a group called the Sports Broadcasters Association, and they met every week at Leone's in the private dining room upstairs. The first time I walked into that room, I was absolutely starstruck. Because sitting around the table were the likes of Mel Allen, Red Barber, Don Dunphy, Ernie Harwell, and Curt Gowdy. Just the icons of my profession.

Phil Pepe: The *Post* was probably most responsible for giving the Knicks the coverage they wanted. The *Post* in those days was the, quote-unquote, basketball paper. Ike Gellis was tremendously responsible and deserves a lot of credit for putting the Knicks on the map. He covered them religiously, gave them good play, and treated that assignment almost as the equal of anything else. He recognized that the time after baseball was open, and he was gonna jump into the basketball thing.

Leonard Lewin: The *Post* was always known as the basketball paper. They traveled and covered all the games. Ike Gellis and Paul Sann, the editors, were basketball nuts. They loved the game.

Leonard Koppett: The *Post* was clearly the basketball paper. This goes back to the early forties. At that time, the *Post* was *the* liberal paper in New York. It's an afternoon tabloid, and its readership had a higher proportion of Jewish readers than any other paper, because of its politics. It's down-the-line, Roosevelt Democrat–in columnists, in editorial position, everything. James Wechsler, who would wind up fighting against Joe McCarthy and Walter Winchell, was the editor. Max Lerner was the top columnist. It's *the* liberal paper. Well, that audience– New York liberal, heavily Jewish and Irish–loved basketball. They've always been basketball fans, but they weren't getting any attention. The *Post* satisfied them with heavy basketball coverage, basically of the Garden games–the colleges and then the Knicks.

Phil Pepe: Back then, the Knicks used to pay to send us [reporters] on the road. By that time, baseball had stopped doing that. In the old days, baseball did it, too. The *World-Telegram*, the *Journal-American*, and the *Post* all accepted these trips, which was the Garden's attempt to get space in the papers. We wouldn't cover if we had to pay for the trips. The papers couldn't afford to send us on the road. The Knicks would pick up all the expenses, and it continued right into the mid-sixties.

Leonard Lewin: At the start, very few newspaper writers traveled with them [the team] during the season. I think only the *Post*. Then when I went out, I only went out because they [the Knicks] were paying my expenses. Otherwise, [sports editor Dan] Parker would never have sent us out. Never. But sometimes some of the other papers wouldn't accept that, like the *Times*.

Leonard Koppett: When I went to the *Post* in '54, I traveled constantly. Wherever they went, I went, for about the next six or seven years.

Phil Pepe: Dick Young used to cover the Knicks. Bill Roeder was the *World-Telegram* Dodger writer, and he covered the Knicks. Lots of baseball writers covered basketball in the off-season. And since the season started later in those days, they finished their baseball coverage and just went on and covered the Knicks. That was very common. But the NBA was really down low on the totem pole in terms of coverage.

Bob Wolff: WPIX had a schedule in which they bought 60 Garden events. Fifteen or twenty might be pro basketball, fifteen or twenty might be college basketball. They carried the track meets, dog show, horse show, boxing, hockey, everything. We had all of these events, all fall and winter, and I did them all.

Leonard Lewin: The day the *Mirror* folded in 1963, I was up at Giants football camp. I came to the office, filed my story, and went home. When I left the office, nobody had said anything. No rumors, no nothing. I got home and I got a call from [boxing executive] Murray Goodman. He said, "Your paper folded." He called to tell me how sorry he was. I said, "*You're* sorry?"

Travel was by train in the fifties, which allowed the press and the players to mingle for hours. They all got to know each other pretty well, creating an atmosphere of trust between the media and players, as well as a host of travel horror stories that live on in memory.

Leonard Koppett: The Green Parrot Café story is all my fault. I wrote about it for the *Post* and Podoloff went crazy! He interpreted it as a whorehouse. But it was a *Post* story originally and was embellished afterward. Here's the way it came about: You'd play a game on Saturday in Rochester. Your next game is Sunday night in Fort Wayne. The only way to get from Rochester to Fort Wayne is to get on the New York Central Railroad in Rochester, on a train going to Chicago. It makes a stop–just for us–at Waterloo, Indiana. That's about 28 miles north of Fort Wayne. The real railroad connection to Fort Wayne was on the Pennsylvania Railroad, which didn't go through Rochester. So we'd get off at Waterloo, and it's about 6:00 in the morning. Waterloo is a little town of a few houses and one main street. You get off the train and trudge through the snow three or four blocks down the street to this place called the Green Parrot. It's like a coffee shop and a general store put together, with a few rooms upstairs. So you'd throw some pebbles at the window, and a lady would let you into the coffee shop and make you some breakfast, and then four citizens with four cars would take the 16 people, including writers, on these snowy roads down to Fort Wayne, about a 45-minute to an hour drive. You'd get to Fort Wayne and play that night.

Harry Gallatin: There was one trip I never looked forward to. We usually played a game at Madison Square Garden on a Saturday night, and then we went down to Grand Central and took the Pennsylvania Railroad to Fort Wayne. We're on the train all night, arrive in Fort Wayne early in the morning. We'd walk down the streets of Fort Wayne with the church bells ringing, to the Van Normand Hotel, and lace up our tennies for an afternoon game. To me, that was the real test. We did that a number of times.

Leonard Koppett: There were other places that were even harder [than Fort Wayne] to get to. Syracuse was on the main railroad line and also had an air connection. But Syracuse, in January and February, was snowbound more than half the time. So you can't get in or out. If you were taking the train back to New York, you'd have to wait for a 1:00 A.M. train coming from Chicago. If they had berths for you, fine. If not, you sat up.

Vince Boryla: We always took the train to Minneapolis. You'd stop at Fort Wayne and Chicago, then take the transfer train to Minneapolis. When we got there, the hotel was about three or four blocks from the railroad station and we'd usually walk it.

Most of the times we were in Minny, it was so cold we almost never left the hotel. We just stayed there, ate there, and went to the game. Then they'd call us in the morning. We'd always wind up taking an 8:00 train or plane, and they'd call us at about 5:00 or 5:30 in the morning and say, "It's 5:30 and 19 degrees below zero." That kind of woke you up a little bit.

Leonard Lewin: Whenever we went to Boston, we'd take the train from Grand Central. It would be my job to stop off at Leone's first and get a big bag of chicken and shrimp that they'd pack for us. I'd take it on the train, and we'd sit up all night playing cards and eating.

Ray Lumpp: We used to go from Chicago to St. Louis, and that would be a five-hour trip by train. So we players would rent a parlor car. Now, Lapchick forbade us to play cards on the train. We'd play poker a lot to pass the time. So we rented off one of the sleeping cars. Now the train was getting near St. Louis and Joe said, "Where's the team? The team's not around." He thought we got off the train. We were all in the parlor car playing cards, all of us except the trainer. Joe couldn't find his team.

Ralph Kaplowitz: We played at Toronto, and at that time we didn't travel by plane. To get up to Toronto, it took us 15 hours to get there, where today by plane you're there in an hour and a half. So they made arrangements for us to go from Toronto to our next game in Providence. Three taxicabs would be set up: one to take the coach and the guys who worked with him, and then two more to take the players. Since Hertzberg, Schectman, Gottlieb, Bob Cluggish, and I were the first team, we were the last to come out of the locker room, and we got into the last cab. Now, somewhere in Canada we were supposed to meet at the crossroads to pick up the sleeper train to Providence. Unfortunately, the third

The McGuire brothers—Al on the left, Dickie on the right—work out in early 1951. Al would join the Knicks later that year.

cab, on the way, stopped going. The engine quit. So we all got out and pushed the taxicab, until it got started. We finally got to the meeting place, but there was nobody there. They left without us.

What do we do? Well, to make a long story short, we got back in the cab and traveled all night until we got to Buffalo at 8:00 in the morning. The driver dropped us off at the railroad station, and now we're looking for a train to Providence. But there wasn't a train until the next day. Then I looked across the street and saw a taxi stand. So we walked over and asked if they could take us to Providence. Well, the guy said, it's a 10-hour ride. We had to get there by 8:00 that night. So we get in and pay him, and the only time we stopped was to go to the bathroom and load up on gas. We got there at 8:30 at night, disheveled, tired, and unshaven. They'd been waiting for us for a half hour. We get out there, we practice for five minutes, and then Cohalan sits the first team on the bench. We figured, OK. At the end of the half, we're losing. Then we come back into the locker room, and we figured that in the second half, he'd put the first team back in. Nothing like that happened. We're sitting on the bench, and the second team is playing. We didn't play one minute. We never got in. And we never questioned it. We never questioned his decision. What his decision was and for what reason, who the hell knows? And did he talk to us? Did he even say a word to us about what happened? No. So how can you have respect for a guy like that?

Vince Boryla: The scariest one we ever had was where we were flying from Boston to New York after a Sunday afternoon game. It was one of the rare times we flew from Boston to New York. We took off in one of those small planes; I think it was a DC-3. It was stormy out and that plane was being tossed around like you can't believe. I think the lights went out and everything. We were rocking and rolling. The plane was flying very, very low. I was just wondering, as a lot of us were, whether we were going to make it or not. I have a very strong memory of that.

Ray Lumpp: There were a lot of delays with bad weather. That was the worst, when you'd get to the airport and you couldn't fly. Then you'd have to take the train to go to the next town.

Vince Boryla: I look back at the way we traveled. Flying was an extreme rarity. Now they grab their bags at the room or the arena, have them taken to the plane, they have a private jet that's set off to the side and so on. And every now and then I hear players complaining how bad a road trip was, and I say, "Oh, my." They should have been traveling when we were playing. But we didn't know any different. It was just part of the job.

In the spring of 1951, college basketball was rocked by the point-shaving scandals that involved many of the nation's biggest college programs, both in and out of New York City. No school was harder hit, none more devastated, than City College, which won both the NIT and NCAA titles at the Garden in 1950.

The scandals would mean the end of college basketball forever as a top-of-the-line, A-list sports attraction in New York. A vacuum had been created on the basketball landscape of the city . . . a vacuum the Knicks were about to fill.

Leonard Koppett: The scandals marked a vital change in the history of basketball. The first two years of the BAA were really of no major interest to any of the papers. They covered it because they had to, but it's a third-string assignment. The main things are the college doubleheaders, the NIT, and the NCAA Tournament. Outside of the Garden and the major college circuits, basketball was completely regional. There wasn't much intersectional play.

The gambling was the thing that took it over the top. What happened was, right after the war, point-spread gambling came into existence. That greatly expanded the interest in gambling, not by professional gamblers but by people who got a kick out of having a bet on a game while they were watching it. At the same time, the abandonment of the center jump and the introduction of a higher-scoring game gave you plenty of room for a point spread, in a way you couldn't have in baseball or hockey. So the gambling became a very large part of the ticket-buying interest. It wasn't necessarily the greatest off-the-court interest.

But anybody who's gonna bet on a game, whether it's $5 or $50, is gonna be more likely to buy a ticket to watch.

You had this panic reaction to the scandals, and because City College and LIU [Long Island University] were involved, everybody blamed it on the Garden, on the evil of the Catskills, on the evil of the doubleheaders. So they pulled their games back to the college campuses, and now the Garden had open dates. And the Knicks started to fill the open dates. Now the focus of attention in New York shifts to the Knicks.

As another year goes by, and then Kentucky and Bradley are sucked into the scandals, the whole league itself takes on greater importance on the sports pages and on radio. Right away, they thought that if the colleges were crooked, the pros had to be, too. But these college kids were getting $150 to throw a game, while the pros were making several thousand. They weren't going to risk professional careers to fix a game. It wasn't as credible as what was happening in the colleges. So having New York–off the college map for several years–now in the NBA Finals, was a great opportunity for the NBA to get more attention.

Ray Lumpp: Originally, the colleges got all the Garden dates and the Knicks would play at the Armory. When the scandals hit, the NCAA said the college teams couldn't play in the big arenas any-more; they had to play on campus. That opened the dates at the Garden, and we'd play more games there than at the Armory. More and more, as our team got better, we started to catch on. And when you're playing in the Finals three years in a row, you've gotta be one of the best teams in the league.

Leonard Koppett: They couldn't play any Finals games in the Garden because the circus had taken over.

If the Knicks had gotten [Long Island University's] Sherman White, if he hadn't been involved in the scandals, the relationship between them and the Celtics and Lakers over the next 10 years would have been different. The Knicks would have been dominant. Sherman White was that good. He was the closest thing to Bill Russell at that moment.

As the news about the scandals got worse and as more and more front pages showed college players being led away by detectives, the Knicks embarked on a remarkable run: three straight trips to the NBA Finals, in 1951, 1952, and 1953. Three shots at a championship. Three chances for a title, for immortality.

They would be turned away all three times.

The first may have been the most heartbreaking. In 1951, against the Rochester Royals, they lost the first three games, won the next three, then lost the deciding seventh game on the road by four points.

The following two years, they fell victim to the dynasty-in-the-making Minneapolis Lakers. They lost in 1952 in seven games, but Game 1, in St. Paul, would linger in everyone's memory. Late in the first quarter, Al McGuire was fouled while making a layup. Everyone saw the ball go in the basket . . . everyone, that is, except the two guys who mattered most.

Leonard Koppett: While the scandals were breaking in February and March of 1951, the Knicks were on their way to the NBA Finals. They knocked off Boston, got past Syracuse, and wound up playing Rochester. And they had the papers to themselves. All the other stories were about the terrible things that were happening to the college kids.

Ray Lumpp: The Knicks had great rivalries in those days. Boston with Cousy. Minneapolis with [George] Mikan, [Jim] Pollard, and [Vern] Mikkelsen. Rochester with [Arnie] Risen, [Bob] Davies, and [Bobby] Wanzer. There were great players at that time.

Vince Boryla: We really had a genuine rivalry with Syracuse. We didn't like each other. We had great battles with them. They had great players: Al Cervi, Paul Seymour, Dolph Schayes, Red Rocha, and John Kerr a little later. They had a fine ballclub.

Ray Lumpp: We're up there for the seventh game [of the 1951 Finals] and we've got the ball up a point or two with the clock running out, and we lose the game. Max let the ball get away out of bounds. Rochester called time, and Davies then got it to Risen, who made the winning shot, and there goes our championship ring. Ned Irish had a plane full of champagne ready for his first championship team.

Leonard Koppett: They [the Knicks] were two points behind, it seemed, the whole last four minutes of the game. It's before the shot clock in those days, so the whole end of the game was foul trading. They just didn't quite catch up.

Vince Boryla: The final game was a three- or four-point game throughout, and I think we got screwed on a couple of calls, but that's neither here nor there.

Harry Gallatin: It really just seemed to me that we should have won that game. It was one of those that you get down to the last moments of the game and you just felt very confident that you were gonna get it done. It just didn't happen. It was very disappointing. We all felt that we were the best team and had proven it. All we had to do was get it done, and we didn't.

Ray Lumpp: I didn't come back on the plane. Connie [Simmons] and I bought cars up there and drove them back. You couldn't get cars in those days in New York; you had a long waiting list. So we went up to Rochester and bought cars from one of the Chevrolet agencies up there and drove them back to New York.

Dick McGuire: I think it might have been Slater Martin [who fouled Al]. But the biggest thing about it is that the guy didn't see the ball go in the basket. They gave him two shots because they never saw the ball go in. But it did go in. So Al made the first and missed the second, and that might have changed the whole thing around.

Ray Lumpp: Al went in and made a layup, and [Stan] Stutz and [Sid] Borgia said, "Two shots." So [Lakers coach John] Kundla says, "Why two shots? The ball went in." Stutz goes to Borgia and says, "Did you see it go in?" Borgia said no. Now, they had about ten thousand people in the stands, they had Commissioner Podoloff sitting there, and they had a third official on the side. But they couldn't rule on it. It had to be ruled by the two officials in the game. And they said that the last time they saw the ball, it was rolling off the rim. They didn't see it go in; they didn't count the basket. They give Al two shots, he makes one, and we lose in overtime. That's the way it goes. Everybody else saw it go in.

Harry Gallatin: I don't remember who the foul was on, but it was fairly obvious. I think at the time, Al had broken his jaw and was wearing that cage. I don't know if the officials were distracted or what happened, but there was no question about it. It might have changed the game, and we all thought at the time that we should have won that, too.

Dick McGuire: Rochester had a very, very good backcourt with Bobby Wanzer and [Bob] Davies. I had Davies. With Minnesota, I played Slater Martin an awful lot. George Mikan and Vern Mikkelsen killed us. Mikkelsen hurt us more than Mikan because he was their second big guy, along with [Jim] Pollard. Their front line was extremely big. Pollard was the first big guy I ever saw who could handle the ball. We'd try to press them, and he'd bring the ball up against our press. A lot of times when we played Minneapolis, they'd try to take me down into the corner. I was really good at stealing the ball, at shooting the gaps and running the lanes. When Pollard brought the ball up, I had no way of getting involved in our pressure. He handled the ball extremely well for a guy 6'7", which today they can just about all do.

Vince Boryla: In those days, to win away from home was just impossible. Except that everybody played well in New York. And the officials always bent over backward for the visiting teams in New York because they wanted to show what great balls they had, you know? Syracuse and Rochester were probably the two most notorious places to play.

Harry Gallatin: When I think about my career, I really feel that we should have won one of those championships. Even against the Lakers, I thought that we were the best team there, at least in one of those years. It was a disappointment in a way, but I also think our team distinguished itself by finishing second a number of times. You have to be pretty decent to do that.

Ray Lumpp: Mikan made the difference. Just like years later, the guy who made the difference was Bill Russell. We could always beat the Celtics in the playoffs, until Russell came. We could *always* beat Boston. We'd go on and they'd go home. But as time went on, when they got the big guy, Russell, he made all the difference.

Coach Vince Boryla lost this battle during 1957 in Philadelphia to referees Norm Drucker and Jim Duffy.

THE LINEUP: Dr. Richard Lapchick; Leonard Koppett; Vince Boryla; Les Keiter; Fuzzy Levane; Richie Guerin; Dick McGuire; Johnny Green; Leonard Lewin; John Andariese; Cal Ramsey; Marv Albert; Al Albert; Steve Albert; Freddie Klein; Al Bianchi; Sonny Hertzberg.

Never dull–but not successful either–the Knicks started burning through coaches quickly starting with the 1955–56 season.

Dr. Richard Lapchick: My father quit the Knicks because he knew he was going to be fired. He knew he had fallen out of favor with Ned Irish. He knew it was going to be embarrassing and humiliating not only for him but also for his players, and he wanted to spare everyone the embarrassment. When he resigned, he didn't have the job at St. John's, but it all worked out for him.

Leonard Koppett: Irish cooled off on Lapchick for various reasons, mainly, in my opinion, because Irish would interfere with the drafting process, always choosing a well-known college player over actual ability. Then he started to second-guess and blame Lapchick for everything when they lost, without knowing what the hell he was talking about. Irish had very little idea of what basketball was really all about.

Vince Boryla: The last year I played [1953–54], I had a bad wrist that turned out to be broken. So [when I didn't play], I sat next to Joe Lapchick, and we talked back and forth a lot. I recommended some substitutions and things like that.

Leonard Koppett: When it came time to discard Lapchick, in Irish's eyes, he made Boryla the coach.

Vince Boryla: I knew that they [Irish and Lapchick] weren't getting along, but you hear that a lot. I never had any aspirations to coach. I really had no thoughts of coaching. Then I got a call from Ned that he was going to make a change, and would I come out and be the coach. So we talked, and I talked to Lapchick, and he knew he was on his way out. So I said, "Well, I'll give it a fling." And it was the greatest thing I ever did, because I coached a little over two years and had another year on my contract, and I realized I didn't have the temperament for it. I made some moves on the club that eventually helped, but they weren't seen that way then because I got rid of some of the guys that I had played with. That was very difficult to do, but it was a necessary thing.

Les Keiter: [Boryla was a] very competitive guy. He took defeats very hard. We lost a game at the Garden on a night that we had to catch a train to Boston right after the game. We were in a losing streak, and Vince sat in the back of the train, in the car where all the players and writers were, and he wouldn't talk to anybody. He put dark glasses on, much the same way Floyd Patterson did after he lost the title to Sonny Liston. He became almost a hermit on that trip.

Fuzzy Levane: I came along in '56, when Joe Lapchick was just about to leave to go back to St. John's. Joe called me up–I had just come back from Milwaukee after coaching there–and he asked me if I was interested in joining Vince Boryla's staff, because Vince was going to be the coach. So I met with Vinnie, and he offered me a scouting job. It was purely scouting. There were no assistant coaches in our day. Red Holzman didn't have an assistant coach until he made [Dick] Barnett an assistant after they got [Earl] Monroe. So I was a scout. I helped out during training camp. But once the season started, I didn't sit on the bench.

Les Keiter: We lost one game in the last second at the Garden to the Celtics. We lost by one point because Bob Cousy, with one second left, threw a laser on the inbounds pass to Bill Russell, who alley-ooped it and scored at the buzzer. Vince Boryla complained that it was an illegal pass from out of bounds and that time had run out. He went absolutely off his rocker. He chased Lou Eisenstein around the court, then charged the officials' dressing room. Vince was pounding on the door. He was gonna kick it down. He got fined and suspended for that.

Vince Boryla: I've never once looked back at my life and said that I would have been happier coaching, because I got that out of my system my first shot out of the box, so to speak. It just didn't sit well with me. I'd take it very personally. You know, I played at about 218 [pounds], but when I coached I got up to 255. I just weighed myself two days ago after I went swimming, and I weigh 223. So I'm down 32 pounds from my coaching days. I just wish I looked as good now as I did then, because the stuff kind of moves around on you. I said to myself, "How can I look like this at 223?"

Fuzzy Levane: Vince stepped down *very* voluntarily [on April 5, 1958], because he had a pretty good contract. Vinnie is a very good businessman, and he hooked up with a guy in Denver. So he left the Knicks to go back there.

I was Boryla's first choice [to succeed him]. Ned's first choice, or choices, were Frank McGuire and Al

Cervi. But Vinnie was plugging for me. And I think the turning point came one night when we were playing the St. Louis Hawks and Vinnie had to go out of town. One of his best friends had died. So I coached the team for that night, and we won. I used one of our substitutes, Brendan McCann, and he did very well. Vinnie hadn't been using him much up till then. After the game, Irish came into the locker room and, you know, [he was] very jubilant. And I think that really showed, in his mind, that I could coach. But Vinnie was 100 percent behind me. That's how I got it.

The parade of Knicks stalwarts of the late fifties begins with a former Quantico marine who became a six-time NBA All-Star during the franchise's bleakest period . . .

Richie Guerin: My plan was basically to go to the NBA. I felt I needed to work on some parts of my game, but my aspirations were to join the Knicks, who had drafted me out of Iona [College], when I got out of the marines.

Sonny Hertzberg: Richie was a strong player for his size at Iona. He would go into the pivot, or go around anybody. He reminds me of the kid who's playing with Boston today, Antoine Walker. He was strong and could shoot and get inside. He did a lot of scoring and was deceiving with his strength. I thought he was a great prospect.

Dick McGuire: At training camp that year [1956], I told Vinnie Boryla that Richie Guerin was a helluva player and that he's a guy you should keep. And all of a sudden, that's the reason I was let go. I wanted to be right, but not that right. And Richie, of course, turned out to be a helluva player.

Richie Guerin: I played a lot of summer league ball with Carl [Braun] and Dick [McGuire] before we went to training camp. In those days, the Knicks used to play a lot of the college All-Stars and former players out at the Malibu Beach Club. They asked me to play with them in some pickup games at Malibu and around the city. So I got to know them pretty well before I actually got to training camp.

Johnny Green: Richie really wanted to win. We all wanted to win, but Richie had that added responsibility of being the captain. And sometimes because of that, he'd take it on his shoulders to do things. Richie was a tremendous player, very dedicated.

Richie Guerin: It was very frustrating because, as good as the seasons I had individually were, it seemed like by the first of the year, we were always eliminated from the playoffs. I always felt that you had an obligation to your franchise, to the people of New York, and obviously to yourself and your family, to do the best you can and contribute the most that you can. It was tough to do that four or five nights a week, when you knew that you had to have supreme efforts from you and the other guys if you were gonna win.

Leonard Lewin: Richie was a rugged player. Dolph Schayes challenged him once to a fight, even though he [Schayes] had a broken wrist and was playing in a cast. He was clubbing Richie with the cast and Richie was fighting him off. Richie was the toughest fighter on the team.

Richie Guerin: Bill Sharman was a great competitor, like I was. When you came into the league in those days, we only had eight teams. And you used to play these guys eight, nine, ten times a year. So when you played them, some rivalries really built up. Billy was a fierce competitor, as I liked to consider myself. He didn't like to get pushed or bumped around, so I used to play defense that way. You were allowed to use a certain amount of contact when you played people. Obviously, Billy didn't like that, so we had a couple of skirmishes. Finally, after the second one, we said to one another, "This is kind of crazy to play like this every night." So we respected each other and said let's just go out and forget the fisticuffs.

Leonard Koppett: Richie was a tremendously versatile, all-around player. He's an In-Between Ike, very aggressive, very competitive. He could shoot, he could defend, he could do everything. But that wasn't gonna make them a good team. The whole team has to be good. So he played in a very unfortunate period.

Les Keiter: Richie was our star player. He was one of the great guards of pro basketball. He was a native New Yorker, and he had a big fan following. He was the key man on the ballclub, no question about it.

John Andariese: Tough. A marine. Tough, tough guy. Nobody could stop him when he put the ball on the floor to go to the basket. Very strong. The waters parted when he put the ball on the floor and went to the basket with those big strides.

Richie Guerin: I played 42 or 43 minutes a game, basically, night in and night out. I felt, like a lot of players feel sometimes, that you had to make a certain contribution if the team was gonna have a chance to win. Whether that be getting 20 rebounds, blocking shots, or scoring 25 points a game, or playing great defense, or whatever it might be, I felt I had to do all of those things. When we'd play Cincinnati, I'd guard Oscar Robertson. When we'd play the Lakers, I'd guard Jerry West. So I also guarded the best guard on the other team, and that takes a lot out of you.

Fuzzy Levane: Richie Guerin should be in the Hall of Fame. Richie was a hard-nosed type of player. When Red [Holzman] was alive, he and I tried to talk the Hall of Fame people into considering Richie, but unfortunately it didn't happen.

Guerin's teammates were equally compelling, with various skills and talents that made the Knicks an entertaining–if not victorious–team.

Les Keiter: I had done Kenny Sears' games in college, at Santa Clara. When he came to the Knicks, they set him up at the New York Athletic Club. He lived there, and they set him up with the best room there. He got a big bonus to sign with the Knicks. I don't think, in all honesty, he ever quite lived up to the hype and buildup. But he was a good, solid ballplayer.

Johnny Green: Kenny was a tremendous shooter, but he was a frail person and couldn't take much punishment. And back then, the NBA was more physical. Kenny got roughed up a lot. But he could really score.

Richie Guerin at work, hooking one over Cincinnati's Maurice Stokes (No. 12) and Jim Paxson at the Detroit Olympia.

Fuzzy Levane: Charlie Tyra had a good little jump shot. He was short of a plugger. He was built like Wes Unseld in a way.

Les Keiter: Willie Naulls had one of the most perfect bodies I think I've ever seen on an athlete. He was big, strong, and soft-spoken.

Fuzzy Levane: We got Willie Naulls in a trade with St. Louis. A solid player, had a good one-handed outside shot.

Johnny Green: Willie was looked upon as extremely talented. And he maybe could have been a superstar if he would push. He had a good outside shot, he could rebound, and he was very talented. But people looked upon him as not playing as hard as he could have. And by not doing that, he was looked at as someone who didn't achieve as much as he could have.

Cal Ramsey: Willie was a great guy, a terrific offensive player. Great shooter out of UCLA. Not a great defensive player. It's kind of ironic because Willie is very big with the church now, but he used to be kind of a ladies' man back in those days. He used to date [actress] Leslie Uggams. That was years ago. But just a great guy, and a good friend.

Johnny Green: Willie Naulls and I became good friends. Willie was a nice, clean-cut person, and I relied on him from day to day. I lived in New Jersey, in Orange, and he lived in Montclair. So I depended on him, and he sort of took me under his wing and gave me advice.

Cal Ramsey: Willie had some career changes. First he got into the fast-food business, then he got into the banking business. He had a bank in California. Then he was in the automobile business, and then he got into the ministry. He's done very well.

Richie Guerin: I had the greatest admiration for both Sears and Naulls. Both of them were single at the time. Kenny stayed at the New York AC most of the time; he had a room there. Willie had a great body. Willie, in those days, liked to play outside a lot. So we had a 6'9" Kenny Sears, who was a real good outside shooter, and we had a 6'7" Willie Naulls, who also loved to shoot the outside shot. Neither one of them gave us an inside presence, and obviously we didn't have an outstanding center. The thing that hurt us the most was the lack of good board work and inside defense and presence. So as a result, even I would go into the pivot at times against certain teams. That was the type of style they liked to play. And while it may have been more successful on teams that had different types of players, it didn't help us as much as it should have.

Fuzzy Levane: Red Holzman's my scout now, OK? And he's telling me about this guy [Johnny Green], 6'5" from Michigan State, who can jump and knock a quarter off the top of the backboard and this and that. So I said, "Red, can he play basketball?" I didn't wanna know how high he could jump. He was our number one draft choice [in 1959]. We were also looking at Rudy LaRusso. Red made the call there.

Johnny Green: I had no contact from the Knicks, only from Paul Seymour and the Syracuse Nationals. When I was drafted by the Knicks, I was stunned.

I guess I was shaking in my boots a little bit. I had heard and read a lot about New York. Then I had to come in and talk to [their] people, and remember that at that time, players didn't have agents. So I had to come in and talk to them myself. And I was always very conscious of that, because here I'm an amateur and I'm going in there talking to pros, in terms of negotiating a contract and all. I looked at myself in terms of, Am I qualified to do this?

The guy that I came in and talked with was Fred Podesta. He was sitting behind his desk, and he had those half-rim glasses on, and a lot of times he'd be looking over the glasses. I remember that image. I didn't know anything about negotiating a contract or what to ask for. This was all new to me. I had no knowledge or experience as far as negotiating. I was just playing basketball because I liked it. And now here's a chance that I can get paid for it, so how much do you ask for?

My mind-set was, if they offer me something, I'm just gonna ask for more. I signed for $15,000, which was not a bad salary on a one-year deal. Now, Oscar Robertson came out the following year and got about $17,000, so I felt I did well compared to some of the other players.

Richie Guerin: Johnny wasn't a very good outside shooter, although he'd probably argue with me [Guerin laughs], but he hung around inside. Before they changed the rules, Johnny would offensive goaltend a lot, where he would go over the rim. If I shot a set shot, he could sort of catch it, almost, and guide it into the basket. You could do that. Johnny was very, very quick and very, very agile inside, but he wasn't an offensive player. He got most of his offense either by being on the break or rebounding and tapping the ball in.

Changes were also afoot in the form of a colorful announcer who had always wanted to land in New York.

Les Keiter: I had been the sports director at KYA in San Francisco when my friend and mentor, J. Elroy McCaw, called me and said, "Les, can you be in New York on Friday?" I said, "No!" This was on Tuesday. I said, "What are you talking about?" He said, "Well, I guess you heard that I bought WINS, and effective with this phone call, you are my sports director." I said, "Elroy, I can't just leave. I have a job at KYA that you got for me, and a house and a family. I can't just pick up and go." And he said, "Les, you always said your dream was to live and broadcast in New York. And now you're the sports director of WINS." That's what brought me to New York in 1954.

Marv Albert: I used to enjoy Marty [Glickman] and Les doing the games. They were so different in style, obviously. When the Dodgers and Giants moved away, Les did re-creations that were enormously popular. I knew Les from my ballboy work, so I would go down to WINS and watch him.

Les Keiter: "In again, out again Finnegan." "Ring-tailed howitzer." "It's in the air, it's in the bucket." People ask me if I did those expressions consciously, and the answer is always no. In those days, sportscasters had styles. They don't have them so much today [because] the owners of teams and networks don't want you to be stylish. They just want you to do the game and sell the product. But in those days we had a style. And my style included those sayings.

Meanwhile, at 178 Kensington Street in Brooklyn, three young brothers shared a passion for the Knicks, a tape recorder, and a dream.

Marv Albert: I was an office boy one summer for the Brooklyn Dodgers, and it was like a dream come true. One of the perks of the job was that I was able to lug my tape recorder to every home game up to a club box that was just to the right of where Vin Scully and Jerry Doggett sat, and I'd be able to do the games to myself on my fictitious radio station, WMPA. My parents got me my tape recorder: it was a Revere reel-to-reel. It was huge, lugging that thing on the subway. The Wollensaks were actually a step up. They were smaller but still pretty big.

Al Albert: I was a gofer on WMPA. Unpaid gofer. We had a little room in our house, which we of course called the Little Room, which essentially became our press box. In the room was a TV set, a table, and a couple of chairs, and that was it. We'd turn the TV sound down and Marv, who was the station manager of WMPA, was the one who got to call the games. I would be keeping stats, and depending on what sport it was, I'd be the one who had to regulate the crowd record. If it was baseball, I'd have the two sticks to [re-create] the crack of the bat. If it was basketball, I could elevate the crowd with the knob on the record player. I could also do the crowd noise myself. I was very good at making that sound; I think that's why I was hired. I would also run into the kitchen for halftime snacks.

Steve Albert: Marv was much older than me. Probably still is, although not according to him. The gap keeps getting narrower every year. I'll be passing him any day now.

Les Keiter: I first remember him as a high school kid. He was the ballboy for the Knicks. One day he asked me if I had any equipment I could spare from the baseball re-creations I was doing on the San Francisco Giants games starting in '58. Marv asked me if I could lend him the wooden block and other things I was using on the re-creations, because he wanted to practice at home. So I gave him some things that I used.

Graceful rookie Willie Naulls swoops over the Hawks' Bob Pettit at the Old Garden during 1956 as Harry Gallatin, Guerin, and the Hawks' Slater Martin (No. 22) look on.

Steve Albert: When we did baseball, one of us would do the play-by-play, one would operate the crowd record, and the third would have two heavy marking pencils that we got from our father's grocery store, which would simulate the sound of the bat.

Marv Albert: Jim Baechtold was one of the better jump shooters in the league. He had a beautiful stroke. He averaged 13.9 points one year [1954–55], and he was a good player. Just from going to games and collecting autographs, [I knew] he was such a nice guy, humble and cooperative. So I got to know him and started the Jim Baechtold Fan Club. And one thing I did to get closer to what I wanted to do was put out the very popular *Baechtold Bulletin*. Due to the enormous success of the Jim Baechtold Fan Club–Bud Palmer used to plug it all the time on the air; I think I pestered him into doing it–I was actually encouraged to start a Knicks Fan Club. There was another fan club for Kenny Sears, and we kind of combined forces.

Al Albert: Our parents were pretty cool with us, because they knew our desires, even though our mother wanted us to be doctors or lawyers. She would say, "What are you gonna *do* with all this sports stuff?" It was our lives.

Marv Albert: Aaron Karlin, the publisher of the *Baechtold Bulletin,* was my piano teacher. I played piano for about 10 years. I can still give you the opening bars of "Malaguena" right now; I can't get any further. One of the perks about taking piano lessons was that he had a mimeograph machine. I also played the accordion and gave practice lessons. I used to go to his office on Kings Highway, and instead of getting paid, I could use the mimeograph machine to print the *Baechtold Bulletin*. So I would put ads for his [music] school in the *Bulletin*, and I know it turned his business around. Pretty small ads, for all he did for me. "Drop in some time." Very catchy.

Al Albert: All of a sudden my big brother is involved with a Knick. And I remember asking, "Have you actually *spoken* to him?" I think that was the first connection I ever made with a team and a player. And that's what our lives became. But I'll

always remember the name Jim Baechtold, and I always had a strong and close feeling toward him because I know that was Marv's first connection with a player.

Marv Albert: I still have people coming up to me now telling me that they were a member of either the Baechtold Fan Club or the Knicks Fan Club. We had about a thousand members at one point, and I often remember the names. We'd have the Knicks Fan Club meetings either at the Garden or at the 69th Regiment Armory, and I'd emcee it. We'd always get two players, and they would do a Q&A with the fan club members. The Knicks were very cooperative with it. So from that I was able to meet Marty Glickman, wound up doing stats for him, became a ballboy, and all that.

Al Albert: It's amazing, when you think of it, what a great education that was. We were learning how to do things, sitting there with the TV set and turning the sound down. And eventually when Marv moved on, I moved into his seat as general manager of WMPA. Marv would not allow a change of call letters, though. Steve moved into the gofer role, reluctantly.

Back at the Garden, Levane would lead the Knicks to a 40–32 mark and a playoff berth in 1958–59. But that would be the lone bright spot of a decade-long dry spell. It would be the only time the Knicks would see the postseason over a 10-year span (1956–57 through 1965–66) in which the club's overall winning percentage was just .379.

Les Keiter: Fuzzy was a players' coach. He was one of the guys. He liked to hang out with the players. And then suddenly he became the head coach, so now he had a lot of officialdom that he never had before. Fuzzy was a good coach, but he didn't have too much more success than Vince.

Fuzzy Levane: When I took over the Knicks, I put in something new. I put in an offense where I had three men outside and two in the corners. I really didn't have a good pivot man, not as good as a Mikan or Johnny Kerr. I'd have the backcourt men pass, then go through and pick for the forward coming off. So every time a backcourt guy passed off, he'd go the opposite way and take his defender that way. Hit and go away, hit and go away, instead of hit and follow, where you'd bring your defender into the play. It was a different type of offense, and the other teams at first couldn't figure out what we were doing. But I knew we were basically a .500 club, because as soon as they found out what we were doing, we were .500 from then on.

Richie Guerin: I don't think it was so much what Fuzzy did above what Vinnie did; it was a matter of some of the new people that they made trades for starting to play a little better together. We had some real good years by some of the individuals, like Kenny Sears and Willie Naulls and myself. We were fortunate enough to play very well and get into the playoffs, but then we got eliminated by Syracuse in the first round.

Johnny Green: We all got one-year contracts. They always said, "We'll talk about next year next year." So when it would come down toward the end of the season, guys wouldn't be sitting down because they'd be playing for next year's contract. You'd be diving for loose balls and the whole bit, because next year's salary hinged on it. And if you were on a losing team, it made it that much tougher to negotiate.

It crossed my mind that I should have had someone to go in there and talk for me. I didn't know anything about negotiation. So it crossed my mind, but I never put it into reality. I think Cazzie Russell was the first player to have an agent talk to the Knickerbockers. But it was something I had in the back of my mind then.

Fuzzy Levane: I got along fine with Ned, the first year. We started off with something like 10 out of 11. That's when I wound up saving Lenny Koppett's life. Lenny was one of our beat writers with Lenny Lewin, Murray Janoff, and Warren Pack, and he was having trouble with his fiancée.

Leonard Koppett: I was single in those days. This is at the start of the 1958–59 season, around October of '58. Fuzzy and I have been close from the time he was a scout, and now he's the coach. I'm

having romantic difficulties with someone I'd been going out with, and it's at the breakup point. The Knicks start the season winning two of the first three games, and now we're going on the road. The night before, I have the final breakup. Now I'm sitting in front of the bus, looking very morose. Fuzzy comes by and says, "What's the matter?" He knows what's been going on with me. I tell him, "Fuzzy, it's all done. It's over. The only thing I can think to do is to kill myself. But first let's see how long you can keep a winning streak going." So they won the next eight games. By that time, I got over it. And I always told Fuzzy that he saved my life.

Fuzzy Levane: Guys liked to play for me. I was a ballplayer once, and I treated them like I would have wanted to be treated. I gave them a lot of leeway, as long as they performed on the court. Today, they make such a big deal. You don't need five assistant coaches. These guys tape everything, they know what these guys are gonna do even when they go to the bathroom. I maintain– and Red had the same philosophy–that basketball is a reaction game. You've got to react to what's on the court, not wait for the coach to tell you what to do.

Leonard Koppett: Fuzzy was very much a let-them-play coach. He wasn't gonna give them complicated diagrams or try to control them from the bench. He got everything he could get out of that team. Unfortunately, they lost the deciding game of the [1959] first round [at Syracuse], but they could have gone further. In those days, winning playoff games on the road was really unusual.

Fuzzy Levane: Coaches then were managers in a way. We knew how to bench-coach, which today is very, very lacking. These coaches today, even with their four assistant coaches and their pads . . . I mean, by the time they write something down, 10 plays go by. I'm not knocking the assistant coaches, but if I had nine assistant coaches, I'd play them because they're pretty good players.

Johnny Green: Everybody was looking for a center if they didn't have Bill Russell or Wilt Chamberlain. So we were pretty much at the bottom [of the standings], and we'd need rebounding.

So my leaping ability worked both for me and against me. I wonder what would have happened if we had a dominating center. In college, I had played center, but in the pros I was a forward. So I had to develop a whole new game as a forward. So on the one hand, it was an asset in that it allowed me not to get cut right away, to be able to develop. But on the other hand, it did kind of hinder me after I got acclimated, because every team I was with looked at me as a rebounder.

Freddie Klein: Everything was against us. Russell was unbeatable with the Celtics. Chamberlain was unbeatable. We were always in the wrong place in the draft. Look at Chamberlain. We didn't even have a chance for him because his pick was territorial and Philly got him.

Fuzzy Levane: When Chamberlain came into the league, forget about it. We were a legitimate last-place team.

Johnny Green: There was Boston with Russell, Philadelphia with Wilt. Then Syracuse, who had a good team. And we were the fourth team in the East. So how far were we gonna go? Then you went out West and you had St. Louis, the Lakers, and Cincinnati. So we could win a game here or there, but wins were hard to come by. And sometimes it was a little awkward because players would say, "Let me do it." And maybe we didn't get the unity that we could have and should have had. Maybe we would have won a few more games. But a few more games . . . we'd still be in the cellar.

Al Bianchi: I hate to say it this way, but we [Syracuse] never really worried about New York at that time. They were always the fourth team in the East. When I went in to do my contract, Danny Biasone would sit there with the cigarette in his mouth and say, "We'll beat New York and get the playoff money, and get the $500," or whatever it was in those days. Our biggest rival was the Boston Celtics. The Knicks were like an aid to us if we slipped. We always knew we could beat them.

Les Keiter: It's tough traveling with a losing team, and the Knicks just weren't one of the top teams. That was a challenge because we were out of

so many games. At that juncture, I was so new in New York and new to doing pro sports. I was so thrilled to be going into Madison Square Garden night after night to be involved with pro athletes. I was thrilled to be a part of it. I don't think I could have been much happier if we had been a winning team.

As the fifties wound down and the situation at the Garden grew more desperate, the Knicks were increasingly frustrated by the players they didn't get.

Fuzzy Levane: I got along with Ned, but there were a couple of things that happened [in 1958–59] where I could have improved the club. I think the most surprising thing was that we beat Syracuse something like nine straight games. And they had Schayes, Kerr, Bianchi, and those guys. That was unheard-of. We just had their number. So I was flying back from the All-Star Game in [Detroit owner] Fred Zollner's plane, and Zollner said to me, "Are you interested in George Yardley, for Charlie Tyra?" I said, "What?" I wanted to stop the plane right there. So I got home and I said to Ned, "We've got a chance to get a pretty good player here." I think Yardley was making about $23,500, and when Ned found that out he said no. It would have messed up the salary structure of the team. So, P.S., one week later, Detroit trades Yardley to Syracuse for Eddie Conlin. We had beaten them nine in a row, remember. We played them three more times, and they beat us the last three games. And in the playoffs, who do you think we play? Syracuse. And they beat us two in a row. We had that team's number. Guerin played Larry Costello tough; Ray Felix played Johnny Kerr even-up; I don't know how. And Mike Farmer did a good job on Schayes. But the guy that gave them that extra edge was Yardley.

Leonard Koppett: In 1959–60, the Knicks finished last in their division. So you'd think that by right, the two teams that finished last in the two divisions should have the first two draft picks. As it turned out, two teams in the West–Cincinnati and Minneapolis–had worse records than the Knicks. So

Big Apple product Fuzzy Levane (left) succeeded Boryla as head coach and signed on the dotted ball for Ned Irish (right) in April 1958.

the Knicks wind up with the third pick, and that's Darrall Imhoff. The first two picks, of course, were [Oscar] Robertson and [Jerry] West. On top of that, you had the [Walt] Bellamy situation the following year. The Knicks had the worst record in the league, but the league gave the first pick to the new Chicago [expansion] team, and they picked Bellamy out of Indiana.

Fuzzy Levane: The lowest team in the league [in 1958] was Minneapolis, and they were gonna take Elgin Baylor. So I went out to Seattle and talked to him and said, "Geez, you don't want to go to Minneapolis. Tell the writers you're gonna stay in college." Because, you see, he had another year of eligibility left. He had been a transfer student and sat out a year. So the papers went with that. Bob Short was the owner of the Lakers. And up until the day of the draft, we thought we had Baylor convinced that Bob Short wasn't gonna pick him. Now, we had the number three choice and Cincinnati had number two. And we had a deal worked out with Bobby Wanzer that if Minneapolis passed up Baylor, we would trade Guy Sparrow to the Royals and switch our picks. The next morning, Bobby [Wanzer] called me and said, "Is everything we talked about last night OK?" And I said, "Fine." But Bob Short fooled everyone. He wasn't gonna take a chance on losing Baylor, so he drafted him anyway.

Richie Guerin: The unfortunate thing of those years was that some of the talent that was drafted–and this isn't a slam against any of the players–was such that we were so desperate to get a big man that even if they weren't quite as good as some of the smaller people, whether they were guards or forwards, the Knicks would go ahead and draft them. They figured that those guys were gonna play center and that's what they needed. As a result, between [Ron] Shavlik and [Charlie] Tyra and some of the other players, it didn't pan out.

The coaching carousel would spin again on December 18, 1959, when Levane was fired after an 8–19 start and Braun was named player-coach during a New England weekend highlighted by what its participants would always refer to as The Last Supper.

Fuzzy Levane: In my second year, I asked for a pretty good raise, like $10,000. I got a raise, but nothing like that. So we start the season 8–19, and Ned makes the change. But the funny part of it is that the fellow he picks to succeed me, Carl Braun, he was trying to unload about a week or two before! And I was saying, "No! No!" But he was never fond of Carl. I even think he was trying to trade him the year before.

Johnny Green: Fuzzy was having his ups and downs because the team wasn't really winning. I only played a half year for Fuzzy, and then Carl Braun became the coach. So the coach's tenure wasn't solid. A lot of times, when you have a team that's losing, nobody's watching your back. Because all of a sudden the players could be thinking that they could be doing better, and then go talking to management.

Leonard Lewin: Carl Braun became the coach on the night Fuzzy Levane had The Last Supper in Boston. Braun and Irish were supposed to join us for dinner after the game. So we all go to dinner with Fuzzy. In the meantime, Irish was signing Braun as coach back at the hotel. We were all sitting around, and then we found out that the bar closed at like 12:00. So we ordered two drinks for Ned and put them at the head of the table. He never showed up.

Fuzzy Levane: We had prepared to have dinner after the game in Providence against Boston [on December 17, 1959]. Ned was invited, and we had his scotch ready. It was Lewin and Pack and Murray Janoff and Lenny Koppett, maybe a few others. We're having a nice dinner, but Ned doesn't show. And I think I had a little inkling, you know what I mean? The week before that, we lost a game to Minneapolis. And I see Fred Podesta and Ned in the hallway and we had a few words. I gave them a little blast. So I think from that point, about 10 days before, I was in the crosshairs, because the Knicks had never been that far under .500 before.

John Andariese: In the fall of 1960, Fuzzy Levane was the coach of the New York Skyscrapers, which was a competing team that played against a Globetrotter-like team, the Harlem Ambassadors. I played for Fuzzy on the Skyscrapers along with Roger McCann. We had a tour throughout the Midwest, and the deal was that if you bought a ticket, you saw two Jewish comedians open the show, followed by Althea Gibson playing a tennis match against Carol Fagaros, who was a blonde bombshell–type player, followed by this wonderful basketball game: the Harlem Ambassadors against the New York Skyscrapers, with me, Roger McCann, and a bunch of medium-skilled former college guys.

Amid the losing, amid the coaching changes and growing front office turmoil, there were the wild and the wacky . . .

Les Keiter: What a fight that was: Woody Sauldsberry against Richie Guerin. I've never, ever seen a brawl that could match that. Sauldsberry and Guerin clashed all during the game, little things back and forth. And all of a sudden, they got into a fistfight. Now, this game was at [Philadelphia's] Convention Hall, which was a lousy place for basketball, but the fans in the first row were practically on the floor. Guerin and Sauldsberry wound up in the third row among the fans, and that brought the fans into it. There were fans punching each other, fans punching the players, and players punching fans. The minute that fight started, I ducked under the table because I didn't want to get hurt. And I described it like a prizefight; I did the blow-by-blow. I remember Guy Sparrow got hit over the head with a chair and blood came down over his head. It went on for about 20 minutes. And the irony of the whole thing was that when the game was over, we had to take a bus back to New York. And they took the Warriors too, because they were gonna play in the Garden the next night. So here were these two teams who just had this terrific brawl, and we were locked together in a darkened bus from Philadelphia to New York. The ride was pretty quiet.

Johnny Green: We played in Chicago once, and they shipped the uniforms on a separate plane,

and they never got there. So we had to play half the game in the Zephyrs' road uniforms. There were other times like that where the game would be delayed for a half hour while we waited for the uniforms to arrive. You had a lot of oddball things happening.

You had two uniforms, and you had to carry your own uniform in your bag. And there'd be a case where a bag would get lost and the player would have to get another uniform and tape on a different number, or turn it inside out. We didn't have a lot of the luxuries they have now.

Leonard Koppett: One night Fuzzy is coaching and they're playing in Minneapolis. They're losing big at the half, and Fuzzy is ripping into them in the locker room. He's chewing out Guerin and going on and on, and Richie's taking it pretty hard. Then Fuzzy turns to Ray Felix and says, "And you! You let [Larry] Foust go around you five times!" Ray holds up three fingers and says, "Three, baby! Three!" Guerin started laughing so hard he almost lost it.

Les Keiter: We had a big dinner party that we had planned for a long time, for a Sunday night after a [football] Giants playoff game against Cleveland. I was involved with both the Knicks and the Giants at the time. So we had this big party with all the Knicks there. Our house had a moderately high ceiling. Felix, of course, was 6'11". And somebody at the party asked him for an autograph, so he took the autograph book and he put it up against our beamed ceiling and signed it. I never saw anybody do that.

Ray Felix was a good ballplayer. Later on, he went to Los Angeles. One day he was driving on Wilshire Boulevard, and somebody bumped into his car. So the guy got out of the car and came over to Felix, who was sitting behind the wheel, and started berating Ray. Felix finally opened the door and got out of the car, and when he stood up to his full 6'11", the other guy quickly bowed out, got in his car, and drove away.

Richie Guerin: In those days, we didn't make an awful lot of money. I had a wife and a few kids and a dog, and we were making payments on a house. And yes, I did buy a Volkswagen. I think the funniest story about the Volkswagen was where we had my wife, myself, my daughter, Carl Braun, Lenny Lewin, and the dog going to the airport to catch a plane to Boston. And when we pulled up to the airport, people must have thought it was a car from the circus with all these big guys getting out and saying good-bye. Lenny wrote a big thing about it. He couldn't believe that we all got into the car. Then I moved up: I kept the Volkswagen, but eventually got another car.

During this time, there was a much more serious issue that would not be acknowledged or dealt with for years: the quota system.

While the NBA had been integrated in 1950 with the signings of Sweetwater Clifton, Chuck Cooper, and Earl Lloyd, many club owners throughout the fifties were reluctant to have more than one or two African Americans on their teams. The NBA's first all-black starting five, in fact, wasn't fielded until December of 1964, when the Boston Celtics started Bill Russell, Satch Sanders, Willie Naulls, Sam Jones, and K. C. Jones.

When New York University product Cal Ramsey signed with the Knicks early in the 1959–60 season, the team already had three African Americans: Johnny Green, Ray Felix, and Naulls. What would transpire over the next month produced a scar that would never fully heal.

Cal Ramsey: I was drafted by the Hawks [in 1959]. I played very well, but I was playing behind Bob Pettit and Cliff Hagan, two of the greatest players of all time. I got cut from them once, and after about two weeks they brought me back. I was playing, and then I was playing center, and then Charlie Share, who had been hurt, came back to the team. And to make room they had to let me go.

So then I came to New York. I had a tryout with the Knicks, and I had an extraordinary practice, one of the best days I ever had in my life. So they signed me, and my first game was against the Lakers in the Garden.

Leonard Koppett: Of course there was a quota system. Certainly. But it was a quota system that

wasn't imposed and enforced, it was a quota system in which the promoters believed. They were as bigoted as the rest of society. They figured if you had too many black guys, the white customers wouldn't come. It's one of the reasons [Ben] Kerner had to trade [the draft rights to Bill] Russell to the Celtics; it wasn't gonna fly in St. Louis, he believed.

Johnny Green: Cal perhaps became a victim of that, because he was drafted by the St. Louis Hawks. And that was probably the worst place to go. He was good enough to make the team, but because of the quota system, Cal got cut. And he realized that he was better than some of the guys on the team. Then the Knicks picked him up.

Cal Ramsey: I only played a few games, but I had some really good games. [Ramsey averaged 11.4 points per game in seven contests with the Knicks.] I had one game against Detroit where I had 15 points and 15 rebounds. Had another against the Celtics where I had 16 points against Bill Russell. I think I scored double figures in every game except the last game, which was against Cincinnati. Shortly thereafter, I was cut. And I can recall Fuzzy Levane giving me the phone call, and at the time Fuzzy stuttered a lot. He called to tell me he had to let me go. That's the way he put it. He sounded like he didn't want to do it. I know, in retrospect, that he did not want to do it, because I was the first player off the bench almost every game I was there. And I performed well, and I know he liked me and wanted to use me. But the powers that be decided that they didn't want me, that there were too many African-American players on the team at that time, and so I was the odd man out.

If you look back, how many African-American players sat on the bench during those years? Most of them were great players; they were starters. There was Oscar, there was Wilt, there was Russ, there was Sam [Jones], there was K. C. [Jones]. Tom Hawkins, too. But very few were on the bench. I was on the bench. I was the sixth man. I was not a great pro basketball player, but I could have been a *good* pro basketball player. I think I've proven that, if you look at the stats. There's another guy who played around the same time who had a similar problem: Cleo Hill, who was a great, great player. He went to the Hawks right after me and had a terrific preseason. But they said he shot the ball too much, and I think some of the players petitioned the coach that he not play. Paul Seymour was the coach, and he said that this kid was good, that they were gonna play him. Players went to management, to Ben Kerner. Not only did they get rid of Cleo, but they also fired Paul Seymour.

Johnny Green: Oh, yeah. We were very much aware of it. If you had three black players on a team, that was a lot. And there were some teams that didn't have [hardly] any, like the St. Louis Hawks. You'd go to Philadelphia and they had three or four. Or Boston; I think Boston had more black players than anybody. But yes, very much so. And as a result of that, you had a lot of talented guys who never got a chance to play. What you didn't have were a lot of black players who sat on the bench. Either you were very good and you played, or you weren't on the team.

Cal Ramsey: I felt that if you were good enough, you were gonna play. I thought I was good enough to play. I wasn't going to be a great, great player, but I knew I could play in the league. I had proven that beyond a doubt. And from what I heard it came from the top, from Irish, that there were too many African-American players [on the team] and that they had to get rid of some. And I know for a fact that Fuzzy, who was coaching, wanted me to play. Why would I be the first player [off the bench] in every game, and then I'm the first player cut? That didn't make too much sense.

Leonard Koppett: That's what Jim Crow was. And the unraveling of Jim Crow was a very slow process.

Cal Ramsey: After I left Syracuse [in 1961], I was very, very despondent because I felt that I should have played. I felt that I had proven I could play in the league. I was sitting on a bench in front of my apartment building, and Dolly King, who had been a great, great athlete at LIU and with the old New York Rens, came up. Dolly knew me very well because he refereed college games when I played. And I'll never forget this. He came up to me and

said, "I know that you feel bad, that you're upset because you feel you should be in the NBA. But you listen to me. You're a really good athlete, but you've also been a very good student. You're very well liked. Trust me. In 10 years you'll be on the same level with all of your friends, like Oscar and Wilt and Satch. Professionally, you'll be able to deal with them." I thought he was crazy, but he felt that I had the potential to move on as an individual, as opposed to as an athlete. And sure enough, he was right.

Following a 21–58 finish in 1960–61, Braun was fired as player-coach and headed to Boston, where he would cap his standout playing career by winning an NBA Championship ring with the 1961–62 Celtics.

To select Braun's successor, the Knicks would dip into the college ranks for the first time since the Lapchick days. On May 8, 1961, 38-year-old Eddie Donovan, who had led St. Bonaventure to a 139–57 mark over the prior eight seasons, was unveiled as the new coach.

Over three full seasons as head coach, Donovan would not win more than 29 games in any one year. His top player at St. Bonaventure, All-American forward Tom Stith, was drafted by the Knicks in 1961 and then contracted tuberculosis, virtually ending his NBA career. At the time, no one could have dreamed that the hiring of Donovan and scout Red Holzman in 1958 would be the first steps–the very first steps–toward the franchise's rise to greatness.

Leonard Koppett: Donovan had brought his St. Bonaventure teams to the Garden several times and was very much admired for what he got out of those teams and for what he was like personally. He was very respected by other coaches and seemed very qualified.

Johnny Green: Eddie liked me, because, win or lose, I played hard. So I did quite well under Eddie.

Fuzzy Levane: After Braun, Ned hired Eddie Donovan, but Eddie had a three-year contract. You look at Donovan's first year [29–51], and he would have been fired if not for the contract. But it wasn't his fault. He didn't have the players.

Johnny Green: Eddie came in and things looked promising. But things never materialized. Then Tom Stith got sick. So things were still kind of helter-skelter. When you're losing, there's always the pressure to do something. And in New York, the pressure was so great it was unbelievable. We had seven or eight papers, and there was constant pressure. It wasn't like a smaller market. There was a lot of tension and pressure surrounding us.

Donovan's Knicks were the party of the second part in perhaps the single most famous game in NBA history–the unforgettable night of March 2, 1962, at Hershey, Pennsylvania, when the Warriors' Wilt Chamberlain scored 100 points in a performance of near-mythic proportions.

Johnny Green: We were pretty much playing the schedule out, and we took the bus down to Hershey. That year, Wilt was having a monster year where he averaged 50 points a game. Now, we had Phil Jordan on the team at center, but he came down with a virus and stayed in the hotel. So Darrall Imhoff and Cleveland Buckner had to play center. Eddie kept shuttling guys in there. Willie [Naulls] played him [Chamberlain], I may have played him a little bit, the guy who sold the popcorn may have played him. But Wilt simply had his way.

Richie Guerin: I happen to think that Wilt was the greatest player who ever played the game. And I told Wilt this several years ago, when I was in Seattle coaching the old-timers prior to the [1987] All-Star Game: I told him that it took nothing away from his talent and ability, I just felt in my heart and soul that if the game was played under normal conditions, he probably would have scored 75 or 80 points. But the way it was played, where they deliberately fouled us in the second half so they could utilize most of the clock on the offensive end, that's not the way the game's supposed to be played. To me, they made their minds up at halftime to see if they could get 100 points for Wilt. He had 41 points at the half. There's no doubt in my mind that they made up their minds to do that. They made a little bit of a farce of the game. Even the officials [Willie Smith

and Pete D'Ambrosio] got caught up in it a little bit. I tried to foul out; I must have committed 10 fouls. But the refs said, "Come on, Rich, if we gotta be out here, you gotta be out here."

Cal Ramsey: I was in a car, coming from a game from someplace in the Eastern League, when I heard that Wilt had scored 100 points. I can recall hearing it on the radio. And one thing that fascinated me was the fact that he made 28 of 32 free throws. I used to work out with Wilt a lot, and we'd go in the gym and he could make free throws when nobody was there. He could shoot. But put him in a game and he'd go 1-for-12 or 1-for-15. But in this particular game, he went 28-for-32, which to me was just astonishing.

Johnny Green: The whispering around the league was that you'd look at the box scores and see that Wilt got 75 points and missed 20 free throws. And we started to think and say to one another, "If he ever made his free throws, he'd score 100 points." And that's what he did. In Hershey, the rims were dead. In other words, the ball would hit the rim and bounce around and then maybe go in. So when you play on a basket like that, it's very friendly. And once you start hitting, the basket seems like the size of the ocean.

Richie Guerin: [Elgin] Baylor's game [when he scored 71 points against the Knicks on November 15, 1960] was in the normal flow, and it was one of the greatest performances I've ever seen in my life. He'd take a shot and if he missed it, he'd be down there, going to the boards, rebounding, and putting it back in. That was just a sensational and well-earned 71. At the time he did it, it was a league record. But the game with Wilt probably would have broken that even without their going out of their way, without trying to do anything. That was my only hangup about it.

The "highlight" of the Knicks' 21–59 season in 1962–63 would emerge only in retrospect. It came on Sunday afternoon, January 27, in an otherwise non-descript 123–110 loss to the Celtics at Boston Garden. Listeners back in New York tuning in to the tape-delayed broadcast on WCBS did not hear the familiar voice of

Eddie Donovan looks over his bench during his first game as head coach, October 19, 1961. Left to right are Johnny Green, Cleveland Buckner, Phil Jordan, George Blaney, and Dave Budd.

Marty Glickman. Instead–and for the first time–they would hear the voice that would provide the soundtrack for the next four decades, and more, of New York City basketball.

Al Albert: It started Saturday night. Marty called from Paris. He was over there looking at some horses, and he couldn't make it back. Jim Gordon had a Rangers game, so we got the call. All of a sudden Marv came in and said, "I'm doing the Knicks game. Come on, we gotta go."

Marv Albert: Marty was reportedly stuck in a snowstorm in Paris on harness racing business. He was the race caller at Yonkers Raceway. So we took an all-night train with my Revere tape recorder, because I wanted to listen to tapes and refresh my thoughts. Al did stats. We were up all night, then slept a couple of hours at the old Madison Hotel.

Steve Albert: When Marv did his first Knicks broadcast, I remember being very upset that I wasn't allowed to go with them to Boston. Al went as the statistician, and Marv was armed with all of his scripts and things that he needed. I was kicking and screaming because my parents wouldn't let me go. They thought I was too young. I really wanted to be a part of it, because I had a feeling it was going to be the start of something big, even at that age. I was just a little kid. I was two months old, and Marv was 36.

Al Albert: The best way to get up there was by train, and I was his trusty sidekick, the gofer and stat man. I remember my parents being very excited. We had to get an 11:00 train on Saturday night. I remember hopping on the train and Marv bringing as much info as he could, even back then–newspapers and whatnot. I slept on the train while he worked. We got to the hotel, this old, old hotel in Boston. When we got to the room, he told me to go to sleep while he worked. Now, it's an afternoon game, so we get up early. I think he worked through the night. He was going on adrenaline and maybe three hours of sleep.

Marv Albert: We went early to the press gate, and here are these two kids, saying "We're here to

broadcast the Knicks game." We really didn't have any passes or anything. I thought my name was going to be left on the press list. I actually had to open up my attaché case, with all these papers and all, and show them the commercials. Then Eddie Donovan happened to come by. I knew Eddie because he had appeared on some of Marty's shows, and he said, "He's OK."

Al Albert: We went up to the press box at the Boston Garden and it was like heaven. It was midway up, overlooking the floor, and it was like you died and went to heaven. It was the greatest spot to announce, right over the sideline and surrounded by the crowd. Marv had all his preparation done, and you could tell that this was the moment. And the game just went like that. It went by so quickly. And I just knew he was on his way.

Marv Albert: It did go fast for me. At the time, I was just trying to break in. I wasn't saying to myself, "Boy, I hope this is the start of this career." You don't think like that. You're just thinking that this was a wonderful opportunity, and I hope I do a nice job. Marty called me afterward and said, "Hey, kid. How'd it go?" And I said I thought it was pretty good. He listened to it and thought it was good, but he pointed out certain things I was unaware of.

Al Albert: The funny thing was, he was doing his first game ever, but for us it was [as if] we had done many games together before. Instead of being in the Little Room, we're now in the Boston Garden. So I think he was as prepared as you could be in that kind of a situation. It was just that now it wasn't off the TV set, it was actually in the Boston Garden with the game in front of him. So I think he was ready and excited and juiced. I know that Marty listened to it afterward, and he knew that Marv was ready whenever needed. And after that, Marv encouraged Marty to look at more horses all over the world.

Marv Albert: By the time I ended up filling in for Marty and Jim Gordon on games, I was fairly comfortable. I had done so many games, even though they were practice games, on my tape recorder, that I had enough confidence in myself. I listen to those tapes now and I say, "Why *did* I have that confidence?" I still have a lot of the old tapes, including my disc jockey stuff from Syracuse. If I want to send my wife out of the house, I'll put one on. The dogs enjoy it, though.

Al Albert: There were no promos for WMPA. But I think my mother slipped in a few promos for her lamb chops.

Donovan's third season as coach, 1963–64, resulted in a 22–58 mark and a fifth straight last-place finish in the East. Two more non-playoff seasons, in which the Knicks would fail to exceed 31 wins, still lay ahead.

Over a four-season span from 1961–62 through 1964–65, the Knicks failed to average even 10,000 in home paid attendance. In 1960–61, they had neither a local radio nor a local television contract. In the New York City sports picture, the Knicks had been rendered virtually irrelevant.

But slowly–very slowly–things were about to change.

Johnny Green: They were making a lot of changes, trying to get a winning combination. There were no untouchables.

Leonard Koppett: The Garden did not choose a really good coach between Lapchick and Donovan. When Donovan became the coach, he had nothing in terms of material. When they made him general manager and got out of his way, he started to put together a good team, both in drafting and trading and in judging what it took to make a good basketball team.

The crowds, the traffic, the marquee, the excitement . . . the Old Garden in its final year, 1968.

THE LINEUP: Marv Albert; Freddie Klein; Johnny Green; Stan Asofsky; John Andariese; Ray Lumpp; Al Albert; Al Bianchi; Leonard Koppett; Spencer Ross; Marv Albert; Ernie Grunfeld; Cal Ramsey; Vince Boryla; Dick Van Arsdale; Bill Bradley; Phil Jackson; Rolando Blackman; Les Keiter; Bob Wolff; Harry Gallatin.

Opened in 1989, the gleaming Worldwide Plaza office-apartment complex covers an entire block of New York City's West Side: bordered by 49ᵗʰ and 50ᵗʰ Streets to the north and south, Eighth and Ninth Avenues to the east and west. And nowhere amid its 50 stories and 1.7 million square feet is there any reminder or indication that this, indeed, is hallowed ground. No sign, plaque, or monument to inform future generations what stood here between 1925 and 1968: not just the country's premier indoor entertainment showplace, not just promoter Tex Rickard's 18,000-seat masterpiece, but the place where the game of basketball grew, matured, and flourished; the place where two generations of New Yorkers fell in love with the sport.

Marv Albert: I sometimes wish that the Old Garden would suddenly reappear. The Garden now is very nice; it's one of the great buildings in the NBA and I'm sure opposing players still love to come here. But the Old Garden was like a classic place. It reminds me of when I used to go to Ebbets Field. If you look at it now, there were probably so many things wrong with that building. The dressing rooms were tiny, and there were a lot of inconveniences. But that lobby area, where, as I learned, a lot of business was going on, was just a great scene at halftime and prior to games.

Freddie Klein: It had a tremendous flavor. We used to gather under the canopy and meet all sorts of gamblers and regular fans and crooks and doctors. It was fabulous. We had Nedick's on one side and Adam Hats on the other.

Johnny Green: You had that long walk where you'd leave Eighth Avenue, but you'd have to walk through that long lobby to actually get into the Garden. You had the little shops on each side, about five or six, including the Nedick's hot dogs. After practice, we'd always go by and get a Nedick's hot dog. Then you had the awning, the marquee.

Stan Asofsky: There wasn't more knowledge and sagacity than under that arcade, by Nedick's. And that's where *Ring* magazine was, right above. You'd get in with your G.O. card. There was more warmth, more closeness. And there were much more knowledgeable fans.

John Andariese: I can re-create the entire feeling of the Old Garden in an instant; being a fan, meeting at halftime in the lobby. The great part of the Old Garden was that everybody piled out into the lobby. Everyone would just drift out there and B.S. about the first half. That was a great meeting place, with refreshments and Nedick's and everything.

Ray Lumpp: We were big in the garment district. All the people in the garment district had season tickets or the best seats in the house. They followed the game very closely. It started with the colleges, and then after the scandals, the NBA took over. And as better and better players came into the league, it turned into a tremendous game. Mikan, Cousy, Davies. Great players.

Al Albert: You know, most people are grossed out by cigar smoke. But for me, it's my identification with being at the Garden. It meant that you were old enough to smoke. You'd see the names on the marquee, you'd have a Nedick's, people just browsing around and at the ticket windows, and people smoking cigars. That's stayed with me. Anytime I smell a cigar now I think of those days at the Old Garden.

Al Bianchi: When we were on the other side of the [Queensboro] bridge, Saturday was a big day. There would be a clinic in the morning with Clair Bee and some of the other college coaches. Then in the afternoon there'd be a pro game, and at night there would be a college game. So it was a full day. That was big-time. That's how we spent our time, either playing in the schoolyard or going over the bridge to watch 'em at the Garden.

In the mid-fifties the Garden started hosting double-headers, which were immensely popular and brought together half the league under one roof.

Leonard Koppett: After the scandals, the pros started playing doubleheaders. The big arenas had conditioned their customers to two games. And the smaller arenas, who didn't need doubleheaders, made money by selling off home games to the bigger arenas that could use them in a doubleheader. Well, when you have a doubleheader in an eight-team league, that means exactly half of all the players in the league are in your building on the same night, and in the same coffee shop or airport afterward. The intimacy of that world, at that time, was enormous.

Spencer Ross: Tuesday night was double-header night at the Garden. The first game started at 6:30. When I was 12 years old, a few of my friends and I would take the subway from Brooklyn to 42nd Street, and then take the local up to 49th Street, then walk up to the Garden. We wouldn't get home until about midnight, because after the game we wouldn't take the subway back from 49th Street. Instead, we'd walk down to 42nd Street, to Times Square right off Seventh Avenue, to a place called Grant's, where you got hamburgers that were in the worst grease of all time. But they were the

best. They were two for a quarter with grilled onions. Oh, it was just fantastic.

Marv Albert: I'd bring my schoolbooks with me on the subway and do my schoolwork going to and from the Garden. It was a different time. And I'd come back after what Marty used to call the "All-NBA doubleheaders" pretty late at night. There was sort of a sense of urgency to get my work done, rather than doing it at home where I'd probably be listening to the games anyway. So I think it actually encouraged me to get my work done.

Ernie Grunfeld: My dad worked in the Bronx, and we used to meet in front of the Old Garden. We used to go see doubleheaders, and my dad was a huge sports fan. Sometimes he'd come late, and we'd miss the first half of the first game because he couldn't get out of work in time. Those were great days. I remember how smoky the Old Garden was, and we always sat way, way upstairs where all the smoke rose. It was a great place with a great atmosphere.

Al Bianchi: The doubleheader nights were a big gathering for the four teams. It was great. We used to hop on the train at Syracuse early in the morning, get down there, play the game, and get right back on the train to Syracuse.

The Garden still made time for the college boys to collect their own memories. For the fans, the pro doubleheaders and the college holiday tournaments mixed with the powerful ambience of the arena to create a lasting impression.

Cal Ramsey: Going to the Holiday Festivals and the NITs, and watching those great Duquesne and Niagara teams, and LaSalle with Tom Gola. I'll never forget that in one game, Duquesne had Sihugo Green, who was my idol, and Dick Ricketts playing for them. And they scored all of Duquesne's points in the first half of one game. As a matter of fact, watching them I was so impressed that I wanted to go to Duquesne. The coach later came down and took me to dinner with Ricketts and Sihugo Green, and I almost had a cardiac arrest. I would have signed on the dotted line right there because I loved those guys so much. But for some reason, they de-emphasized basketball the next year, so I wound up going to NYU.

John Andariese: As a [high school] senior, I was All-City, and I played in the [1956] *Herald Tribune* Fresh Air Fund Game at the Garden. I played for the Brooklyn-Queens team against Manhattan–the Bronx–Staten Island, my first game ever in the Garden. The year before, as a junior, I had tickets to the game. Great seats. Then I got sick the night of the game, and my mother wouldn't let me go. I'll never forget sitting at home. I remember what the radio looked like, sitting at home in the kitchen in Brooklyn listening to Marty Glickman do the game. I was just distraught. And I remember saying to myself, "The only thing that can make me get over this is if I play in the game next year, as a senior." And the next year I did make it. Sam Stith and I were the only two guys in the game from Catholic high schools. In that game, I was on the same team with Doug Moe and Tommy Davis. Satch Sanders guarded me. It was the ultimate honor. The next game was the East-West college All-Star Game, and [Bill] Russell and [Tommy] Heinsohn played.

Vince Boryla: You'd come in the back door and go around to the locker room. You didn't have to walk upstairs or take a lot of elevators like they do at the New Garden. The court was there, and the second and third levels were almost built into the court, only higher up. It was the most imposing building I ever played in.

Spencer Ross: People don't realize that there were no escalators at the Old Garden. You climbed stairs, something like nine floors up. The side court at the Old Garden was wonderful for basketball. If you sat there for hockey, which has a bigger surface, you couldn't see the ice unless you sat in the first row. So for hockey, you wanted to sit in the end arena.

Leonard Koppett: The Old Garden was just great for basketball. It had been built originally for boxing and hockey. For boxing, of course, the floor would be filled with ringside seats. For hockey, the seats upstairs were such that you couldn't see

the near side, under you. If you sat in the end zone, you saw the whole rink, although one goal would be pretty far away. The way the Old Garden was built, at least 60 percent of the seats were on the ends. The sides were narrow and the ends were fat. It isn't like the present Garden, which is an even bowl.

Freddie Klein: A lot of smoke, cigarette and cigar smoke.

Stan Asofsky: And that stench. That beer stench.

Ray Lumpp: At halftime, it was like going into a casino. Everybody had a two-dollar bet or a five-dollar bet. At halftime, you'd hear people saying, "Hey, give two, take four," and like that. It wasn't big-time gambling, it was more small-time. But it was there. And New Yorkers loved to have a little action. The games were being bet on, no question about it.

The crowd, the referees, the Garden staff, the floor, the locker rooms, the atmosphere–they all made the building special.

Leonard Koppett: The crowd reaction in the Garden would be incredible. A team would be 10 points ahead with 30 seconds to play, and people would be going crazy because the spread was 9 points. So if either team scored, the bet would be tilted the other way, even though the game itself had been decided.

Marv Albert: John Goldner was my boss when I was a ballboy. John was great, but I think he was a little skeptical of me at first because I was juggling so many things at the time. I would keep stats sometimes and do ballboy duties other times. Curt Block, the legendary PR man from NBC, actually preceded me as a ballboy. Curt became a standout player at Hofstra.

John Andariese: To anybody trying to sit courtside, John Goldner was a central figure in your life. Always in a suit and tie, always kind of a stern man. He would pick out those who didn't belong in the courtside seats. I mean, when you sat courtside to watch Hot Rod Hundley drop in 40 or 50 against St. John's, or Tom Gola with LaSalle, the

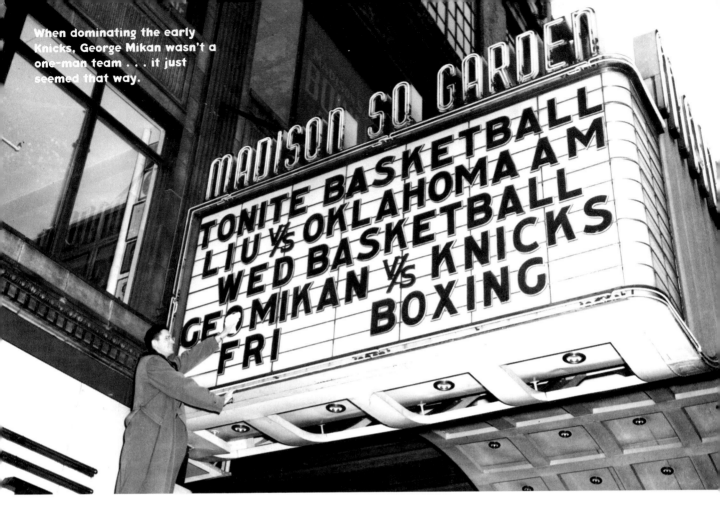

When dominating the early Knicks, George Mikan wasn't a one-man team . . . it just seemed that way.

Garden was a major part of your growing up. And you never had courtside seats. What teenager did? But there would be games when people left early, and if you got the chance, you'd do what any kid would do: try to sit down closer. And when that would happen, you would be confronted by the policeman of courtside seats, John Goldner. And he did it very simply, too. There was no question, no arguing. The trick was not to be spotted by him. He'd walk around courtside and then just point right at you, followed by the baseball umpire's sign: You're out!

Freddie Klein: [Referee] Sid Borgia once called a foul on Wilt Chamberlain. And Chamberlain bounced the ball hard, toward the top of the Garden.

And Sid told him, "If that ball comes down, it's a technical foul."

Stan Asofsky: Earl Strom was our favorite. He was a great referee, and he once invited Freddie and me to Carlisle, Pennsylvania. They were having a big dinner honoring him, and we were going to sit between Chamberlain and Julius Erving. And the reason was that he wanted us to harass him, to tell bad stories about him, because everyone else was there to give him plaudits and accolades. We didn't go, though.

Freddie Klein: We used to kid [referee] Mendy Rudolph because we knew he gambled a lot. So we'd say, "Mendy, who's gonna win the game?" He'd turn around and say to me, "The team that scores the most points, schmuck."

Stan Asofsky: One of our favorite ballplayers to razz was Rick Barry. Freddie used to say that Rick never committed a foul in his entire career.

Freddie Klein: And neither did Billy Cunningham.

Marv Albert: I was the visiting ballboy before I became the Knicks ballboy. That was a great experience in seeing all the coaches and all the players. I don't know what it's like now, but some coaches would let me stay in the locker room while they were talking to the team. Not everybody allowed that. You really got an insight in terms of what was going on with the game.

Steve Albert: My first two years I was the visiting ballboy. The Celtics came in one night, and they had these great warm-ups with their names on these cloth plaques that would snap on the backs of the jackets. And one of the most valuable was the one that said "Havlicek." We come back after the warm-ups into this small locker room, and the trainer, Buddy LeRoux, who went on to own the Red Sox, comes up to me. And he said, "We're missing [John] Havlicek's warm-up." And I went, "Oh, my God." I run out there and look for it, and it's gone. Completely gone. Buddy was not a happy man. He climbed all over me, just all over me. I'm on the verge of tears; I'm thinking this is the end of the world. I'm gonna lose my job because I lost Havlicek's warm-up. It was probably stolen while I looked away. Now Havlicek, unbeknownst to me, sees all this. He's sitting at his locker, and he sees what's going on. Then he comes out later—like in the Mean Joe Greene commercial. He comes out, puts his arm around me, and says, "Don't worry about it, kid. He loses his temper sometimes. Don't let it get to you. I'll get another warm-up." He just made me feel so good. I never forgot that.

Dick Van Arsdale: I loved the old building. I loved the doubleheaders on Tuesday nights because I'd be able to see my brother [with Detroit] maybe 20 times that first season. I liked it so much better than the New Garden. The ambiance, the smell of it. The rims were a lot softer than in the New Garden. I never liked the New Garden, I just thought it was a very tough place to play. But the Old Garden had a character and a history all its own.

Johnny Green: It really wasn't a good floor. It had dead spots, and that particular floor was just a thin layer of board. It had to be very portable. And if the boards were two inches thick, that was a lot. So you'd wind up with a lot of dead spots because the boards would be set up directly over concrete or the hockey ice. The floor had no spring to it.

Steve Albert: We used to shoot around early, and just feeling how soft those rims were–oh, the greatest. And the sound the ball would make when it went through the hoop. It was a great sound. I didn't hear it often enough. I heard "clang" a lot more.

Bill Bradley: I remember how tiny the locker rooms were, and the history that was there. The rims were soft, and the floor was sometimes hollow. You could sit in the upper deck and actually be closer than a lot of people in the lower deck. And I think of all the people who worked there: John Condon, Dr. Yanagisawa, and all the guys in the back who were sort of roustabout guys.

Phil Jackson: They said Feets Broudy had the most educated finger in the NBA, and perhaps he did. Feets was really renowned. He loved basketball. If there's a home court advantage, he found a way to bring the home court advantage to the clock.

Bill Bradley: Feets wasn't the Old Garden or the New Garden, he was *the* Garden. I had a little thing with him before every game; I'd give him my towel. It was a little superstition. He was a great friend, totally dedicated to the Knicks.

John Andariese: The voice of John Condon always permeated the building, like the paint on the wall. It was just always there. And the thrill of having him announce your name as a player . . . that was another level of ecstasy.

Rolando Blackman: That was a big deal for me, because growing up and listening to his voice all through the times the Knicks were winning championships, he was the voice of the Knicks. And I just wish he could have said my name in the starting lineup as a Knick. People may think that it was kind of silly, but it was a real big deal to me.

Spencer Ross: In the early days when they were doing cable TV, there was a time when Marty couldn't make the game. They were gonna bring somebody else to do it, but Marty said, "Don't bother, it'll work. All we have to do is pick up the PA feed with John Condon." And that's what they did. They did the entire game off the PA system, because John's voice was very simple and distinct. It was, "That was Walt Frazier . . . New York leads, 10–6." Or "New York foul by Walt Frazier. That's his first and the team's second. Elgin Baylor on the line, two shots . . . " That was it.

Marv Albert: The broadcast location at the Old Garden was outstanding. It was low; it had the overhead look like the Boston Garden did.

Les Keiter: The Old Garden was a particular favorite of mine because I spent so many nights there. It was idyllic from a broadcaster's standpoint. We had our broadcast booth on the second deck, looking straight down. It was a very narrow booth. The vantage point was perfect. For me, the Old Garden was a ball.

Bob Wolff: It was the perfect setting to broadcast. It was like sitting in your living room, only raised. The seats were banked so high, it was like being on a cliff. There was a little ledge in front of the balcony where we sat. And if you couldn't call a game from that position, you couldn't call a game. That was the perfect setup. When we moved into the present Garden, we were so high that you couldn't tell Frazier from DeBusschere.

Leonard Koppett: In the Old Garden, the basketball press table was at courtside, the whole 49th Street side. The scorer and the player benches were on the 50th Street side. So you were really in the game. At every timeout, you were chatting with the officials. Because basketball was considered, in newspaper terms, a second-ranked sport, the people covering it weren't the biggest big shots, journalistically. Obviously, the people playing and officiating knew they weren't big shots, either. So there was much more interaction.

John Andariese: When I was at Fordham, many times the Garden allowed the college teams to practice there on Saturday mornings. That was like eating ice cream all day. I mean, you're playing in the Garden! The floor was soft. It had a lot of give to it. The rims were nice, and you were where the greatest of the great had played. It was thrilling.

Steve Albert: The unbelievable joy of getting there early and being allowed to shoot around, and then having the players, one by one, trickle out. And then feeding the ball to some of the all-time greats: Jerry West, Wilt Chamberlain, John Havlicek.

The Old Garden–actually, the third of the four buildings to carry the Madison Square Garden name–perished under the wrecker's ball in late 1968. And yet, nearly four decades later, the memories grow even more vivid among those who were fortunate enough to call it home.

Harry Gallatin: It's kind of a shrine to me, and I think it is to a lot of players. When they came into Madison Square Garden, they always seemed to want to play their best. It was the Mecca of basketball, and we always felt that teams played a lot better against us in the Garden than they did when we went to their court. We always had that in the back of our minds, and we knew that once teams came into the Garden–where it all started, even though Dr. Naismith started [invented the game] in Springfield–we knew that there was something about playing in New York, in the Big Apple, that means a lot to most players.

Dick Van Arsdale: God, that office they had in the Old Garden. I remember the linoleum floors. And I think there were only three offices: Eddie Donovan's, Frankie Blauschild's, and Jimmy Wergeles'.

Marv Albert: As you walked in, the Knicks offices were to the left of the lobby. There was a tunnel that went past various entrances to the arena, on the loge level. The offices were in there, and I'd get so excited going into the office. I was so obsessed with wanting to be in the business as either a sportswriter or broadcaster. [Trainer] Donnie Friederichs' wife was the office manager, and she worked for John [Goldner]. She ran the office.

Clean-shaven rookie Phil Jackson throws it down against the St. Louis Hawks during February 1968 in the Knicks' next-to-last game at the Old Garden.

Leonard Koppett: At halftime, you congregated in one of two places. In a few steps, you'd be out in the Eighth Avenue lobby, where everybody knew the rounds. Or you went back to the 49th Street side where the club offices were. And in one or two of those offices, you'd sit around and bullshit.

Spencer Ross: Tuesday nights were always an exciting time, walking through that rotunda right in front and stopping at Nedick's and getting a couple of hot dogs with an orange drink. Tuesday nights had the big crowds. On Saturday nights, even when the Knicks had a good team, there were eight or nine thousand people there.

Al Albert: When Donnie Walsh was involved with the design of [Indiana's] Conseco Fieldhouse, he wanted to make sure there was a big entrance place because he, too, growing up in New York, remembered what the Old Garden was like. Just the scene. Every game, you felt like you were going to *the* event.

Freddie Klein: It's a social thing. I like to be here and talk to people. If they lose, they lose. And if they lose, I always figure that the other team played better. There was more love for the game back then, too. Guys didn't get paid a lot of money, but they loved the game. Now, everything's a business.

Bob Wolff: I had just completed three years with NBC, doing the Baseball Game of the Week. I was also doing the NBA as their lead announcer. I had the job that Lindsey Nelson had when he went to the Mets. NBC lost the [baseball] contract in '64 and ABC picked it up, and I became one of their announcers but not their lead announcer. At the same time, the New Garden was going up. I was still doing all the Knicks and Rangers games, so the Garden said to me that they could use me to make the transition in publicizing the move from the old arena, selling tickets there, to the new arena.

Freddie Klein: We were just so used to that place, it was like our place. This place [the New Garden] was much colder in the beginning. It's OK now, though.

Stan Asofsky: This is more of a corporate crowd. The old building had more people indicative of us, more like us.

Bob Wolff: When we moved out of the old building, the big thing was that every sport had a special farewell night. Every event had a closing night in the old building and an opening night in the new building. And that opening night, the show with Bob Hope and Bing Crosby, was unbelievable.

Freddie Klein: If you loved pro basketball, you had to go to the Garden. It was as simple as that. It was a lot more closed then. Today, you can watch so much. If you like basketball, you have anywhere from 5 to 15 games a week on cable TV. But back then, going to a Knicks game was an event. It was like a private club, like it was our little secret. Everyone who came over from the Old Garden understood that.

Bob Wolff: In many ways, a lot of the people who were planning things for the new building were keeping them a secret. So this is at the first meeting with all the bigwigs there. I said, "I'd just like to ask this: Where's the press box?" There was silence in the room. So I said, again, "Where are all the press going to be seated?" They told me they had a new plan that would work well. Somebody said, "We have figured out that most of the Garden time is not spent watching the Knicks and the Rangers, it's at all the other events. So if we make a press box and press row for the Knicks and Rangers, we're going to waste a lot of seats. What we plan to do for Knicks and Rangers games is to put planks down across the seats for the media, and remove them afterward." So, naturally, I said, "What happens if someone in the middle of the row has to go to the bathroom? Does everyone have to lift up the plank for the whole row for this person to get out?" Now there's the same silence. Then I explained that as an announcer, I'd have to get up and move around to do stand-ups before the game and at halftime, so how would that affect me? And where would the cameras be? Same silence. At this point, it behooved me to have a private talk with Irving Mitchell Felt and say, "We're heading for disaster."

Johnny Green: If you go to the Garden now, I think there are maybe three ushers who're from the Old Garden. I see them sometimes when I go there. But the numbers are growing smaller.

Bob Wolff: We had so many problems with television in the new building. One was that, for decoration purposes, the New Garden had all these thin poles that went up and down near the roof. So when you sat up high, all you saw were these poles. It was as though you were looking through a giant crossword puzzle. So we had to learn to shoot around them. Another problem was that in the Old Garden, you could look right straight down. But in the new building, if you're sitting a little bit up in the stands and the puck is up against the near sideboards, you couldn't see it. We never did fix that. But the worst thing was that, to make it easier to do basketball, they would suspend a little booth from the roof. The problem with that was twofold: One, to get into the booth they would suspend a rope ladder down and you'd risk your life scrambling up. Furthermore, when you're up there and you had to go to the bathroom, there were no facilities. That made it even worse. We survived, but barely.

With Donovan promoted to general
manager, Gallatin took over as coach
in early 1965.

THE LINEUP: Leonard Koppett; Leonard Lewin; Richie Guerin; Harry Gallatin; Willis Reed; Dick Van Arsdale; Red Holzman; Dick McGuire; Johnny Green; Phil Pepe; Bill Bradley; Phil Jackson; Walt Frazier; Marv Albert; Bob Wolff.

As the country was convulsed by social tumult during the sixties, the Knicks experienced the beginnings of their own revolution. The building blocks for the franchise's most successful period were assembled starting in the mid-sixties–but not before a few false starts and other big changes.

Leonard Koppett: The front office was doing all the drafting. They were dictating the drafting. And if you look at all those names, they were all people who had done something in a college game at Madison Square Garden. Go explain that to Irish and Fred Podesta. That's basically what it was. Finally, when they got Donovan in there, they started choosing wisely. All of a sudden, they got Cazzie Russell and Bill Bradley and Willis Reed.

Leonard Lewin: Ned and Freddie Podesta were in charge of the picks. Everybody else used to wait until they told them what to do. He'd tell them who he wanted drafted. They picked name players who were out-of-towners.

Over a seven-year period, from 1958 through 1964, only once did the Knicks fail to secure at least the third overall pick in the NBA Draft. Yet the list of selections from that era became a litany of players who simply didn't pan out.

Mike Farmer from San Francisco in 1958. Tom Stith from St. Bonaventure in 1961, felled by tuberculosis. Paul Hogue from Cincinnati in 1962, dogged by bad knees. New York City product Art Heyman from Duke in 1963.

Jim "Bad News" Barnes from Texas Western, for whom the Knicks passed on Willis Reed in 1964. At the same time, the Knicks passed over a veritable NBA All-Star Team: John Havlicek, Lenny Wilkens, Nate Thurmond, Guy Rodgers, Rudy LaRusso, Satch Sanders, Zelmo Beaty, Kevin Loughery, Chet Walker, Tom Meschery, Gus Johnson, Jeff Mullins, and Paul Silas. Of all the Knicks' first-round selections during that span, only Johnny Green, in 1959, made an impact with New York.

Heyman's arrival in 1963 signaled the departure of one of the greatest Knicks of them all.

Richie Guerin: I went to Eddie Donovan myself. I thought I still had a lot of good years left to play with the Knicks, and I really felt in my heart and soul that I could have been a big help to Artie as well as the team. I went to Eddie and I said, "Look, I have a lot of years left, certainly three or four more good years. I'm not gonna take a back seat and come off the bench with this team. If you want to start Artie, that's your prerogative. But I'm certainly not gonna be a sub." And he said, "Oh, no, no, Rich. You're still in our plans." I said, "OK, but I want to be up front with you and you to be up front with me. If that's the way it's gonna go, then try to make the best deal for me because I'm not gonna be a happy camper."

As we got closer to the beginning of the [1963–64] season, it started to feel like something was going to happen. I wasn't playing as many minutes, and there was always the excuse that "you're in good shape, but we have to take a look at some of these young guys." On opening night at the Garden, I only played 10 or 12 minutes. We played in Cincinnati next. I played about 20 minutes, and right after the game Eddie told me I was traded. And both of us sat there and cried. I had the biggest admiration for Eddie Donovan. I just wish it would have been done before the season started. My wife was pregnant at the time with our last daughter, and I was in St. Louis when she was born in December, so the timing wasn't the greatest. It was sad to leave. I felt in my heart that I still could have been an asset to the team, but I guess they looked at it as a rebuilding phase and they had to start someplace.

But now Irish's attention was about to be diverted elsewhere. In late 1960, plans were announced for the construction of a new Madison Square Garden, to be built atop a leveled Penn Station on Eighth Avenue between 31st and 33rd Streets. Now there was an arena to build, and new business to tend to, and Irish decided that it was time to let someone else handle the construction of his basketball team.

It was a simple, almost unnoticed announcement. On January 3, 1965, after compiling an 84–194 record as head coach, Donovan was "promoted" to general manager, while Harry Gallatin returned to the Knicks as head coach. Almost as an afterthought, it was noted that Donovan would preside over player personnel matters, while Irish and Podesta would turn to the business end and to solving the inherent problems of building a new Garden.

At the time, it was perceived as a demotion for Donovan. After all, he had been let go as head coach, and the concept of promoting a man who had produced three straight last-place finishes and a .302 winning percentage didn't seem plausible.

No one could have dreamed that, from this point on, the Knicks wouldn't take a backward step for more than a decade.

Leonard Lewin: It all changed when Donovan came in. He and Holzman would sit and watch films of the college players, and I'd sit with them. In fact, I was with them when they were trying to decide among [Jim] Barnes, Willis Reed, and Luke Jackson. Philly decided on Luke Jackson because he was a better athlete. The Knicks took Barnes and didn't take Willis until the next pick. Willis was always mad at the Knicks for that.

Leonard Koppett: One thing that helped Donovan was the fact that Irish and Podesta were older now. They were now getting involved with plans for a new Garden, and paying that much less attention to the moment-by-moment of the Knicks. The same sort of thing happened with the Yankees when Steinbrenner was suspended: the baseball people were able to build something that he had stopped interfering with. When you have interfering ownership, anything that distracts them is good for the team.

Harry Gallatin: I really didn't recognize at the time that it was going to occur. I still think that Ned and Fred had their hand in it, but it was a turning point in that way. An awful lot of times, the publicity that certain players had might not have influenced Eddie's decision on who he drafted. Eddie was very aware of good players and had a number of contacts with coaches. That helped considerably. I would tend to trust a coach's opinion, as opposed to someone who was thinking about the publicity.

Leonard Koppett: It's not that they [Irish and Podesta] wanted to get out of the business, it's that their attention was taken up by more important things, like the new building. Also, I think they were tired of getting their brains beat out with last-place clubs, and it wasn't any fun.

Leonard Lewin: Ned made the decision himself [to take himself out of the basketball end]. Nobody had any influence on him.

Leonard Koppett: I don't think it was a philosophy as much as it was judgment. Eddie had good basketball judgment. He could tell what a player could do and how it fit with the team. When Eddie was the coach, he didn't have any players he could do anything with. But as general manager, he was able to gradually supply the team with better players.

And so, one by one, they arrived: Reed in 1964, as a second-round pick following the selection of Jim Barnes . . . Indiana's Dick Van Arsdale the following year . . . veteran sharpshooter Dick Barnett in a trade with Los Angeles in 1965 . . .

Willis Reed: Harry [Gallatin] was a tough guy. He believed in doing it right. I remember the year after he took over for Eddie, when we went to training camp, we didn't win many games but he worked us really hard.

Dick Van Arsdale: I knew they were looking at us, my brother [Tom] and me. We had dinner with Red Holzman and Harry Gallatin in Indianapolis before the draft. And that was really impressive to us, that they would take us out. After the draft, I got a call from Eddie Donovan, who said, "We've drafted you; you're going to be a Knickerbocker."

Harry Gallatin picked me up at the airport and took me downtown. They put the rookies up in a place called the Paramount Hotel, which was on 46th Street down from the old building.

Willis Reed: Johnny Green and I laugh about the fact that he had to go out there and play with four rookies, with Jim "Bad News" Barnes, Willis Reed, Howard Komives, and Emmette Bryant. He said, "I should have gotten paid twice the money I was getting paid."

Dick Van Arsdale: They had a rookie free-agent camp that [1965] summer, like an open tryout camp, at the 69th Regiment Armory. There must have been 150 guys there, and some of them couldn't walk and chew gum. I mean, you saw everything at that workout. Dave Stallworth and Barry Clemens, who were also drafted that year, were there. Bill Bradley had been a territorial pick but had elected to go to Oxford. And the thing that impressed me was that Willis Reed and Emmette Bryant, who were

second-year guys, both participated in it. And you talk about some bad players; there were 150 guys there, and some of those guys were just horrible. That was my indoctrination to New York.

The neat thing about playing in New York as a rookie was they gave us rooms at the Paramount. They were eight-by-ten, or even less than that. They were so tiny, but they were free. I didn't have a car, so we'd walk to the games, walk back, and everything we did was right around Times Square and the West Side. We'd go to Mr. Laffs and everything. I hung around with Butch Komives a lot, Stallworth, Clemens, and Willis Reed. All we did was play basketball, eat, travel, and drink beer.

I started out in training camp [rooming] with Tom Gola. I loved him. He was an old veteran, a nice guy. The guy I probably roomed with more than any other was Butch Komives. One of the toughest guys I've ever met in my life.

My first year, I signed a contract for $12,000 with a $1,000 bonus. Second year, I signed for $17,000, and at the end of the year I was so good that Ned Irish gave me a $3,000 bonus. The third year, I signed a deal for $30,000 a year for two years. That's when the ABA started and Tom and I were looking around a little bit.

Red Holzman: When we first got Dick Barnett, everybody said he was a flamboyant guy, with the "Fall Back, Baby" stuff and everything. But they didn't realize Dick was a very intelligent player. He could play any type of game you wanted. Strong, strong guy.

Dick McGuire: Dick Barnett was a much, much better player than he ever got credit for. Red thought he might have been the best player on the team, defensively. He always played the toughest guard. That way he gave Walt [Frazier] the chance to roam around and steal the ball.

Red Holzman: He'd been there [in Los Angeles] a long time, and he wanted to go someplace where maybe he'd have a chance to win something. He figured he'd been there long enough, similar to what Kareem did when he went to the Lakers.

Dick Van Arsdale: What happened after a few games was that they traded Bad News Barnes,

Johnny Egan, and Johnny Green to Baltimore for Walt Bellamy [on November 2, 1965]. Then I moved into the starting lineup, ahead of Stallworth. I knew my role was to defend, play the small forward position. I wasn't a great shooter, but I worked my butt off guarding people. I averaged about 12 points that first year, made the All-Rookie Team, and it felt like I'd died and gone to heaven.

Johnny Green: It was the first time I had been traded, and it had a tremendous impact. But I could see the move from the management's point of view. I knew about the Walt Bellamy situation, and I was hoping we would be able to get him. I just didn't think I'd be involved in the trade.

Then, in successive years, the Knicks drafted perhaps the two most celebrated college players of that era. In 1965, with their last-ever territorial draft pick, they selected heralded Princeton All-American Bill Bradley. The following year, they used the number one overall pick on the consensus College Player of the Year, Michigan's Cazzie Russell.

Ironically, Bradley and Russell had already been linked in New York basketball legend. In the 1964 ECAC Holiday Festival at the Old Garden, the two staged an unforgettable duel in the semifinal round. Bradley scored 41 points to lead undermanned Princeton to a 12-point lead over the heavily favored Wolverines, but he fouled out with just under five minutes left in the game. Then Russell took over, scoring 9 of his 27 points in the final three minutes to key a 17–1 Michigan closing run that led to a pulsating 80–78 win.

Now they would be Knicks teammates—that is, if Bradley decided to turn pro. He had earned a Rhodes Scholarship and was headed overseas to Oxford to study and mull his future. It would be more than two years before the Knicks would see him again.

Harry Gallatin: I was on board when we drafted Bill Bradley. That was a decision that I fought with the bosses on, because he was going to Oxford at the time. His name was in the draft, and I talked to Ned Irish about him. Of course, Bill was from Crystal City, Missouri, and I was the coach at Southern Illinois–Carbondale before I

went to the Hawks, so I knew all about Bill and his aspirations and what kind of player he was. When his name came up, I went in specifically to talk to Mr. Irish about drafting him, even though he was going to go to Oxford. I said, "You will never waste this choice on this player. He will be one of the best players in the league." And he turned out to be that.

Phil Pepe: You can't imagine how big a star Bradley was. He was the Michael Jordan of his day, as a college player. He was a one-man team. And here he was with four other students. He was exhausted when that game was over, and he practically beat Michigan singlehandedly. He fouled out toward the end, but he was all over the court. He was brilliant. And I'll never forget Lenny Schecter writing a column after that, saying that someday this guy was going to be President of the United States. And he almost was.

Dick Van Arsdale: Bill really made our world championship team when we went to Budapest in 1965. He was the glue of that team. We had Bill, Billy Cunningham, Lou Hudson, my brother [Tom] . . . we had a hell of a team and we just kicked everybody's butt over there, basically. Tom and I spent a lot of time with Bill, and we said that when we got to Europe, we were only gonna speak French, because we'd all taken French in college. Well, we couldn't hold a candle to Bill. And wherever we'd go, he'd go off to the consulate and visit. He just knew what he wanted, always the politician.

Bill Bradley: One always wants to test one's ability against the best. In my case, that was probably the main reason I decided to play professionally. When I was thinking about it when I was a senior at Princeton, I had a good senior year, and then I decided I wanted to get away from all the public acclaim that surrounded the Princeton years. So I went to Oxford to gain perspective. While I was there, I came to realize that I really loved the game, and not to play professionally would be to deny a part of myself that possibly was more fundamental than any other part; and that the challenge was to test yourself against the best.

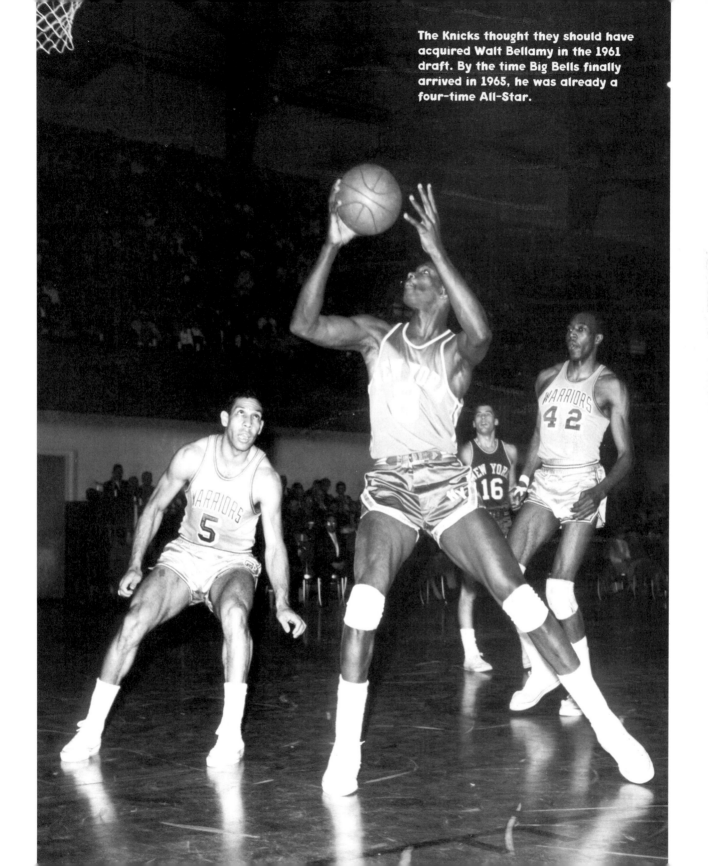

The Knicks thought they should have acquired Walt Bellamy in the 1961 draft. By the time Big Bells finally arrived in 1965, he was already a four-time All-Star.

Bradley would finally arrive in December 1967. After a memorable press conference at Leone's that would yield both a new contract and a new nickname, he would struggle through his rookie season.

Leonard Lewin: They gave Cazzie Russell a deal worth about $100,000 total. Then they gave Bill about $125,000 to make him the top-salaried player on the Knicks. So at the press conference at Leone's, I called him "Dollar Bill" in my story that night. And the name stuck with him. I told him when he was running for president, "If you become president, I become famous."

Bill Bradley: People always ask me how I got the nickname Dollar Bill and I mention three possibilities: First was the size of the initial contract. Second, my teammates said that I still had the first dollar I ever earned. Third, I often took the last-second shot. Those are the three possibilities. I guess Lenny coined it in response to the contract.

Leonard Koppett: Bradley was gonna come in as a backcourtman. But he couldn't be an NBA backcourtman; he wasn't that quick. Then he found his right place, where he wound up, in the corner.

Dick Van Arsdale: Bradley came midway through my third season. And I think I was a little bit naïve at that point. I had a great second year, and I thought I was secure. If you look at the expansion teams today–when I left New York, I was averaging over 30 minutes a game. So it wasn't like the expansion of recent years. I thought at that time that I was gonna be in New York for the rest of my career. Because I didn't think Cazzie was better than I was, and I'd played with Bill in Europe. I think that Bill Bradley is one of the most brilliant players of all time in what he did with–and I don't mean to demean him at all–a limited amount of physical ability. He was just so smart and great to play with. But at that time I wasn't worried about anything, because I thought I was here to stay. In retrospect, I understand what happened. Cazzie had the big contract, and Bradley wasn't going anyplace; plus he fit in so well and could play with anybody. We were all playing the small forward position, so I was the expendable guy.

I was very surprised, at that time. But when I think about it today, I shouldn't have been surprised. I got a call from Eddie Donovan the day of the [1968] expansion draft, and I was shocked when he told me I was going to Phoenix. I called my wife, who was a schoolteacher, and the first thing she did was start crying. It was not a good time for me. It hurt, you know. I had spent three good years there and then had to leave.

Dick McGuire: I was playing Bradley more as a two [guard], where he ended up being a much better player as a three [small forward]. As a two, he had trouble beating guys, where he didn't have that trouble as a three. And the threes didn't play him as hard as the twos played him, so he could get his outside shot. And Bill became a great player.

John Andariese: I was sitting courtside shortly after Bradley became a pro. They were playing the St. Louis Hawks, and Joe Caldwell was guarding him. And I remember thinking, "How can this guy survive what Caldwell is doing to him?" He was just manhandling Bradley. But, Bradley being Bradley, he found a way.

Bill Bradley: The first year was really a nightmare for me. I came in as the so-called white hope, and I knew I wasn't. I was playing guard, and I knew I was out of position and was an utter and total failure. The iron rule of celebrity came into play because I had skyrocketed so high and had so much publicity, so when it turned sour it really turned sour. People literally spit on me, threw coins at me. I'd be accosted in the street. It was a very tough year. The following year, when I got the break and moved to small forward, it was a totally different experience. It was like returning home. But the first year was very tough.

Dick McGuire: Bill had problems defensively playing the two. Because they were quicker than he was. If you're quicker than the guy who's playing you, it's a lot easier than being slower than the guy who's playing you, because it's tough to put the ball on the floor and all that. And Bill struggled defensively. Now, at the small forward we had Cazzie Russell, and all of a sudden, we're playing Cazzie [as a starter]. So there wasn't that much of a place to play Bill except as a two. And finally Cazzie got hurt and Red moved Billy up to a starting forward, and we went off from there.

Bill Bradley: My first year, everybody and nobody were my friends, meaning that I had no complaint about any team member. I was learning an awful lot about the league, about the travel, about the game, and everyone was helpful. Ultimately, you have to have a few years of interaction with someone before they're really your friend. At the end of that first year, Phil Jackson was also a rookie, and he asked me to come out to Williston, North Dakota, to a banquet honoring him. I went out and did that, and I also taught school in Harlem after the second year. But I had no one friend at that stage.

Willis Reed: One day Bradley comes up to me in the airport and says, "Willis, can I talk to you?" I called him Bradley then, so I said, "What's up, Bradley?" He walked over, looked around, and said, "Listen, you call all the guys on the team by their first name, and you always call me Bradley." I said, "Yeah, so what?" He said, "Would you please call me by my first name? Would you please call me Bill?" I said, "OK, Bradley!" But today I call him Bill.

Dick Van Arsdale: When Bill came in to sign his contract, he walked out onto Ninth Avenue and was almost hit by a car because he wasn't paying attention. He was known to be a crappy dresser then, too. But a wonderful guy.

Bill Bradley: It was early evening. I was living at 57th and Eighth, and I was going to have dinner with my Italian basketball coach, who was in town. I had played in Italy for one of the years I was at Oxford. Naturally, I was late. So I crossed Eighth Avenue at 57th, on the north side. It was raining and I was going against the light. Suddenly, out of the right-hand corner of my eye, I see a car. It's going about 20 or 30 miles an hour. Just by instinct, I jumped up and to my left. Luckily, it was an MG, and I rolled over the car and fell into the street. The driver stopped; she was a young woman. Then I walked down to St. Clare's Hospital for x-rays. There are no broken bones, but I have two severely

sprained wrists and a contusion of my hip. So I'm out, after I'd only been there about a week or two. The hip wasn't as bad as my wrist, because I couldn't shoot. Dickie and Irish didn't say anything. I guess they were just glad I wasn't killed, because I could have been. I've often thought that if SUVs existed then, I'd have been dead. Or even if it was a bigger car. I was just lucky it was an MG. And it was just instinctive, jumping up. The young woman was absolutely positive I was going to sue her, which I never did.

With the fifth overall pick in 1967, the Knicks drafted Southern Illinois' Walt Frazier, who only weeks before had earned MVP honors at the National Invitation Tournament at the Garden. The second round brought a gangly, introspective forward from North Dakota named Phil Jackson. The impact of the two rookie roommates would be felt for decades to come.

Phil Jackson: I had quit baseball, where I'd had interest from the Dodgers after my sophomore year in college. I was really interested in baseball, but then basketball became more of a success story for me. I grew from 6'5" to 6'8" during my college years. My senior year, I averaged almost 28 points a game, and I was among the top small-college scorers, so I knew I was going to have an opportunity. Yet I had never seen a professional ballgame. I had seen some on TV. They had a Sunday game on ABC in the sixties, and they showed the Finals, and that was it. But I listened to the All-Star Game when it was broadcast. I was aware of all the players, but I didn't know the game. I hadn't seen the game often enough to really know it. I came into the [pro] game very naïve.

Red Holzman had come to scout me at an NCAA Tournament, and I'd had a miserable game. I played short, just 20-some minutes, and fouled out. And he left and had gone on to another tournament. Then I scored 50 points the next night in the consolation game. So I was surprised when the Knicks picked me, because Red hadn't seen that game. I got a call. I also got a call from the ABA; I was drafted by the Minnesota Muskies. They had a territorial pick, and Minnesota was just a couple of hundred miles away. So I had that going for me.

I made a trip to New York over Memorial Day weekend [in 1967]. I decided not to play baseball in my senior year and pursued the Knicks when they offered me a two-year guaranteed contract for a total of $25,000, with a signing bonus. When I went to New York City, the circus was in the Old Garden. I stayed at the Paramount Hotel and went to the circus. One of the players, Neil Johnson, took me out to dinner and then said, "We'll go hang with my guys. If you need some money, here's twenty bucks." So I kind of wandered in Manhattan that Saturday, for the largest rally for the Vietnam War up to that time. There were 500,000 marching in support of the Vietnam War. There were firemen, policemen, and sanitation workers, and their unions all rallied behind. There was a furor; it was quite an active weekend. So I had a wonderful time in New York City, except that a taxi driver bilked me out of about twenty dollars by driving me over the Triborough Bridge to the Grand Central to get to Kennedy Airport. When I got to the airport he had used up all of that twenty dollars and I had nothing left for a tip, and Neil Johnson was back in Washington Heights.

Dick McGuire: I don't think I played Phil all that much. I think Red was the one who started playing him a lot, especially in the press. He used Phil as the front man. He was all arms and was all over you, and made every pass a tough pass. All of a sudden, you couldn't get it to the guy, and now you have to lob it. And Red did a hell of a job. He put the press in, and we pressed very, very well.

Dick Van Arsdale: Phil had the coat-hanger shoulders and the long arms, and he was basically a bench player who would come in and rebound, block shots, and bang.

Walt Frazier: Phil was from North Dakota, so he liked to sleep in a cold room. I didn't like it really hot, but I didn't like it that cold. He usually won out. I used to come in right after the game and go right to bed. Phil would go out, come back later, fall asleep; and then I'd be wide awake. So I learned that you gotta relax in this business. You gotta let

the game go and not take it so hard. Then I started hanging out after the games, too, and I started sleeping better, because I saw how it was working for Phil.

Meanwhile, the coaching situation was as jumbled as ever. Gallatin lasted just 11 months before he was replaced by Dick McGuire on November 29, 1965. In 1966–67, Dickie led the Knicks to their highest win total (36) and first playoff berth since 1959.

But the following season, as the Knicks were preparing to move into the New Garden on 33rd Street, McGuire could not survive the increasing pressures of a 15–22 start. On December 27, 1967, moments after a loss to Philadelphia, he would exchange jobs with the team's longtime scout. Red Holzman would be the new man in the hot seat.

Dick Van Arsdale: I was Harry's kind of player because I was kind of fearless, aggressive. I'd go through a wall for a coach. My first training camp was at Fairfield University, and there was a step pyramid drill, where you went up steps on one side and down steps on the other side. I'd lead the charge up the steps, and I never got tired. I'd just go on forever. I think he liked that.

Willis Reed: One thing that Harry used to tell us was, "You know, some of you guys, when you get that check at the end of the month, you need to cover your faces because you know you don't deserve it." I never forgot that statement. He was always philosophical about things like that.

Dick Van Arsdale: Harry was a very demanding coach. That first training camp was as tough a training camp as I experienced in my 12 years in the NBA. He just drove us. Run, run, run. It was very difficult. And training camps back then were a lot longer, about 10 or 12 days of two-a-days. I thought he was a pretty good coach.

Dick McGuire: I came back to New York and tried to sell insurance. What you are, basically, is a door opener. I couldn't sell a stamp. I couldn't close on anyone, but they used me as a door opener more than anything else. I did that for a year or so, made a living doing it, mostly at a discount or selling to my friends. And the only thing I enjoyed about the whole damn thing was that I played for the company basketball team.

I was selling insurance, and somebody told me that they [the Knicks] are gonna speak to me about it [coaching]. I came in, saw them, and thought I'd give it a shot. Probably Podesta was the guy that called me, but Ned was the one that told him what to do.

Dick Van Arsdale: Dickie [McGuire] is one of my all-time favorite people. But Dickie, by his own admission, was not really cut out to be a coach. Everybody loved him, but Dickie was like one of the boys. He wanted to roll the ball out and play. He expected everyone to know how to play, because he knew the game so well.

Bill Bradley: He was only the coach for about a month, so I didn't really have any experience with him. I like Dick; he was a great player. He knew the game, and I always loved to talk about the game with him, and he was certainly kind to me as a coach. But he had a difficult situation on multiple levels.

Dick Van Arsdale: Before a game, coaches always put the names of the starters up on the board and give defensive assignments. Dickie would look at Bellamy and say, "Bells, you take whattayacallit." Or, "Willis, you got whattayacallit." And then, "Van, take whattayacallit." Everything was "whattayacallit" with Dickie. Everybody loved him, but you knew it wasn't going to last too long.

Leonard Lewin: I remember the night they fired him. His kids and [wife] Teri were standing in the hallway crying. In fact, Red Holzman was sitting during the game with [his wife] Selma and my wife. He said to them, "Wait for me, I've got to see Ned after the game." When he came back, he told us he was hired as coach.

Phil Jackson: I think if you compare the Knicks [of that era] to a present-day club—and I'm just talking about talent—you would say they were similar to, say, the Clippers or the Grizzlies. They had been drafting pretty high and had great draft picks, so they were loaded with talent but didn't have leadership. They brought in Walt Bellamy and

Dick Barnett, who were kind of elder statesmen, to try to balance that out. But with Dick Van Arsdale and Cazzie Russell scrumming for a starting position at that time, and then Bill Bradley coming in, it was a situation of [having] more talent than time to be played. And Red figured that out by just saying, "We're gonna press full-court." So then we had a second unit comprised of myself, Walt Frazier, Emmette Bryant, and Van Arsdale. And we were good. In the second half of the year [1967–68], we were able to be the most successful team in the league. So there was hope.

Dick McGuire: I don't think I was ever meant to be a coach because I'm not going to yell at all. I always thought that if you treated guys well, they'd all play hard for you. Forget that, that's not true at all [McGuire laughs]. People are people and you are what you are. It's tough. And one guy I'll always remember is Dick Van Arsdale. I would take Dick out and I'd say, "Dick, I'm sorry. I'm taking you out because you're the only guy who doesn't make a scene when I take you out." Once in a while I gotta be right, you know?

As the team was coming together, the one-word phrase that would become synonymous with its success was about to be coined.

"Yesss!"

The play-by-play report from the March 23, 1968, playoff game against Philadelphia–the first postseason game ever at the New Garden–reads, "Barnett jumper from right corner" with one second remaining in the first quarter. Just one basket, one among thousands, but the reaction to it would echo for decades in every schoolyard in the city.

Marv Albert: Sid Borgia was a very colorful referee. When a player scored and was fouled, he'd say, "Yesss, and it counts!" He had all these flamboyant ways about him. So it came from that. I picked it up during my ballboy days, sitting near the court and hearing it.

Dick Barnett hit a "Fall Back, Baby" fling at the buzzer to end the first quarter, and it just came out. Then I started to incorporate it [into the broadcasts],

Dick Barnett snatches a rebound away from Philadelphia's Wally Jones.

and the fans would repeat it back to me. For whatever reason, it just caught on. And when you try to look for a catch phrase, whatever the sport, it's usually forced. It just happened to work in basketball at a time when the Knicks were becoming very popular and very good.

Two years earlier, New Yorkers tuned in to Channel 9 for a Knicks road telecast that featured an announcer who stayed home. The date was March 5, 1966. It was snowing in New York, and getting worse by the minute . . .

Bob Wolff: I was doing a 1:00 Fordham-Manhattan game at Rose Hill, then the Knicks at Cincinnati that night. I did a lot of those two-events-in-two-cities days. I always double-booked my travel, and I never missed. I figured on this one I could get to Cincinnati for the 8:00 game there. But after the game at Fordham, the snow started to come down and it's getting worse and worse. And if they're not flying, what do I do? So [my wife] Jane picked me up, and we went to the airport, and this flight is cancelled and that flight is cancelled. Now the airport was practically closed, and I asked, "Is there anybody here who would dare to risk flying me in a private plane?" They said I had to be kidding. So I didn't know what to do.

Jane was the one who suggested going to the Empire State Building, where the broadcast tower for WOR was. I could look at the picture there and do the play-by-play off the picture. They had a little cubbyhole of a room, and they put a microphone in front of me. They could relay the picture and crowd noise audio from Cincinnati. So I called [Knicks publicist] Frank Blauschild and said, "Frank, you have a telephone by your side. We're gonna be in constant communication. Don't let it stop. All I can see is what's on the screen, so if you see a sub coming in, or need to give me stats, keep telling me that in my ear."

So I started out the broadcast saying, "Tonight's game is coming to you with the video from Cincinnati, where the Royals meet the Knicks, and the audio being transmitted from the Empire State Building." The game unfolds and it's an overtime game. Cincinnati won on Jack Twyman Night. At the end of the game, I repeated that the video came from Cincinnati and the audio from the Empire State Building. That was it, and I walked out into the night. And I said to myself, "That would be a great story."

But I couldn't tell anyone, because my bosses would say, "How come you didn't tell us first?" Also, this may kill any broadcaster from ever going on a road trip again. They'd figure that if I could sit there and do a game off TV, why should they pay for me to travel? So I kept it quiet for about 20 years.

Dick McGuire's 1966–67 team had broken a seven-year postseason dry spell. The following year, with Holzman taking over in December and the New Garden opening two months later, the Knicks went 43–39 and took defending champion Philadelphia–the 76ers of Chamberlain, Greer, and Cunningham–to six games in the first playoff round.

Dick Van Arsdale: We were getting a lot better. I knew with the players we had, we had a pretty good team. I thought it was only gonna get better from there on out.

But the first weeks of 1968–69 were disastrous. The Knicks started 6–13, and nothing was working. The Bellamy-Reed frontline tandem, with Willis playing out of position at power forward, was inconsistent. Bradley continued to struggle in the backcourt, while Frazier and Howard Komives fought for minutes.

Meanwhile, out in Detroit, the Pistons were having problems of their own.

With an undersized team, coach Paul Seymour coveted a big man. And not just any big man, but Bellamy, a four-time All-Star by the time he arrived in New York. So Donovan received a call from Ed Coil, the Pistons' general manager. And then another, and another. Was there anyone, Coil wanted to know, that the Knicks would take for Bellamy (except, of course, Detroit's outstanding–and untouchable–youngster, Dave Bing)?

There was, in fact, one Piston who Donovan liked as much as Seymour liked Bellamy. Donovan had tried to acquire this player several times in the past. But this was a Detroit guy: Detroit-born, Detroit-raised, Detroit-schooled; a rugged, bruising, blue-collar guy who personified a blue-collar town. A perennial All-Star, and a man held in such high regard in his hometown that the Pistons actually made him player-coach at the ripe old age of 24. So whenever Donovan asked Eddie Coil about this guy, Coil naturally wouldn't listen.

But now it was December 1968, and Paul Seymour needed Walt Bellamy like a pair of eyes. And now Eddie Coil was listening.

Willis Reed: We had a Tuesday night game at the Garden, then we went on the road. [In that Tuesday game] Bellamy got in foul trouble, and I played center most of the time and had a good game. Red came up to me on the plane and said, "How'd you enjoy playing center?" I said, "It was all right." He said, "Who knows? You might be playing there more." I thought Red was jerking me around. He always used to be giving you that kind of stuff. He'd give you a key from the hotel, put it in your pocket, and say, "You're my key man" and all that stuff. But sure enough, we get to Detroit and on Friday night, Bellamy and Komives have Pistons uniforms on and [Dave] DeBusschere's got a Knicks uniform on!

Walt Frazier: We're in Detroit. I'm lying in bed watching television, and the news comes on, and I say, "Oh, shit!" Because that changed my whole life. Now I'm a starter.

Willis Reed: I think it worked out pretty good for us. Maybe we didn't win with it because we didn't quite have all the pieces yet. It wasn't that Bellamy and I couldn't play together. At that point, we had never made a commitment to give Clyde [Walt Frazier] the basketball. I wound up making the All-Star Team at the forward spot and the center spot, so it wasn't bad. It's just that we hadn't become a good team yet.

Marv Albert: There was such a high level of intelligence on that team. You hear all the talk about "five coaches on the floor." You could see it. But it really didn't happen until the DeBusschere trade. There was a missing piece, Dave being the great team player he was.

Willis Reed: Playing forward was a new experience for me. It was more about helping me learn some other things about the game. Was I a great power forward? I was probably a *good* power forward. I didn't have the long range that, say, we got when we got DeBusschere, who could play power forward and shoot long outside shots and handle the ball like a guard. I did not have those capabilities.

It would simply be known as "The Trade": Bellamy and Komives to Detroit for Dave DeBusschere, 6'6" and 220 pounds of the best defensive power forward in the NBA.

For the Knicks, it was a trade that worked on so many levels it was almost incalculable.

The cast was now complete.

Willis Reed: Most people look at that trade in terms of us getting DeBusschere and me going back to center. But I thought that the most important part of that whole thing was that we made a commitment that Clyde was going to be our point guard. That gave the team some stability because when Komives played the point, he was not a pure point guard. He was more of a shooter, and he just didn't have the skill level that Clyde had. Clyde could make the pass. He was so great off the penetration. When we made that whole switch, with me going back to center, I found myself getting three or four easy layups a game because he'd just penetrate and pull that big guy over and lay it off to me.

Leonard Koppett: When they got championship material, they became a championship team.

Forevermore, the DeBusschere trade would be hailed as the "missing piece" of the Knicks puzzle. And in one very important way, it certainly was; a roster of championship potential was now in place.

But there was still one more vital change, although no one realized it at the time.

A month after the DeBusschere trade, on the night of January 21, 1969, Cazzie Russell suffered a broken ankle diving for a loose ball against Seattle. Cazzie had been the starting small forward, but now he was out for the rest of the regular season. Limited in his options,

Cazzie Russell's broken ankle—he's carried off by Knicks trainer Danny Whelan and Sonics trainer Jack Curran—opened the spot for Bradley in the starting lineup in early 1969.

Holzman moved Bradley–the third guard behind Frazier and Barnett–into Cazzie's starting forward slot.
And Dollar Bill struggled no more.

Bill Bradley: I always respected Cazzie as a human being. We were competitors, and sometimes it was tense, but we had a sufficient amount of respect for each other. And we both wanted, above all, to win a championship. So if I'd start and hit a bad spell, Red would send in Cazzie, and if he hit five in a row, I'd actually feel good because that boosted the team.

Dick Van Arsdale: Cazzie was a great shooter. He wasn't a defender, but he could score. I got the impression that Cazzie was the kind of guy who wasn't going to wait, he wanted to play right away.

Bill Bradley: DeBusschere coming added a great deal. And then the thing that really put the team in place was a period in my second year [1968–69], after Cazzie was hurt, where five guys played over 40 minutes a game for 20 or 30 games.

There was no question that this was my chance. First of all, I was in a situation where I had to play, and there was playing time available. I was familiar enough with Red's system that I knew exactly what my role was, and I was determined that I was not going to fail.

One game, out in San Diego, we had played on a Saturday night and had gotten into San Diego on Sunday around noon, and I had a tuna fish sandwich. And by game time, I was sick as a dog. During the game, I would actually come over to the bench and upchuck, and then I'd dry heave at the foul line. Red and Danny [Whelan] were saying, "Don't you want to come out?" And I'm yelling, "No! No! I'm not coming out!" In other words, I was gonna prove to them that I wanted that position and I was gonna make it for the team. I didn't care if I was sick or not. And after the game, in the airport, Willis and DeBusschere were laughing at me because they knew exactly what I was doing.

Phil Jackson: It [my back injury] was a sequence of events. I went up for a shot late in a ballgame against Phoenix in January [1969]. I got pushed in the back as I was looking to release the ball, came down a little crooked. So I was gimping around, had some tightness. [Trainer] Danny Whelan would stretch you out and readjust you. I went out for the next game, at San Francisco, a drafty, cold building. I wasn't properly loose, and I came in and shot a turnaround jumper. And my defender made me turn just a little bit, so when I landed, I landed on my heels. And the jolt was enough to crush my disc. Right away, I got a shot of pain and came out. I went back during the second half, but then I started realizing how bad it was. I couldn't sleep for the next couple of nights.

And within a week after that, Cazzie broke his ankle, and he was in the same hospital I was. I was in traction for my back, and he came in with the broken ankle. We were already one man short due to the DeBusschere trade. Suddenly we're down to a nine-man basketball team. And it was the making of our team, because a five-man group had to figure out how to play together, playing 40-plus minutes together.

Bill Bradley: We had that game in the Garden in '64, Princeton versus Michigan. Michigan is number one. I foul out with about two minutes to go, and we lose. Cazzie had hit the winning shot. That echoed when we played them again in the Final Four, and they won again. Then, when we came to the Knicks, he's a forward and I'm a guard. They switched me to forward after Cazzie broke his ankle, and then when he came back, we were in a competition for that slot. I think it made us better because of the competition.

Dick Van Arsdale: It was a difficult transition for Cazzie that first year. He had trouble with the defensive part of the game.

Bill Bradley: Even in New York today, I'll run into people who'll say, "I was a Cazzie guy." There were Cazzie guys and Bradley guys. That was a little ridiculous.

Rebounding from the slow start, the post-DeBusschere Knicks finished with a club-record 54 wins, then pulled off a stunning four-game sweep in the first playoff round against the NBA's winningest team, the Baltimore Bullets.

"Dollar Bill" hooks one over Chicago's Barry Clemens during his sophomore season.

But in the Eastern Finals, they would fall in six games to the veteran Boston Celtics, who were on their way to their 11ᵗʰ and final championship of the Bill Russell era. A groin injury hobbled Frazier midway through the series, and only one of the Celtics' four wins was by more than eight points. The series ended with a one-point loss at Boston on a gloomy Friday night, April 18, 1969.

And on that night, in the losers' locker room at the Boston Garden, the 1969–70 season began.

Walt Frazier: I had strained my groin. I tried to go, but it was just too painful. I played well sporadically, because I really didn't have any lateral movement. It was disappointing.

Everyone was talking championship, because we felt we were on a par with the Celtics. Even with my being injured, we still gave them everything they could handle. We weren't in awe of them anymore. So we were all talking, "Hey, this could be the year." The confidence level was tremendous.

Bill Bradley: We knew, when we lost to the Celtics, that we were coming back the next year. We knew we shouldn't have lost to the Celtics; we beat them six out of seven times in the regular season. But we lost in the playoffs because of their experience, and Bill Russell and the whole thing. But we knew at that moment that we were the best. Or at least we *thought* we were the best, and we couldn't wait to get to training camp the next year.

Before Clyde was Clyde: Frazier lays one in against the Hawks during his rookie season.

THE LINEUP: Willis Reed; Walt Frazier; Harry Gallatin; Fuzzy Levane; Dick McGuire; Johnny Green; Dick Van Arsdale; Phil Jackson; Marv Albert; John Andariese; Richie Guerin; Phil Pepe; George Kalinsky; Don Chaney; Mel Davis; Cal Ramsey; Mike Glenn; Bob Wolff.

They joined the Knicks three years apart during the mid-sixties, products of the Deep South, with little national fanfare as college players. But by decade's end, Willis Reed and Walt Frazier would emerge as the most visible, most enduring, most popular, and most important members of the Knicks' greatest teams.

Willis Reed: If I had a chance to play at the next level, I picked the right guy. I picked Fred Hobdy at Grambling. They played running basketball; they played man-to-man defense. He had played center himself and did a lot of work with big people. Most guys pick a school. I picked a coach.

Walt Frazier: Whenever I read a college magazine, I wasn't even listed in there, so I never thought I had a chance to be a pro. The only time I thought I maybe had a chance was in the NIT, when all these coaches were asking me if I would be willing to leave school to turn pro. I had another year of eligibility left. That's when it kind of dawned on me. And then with some of the guys I read about, I was having good games against them. So I figured maybe I had a shot.

Harry Gallatin: One of the things that I always felt was important as a coach was to work out individually with some of these players, which was a legal thing. So I went down to Grambling and worked out with Willis, before we drafted him. I did the same thing with Zelmo Beaty, who played at Prairie View, and Paul Silas, who played at

Creighton. I was young enough at the time to go and be able to challenge these guys a little bit and find out what kind of heart and moves they had, and whether they'd be able to get along and be a part of a good team.

Willis Reed: The day of the draft, I was doing my student teaching at Webster High School in Linden, Louisiana. I was in the gym working with some kids, and I got a call from Eddie Donovan. He said, "Hey, Will! Just wanted to let you know that we've completed some rounds, and we've taken you number ten in the draft." I wasn't happy with that because I thought I should have been a first-round pick. I thought I should have gone a little higher than that, and I kind of thought I was going to get drafted by Detroit because Earl Lloyd had seen me play some of my best games. But a lot of times you find out that destiny is not where you think it is. Destiny has its own role to play in your life.

Fuzzy Levane: As far as drafting Willis, they were the luckiest team in the world, because they drafted Bad News Barnes first. And they were lucky enough that eight other teams passed up on Willis, including my friend Mr. Auerbach, who picked Mel Counts. When Willis was still there in the second round, they grabbed him like Nedick's.

Walt Frazier: I had an agent. That day I went to class, came back, and I was shocked. Because I had never heard from the Knicks. The Knicks never talked to me. I had worked out a three-year deal with Seattle on the phone. Seattle had the sixth pick, right after the Knicks. Seattle said that they'd draft me, and we had already worked out a deal. So when I came back from class, my agent had this dumbfounded look on his face. And he said, "You've been drafted by the Knicks." And I said, "Why?" Because I knew they had all those backcourt guys. I felt terrible because I figured they drafted me just to trade me.

Harry Gallatin: We were really sold on Willis Reed. Just a perfect gentleman, and he had all kinds of talent, inside and outside. And the biggest thing was that his heart was as big as his chest. To me, that meant a lot when it came to playing basketball.

Walt Frazier: When I first came to New York, Willis picked me up at the airport. He had a convertible, so I ended up getting a convertible. He had a big impact on me as a person and as a player, with his professionalism and tenacious work ethic.

Dick McGuire: When we got Walter [Frazier], Walter was the best player we had in training camp [in 1967]. And then he got hurt in an exhibition game out on Long Island and was out for quite a while. He was the best runner, handled the ball extremely well. A very, very good player. He would have been a starter had he not gotten hurt.

Johnny Green: Willis came in, and, during his rookie year, he had one game where he had something like 46 against the Lakers. So you could see that he was starting to surface.

Dick McGuire: He [Reed] was such a good competitor, he hated to lose in practice. He was that good a competitor. He just loved to play and played hard all the time. And he was a great shooter for a guy his size. Facing the basket, he had a nice little

jumper. We knew he was going to be good, but I never knew he was going to be as good as he turned out to be.

Willis Reed: My first year in the league, I scored my fewest points against Wayne Embry, because he would just hold you and he wouldn't let you go. Wide Wayne! The first time I ever played against Wilt, I had something like 32 points. I looked down at the stats and he had like 56, and if he had made his free throws he probably would have had 60. He was so domineering physically.

Walt Frazier: I remember thanking God that I signed a three-year contract. I didn't think I was going to be around long. At that time, I was a jack of all trades and a master of none. I was passing when I should have been shooting and vice versa. After a while I was saying to myself, "Man, why did I go to this team? It's such a selfish team." Cazzie and Komives hated each other. They wouldn't pass the ball. Bellamy and Willis were fighting over the same rebounds because Willis was playing out of position. It was just chaos. Willis wasn't used to a guy going up the chute and then dishing off to him. So I'd do that and the ball would go out of bounds. Nobody was ready for that. My only savior was defense. That's where I had my confidence. I was a good shooter in college, but I was nervous with the Knicks and I rarely shot the ball. So I really worked hard on defense.

Dick Van Arsdale: Frazier had a difficult time his first year. But there was a grace about Walt that everyone saw eventually. He was really smooth, and he made the game look easy. When you watched him, you said to yourself, "Here's a guy who's not real quick or fast." But he was a great defender and had great anticipation. You could see he had a grace that told you that he was gonna make it eventually.

Walt Frazier: I came in early to New York, and I played against Dick [McGuire] and Bill Bradley and [Dick] Van Arsdale. And I was thinking, "Man, this game is so physical." I mean, pick-and-rolls and all that. I had my doubts, man. And then my injury really set me back. I turned my ankle pretty bad, so I was on the injured list to start the season. So I was the forgotten guy, because everyone was waiting for Bill. That took a lot of pressure off me.

Essentially, when I was in the game, I'd bring the ball up to the halfcourt line, I'd pass it, and I never saw it again. That was it. I didn't see the ball anymore. Barnett didn't want to handle the ball. That's why we worked so well in the backcourt, because he didn't want to handle it and I had it most of the time.

Willis Reed: In my third year [1966–67], I became the captain. Dickie McGuire walked in and said, "Ownership has decided that Willis Reed's going to be the captain of the team." There was never a vote or anything. I thought it was amazing. I had never heard of anything like that. I thought it was a great honor, but I also thought it was an amazing thing. Because I had played on teams where if you play good and you do all the right things, maybe you were lucky enough to become one of the guys who's chosen by the group to be one of the leaders. But that was a decision that came from upstairs.

Walt Frazier: Willis would always take the rookies under his wing and show them around. He would loan you his car or money. Barnett probably owes him a hundred thousand dollars. So the Captain was very generous. That was his personality. You'd say, "Willis, can I use the car?" and he'd say, "Yeah, man, it's in the garage." When I got to be a veteran, I could never be as compassionate as him.

Before long, their given names would no longer be needed for instant recognition. They would simply be Clyde and the Cap'n.

Mel Davis: Here I am, a rookie, and I missed training camp. I don't know the plays, I'm not in shape, I don't know really where I fit in. Red was just gonna let me find my way, once I got in shape. But I was very lucky to have Willis Reed as my roommate. He took me under his wing and explained to me that I was the last man on the team for that very reason. I had to work my way into the system and prove, not only to the team but also to the coach, that I belonged here. Willis told me to be focused, work hard, be the first one

there and the last one to leave. He gave me a lot of advice that I teach to my kids today.

Willis Reed: I had been the captain of every team I had played on at some level. So I had seen what captains do and what leadership meant and stuff like that. And I played for some coaches that were pretty demanding in terms of what people had to do and be responsible for. I think all those were characteristics that I gained from some of the coaches and from those people.

Mel Davis: The advice he gave me was invaluable: Treat people the way you'd like to be treated. Always be in shape, take care of your body. Eat right, rest right. Get a feel for the game, get a feel for the city you're going to. And, first and foremost, remember that you're a professional. You're not an amateur anymore, playing collegiate basketball. You're a professional now. Treat it as such. From that relationship, we have a strong friendship right now, one that's everlasting.

Cal Ramsey: I had a lot of respect and admiration for Willis Reed. He did something that was rather unusual when I first got the television job. He came to me and said, "Look, man. If you ever need my help for anything, any information about the players or the team, I'm here for you." I thought that was very nice. Classy, classy guy.

There was one endeavor at which Reed wasn't quite so successful. But he took it in stride . . .

Willis Reed: The Beef 'n Bun Restaurant! I learned a lot about real estate from that. I got into it with a few guys and said, "Well, if we can get this place to Seventh Avenue, we'd have it made." And we were about one block too far south and one block too far west! It was good, but we didn't have the traffic. Game days, it was a great spot. But it had to be a great spot every day to make any money, and it wasn't. But we had some fun with it. [Greater Metropolitan Radiology now occupies the former site of Willis Reed's Beef 'n Bun at 254 West 31ˢᵗ Street.]

Another fun thing I did was my basketball camp [at the New York Military Academy]. It's amazing how many guys I meet now that say, "Hey, I went to your basketball camp." Now they're not basketball players anymore.

One flamboyant, one stoic. One supercool, one rock-solid. One audacious enough to author a book called Rockin' Steady: A Guide to Basketball and Cool, *and one who would pass the half hour before tip-off by leafing through* Field and Stream.

Phil Jackson: Walt was perhaps not as street-slick, but his father was very much a man of Atlanta. Walt was the only boy in a family of girls. We had a friendship because we had played against each other as juniors in college. I had to guard him, at 6'7", and he was a forward at 6'3". That was an interesting matchup because the notoriety was following us both at the time. Then we got to the Knicks and we were paired up together. We were both from pressing defensive college teams, so we naturally fit well together on the court.

Walt Frazier: My sophomore year in college, I was a Little All-America second team. Then I started hanging out, not going to class, and the next year I was ineligible to play. So as a punishment, the coach made me play defense every day in practice. Being a pragmatic person, I never blamed him for my own folly of not being eligible. And I said, "If I gotta play defense, I'm going to be the best damn defensive player around." So I mastered the stance and all that. And the way I'd get back at them was, during scrimmages, I'd create so much havoc out there the coach would have to say, "Hey, Frazier! Sit down!" That was the year I fell in love with defense, because I never played offense for a whole year.

Phil Jackson: Walt was very cool, quiet, self-contained. The first time we went out to San Francisco, we walked the streets and the hills and got leg-weary. During that walk, Walt wound up buying a hot diamond ring from a guy. And he took it into a telephone booth to see if it would scratch the glass. It was a dud; he got taken. So I don't know how sharp or savvy he was, when you think about it.

Marv Albert: You could see he was uncomfortable when he first came in, because he didn't start.

Bradley was in the backcourt and having problems. Red handled it very well, incorporating Clyde into the lineup. Right away, you could see the body language and everything. They knew it too, the way he handled himself on the court. Off the court, in a locker room of great talkers, he might have been the best.

Walt Frazier: I lived in the New Yorker Hotel my first couple of years. The Knicks used to pay for everything but your incidentals. Barnett and Bellamy lived there a while, too. It was funny, because your room was predicated on your status on the team. So in my first year I had a room where I could lie in bed and open the door at the same time. Bellamy, meanwhile, had a suite, and the other guys had bigger rooms. I remember I had two clothes racks in my room, plus I used the shower stall as a clothes rack. Then as I started to progress, they gave me a larger room.

Phil Jackson: I smoked a pipe at the time. I'm sure that's strange to people because pipes were so associated with marijuana. I had no knowledge of what marijuana was at this time, but I did smoke a pipe. Walt convinced me that that wasn't too cool. Not for him. He was very much into the health aspect of living. Our relationship continued until I was injured the next year. I started to miss games, and things changed up as I didn't travel.

Walt Frazier: I used to be afraid to go to sleep on an empty stomach. My motto used to be "What is a meal without dessert?" I used to love pie à la mode and all that stuff. I used to just pig out.

Across from the New Yorker, they used to have Nedick's open all night. I used to go over there all the time, for the big fat fries and hot dogs. I also loved the Chock Full o' Nuts hot dogs. They were right on the corner. It was an eating frenzy.

Dick Van Arsdale: [Willis was a] great competitor, fabulous teammate. He wanted to win so badly. One of the hardest workers I'd ever seen. He'd just do anything to win. Great, soft left-handed jump shot. I had so much respect for Willis because of his desire to win. Just coming to that rookie camp at the Armory in his second year told you everything about Willis. He was the leader right from the start.

Walt Frazier: Willis got me my first date in New York. A girl named Joan. I'll never forget that.

John Andariese: I remember watching Willis Reed clean out Rudy LaRusso and the Lakers. I was in the side promenade for that game.

October 18, 1966, at the Old Garden. After that night nobody messed with the Cap'n again . . . almost.

Willis Reed: All I know is, Dolph Schayes, who was the supervisor of officials, wanted to put me out of the league! We filmed all our games, and they showed on the film that when we were coming up the court, Rudy threw a haymaker at me. And that's how the fight started. And then I was protecting myself. I have in my scrapbook a picture of [the Lakers'] Darrall Imhoff holding me in a bearhug and Rudy squaring off to knock me out. So it was an unbelievable thing. When it was all said and done, it was scary to me. Because what happened was that I ended up fighting the whole team by myself, because there was nobody helping me. But I had played football, so I had no fear. One thing that football gave me is that, once you walk off a football field, ain't nothing in the world you fear. Because you know what pain's about, you know what it is to hurt; you know what it is to hurt people, and you know what it is to get hurt.

Rudy had a great reputation, and he was a really good player. And I remember I kept complaining to the officials [Mendy Rudolph and Richie Powers] that the guy was climbing over my back and every-thing. "Shut up and play basketball!" That's what they told me. "Shut up and play basketball!" So I said to myself, "Shit, at some point I'm going to take care of this." So under the boards, I elbowed him. Nothing vicious. And going up the court, that's when he threw the haymaker at me.

I said I would never let that happen to me again. If I ever get in another fight, I'm going to have better control. But I was in a situation where . . . I went over by the bench and John Block threw a punch at me, and I just ducked his punch, and then I hit him and broke his nose. There was no help, I'm telling you!

You know, I had another fight with Rudy. He was playing with San Francisco. Jack Madden was the referee. On one play Rudy went up over my back to knock a rebound out of my hands. And Clyde Lee, who always had his hands up, caught the ball and laid it right up. I looked at Jack and he's taking off down the court. I know he saw the guy foul me, but he didn't call it. So I was so pissed off that I came up the court and caught Rudy with an elbow. And Jack never saw it. He turned and saw Rudy crumbling, and he knew I hit him. After that, I never had another fight until I had the one with Lou Hudson, of all the guys in the world.

Johnny Green: You started to realize that, "Hey, we've got a warrior here." So that's how the Knicks looked at him, that he wasn't afraid to mix it up and that he could play. At that point, they thought that if only they could get a center, it would be all right. That's how the trade for Bellamy came about. But that actually set Willis back, because now he has to play power forward, out of position.

Willis Reed: This [the Hudson fight] is in '68, and we're playing the Atlanta Hawks at Georgia Tech. We were running a play for Bradley, two-three-out. And Bill is wearing Lou out. I mean, he is killing him. Richie Guerin was the [Hawks] coach, and you can just imagine, Richie is fucking losing it. So Bill scores about four baskets, and then Lou catches me with an elbow coming across on the screen. So we're lining up for the free throw and I say to Lou, "If you do that again I'm gonna kick your ass." I figured that's the end of it, because Lou Hudson never fought anyone. Now we get to almost the end of the half. We run the play again: DeBusschere sets the screen in the middle of the lane, then I come in. Lou doesn't even try to come over the screen; he takes his fist and beats it right in my chest. I acted like I was shot! I don't want to fight him, because he's a nice guy and he's not a guy I'd want to fight anyway. If I was gonna fight with anyone on that team, it would have been Bill Bridges. So me and Lou get into this fight right in front of their bench, and Richie and Bill Bridges and all their guys come right at us. What happened

Willis Reed in 1969–70: regular season MVP, All-Star Game MVP, Finals MVP, and NBA Champion. Hey, you'd be smiling, too.

then was me and Nate Bowman fighting the whole Atlanta Hawks team. And at halftime I started yelling at the guys in the locker room, and I said, "Fuck, we play together, we fight together!" And the moral of the whole story is that if you're ever gonna start a fight, don't start it in front of the other team's bench.

Richie Guerin: Nate Bowman came over and got a little involved with Willis. Then some of our fans ran down and sort of cracked the both of them from over our bench. A couple of the fans came down and got into it, which obviously is a no-no. Willis said to me later, "Next thing I know, I'm getting cracked in the head by some fans. I said to Nate, 'Don't get in trouble here. We gotta get out of here.'"

Frazier didn't try to outmuscle his opponents; instead he tried to outwork and outshine them in every other way. Having a splendid nickname only served to drive the point home.

Walt Frazier: When Red took over, he stressed defense. And that's when I started to play. He had us picking up from end line to end line. But even under Dick McGuire, I'd play in the second quarter, sometimes in the fourth. Maybe 10 or 12 minutes total. And whenever, say, an Oscar Robertson got hot, I'd be in there on him. Or a Jerry West. And I'd relish that role, trying to guard those guys. I took a lot of pride in my defense.

Phil Pepe: One day they're in practice and Clyde comes down and does one of his looking-one-way, passing-the-other things, and he throws the ball and it hits Nate Bowman and rolls out of bounds. And with this deadpan expression and way of speaking, Barnett looked at Clyde and said, "Baaaaad pass. You hit him right in the hands."

Walt Frazier: I wasn't playing well. So in order to pacify myself, I always bought clothes. I'd go out and dress up, then go back to my room and look in the mirror and say, "Well, at least I still look good." So this particular time we were in Baltimore and I'm shopping, and I see this Borsalino hat. It was brown velour with a real wide brim. I tried it on and liked it. The first time I wore it, guys were laughing at me.

Everybody was pointing at me and stuff. I was a little self-conscious, but then I said, "Hey, man. I like this hat. I think I look good in it, and I'm going to keep wearing it." And as fate would have it, the movie *Bonnie and Clyde* comes out [in late 1967], and then I'd walk in the locker room and they'd go, "Hey, look at Clyde."

I always liked clothes, and I was buying them and wearing them. But only once I started to play well did the writers start to focus on my clothes. I really wasn't doing anything different, except now I was doing it on the court. Then the writers would start to say that this guy wears this, he does that. So the media catapulted it, as well as George Kalinsky. He did a few shots of me in the car, and one with the wide hat that became a classic, and some casual shots. And they'd eventually wind up in the paper.

George Kalinsky: Clyde kept coming up to my office—he was very introverted then, as he is now—and he was trying to figure out a nickname for himself, because he wanted to do something different. Eventually, Danny Whelan came up with Clyde. So he came up one day and he's wearing this green outfit with a green hat and green alligator shoes. I said, "Oh, my God, this is it. Let's go downstairs and take a photograph somewhere." This is in 1969. We went right outside 4 Penn Plaza, and I took the picture of him leaning against the lamppost. Then the Knicks started winning, and magazines like *Newsweek, Life,* and *Look* started calling me for photographs. When *Newsweek* called, I asked if they were interested in any photos off the court, because this was something new. They said, "Sure." And one of them was the Clyde photo. So they run a big photo montage with action photos of everyone, plus this picture of Clyde. Then we got about 200 letters, mostly from girls, wanting this print of Walt Frazier. And right around that time, there was a novel out called *The Pimp,* and they copied the photo, the pose. It was a best-seller at the time. So now you saw that book all over the place, with this copied pose.

Don Chaney: The one thing that annoyed me about Frazier was the fact that, when things were really going bad for the Knicks, and for himself, he always had that same coolness and confidence as if everything was just right. And it just drove me nuts. He wasn't rattled about anything. If he was having a really lousy game, the perception was that he was having a 20-point night. He always had that appearance that he was in control.

Walt Frazier: It was magic, the things that happened [after I became a starter]. I saw that the guys had confidence in me. They wanted me to have the ball. Dick [Barnett] didn't want to handle the ball, so Red just said, "Go get it, Clyde." I knew my role. My role was to hit the open man, play some defense.

[After the DeBusschere trade] it was like someone pulled a veil off my face. I found myself penetrating inside, and then I copied Barnett's move where he faked guys into the air. So I added to it; I'd fake them and jump into them, but still try to make the shot as well. So all that started happening to me overnight. All of a sudden I was penetrating, dishing off, finding Willis for easy baskets and stuff.

Don Chaney: There was a respect at the time for Frazier, but at the same time, because of the tradition, there was also a deep hatred. So when we [the Celtics] competed against the Knicks, we had respect for them because Frazier was a great player. Not only that, he was always in the news, in the papers, in magazines, and on TV—not only for his on-court play but for his off-court play as well. He had the furs and the cars and everything. We were totally the opposite. We were generic, basically.

Walt Frazier: It was something I relished. I liked being Clyde. Clyde was a good name for me. All of my endorsements were related to Clyde. The kids loved Clyde. And even now, people never call me Walt. It's always Clyde.

I started going to Lester the Tailor because of Barnett. When I was in college I wore penny loafers and button-down shirts like everyone else. Then, coming to the Knicks, all the guys were good dressers. So I used to go to their shirtmaker, this guy Artchiller Freetman in Brooklyn. He used to make the shirts with the monograms on them. But I always liked the way Barnett dressed, and I found out he was going to Lester. At that time, he was right in midtown. So I started going there to have my suits made. At the peak, I think I had about 50 or 60 suits. Same amount of shoes.

Phil Pepe: Clyde was the focus of most of our attention. Very quotable. He had good lines and that flamboyant style as a player and as a person. He was a delightful guy to be around.

Mike Glenn: Walt Frazier was a huge shadow [to any player coming out of Southern Illinois], but it was a good shadow. We had very good physical trainers at Southern Illinois, and they'd tell me what Walt used to do, what exercises he did, and how he got so strong. I was trained in all these facets while I was still at Southern Illinois. I knew so much about Walt Frazier–reading his book, talking to people who knew him–that he was an inspiration. I remember when he came back to Southern Illinois when they retired his jersey. We played against Florida State, and we just knew we could not lose. No way. Not with Walt Frazier in the house.

Don Chaney: It was a little awkward because once I committed to coming to New York, I realized I'd have to see Walt Frazier every day! That was hard; that was very hard. We've always had a mutual respect for each other, even when we were competing. But there was a certain demeanor we established with each other as players, that we acknowledged each other but that was it. He was the enemy. And coming here, knowing that instead of being a Celtic I was a Knick, that was very difficult for me. I was very uncomfortable because it stayed with me all those years. It was the strangest thing. And then speaking to former Knicks players, I was very uncomfortable. It was like you'd been in a battle all your life with the person, and all of a sudden this guy's living in your house. I've probably adjusted and felt comfortable around Walt Frazier just in the last two years. It's really strange. The competitive juices just flow every time I see him. It's just something you can't overcome right away.

Frazier strikes again, this time against Detroit's Otto Moore.

Spoils of victory: the Cap'n and
the coach accept the Walter
Brown Trophy, emblematic of the
Knicks' 1970 NBA title. That's Ned
Irish on the far right.

Bob Wolff: Walt Frazier, I thought, was the most amazing of them all. Frazier was always portrayed in the papers as this flamboyant man-about-town with the fur coats and all. In person, he was very soft-spoken. And on every trip, he always brought along two or three books, like *Fifty Ways to a Better Vocabulary* and *How to Increase Your Word Power.* All these books on reading and vocabulary. And I thought that here's a guy who's really starting from scratch, trying to learn how to speak in public. And lo and behold, doggone it, I found that he's using these words now to do something different. And not only does he use them to become a character and personality, but the truth is he has a wonderful vocabulary. He's using words the average broadcaster doesn't even throw in.

Marv Albert: Clyde was the guy I'd always go to for postgame sound. He was so refreshingly honest and said everything so well. When he first came up, I remember going to his press conference and sitting there at the table with him. He was such a good guy. This was before all the Bonnie and Clyde–type image stuff came in. Eventually, he knew that was good for him and his career. He had delivered by then.

Walt Frazier: The Clydemobile was a Silver Shadow Cloud III Rolls Royce. I used to buy Caddies all the time, but how far do you drive in New York? So after two years I'd have less than 15,000 miles and I'd try to trade it in, but it wouldn't be worth anything. I never liked Rolls Royces because they were always black or gray. Then one day I was walking on Third Avenue and there was a steel gray Rolls there, and somehow it was illuminated by the sun. And I was looking at the lines on the car and admiring it, and I thought, "Wow, that's a cool car." Then I went to the Rolls place, but I asked the guy if he could jazz up the colors a little. So he did that, made it brighter, and then he put the Landau bars on the back. But something was still missing, and then I said, "What can I do with these tires?" So the guy said, "Put the gangster whitewalls on there." So that did it. That made it the Clydemobile. Once he did that I went, "Yeah! That's the car I like."

I had a lot of fun with that car. I used to go down to Atlanta with it, and the looks and stares you got in the seventies . . . I remember going into a gas station, and it was like in a movie. I used to carry a jump rope in the car, because your legs get tired from driving so long. So I pulled into the gas station and told the guy to fill it up. And I got out to jump rope and he got in, and the guy was like, "What the hell is this?" He was climbing all inside the car, and I'm going, "Hey man, just fill it up!" It was unreal how people would stare and point at that car.

I had it up until last year [2001]. I sold it to a huge Knicks fan here. I kept it in Atlanta for a while, then I had it at a friend's house in New Jersey. But that's why I decided to sell it, because you can't let a car, any car, sit and deteriorate. So this guy who's a big Knicks fan bought it. That was a tough decision, man. Thirty years. That car was like my wife. And I wasn't there when he took it. I just couldn't see it go. I just told him where it was and that was it.

The Clydemobile was distinguished–temporarily–by a set of one of the first vanity license plates in New York history: "WCF," for Walt "Clyde" Frazier.

Walt Frazier: And they got stolen in Atlanta, of all places! I took it to Underground Atlanta and somebody stole the plates right off the car. Never had that trouble in New York.

Red Holzman at work.

THE LINEUP: Willis Reed; Fuzzy Levane; Phil Jackson; Leonard Lewin; Dick Van Arsdale; Bill Bradley; Leonard Koppett; Marv Albert; Jerry Lucas; Mike Glenn; Cal Ramsey; Bob Wolff; Mike Saunders; Phil Pepe; Spencer Ross; Freddie Klein; John Andariese; Bob McAdoo; Dave Checketts; Ernie Grunfeld; George Kalinsky.

In 1967 a watershed event occurred for the Knicks: the hiring of Red Holzman as head coach. He was a brilliant tactician and innovator, and he knew how to motivate people–especially his players.

Willis Reed: Red Holzman was the first man I ever met in the Knicks organization. I met him my senior year at Grambling. I saw him in his gray, striped suit, with a London Fog tan raincoat and a cigar, leaning against the wall watching us play.

Fuzzy Levane: I brought Red into two places. First, I brought him to Milwaukee after he'd been released by Rochester. I got Red to be my 10th man there. Then Ben Kerner fired me for my own good. When I got the job with the Knicks, Red called me and asked me for a job. But Ned [Irish] wanted to bring back Sonny Hertzberg [as a scout]. I said no, I wanted Red. So I had Vinnie [Boryla] speak to Ned, and Vinnie told him, "Let Fuzzy have who he wants." That's how Red got to the Knicks.

Phil Jackson: I participated in something called Boys Nation, which was an American Legion–sponsored political week for juniors in high school. I was a counselor and a chaplain. It just so happened that Mayor Lindsay was there that day from New York City. Red Holzman flew out, and we signed the contract right there in Fargo, North Dakota. And that's how my relationship with Red began.

Leonard Lewin: He didn't want to coach. Every time they approached him, he turned them down. He said he was happy in the job as a scout. What made him change was Ned. Ned and Eddie [Donovan], I guess.

Willis Reed: The one thing that Red had that no one else had, was that he had the luxury of being involved in drafting and being involved in acquiring all the players on the team in trades. So he knew a lot more about them–their temperament, their basketball ability–than anyone else. That gave him a tremendous advantage when he became the coach, and he used it very well.

Dick Van Arsdale: Red was an outstanding defensive coach. When I was a rookie, Red was responsible for helping teach guys how to get over a pick. He was adamant about not switching, and staying with your man. With Red, you busted through picks. You didn't go around a pick, you just led with your leg and popped over the pick.

Phil Jackson: The first practice we had [under Red], I missed. I was sick. And I heard that we were gonna play full-court basketball. And it wasn't just full-court basketball, it was *pressure* full-court basketball. So for the second practice, I come in and we're playing full-court, and we press from the moment we roll the ball out until the end of the practice. It was a great conditioner for a team that might have been a little out of condition. Secondly, it let him know who wanted to play hard and who didn't. And it gave an opportunity for us to have more than five, seven, or eight guys on the floor. It gave him the opportunity to play 10 or 11 guys.

Leonard Lewin: Red applied the intelligence he learned from Nat Holman at City College. Give-and-go and a lot of tricky stuff, like the weave.

Bill Bradley: There was a period after Red took over where we practiced 19 out of 20 days, something like that. I also remember Sunday workouts at St. John's. He was basically trying to get across to us that we win with defense and helping out; face the ball, hit the open man–the basic fundamentals. He got us to function more as a team. I think we did that, but a month or two is not really long enough to make that happen. I think it really started the following [1968] training camp.

Willis Reed: Red gave us a lot of freedom on offense. He didn't give us any freedom on defense. He was very demanding about how we played defense, very specific about how we would play defense and what responsibilities everybody had. But on offense, that's the one carrot he would give us. He'd say, "Run anything you want to, as long as it works."

Leonard Koppett: Red understood, completely, the aspects of basketball. After all, he'd played for Holman at City College. He understood what the basics of basketball were: defense creates offense, and that movement–endless movement–is the nature of the game. Hit the open man; but to hit the open man, somebody's gotta be open. And the only way anyone was gonna be open was if everybody's moving, not if just one or two guys are moving. He was able to instill that in all of them, in practice and in games.

Phil Jackson: We had two systems: a high-post system, and a 2-3, center-in system. And that was basically it. We had some specials that we ran off it, probably like six or eight pages that I wrote up. Not

like we have in this day and age. We were a pretty basic team. In the process, he would talk about basketball to me. Little things about people and personnel. Red had a way about him that was endearing to me.

Dick Van Arsdale: In training camp, Red liked to run up and down the court and play. He had a thing where he kept a ball in his hand by the side of the court. And if you ran down the court with your head turned away from the ball, if you didn't see the ball in transition, he'd throw the ball off the back of your head. Today, guys don't see the ball in transition; they have no idea where the ball is. Drives me crazy. But Red was a stickler about that.

Marv Albert: It's interesting now to hear the comments of the guys he coached, who I think have even more respect for him now than they did when they played for him. Guys like Clyde, Phil, and Willis think back and they realize what a great coach he was. He was the best possible coach for that team. His personality was such that he was laid back, but inside he was burning. He was a very fiery guy, but he kept it inside.

Jerry Lucas: The thing about Red was that he understood individuals. Obviously, he was a great basketball mind. That's a given. But his real strength was that he understood individual players. He understood their psyches. He understood the buttons that needed to be pushed on each individual player. A lot of coaches that I had seen and a couple that I had played for did not have that particular ability. They seemed to handle every player the same way, across the board. That was how they coached. But Red was particularly adept at knowing how to handle individuals on an individual basis. It made a tremendous difference.

Bill Bradley: Red was always very direct with people about what he wanted, what he expected, where the boundaries were. And you were expected to abide by those boundaries.

Phil Jackson: He was very demonstrative; he was graphic in a lot of his details. He once stood up and took copies of all the plays that we had, and he made the motion of wiping his butt [with them] and said, "This is about how much good these things are," and then he threw them all on the floor. He said it was all about defense, and we were gonna learn how to play defense together. Because once you learn how to play defense, you can play offense.

Mike Glenn: He let guys have input even on defense. He always had the last say, of course. But Red was a stickler on one thing, which has stayed with anyone who ever played for him: "See the ball." Defensively, at all times, you had to see the basketball. I don't think I've ever had a camp where I didn't encourage my kids to see the ball. And now I hear Phil Jackson say it, I hear Jim Cleamons say it. Anybody who's ever played for Red knows that.

Willis Reed: Red's philosophy was that anyone could dribble the ball off the rebound, take the ball and go with it. The only guys he'd tell not to dribble were me and Phil. Phil used to kick it out of bounds and everything. Phil would think, "Hell, I'm no center. I can handle the ball like DeBusschere and these guys . . . "

Cal Ramsey: He had great self-confidence. He knew what he was doing. If you notice, he never had a pad for diagramming plays. I can recall sitting by the bench, and at timeouts Red would talk primarily about defense and matchups and then say at the end, "Now, what do you guys want to run?" He let them call it and they did–Bradley would say "BF21" or whatever–because they were so well-prepared.

Dick Van Arsdale: He was a tough sucker. But you have to know who the boss is, and he was the boss.

Phil Jackson: Cazzie was kind of a spoiled cat. He had the most money; he had the big contract and was in the second year of it. Bradley had gotten more money, but he was still coming in as a rookie who was maybe two months behind at this point. We had a game in Philadelphia–they were the champs–and Cazzie shows up in his car. Red comes over to him and says, "Caz, how much did it cost you for tolls to come down here?" Cazzie thought about it and got all the numbers together, and it's about five dollars. So Red says, "Take the

five dollars off the hundred I'm gonna fine you. We take the bus together everywhere we go. We don't take separate cars." So the same thing happened a week later in Boston. We had this raggedy hotel, the Madison Hotel, right next to the Boston Garden. Cazzie dressed over there and came over to the arena and came late. And Red hit him up again. He said, "We come over here together, we dress together, we shower together. This is about being together."

Holzman knew what buttons he had to push to power his team. But he rarely shared that knowledge with anyone outside the organization, especially the media. Indeed, Holzman always kept the local media guessing.

Leonard Lewin: Red would never tell you anything. He would never say anything. You could say anything you'd want to him, but he wouldn't tell you anything about the game at all. That's the way he was. I guess [his wife] Selma did all the talking.

Cal Ramsey: After the game I'd sit in there with Red when the media came in. And I swear, almost every game, when they won, Red said, "Boy, the players were great. They did a great job, blah, blah, blah." When they lost he said, "Man, I didn't do a great job." He took the hit, and I thought he was terrific for that.

Leonard Koppett: Red was a person who didn't like the spotlight. He knew what coaching in New York meant, as far as being in the spotlight. After all, he had coached before. But in the end, his basketball instincts and desires overcame his reluctance to carry the public burden. And there was no better basketball mind, ever, than Red Holzman. He not only knew it, but he could convey it to his players.

Bob Wolff: After one of the games, I went into Red's little cubicle, where he was speaking to the press, maybe three or four guys. And these guys had their notebooks out and were taking voluminous notes on what Red was saying. I was spellbound, because Red wasn't saying anything. Which, of course, he did extremely well. So when it was over, I

As animated as he could be during games, Red Holzman kept things fairly close to the vest off the court.

said, "Red, can you tell me what you just said that was newsworthy?" I'd kid around with Red, because he was just a master at that. He'd say, "Well, our guys did this, and they did that, and it was a fine effort from so-and-so . . . ," win or lose. It never changed. Then he'd go into what he was going to eat tonight, that he saw a good movie last night. He was unflappable.

Mike Saunders: Red always had the same lines to the media: "The other team was a good team." "The other team was well coached." He never said anything, but it was all purposeful.

Phil Pepe: He was terrific to be around, but you couldn't get anything from him as far as something that would help your story. He wasn't a guy

you'd run to, like Casey Stengel was. He wasn't someone that you had to talk to before you wrote your story, because he never said anything. He was very protective.

Cal Ramsey: In 1970, Jim Wergeles and Red asked me to take a job as Red's stat man, because I used to go to every game. I'd been out of the game, but I wanted to be around the game, and a lot of my friends were still playing, like Satch, Oscar, and Wilt. So I came to almost every game at the Garden. Of course, Red knew me from my days at NYU. So I took a job as Red's stat man for two years.

Spencer Ross: I was just starting out at WINS. I was going down to Baltimore to do a Knicks game. The night before, I did a telephone interview with Red that was very funny. Just a lot of kibitzing that went back and forth. At that time there was an FCC rule that you had to tell someone when they were being recorded before you used the stuff on the air. And I thought that I had told Red, so I really wasn't concerned. He was just doing some really funny things in this interview; it wasn't Red's personal face that you normally saw. He just had a lot of fun doing it. So when I got to Baltimore for the game, I talked to Red and told him, "That stuff went over really funny." He said, "What are you talking about?" I said, "That stuff we talked about." He said, "You put that stuff on the air?" And he went nuts with me, he really did. I was so apologetic to him, I really couldn't stop apologizing. Because I knew he was right, and I felt I'd betrayed a confidence, even though it was an honest mistake. Then, when the game was over, I sort of wanted to stay away from Red. But he sought me out. He wanted to make me feel comfortable. And not only did he tell me to relax, that everything was OK, but now *he* couldn't stop apologizing. There was a tremendous warmth that he exuded.

Freddie Klein: Red Holzman used to call my office and say, "Let me speak to the putz."

John Andariese: I was a million miles from Red [in 1972]. I'm not sure Red knew I existed. Red was not the Red I got to know years later. He was very private, very quiet. I don't think I ever spoke to him [the first year]. He didn't allow you in. I respected him as the genius coach of a championship team. Why would he want to talk to me? Who was I?

Phil Jackson: We had Nate Bowman, who everybody loved. Nate loved to look in the stands and eye girls. He was a ladies' man. I never saw him look at anything he didn't make a play for. He caught my eye in a timeout and said, "Check out 10 rows back behind our bench." And Red caught me looking back there. He came over, jumped in my face, and said, "How much time's left on the clock?" And I happened to know. I said, "Two minutes and 20 seconds." He said, "I don't mean that. I mean the 24-second clock." Well, he had me either

way, because as a college player, you weren't thinking about the 24-second clock. So I didn't know, and he said, "I saw you looking into the stands. I don't want you to be missing out on anything." So we knew he was about discipline and some kind of order.

Spencer Ross: He could be tough. He once said to me, about talking to the media, "The thing that bothers me the most is that you guys ask the same questions all the time." And I said, "Red, realistically, it's the same game every time." And he laughed. He understood.

Leonard Koppett: That's what an intelligent coach does. In his own quiet way, that's what John Kundla did when he had a great team in Minneapolis. You never saw many quotes from Kundla on anything. Why would you? The main thing was what Red could get across to his players on how to play.

Phil Pepe: We'd go out to dinner, and it was almost a command performance. Red would take the writers and Danny Whelan, Frankie [Blauschild], and Jimmy [Wergeles], and we'd go out to dinner on the road. And Red would be insulted if, for some reason, you didn't go. He'd always say, "Remember, when there's food on the table, anything that's said is off the record." But it wouldn't have mattered, because he never said anything anyway. He'd spend two hours talking, and nothing was worth writing. That's the way he was. But he was a very interesting guy and a fun guy to be around.

Leonard Lewin: Racetracks, restaurants, and old movies on TV. And then back to the room to drink. We left in our trail a fleet of hired cars loaded with empty glasses under the seats.

Leonard Koppett: That was the way we lived. It wasn't peculiar to Holzman. You're traveling around the country and it's all one-night stands. So what are you gonna do but watch television and maybe go to the racetrack?

Cal Ramsey: After every home game when we had a road trip [next], there would be a bus to take us to the airport. And I would get Red a scotch and soda and bring it to him on the bus. That was my job.

Phil Pepe: He'd get on a plane, and he'd always have his scotch and his *New York Times* crossword puzzle. And he liked to do movie trivia.

Leonard Lewin: We used to have contests, watching the old movies. Red would say, "Who's that?" and you had to name the guy he was pointing to. He could name them all. Nobody else could.

Cal Ramsey: One night in Kansas City we were looking for a good Italian restaurant, and we wound up at a place that served plain white bread, so you knew it was gonna be a bad evening for Italian food. And it was. It wasn't a good place at all. I don't know who Red blamed, Frankie or Danny or whoever. But man, he was pissed.

Holzman always got his point across to his team, usually in a simple, understated manner that resonated with the group.

Bob McAdoo: Red was very low-key. He wasn't the guy I thought he was. I thought he was a rough, tough type of coach, and he wasn't that at all. Being in Buffalo and watching him from the sidelines, he looked like a tough taskmaster, which he probably was in the earlier years. But he wasn't that with us, and that was OK. I was used to coaches who were taskmasters, like Jack Ramsay and Dean Smith before that. Practices were low-key with Red. There wasn't a lot of preparation, which was also different for me because Dr. Jack prepped you a lot before games. Red was a Hall of Fame coach and a championship coach, and he knew his stuff. But he was very low-key about it.

Phil Jackson: Ever since I'm injured, Red has me go out and scout. If we're on the road and if the home team has a game the night before we're supposed to play them, Red says to go over and catch that game, and put some stuff on the board tomorrow. Red never Xd and Od. He never drew or diagrammed any plays. I don't know if he used salt shakers or something on the table; I just never saw him do it. He told me point-blank, "I've never drawn plays. I just don't do that." But he asked me to draft up a team book. So whenever we'd get a new player,

they'd come see me and I'd have this mimeographed book of plays.

Mike Saunders: Red was anything but simple. That kind of belies who he was and how he coached. He knew everything that was going on; his practices were well constructed. It wasn't like he just rolled out the balls. Not at all. When he first walked into practice, he'd make sure the game clock and the shot clock were on. Then he went through a lot of scenarios, different plays they'd run at the end of the game. It's wrong to think that he was very simple as a coach. He wasn't.

Spencer Ross: Red Holzman would never allow a team of his to have the ball with 41 seconds to go in a quarter and not make them fully understand that the best thing to do would be to get a pretty good shot off one pass, so you'd get a two-for-one. Nobody thinks two-for-one anymore.

Bob McAdoo: The only thing Red wrote on the board were the matchups. And sometimes he wouldn't even do that. He'd look at you and say, "Bob, you've got so-and-so." Or, "Clyde, you've got so-and-so." And, "We'll do this and that," and then we were out of there.

Phil Jackson: We had a routine when we went on a plane. Red would sit in the back of first class, and sometime before the plane would come in, he'd come down the aisle and say, "Well, what do you guys think? Should we practice today?" And then he'd make the decision, yes or no. Finally, I got curious and I asked him, "What makes up your mind?" He says, "DeBusschere. If DeBusschere says we should practice today, then I know he's feeling really spunky and we should practice. But if he says no, then I know he *has* to practice because he's feeling kinda luggy." So I learned about Red's managerial skills and how to handle people. He had a barometer that he used all the time that was very unique.

Mike Glenn: Red wanted you to be a student of the game. More than any coach I ever played for, he wanted guys to talk about the game. Red allowed his players to mature and utilize their intelligence and knowledge more than most coaches. He had no inferiority complex whatsoever. He'd say, "How you guys gonna handle that pick-and-roll?" Or, "I don't wanna call a play. Any play you call will work. You just have to execute." I appreciated Red so much for that. Afterward, it was so hard for me with coaches who would try to be domineering.

Bob McAdoo: Plus, Red had players. That helps. He had Willis and Clyde and Earl and DeBusschere and so on. He had *players*. So if you're the coach, you can just let those guys play.

Red could be beguiling, compassionate, sagacious, and downright heroic.

Leonard Lewin: We used to go to every racetrack. All the newspapermen and Danny Whelan would go. And he always played the same numbers: 2-4-4-2. Those were his favorite numbers.

Phil Pepe: He'd come up with these crazy statements, these Redisms, like, "Never trust your hair to a bald-headed barber; he has no respect for it." I once did a column where I listed about a dozen of them. There was, "Never take medical advice from a waiter," and "Never accidentally raise your hand when the check is coming." He'd also say, "My father used to say, 'If we live, we'll do it tomorrow. If not, we'll do it the next day.'"

Spencer Ross: He was a people guy. He understood that, as good as anybody was–and he was as good as anybody–he understood that everybody was replaceable. He had a humanist way about him.

Marv Albert: I think Red mellowed over the years. He was a different Red than we saw as a coach. He was very set in his ways. We used to have a kidding-around relationship when I was doing the sports at 6:00 and 11:00 on Channel 4. He always used to say, "No, don't talk to me. I'm a bad interview. Talk to the players." And it got to the point where I encouraged him to come on, and he'd get better and better. I'd always rate his interview afterward, and he'd always wait for that. He was almost grandfatherly; it was that type of relationship.

Phil Pepe: He had a thing where he'd sing, and I'd sing this to my kids, and to this day they still remember it. He'd sing a song that he wrote, and it

went: "George Washington Bridge, George is washing the Washington Bridge. The Washington Bridge is being washed by George Washington, who's washing the Washington Bridge." I don't know what it means; it's the dumbest thing I ever heard! But when I think of Red, I think of that. And there was another one: "It looks like rain in Cherry Blossom Lane. In Cherry Blossom Lane, it looks like rain." What the hell is that?

Phil Jackson: As we got going and I received more responsibility as a player, there were things he'd tell me that became significant to me. Little things like, "If you want to coach, this is what you do . . . " He told me that one of the best places to coach is Puerto Rico. It's a game and a place where the energy is so intense, the language skills are different. It's just basketball in its rawest form, and you learn to coach off the seat of your pants. And I ended up coaching in Puerto Rico for four and a half years because when the opportunity came, [I knew] he'd tell me to go there if you get the chance to do it.

Mel Davis: For me it was an ironic situation because Red was the general manager and the coach. We had some difficult times with negotiations in the office, and then coming down to the court, I think that might have been held against me, because I wanted what I wanted; otherwise, I wasn't going to play for the Knicks. But in retrospect, I think he respected me. And I respected him and liked him. I know he wasn't a "rookie" sort of a coach, he was a "veteran" sort of a coach. And that's OK. We had some good times and some long discussions.

Mike Glenn: Red used to tell Sugar Ray [Richardson], me, and all the young guys that the Knicks uniform means something. And when you're wearing that uniform, you will represent the New York Knicks appropriately, on the road and anywhere you are. It was a matter of professionalism.

Spencer Ross: They say there are very few people who ever had an original thought, no matter how much they've accomplished. Red invented certain things. Red invented putting in a guy like Mike

Riordan to give the foul. Red basically invented the offensive-defensive changes. Nobody's ever done it quite as well as he did down the stretch. Guys today still emulate him.

Leonard Koppett: Red's virtue as a coach was proper analyzing of the contributions each particular individual could make, and how to integrate that into a team.

Jerry Lucas: Think about the backgrounds of all the players, where we all grew up, where we were from, the kinds of lives we led, where we had been. We were all different people. Red had the knowledge and the ability to handle that situation. That's what set him apart from other coaches, and I think that's something that Phil Jackson learned at that time in his life and was able to mold into his career. And that's what made him one of the greatest coaches of all time.

Phil Jackson: I was his whipping boy. If he needed somebody to rally the troops around, he could start yelling at me about a variety of things—whether I gambled on defense or I made a mistake on offense or took a shot that maybe I shouldn't have, or whatever. And I was the combative one. I would come back and say, "That's bullshit!" or something like that. And then we'd get into an argument. Then DeBusschere and Bradley would get me aside and say, "Don't argue with him. Don't say anything back because he just needs someone to vent toward." And I didn't like to be the one who was vented at. But with my pecking order on the club, it was natural to do that. And as you find out when you're the coach, it's nice to have a player you can use to be a motivator on the team.

Mel Davis: He was very instrumental in me going back to school and getting my master's at Fordham University. He was my personal reference. So in one instance, he ended my career with the Knicks, but on the other hand he helped me further my education, and now here I am running the NBA Retired Players Association.

Bob McAdoo: One of the things I picked up from Red was to not overcoach. Red didn't overcoach, but he probably didn't have to. The league was different then. When you look back, all the guys

were mature coming in. When Spencer [Haywood] and I left college early, we were the exceptions to the rule. But it's a regular deal now; a lot of the league is like that. We knew how to play the game coming in. Guys coming in now can run and jump out of the gym, but they don't have a clue about cutting backdoor, about how to get in a defensive stance. They don't have a clue. So there's a lot of overcoaching now, which I'm basically not a fan of. But Red and Willis, and other coaches I had, like Dr. Jack and Pat [Riley], weren't like that.

Dave Checketts: Red was the finest human being I've ever known. I can say that without hesitation. Right after I was named president [of the Garden], I called him and he said, "Well, you know I'm here if you need me." I said, "No, no, no. I want you to be *here*. Because I *do* need you." So we went to lunch together, and that was the start of a great, great friendship. He was a man of tremendous patience. Very tolerant, very even-handed, and a great advisor to me at the most difficult times, with every difficult problem.

Ernie Grunfeld: That was one of the greatest experiences I ever had: meeting Red Holzman and having a working and personal relationship with him. His great humor, his wit. He had a sagely way about him, but he was never overbearing. Not only did he have a great amount of knowledge, but he knew how to share it with you without being overbearing. I loved the man.

Dave Checketts: My favorite memories are him at training camp, and at the playoffs, and the dinners. He was a very, very special man. He made a big difference.

Ernie Grunfeld: He had a very calming effect on our organization in a very subtle way, because he'd been through everything before. He'd been under the microscope. He knew how to help us through the tough times. Having Red with us showed others that we were all about success and about winning, and we had our greatest winner still with us.

Dave Checketts: At one point, I was really frustrated with Greg Anthony after we drafted him. Greg was talented but not overwhelmingly so. He was quick, physical, and a good defender. But he had been acting up like a wise guy, and over dinner one night I said to Ernie, "We ought to trade that little so-and-so." And Red looked up at me and said, "You know what? He *is* a little a-hole. But, Dave, he's *our* a-hole." I told that story at Red's funeral, but I used the word *putz* because Red loved that word.

George Kalinsky: When June and I got married [in October 1998], we invited Red to the wedding. He said he really wanted to come, but it looked like he might not be able to because of the leukemia. I said to him, "Red, whatever it takes, please come. I'll make sure you're taken care of. I'll have a car for you and everything." Then I spoke to him the night before, and he said he wanted to come. So I sent a car and he came, and Red was one of the last people to leave the wedding. He really enjoyed himself; Willis and DeBusschere and some of the others were there. And when we came back from our honeymoon, Red's funeral was just a few days later. Our wedding was the last time he left the house before he went into the hospital for good. For our wedding gift, he sent us a check with a note. The note said, "Dear June and George–This is the best I can do. I don't know about these things. If Selma were alive, she would have known what to do."

Bradley finishes off a fast break against Baltimore at a packed Garden in 1969.

THE LINEUP: George Kalinsky; Willis Reed; Freddie Klein; Leonard Lewin; Bob Wolff; Walt Frazier; Richie Guerin; Dick Schaap; Phil Berger; Mike Shatzkin; Stan Asofsky; Phil Jackson; Marv Albert; Steve Albert; Red Holzman; Cal Ramsey; Dave Checketts; Bill Bradley; Bob McAdoo; Jerry Lucas; Leonard Koppett; Mel Davis; John Andariese; Mike Saunders; Earl Monroe; Dean Meminger; Mike Glenn; Hubie Brown; Dancing Harry; Don Chaney.

From 1969 to 1973 the Knicks were the toast of New York, winning championships and the hearts of New Yorkers. There was something about this team that made everyone care just a little more. Entering the 1969–70 season, the Knicks had the feeling that this could be the year.

George Kalinsky: When my son Lee was in the third grade, he had show-and-tell at his school. This was during one of the two championship years. And when the teacher gave Lee his turn, he said that he would tell about the dinner he had last night, sitting at the table with the starting five of the Knicks. So we get a call from the teacher saying, "You better come to school. There's a problem with your son. He's hyper and he's hallucinating." What's the problem? "Well," the teacher said, "he's telling the class—and he's not embarrassed to make it up–that he had dinner last night with these five guys." Who, of course, were the talk of New York at the time. So we said, "Well, that's true." Then the teacher accused *me* of making it up.

Willis Reed: We knew, going back to Boston in April the year before, when we got beat when Clyde had the groin pull, and with Russell saying he was going to retire, that we had a chance to win this year. Because we were good enough; we believed we were good enough.

Freddie Klein: Everybody on that team identified with someone. Bradley was the Ivy Leaguer. Barnett was cool. DeBusschere was the beer-drinking hard

worker. Willis was the strong, silent leader, the captain. Clyde was flashy. They had something for everyone.

Leonard Lewin: Frazier was a live wire. Willis was the guy who carried the team. They got Dick Barnett from Los Angeles, and he was a weirdo. He was always involved in something crazy. The first time I ever saw him, he came in dressed with a homburg, a walking cane, and a pair of spats. Bradley was Bradley. He never had any money in his pocket. Everyone had to lend him money, even after signing the big contract. He lived at the Capital Hotel, a block up from the old building. Then DeBusschere came and introduced everyone to drinking beer. But they were drinking beer before.

Bob Wolff: These guys were so smart. There's never been an aggregation in any league, any sport, where you could find such outstanding wisdom.

Except for the return of Dave Stallworth, who had been sidelined for two years with a heart ailment; the addition of St. John's rookie John Warren; and the loss of Phil Jackson for the season due to his back injury, the Knicks team that took the floor for 1969–70 was the same squad whose prior season had ended in the gloom of the Boston Garden locker room.

This year would end far differently.

The Knicks served immediate notice as to the kind of year it would be. They won their first 5 games, lost to San Francisco at home, then ripped off what was then an NBA record 18 straight wins to start the season at a staggering 23–1.

Three games during the year's first half would symbolize their regular season.

The first came on Thanksgiving Eve, in Atlanta, when they victimized Richie Guerin's Hawks to the tune of 22 turnovers (before that was an official statistic) en route to a 30-point win, their 17ᵗʰ straight triumph.

Walt Frazier: I remember I stole the ball so many times I told the guys [Hawks] to hold on to the ball, I'm tired. All that going back and forth. And whenever I'd go down to Atlanta, my mother would always tell me, "Go see Grandmother, go see these people, go see these other people . . ." I'd eat at every stop along the way, so then I'm exhausted. Finally my mother would say, "Don't let the Hawks beat you." And then I'm running around all night on a full stomach.

Richie Guerin: Maybe I brainwashed myself about that game and put it out of my mind right after that. I really don't remember that.

I had great admiration for that Knicks team. Red Holzman was a very good friend of mine, and they played the game the way it was meant to be played. With the type of talent they had, they played the way it should be played.

Two nights later, going for their 18ᵗʰ straight victory, in Cleveland against the Cincinnati Royals, they were all but finished. Oscar Robertson scored 33 points before fouling out with just under two minutes left, then player-coach Bob Cousy inserted himself into the Royals' lineup. With 16 seconds left and Cincinnati leading 105–100, Reed was fouled by Tom Van Arsdale . . .

Willis Reed: Oscar fouls out and Cousy comes in. We're down five with 16 seconds to go. I got fouled and made two free throws. Cousy inbounds the ball and DeBusschere steals, goes in, and actually dunks the ball with both hands. Then the next play comes in;

they get the ball to Tom Van Arsdale, and Clyde steals the ball. He drives in and gets into the lane, shoots, rebounds, shoots again, and that's when he got fouled.

Walt Frazier: They called timeout to try to ice me, and when I went to the bench, no one is talking to me! It was like I had already made the shots. Red is talking about what we're going to do after I make the shots, and I'm saying, "Hey, I haven't made them yet!" So then I went to the line and I'm saying to myself, "Well, if I don't make the shots, I can't go in *our* locker room, that's for sure." Once I made the first one, the second one was easy. That was unbelievable. I remember Red said, "Let's get out of here before they recount it." So we all ran off the court, and that was probably the most jubilation we ever showed as a team. I think we were happier then than when we won the championship.

Bob Wolff: After the game, we stayed in a hotel right across from the Cleveland Arena. I was standing there with Cousy, ready to get on the elevator. All of a sudden the elevator door opened and I decided I didn't want to get into the elevator and make small talk with Bob Cousy. Not after that game. After the 18ᵗʰ straight win, they had a really off night and got drubbed by Detroit.

And on Christmas night at the Garden, Komives fed Bellamy for a layup with one second left to give Detroit a 111–110 lead. Burned by their former teammates, the Knicks came out of a timeout needing a yuletide miracle.

Willis Reed: Barnett set a backscreen on Bellamy, Frazier threw me the ball, and I caught it in the air and just laid it up. There were certain plays that we ran in certain situations, and in this one we had to get the ball to the basket for a one-second shot. And I don't think we ever ran it again. Or if we did, it never worked again.

With a New York team dominating the NBA, it didn't take long for Madison Avenue to hitch itself to the bandwagon. First came the Vitalis commercial, with reserve Donnie May getting caught using the greasy kid stuff.

Then came the books. DeBusschere coauthored an insider's diary with Dick Schaap, appropriately titled

Dave DeBusschere beats Portland's Sidney Wicks to the rebound.

The Open Man. *Team photographer Kalinsky and the injured Jackson teamed up for a unique (for that time) coffee-table-style photo essay called* Take It All! *A fan— first-time season ticketholder Mike Shatzkin—came up with* The View From Section 111.

But the most penetrating and enduring of the Knicks books would be Miracle on 33rd Street, *the work of an irreverent freelancer named Phil Berger, who portrayed the Knicks as human beings with all-too-human frailties and insecurities. Berger's work, willingly or not, also made stars out of longtime superfans Asofsky and Klein.*

Walt Frazier: They brought us the Vitalis deal, and Red decided that everybody would share

in the money. But I think only the starting five ran out, and Donnie May. So we protested, but in vain.

Dick Schaap: *The Open Man* came about because of the success of *Instant Replay*. Dave DeBusschere, I felt, was the basketball version of [football's] Jerry Kramer. A very, very good player; but at the same time, he was not a superstar. He wasn't a Chamberlain or a Jerry West or an Oscar Robertson. He was a Gus Johnson type. Better than good. Real, real solid. The kind of guy who had a work ethic that made him really respected.

Phil Berger: I happened to be thinking that nobody had done a book like that on a basketball team, traveling around with them. It was semivirginal territory, so to speak. Also, I had a passion for the game, having played in college.

Mike Shatzkin: It helps to have a father in the publishing business, which I had. Now, my father didn't publish the book, but I knew how you do it. I knew about writing a proposal and submitting it to an editor. It wasn't the first time I had ever done that. So I did it, and I got a $2,000 advance from Prentice-Hall, which more than covered the cost of the season tickets. That's how it happened.

Dick Schaap: I didn't want to do a flashy guy with great skills, a Frazier or a Reed. Dave's skills were not that evident. He was the perfect guy to do a book with on that team. He could afford to be candid. I have a rule with any book I write that a subject must be willing to judge himself as harshly as he judges others.

Mike Shatzkin: I got the season tickets partly because I thought they were going to win that year. I sold the book based on what was not, I think, my perception alone that they might win. I can't remember exactly when the contract came through, and it might even have been that they were into that initial winning sprint. It might have been obvious to more people than me that they had a good chance of having a good year. In retrospect, I'm not sure it was the best thing for me, because my book got lost and I don't think all these [other] books were planned, necessarily, in September. I guess Phil Berger's must have been, because he couldn't have jumped into it in November.

Phil Berger: They were a team of sharply contoured personalities, as if a novelist had put them together. Their personalities were unique and larger than life. It ended up that I kind of hit the jackpot in that I had great personalities and people to work with, and a championship year on top of it.

Freddie Klein: Phil [Berger] approached us. He told us he was writing the book. He knew we were big fans and he came down and sat with us.

Stan Asofsky: Phil had these little cards [he wrote on], and he realized there was a lot of [funny] material, so he kept on using us. So I was the comic relief, and Freddie was the straight man.

Phil Pepe: Berger was a strange duck. He was never around. He went his own way, he wasn't part of the group of the beat writers.

Stan Asofsky: Phil had this old place in the Village, and when we got out at night, there were male and female hookers in the police trucks and everything. It was crazy.

Mike Shatzkin: I have to say that, in fairness to [Jim] Wergeles and [Frank] Blauschild, I don't think I projected a particularly professional demeanor. This is 1969, and I was just out of UCLA. I had a huge mop of curly hair, and kind of a hippie-like appearance. The beauty of the book, for me, was that it required very little in the way of planning or organization. I just showed up at the games, took some notes, and when I went home afterward I just sat down at the keyboard and wrote. In fairness to them, if they were being professional about their jobs and trying to figure out who needed the access, from the standpoint of their bosses who were running the New York Knicks, I don't think they hurt the Knicks a lot by not giving me more cooperation. What was interesting were people like Holzman and Willis, who were so kind and seemed to know that, here's this kid who really doesn't know what he's doing, but that doesn't mean we won't be nice to him. That sort of compensated.

George Kalinsky: There's no question, I rode the wave big-time. In the championship year, when about 12 or 13 books came out, all of the publishing houses were calling me for photographs. Then I'm sitting with Phil Jackson one night and I say, "Hey, how about if we do a book?" And we're already in the first playoff round. I figured if I was contributing to everybody else's book, why don't I do my own book? So I spoke to Phil about it, and we started looking for a publisher, but I didn't think there were any publishers left. Then I ran into Leonard Koppett, who told me that he was the basketball consultant to Macmillan. I told him of my idea to do a book that would be mainly a photo book, with Phil writing the text. He said, "Great." There had never been a photo essay book like this before, and when *Take It All!* came out, the *Wall Street Journal* said, "That's a new art form."

Phil Jackson: I needed something. I was going crazy, going to games, sometimes sitting in my seat, sometimes sitting on the bench. I needed something to keep me involved and active, so I got into photography. Of course, George was there, and we started this relationship. And I suggested to him, "Why don't we do a book?" So we started exchanging ideas, and we went up to Macmillan and they picked it up. Leonard Koppett edited my writing. I think I have about six of my pictures in there and George has nine hundred. It's still a book that I thought was really kind of good about that whole time.

George Kalinsky: Phil was the one guy you never saw in a suit; he was always in sandals and shorts or dungarees. Koppett made a connection for us with the publisher at Macmillan. So I called the guy up in the middle of the L.A. series–that's how deep we were into it–and I told him that they were the only publisher in creation that wasn't doing a Knicks book. He told me to meet him on such-and-such a date. Now I'm worried about what Phil is going to wear. That day, Phil meets me downstairs dressed in shorts, sandals, a T-shirt hanging out, and I'm thinking there's no way we can walk up to this guy's office with him dressed like this. I'm in a suit, and I said, "Phil, I don't think that a hippie from North Dakota is gonna be able to get a book deal dressed like this." Phil said not to worry about it. We go up, walk in, and sit down. We introduce ourselves and start talking, and within the first 30 seconds, it turns out that this senior editor is from North Dakota and he's a big Phil Jackson fan. So I'm sitting there saying to myself, "It's a deal!"

Phil came over to my house, and in my den I had all the pictures laid out on the floor. Phil just lies down on the floor with a legal pad and says, "Let's do it." This is on a Saturday afternoon. By Sunday night, we had the book finished.

Mike Shatzkin: Meeting Willis for a hamburger in the place around the corner from the Garden . . . I mean, we sat at the counter an hour and a half before a game and talked! What was interesting was that Willis talked about how he never wanted to be a coach, he just wanted to be a player. He expressed no interest in management or coaching or anything like that.

Phil Pepe: That team just captured the imagination of the city. Remember, too, that was the year the Mets won and the Jets won, and I guess the city was really in a euphoric state. Now it looked like the Knicks were going to do the same thing. I think the Mets and Jets really helped the Knicks get so much attention, because now the whole city was into sports. There was a lot said about how it was New York's year. Plus, that team was so special. When they won 18 in a row, including the comeback, to win that last game against Cincinnati, everything was breaking right.

Bob Wolff: I've never seen it where the acclaim for a team was greater than it was for that 1970 team. It seemed like all the players wrote books. The reporters, the noise in the Garden. It was like the finals of the NCAA every single night. Columns, books, appearances–all that. And because it was New York, people thought that this was the way it was for all of basketball. So everyone bought in: the networks bought in, the big sponsor money came in. And that really solidified the league.

After winning a club record 60 games, the Knicks faced the Bullets of Wes Unseld and Earl Monroe in the first playoff round. The team that the Knicks had swept away the year before took them to seven games this time, before New York won the deciding game at the Garden. Monroe averaged 28 points for the series, with 32 in the Game 7 finale, but Frazier was able to hold him off just enough for the Knicks to prevail.

Willis Reed: I used to block Wes out, and all of a sudden I'd look up, and I'd be looking right up through the nets. Wes had [huge] arms like this, and he'd just take his thumb and walk you right up under the hoop. And so you're looking right up under the basket and the rebounds would be bouncing over your head. I'd be there like, "Holy shit, we gotta stop this from happening."

Walt Frazier: You know, I was always the last guy to leave the locker room, looking in the mirror, making sure my sideburns were straight and everything. So Red comes in and says, "Clyde, forget about scoring. You just need to stop him [Monroe]. Concentrate on defense. Don't worry about scoring."

Earl was probably my toughest matchup, because not even he knew what he was going to do. So how could I know?

Milwaukee, behind rookie sensation Kareem Abdul-Jabbar (still known then as Lew Alcindor), was next. The Bucks were hailed as the team of the NBA's future, and, indeed, their time was coming. But now, the Knicks handled them easily in five games.

Willis Reed: He [Kareem] wasn't able to play at my level at that time. But a couple of years later, after I retired, I told him, "I'm glad I got out of the league before you learned how to play this game." Because he turned out to be a magnificent player.

The Knicks had earned their first trip to the NBA Finals since 1953. But this team, which, except for Jackson's, didn't have a serious injury all season, was about to have its luck, and good health, run out.

Willis Reed: I had been having problems with my left knee. My left knee had really been bothering me.

The Los Angeles Lakers had won the Western crown for the third straight year, despite the loss of Wilt Chamberlain for virtually the entire season due to a knee injury. But Wilt was back now, along with Jerry West and Elgin Baylor, and they seemed poised to give Los Angeles its first NBA title after six Finals losses.

The teams split the first four games. The Lakers won Game 2 at the Garden, while the Knicks won Game 3 in overtime at the Forum, despite West's legendary half-court shot that forced the extra session.

Eight minutes into Game 5, already trailing by 10 points, the Knicks' title dreams all but vanished. Trying to drive around Chamberlain, Reed suddenly crumbled to the Garden floor. It wasn't his balky knee, as he first feared. Instead, it was a severely pulled right thigh muscle. He was finished–for the game, and maybe for the series.

But the Knicks weren't out of it yet. Employing a 1-3-1 defense with DeBusschere assigned to lean on Chamberlain, the Knicks rebounded from a 13-point halftime deficit. With their captain listening in the locker room via a special radio hookup, they outscored the Lakers 32–18 in the fourth quarter and won, 107–100.

Willis Reed: Everybody talks about Game 7. But Game 5 was really the most significant game of that series, because we were way down and came back and won. It's a game we probably shouldn't have won, and I think that if we had played that game anyplace other than Madison Square Garden, we probably wouldn't have won. But those guys really gave it up that night, heart and soul. Everybody contributed to that win.

The Knicks, one win away now, headed back to Los Angeles for Game 6. But almost from the start, it was obvious that they would be without their most important player.

Willis Reed: That injury was so fresh, so new, that I had a significant amount of pain when I did play. There was no way I could have done anything in that game [Game 6]. I left that night, right after the game. I came home and started doing all my preparations to get ready for the last game.

Without Reed in the middle, Chamberlain poured in 45 points and led the Lakers to a 22-point rout.

So the season came down to one game, Game 7 at the Garden; one night, Friday, May 8, 1970; and one question: Would Willis play?

Willis Reed: I came in on Friday afternoon, when nobody was around. I had whirlpool treatments, heat and ice. Bigtime [Danny Whelan] was treating me like a little baby, you know. I went out on the court, and I was still in a lot of pain. I found that I could drag the leg, but when I flexed the leg to try and pick it up, it really hurt, because of the muscle tear. But if I could pull it along, drag it along, leave it straight, I could do that. But jumping was almost impossible.

Phil Pepe: They win the game where he gets hurt, then they get blown away in the next game. You figured he wasn't going to be able to play in the seventh game, and even if he was, he wasn't going to be 100 percent. And how do you stop Wilt Chamberlain? It was tough enough to stop him *with* Willis. That was always a concern anyway. But without Willis, you figured there was no way they were gonna duplicate what they did in the fifth game. In the fifth game, they were playing on emotion and adrenaline. But by the time the seventh game rolled around, you figured they weren't gonna be able to handle Chamberlain.

Marv Albert: Because ABC showed the game on tape delay in New York, it was one of the largest radio audiences ever, at that time.

Willis Reed: I knew I was going to try. I knew I was going to go out there. I didn't know whether or not I was going to be successful. But I knew that the team needed me to be there, after what Wilt had done to us in Game 6. There was no way they would have had any level of confidence if I didn't show up. And I knew I wasn't going to be able to play Wilt. But I knew I could help DeBusschere, Bradley, and Barnett get some easier shots, because I could set the screens, and Wilt wasn't going to come out off the screens. But as far as stopping Wilt [one-on-one], I knew that was going to be an impossible task.

Phil Jackson: I still have a picture that Red told me not to use. Spike Lee offered to pay $10,000 for it. I said it's probably worth 10 times that. It's Willis with the spike in his thigh. They left the needle in his leg and they changed the cartridge when he got the shot. I took a picture of that, but Red said I couldn't ever use it because it was unfair. The press didn't get a chance to take that, so I shouldn't either. I've always respected him for that. I have that [the negative] and I want to get it developed and give it to Willis before it's too late.

Willis Reed: He [Dr. James Parkes] had first started working on me, giving me injections for my hip, with carbocaine. He had this damn needle–

I mean, it was that long. Man, it was a big needle. So he would say to me, "Willis, when this is all over I'll let you stick me with it." I said, "OK, don't forget that!"

They actually had to hold the game up, and then Red said, "Hey, guys, we've got to go with or without him." So they left me in there to finally get the rest of my shots.

Steve Albert: When Willis came out, I had just come out to the bench and gotten the water and towels and everything ready. I looked out to the Lakers, who were warming up, and they all, to a man, turned around and stopped shooting and looked at Willis. And their jaws dropped. The game was over before it started. They were just taken out of it mentally, with that crowd so loud.

Willis Reed: I heard the roar of the crowd. I saw the ovation. And I'm saying to myself, "This is a hell of a predicament to be in." Because here I am. I'm going to try to play the greatest offensive center to ever play the game–a guy who just got through getting 45 against us–on one leg. And the crowd is yelling, "Hey, everything's all right, the Captain is here!" And I'm thinking, "Holy Christ!" You know, when you're dreaming of playing for a championship you're thinking about scoring 32 points, having 20 rebounds, flying all over the place, and all that stuff. But here it's like an invalid trying to play against this guy!

When I walked on the court I knew I had to be very careful. I had to not show the players that I was still in a lot of pain. Had to show them there were some things I could do and not let them think there were things I couldn't do. And I think I pulled it off pretty well. I shot some shots, and I was moving a little gingerly.

Walt Frazier: When I left the locker room, again Holzman said, "Clyde, just hit the open man. Get these guys involved."

Willis Reed: Clyde gave me the first ball, and I made the basket. Second time, I got the ball from Barnett. So I got it from two different guys. That's the kind of team we were. And if you look at it, in the first 10 possessions I think everybody on our team dribbled the ball upcourt, except Willis Reed.

Eighteen seconds into the game, Reed's jumper from the top of the key gave the Knicks a 2–0 lead. A little more than a minute later, another Reed jumper made it 5–2.

Willis Reed didn't score another point for the rest of the night. He didn't have to.

While Reed's performance–four points and three rebounds in 27 minutes–gave the Knicks their early emotional lift, it was Frazier who authored one of the greatest one-man shows in Finals history. Over 44 minutes, he scored 36 points, going 12-for-17 from the field and 12-for-12 from the line, and adding 19 assists and seven rebounds. Much of that came at the expense of Lakers rookie Dick Garrett, Frazier's old teammate at Southern Illinois.

Some observers, including Bill Russell (who was watching the game on television), theorized that Chamberlain, who had shredded the Knicks in Game 6, was not as aggressive as he should have been against a hobbled Reed in Game 7. In hindsight, maybe it mattered, maybe it didn't.

Marv Albert: So much has been made of what Willis did, and it was very inspirational. In an NBA game, when the score was 7–2, do you think it was over? Just limping around and hitting the two shots, Willis gave them such a lift. And then Clyde had one of the greatest games in the history of the NBA Playoffs. I mean, he just took them apart.

Walt Frazier: In that game, I *was* the open man. Every time I came off a screen, there I was. I was uncontested. It was ironic how that evolved.

Willis Reed: I've heard that [the Russell theory], and I disagree with it. And I disagree very vehemently. You see, Clyde had this great, great game. So for most of the game, the Lakers never got into the flow of their offense because he created so much havoc out there, on both ends of the floor. So they were never able to get into the flow of walking it up, bringing it down, and getting the ball in to Wilt. It just didn't happen. The flow of the game was just not that way. And being a big guy, I knew at Grambling that if we played a running game, I didn't get many shots. If we played a slowdown game, I got a lot more shots. So the Lakers never got into their half-court offense because they weren't very quick that night, and that was directly because of the way Clyde

played, with the turnovers and all the havoc he created on the perimeter.

Walt Frazier: I hated that [going against Dick Garrett]. I was happy when they took him out of the game. That's one reason I was never friendly with players. I always kept a gulf between myself and [opposition] players, because of that. With Dick, I was delighted when they took him out of the game, because I felt for him. We hung out during that series. He took me out in L.A., and I did the same in New York.

The Knicks never trailed. They led 69–42 at the half, 94–69 after three. It ended 113–99. Twenty-four years after Ned Irish had been dragged into a new league he initially didn't want any part of, New York had its first NBA Champion.

Steve Albert: When there were a couple of minutes left in the game, Danny [Whelan] signaled to me to collect all of the warm-up jerseys and pants and get them into the locker room because it was going to be a madhouse. Everyone was gonna pile onto the court, which was the case. It's a good thing I did that or I'd have been run over and lost everything. All of that stuff would have been souvenirs.

Walt Frazier: *Sports Illustrated* recently did an article on that [Frazier's success in Game 7]. It mentioned that perhaps that's the most underrated game a player ever had in the NBA. And then, too, with [ESPN] Classic Sports, they show that game quite frequently. So now a lot of people say to me, "Wow, I didn't know you had a game like that." But I know if Willis didn't do what he did, I wouldn't have been able to have the game I had. He got the fans involved and gave us confidence just by his coming onto the floor. But at the time I was very upset, because I was just a young player and I was looking for recognition.

Willis Reed: The only thing we were trying to do was win a championship. That's the only goal that was significant. It wasn't about anything else. Because we were trying to do something that had never been done by a Knicks team. And we felt like it was our year. We had a Cinderella year. We had some great games, some great comebacks. We won 18 in a row and all that stuff. And then I screw around and get hurt. That kind of changed the lay of the land. But when you walk away from it, you realize that we came to training camp for one thing, and when it was all over we walked away with what we came to training camp for.

Marv Albert: What was most significant for me was, after all those years of being a Knicks fan when they usually didn't make the playoffs, I couldn't believe–stepping away from being the broadcaster for a moment–that they were going to win the championship. It was beyond everything.

Willis Reed: I was in so much pain. That night after the game, we had a party at the Four Seasons. I went and I stayed a while. I was in pain when I was playing, but once that carbocaine wore off, I'll tell you, it was rough.

Freddie Klein: That feeling when they won . . . I was in shock. You know, I can only remember Willis walking on the court and making the two shots and nothing after that. It was anticlimactic. Everything had been building up so big, I really don't remember. I was in a fog. I didn't even realize until after the game that Willis had played 27 minutes, when at one point it didn't look like he was gonna play at all.

Marv Albert: We had agreed to do [a series of PlayWorld toystore appearances the next morning]. And when you think about it now, they would have agreed, even with the possibility of them not winning! I was picked up early in the morning, and then we picked Red up in Cedarhurst, and then we went to Willis' apartment in Queens. And we toured three or four PlayWorlds on Long Island. It was unbelievable. What a great promotion it was for the PlayWorld ad people who put this together. It was in the papers; it was all over the radio. There were turnaround crowds everywhere. We were all supposed to speak, but we couldn't. It became a pep rally. It was amazing, for that time.

Willis Reed: May eighth, I'll never forget. You see that [picture of a] little girl right there? That's her birthday. She was five years old that day. The day she was born, I had a headache and was in a lot of pain. And five years later, we won the championship and I was still in a lot of pain. Isn't that amazing?

Collectively the champion Knicks functioned seamlessly, beating their opponents with precision and will.

Phil Pepe: If you looked at them individually, they weren't all that overpowering. They were small and slow. The only guys who were oversized were the guards; Barnett and Frazier were big for guards of that day. Everybody else was undersized. They say Willis is 6'10", but he's really about 6'7". DeBusschere was about 6'4", playing a power forward. You couldn't do that today. Bradley was 6'3", slow, and couldn't jump. And yet when you put them all together, everything worked.

Bob Wolff: A big reason those teams were so great was that, no matter what position they played, they all had this in common: great hands and great basketball knowledge. The hands were important because they kept the ball moving quickly. And as a consequence, they could find the free man more quickly than any team around. They were not typecast by numbers. They were typecast as a team that could operate as a unit.

Dick Schaap: It was the mix that made them so interesting. You had a Joe Namath–type character in Frazier, although he really wasn't that way. He was always very shy. His image was not what he was really like. Bradley was an intellectual in an athletic sense. DeBusschere was quiet. Willis was the leader. That team really reflected New York. You had every kind of ethnic group, including a Jewish coach. Every minority was represented.

Leonard Koppett: I thought at the time that it was the best five-man basketball team I'd ever seen, even better than the Celtics in terms of integrated unity. They didn't have a Bill Russell, but it was the best style of five-man basketball I'd ever seen.

Willis Reed: We didn't have any great, great superstar players where one guy got all the shots. It wasn't that kind of a team. I remember that DeBusschere and Bradley used to kill Milwaukee. Don't ask me why. There were certain teams that Barnett and Clyde always used to have great

games against. When we walked on the court, we knew that, say, against this team our guards would have the best games. And it wasn't guys getting 40 or 45 points, it was guys getting 22 or 25. We had a lot of guys who could score 20-plus, including some guys on the bench who could do it if they got enough shots. That's what made us a good team, because you could not defend us. You could not take away. You might be able to stop this one guy, but that's OK because somebody else will make the basket.

Red Holzman: On the first championship team, we had three guys coming off the bench in Cazzie, Riordan, and Stallworth. Mostly, I was an eight- or nine-guy coach. Those guys in 1970 were used to playing 40 minutes a game.

Cal Ramsey: The thing that was so dynamic about that team was that every player that started, with the exception of Willis Reed, had played guard in their careers. DeBusschere had played guard in college at Detroit. Bradley handled the ball all the time at Princeton. Frazier and Barnett, of course. They all played guard, which meant that they were all very good passers. They were not afraid to share the ball. They were all good shooters, and any one of them could take that last shot. That might have been the difference between them and a lot of teams: the fact that they all could pass, could shoot, and would shoot.

Willis Reed: There were only two positions on that team, I think, who we couldn't play without. We couldn't play without Clyde, and we couldn't play without me, consistently, and win. In any other position, we had good enough people behind the guys. But in that league, how many great, great point guards did you have, and how many great, great centers did you have?

Marv Albert: I realized they were special. They weren't the closest bunch off the court. There was talk about 12 different cabs and all that, although it wasn't that bad. DeBusschere and Bradley were close. Phil and Bradley. Clyde was as he is today, very laid back. Willis was very private. But they had a nice rapport. They wanted their space, but there was great respect among them. Red and Danny had a lot to do with it.

Phil Pepe: The thing that I always marveled at with that team was, when you looked at them playing on the court, they looked like they were five people molded into one. They were close and they saw each other. They looked for each other on the court. And yet when the game was over, there were no close relationships as far as I could tell. You'd see Bradley with DeBusschere occasionally, but Bradley had his own agenda. He'd go into a city and wind up with some sheik or a sultan. He was planning his future even then. But occasionally he and DeBusschere would go out to dinner. Willis would always be with the rookie, like John Warren. Other than that, everybody was a lone ranger. They'd all go their separate ways. They didn't pal around like baseball players.

George Kalinsky: They'd leave the locker room, and for the most part, there weren't any two guys who left together. At least [not of] the top five or six guys. But they all respected each other. It was like working in any other business. And most of them were married and were family people.

Bob Wolff: When that team traveled, they'd get on the bus, and they all spread out and had their regular seats. And they all had separate personalities. They were individuals who came together as a team and then went their own ways. When they put the uniform on, they were a team. Then they'd disappear into the night. They were unique.

Marv Albert: At times I've felt, listening to the tapes of those games, that I might have been a little bit over the top [in favor of the Knicks] in terms of what I felt was right. Even though, if certain guys didn't play well, I would always say it was the case. It was easy because they were such a good team, it didn't happen that often. The new style of broadcasting was beginning to come in, where there was a little bit more objectivity, and I felt very strongly about that. But it was probably the right style for that time, for the love of the team and the way things happened. There's no question there was more of an emotional attachment back then. I still get excited for the Knicks, but it's more controlled.

Off the court, the Knicks were an eclectic group, representing a range of backgrounds, personalities, and interests.

Walt Frazier: Barnett was wild. Every town he went in, he had buddies. It was like Grand Central Station. The phone never stopped ringing from the moment we got in town. Guys would come by to tell Dick where the parties were, and this and that. But with Phil [Jackson], we just went out all the time. We'd go cultural shopping in all the big cities. We'd just put our bags down and go out. Phil liked to go out and just walk around the town, so I'd do that with him.

Cal Ramsey: My closest friend on the team was Barnett, because I came out of school the same year he did. Barnett lived in my apartment in Syracuse, and we roomed together. And when I went into the army, he stayed with my mom at my place because he was new to the East Coast.

Phil Pepe: The guy who was the most fascinating to me, although he wasn't the best interview, was Dick Barnett. He was almost like a mysterious figure. He had this laconic way of playing and a droopy expression on his face, and you'd think he was in another world or from another planet and not very bright. But he was *extremely* bright. And as it's turned out, he's a doctor [of education] today. A brilliant guy, and we never appreciated it. But there was a mystique and a mystery about him that I could never penetrate. I don't think anybody ever did.

Bob Wolff: Dick Barnett was like a droll comedian, like the Bob Uecker of his time. He spoke slowly, and at the end he always had a good punch line. We were at a banquet honoring Red once and Barnett said, "In Boston, we stayed at a hotel that was attached to North Station. And across the street was a burlesque house. Red told us not to ever go to that burlesque house or we'd see something embarrassing. So one night I went in, and he was right. I saw something very embarrassing. I saw Red Holzman sitting there."

Dave Checketts: Basketball in Utah is a lot like basketball in Indiana—there's a basket on every house. We'd go out at all hours of the day and night in my driveway. Basketball was everything to us. But my team—as opposed to most of the kids in the neighborhood who were big Lakers fanatics—was the Knicks. When I was outside shooting around, I was always Dave DeBusschere. He was my favorite player as a kid, rough and tough. I just loved the way Red conducted himself. The Knicks were such a smart team, such a great passing team and a great defensive team. I was in love with that championship club, both times, and heartbroken when they didn't win. That was my first connection with the Knicks.

Bill Bradley: Dave is a hardworking, straightforward, meat-and-potatoes, go-out-and-do-the-job, have-a-beer-afterward, go-out-and-think-about-the-game guy. He was a very experienced pro, and that was very important to me, but he was also a dear friend. Anytime you live with somebody as much as you did with a roommate in those days, you get to know that person very well. And we just had a great personality mesh. He was always the guy who was experienced, and I was the guy who was learning from him. On the court we had our distinct roles, and he was always somebody with whom I had a free flow of information: he'd suggest this, I'd suggest that. We talked about the game a lot.

Bob Wolff: Bradley brought in the touch pass, where he didn't even look. He just flicked it off his fingertips to the next guy in line.

Bill Bradley: Phil Jackson was somebody who was his own special person. We got along extremely well. He was interested in a broad range of things. He was much more of a free spirit in those years than Dave. But he had an underlying tenacity, a knowledge for the game, and a commitment to winning. He had an appreciation for individuality that presaged his later years as a successful coach.

Phil Jackson: The Windmill Effect was all Marv Albert. I was basically brought up in basketball by Bill Fitch, where you play full-court pressure in practices, three-on-three, and it was hell. It was kind of like a hockey game. Everything was about putting pressure on the ball. So that got to be something I did well and something I became renowned for. It was one of the aspects of my game that was probably the most noticeable.

Bob Wolff: Bill Bradley used to read me political dissertations that he had written, and ask me what I thought of them. He'd write these pieces using all these political terms and ask me to critique it.

Bob McAdoo: Bill Bradley was probably the best at moving without the ball, just perpetual motion all the time.

Bob Wolff: I would be trying to get baseball scores and Bradley and DeBusschere would be kidding me, saying, "That sport's done. Nobody cares. What's wrong with you?"

George Kalinsky: After Clyde [and his outfits] started getting publicity, the other guys wanted to be a part of it. Willis was very conservative, and Bradley was too. Barnett was pretty fashionable. Phil Jackson was the one guy who was a hippie.

Bill Bradley: I stand accused! I stand accused! My wardrobe used to be blue jeans and an army jacket. Then Barnett took me down to Lester, his tailor, on 47th and Broadway. Lester measured me, and I got a few suits from him. I wore them about three times.

Bob McAdoo: I remember playing against Walt Frazier in my rookie year in Buffalo [1972–73], when they were just so tough. He was so tough to stop, it was almost like he was scoring at will.

George Kalinsky: Nate Bowman was very graceful. He wasn't as strong as he might have appeared. He blended in as part of the team. He was so graceful in his movements, and his muscles were toned as if he were a thoroughbred horse. Somehow, everything he seemed to do, photographically, came out great. He wasn't a great player–he was an average backup center–but photographically, he was terrific.

The attribute that everyone agreed set the Knicks apart from the rest of the league was their intelligence, both on and off the court.

Jerry Lucas: The Knicks played the kind of basketball that I really appreciated, really enjoyed. I loved every aspect. That team was the most intelligent team that has ever played the game of basketball. Not only from a basic IQ standpoint, if you will, [although] we had Rhodes Scholars, and people who would go on to get doctorates, and Phil Jackson,

who would go on to become a great mind in the game. But beyond basic intelligence, the thing that was so overwhelming was the incredible basketball knowledge that team possessed. It was just phenomenal. Everybody knew the game. They knew how to play, how to win, and the nuances of the game. So much so that at every halftime, Red Holzman, who understood people and individuals, would ask *us* how things were going and what *we* felt we should do in the second half. He also appreciated the knowledge that team had.

Bill Bradley: The first championship year was the first year that the Knicks were the toast of the town, so it became a very heady thing. It was the year the Mets and Jets won, so New York was the sports capital of the world. The Knicks performed incredibly well; we won a lot of games in a row, and the Garden was a special place. There was the first-round playoff with the Baltimore Bullets that was an intense, man-for-man matchup. And the real reason people remember it is because of the series against the Lakers, and Willis, and the fifth and seventh games. I read that in a recent poll, Willis walking out for the seventh game was voted the second greatest moment in the history of New York sports.

Phil Pepe: It was a great team to cover. They were all very cooperative, all very interesting. Bradley had his thing, and DeBusschere probably spent more time with the writers than anyone. We'd be in the coffee shop having breakfast, and DeBusschere would come down and sit down with us and just shoot the breeze.

Bob Wolff: Dave DeBusschere would always bring two or three novels to read on the plane. In the earlier years, when Cazzie Russell was there, he was always sort of a man-about-town, making all the noise. Willis Reed was quiet. They all sat in their own little spot.

George Kalinsky: I considered myself part of the team. I worked out with them; in fact, I hurt myself twice while I was working out. I tore an Achilles tendon and leg cartilage. The key thing was that I felt that they were my friends. We were all around the same age. And one interesting thing was that if one guy was in trouble, like an injury or an illness, everybody else called. Those players didn't have the kind of ego of, "We're players." Even Red. I remember I had some kind of illness and the first thing you know, Red called me. Then Willis called. Then Bradley. And everyone did it for everyone else.

Phil Jackson: In 1970, Eddie Mast came in as one of the youngest players ever to play for the Knicks. He was a 21-year-old kid coming out of college. He had a great love for the game, and he just kind of bloomed at the end of his senior year [at Temple]. People noticed, and he got his opportunity with the Knicks. He was with us for a couple of years. It was right after my rooming with Walt Frazier and before I started rooming with Jerry Lucas. He was a city kid from Philadelphia who loved music, played music. He'd venture out and ask to play as a guest guitarist when we were on the road. He took me around to all kinds of clubs to listen to music. The two things he loved most were basketball and music. Eddie was playing basketball when he died, and he was playing music right up until then. When I went to his funeral, I never saw a more diverse group of people. One-third of the people in the church, I'm sure, were black or people of color. Simply because that's who he was. He was a person who loved people who were associated with music and basketball. He coached in high school; he played overseas. He played as long as he could. He just had an attitude about the game that, hey, this is fun and I'm gonna do it as long as I can. It ultimately cost him his life, but it also gave him his life. [*Editor's note:* Eddie Mast died of a heart attack while playing recreational basketball.]

Phil Pepe: They were a tremendously intelligent group of guys individually. Look at what they all became. They all reached tremendous stature in their post-playing life. Two of them became general managers, some of them became coaches. Bradley was a Rhodes Scholar and a senator, Barnett gets a doctorate. Just tremendous intellect on one single team.

Leonard Koppett: The point is that this was a collection of very intelligent and articulate

people. They knew what to say to stay out of trouble. I remember having a fight with Bradley. He was talking about something and he gave an answer like, "We used a zone offense." I said, "What the hell is a zone offense?" What he meant was, the offense they used against a zone defense. But I hadn't heard it before. You could have those kinds of exchanges back then. I don't think you could do that now.

Phil Pepe: They were more intelligent, because all of them went to college. So they were more sophisticated and more worldly. They understood the relationship between the press and the players much better than baseball players. And they weren't spoiled yet. They weren't getting the attention that the baseball players got. And I don't know if it was spelled out or implied, but there was a feeling of, let's be good to these guys [the press] because we need their coverage and attention. I sensed that a little bit.

Mel Davis: What did I learn from those guys? Transition. Perseverance. Commitment. Enduring and beating the odds. All those things combined. Those qualities translate into everyday life.

Bob Wolff: The guiding influence for all of this, all of the banter and kidding around, was Danny Whelan. Danny Whelan was the needler. With him and Holzman, it was like Edgar Bergen and Charlie McCarthy: Red would think it, and Danny would say it.

Bill Bradley: He [Whelan] was a great guy. He knew athletes. He'd been with the Pirates; he had a lot of great stories. He knew when you were seriously hurt, and he knew when you really weren't hurt but you thought you were. He was just a great spirit in the locker room. Always had a joke or something funny, telling some story. He really engaged the players as well as being a hell of a trainer. He was also Red's drinking buddy on the road, so that was important, too. He kept the players and the coach happy.

Marv Albert: Danny was a very funny guy. He was like a stand-up comedian. I'd sit with him all the time, and he'd do impersonations of all the guys. He had a way of seeing things differently, and

I think he brought that over from his years with the Pirates. I used to love to listen to his Roberto Clemente stories and all his baseball stuff. What a nice guy.

As the championship team developed, the media covering the Knicks underwent a few changes, including the addition of two broadcast analysts who would become fixtures of the Big Apple hoop scene.

Marv Albert: I realized the significance of those broadcasts by what it led me into. There was such a reaction to it. When I was doing it, I was thinking, "I'm so happy to be doing this. I'm really lucky," and so forth. But in the early seventies, suddenly, Wellington Mara comes to me and asks me to do the Giants after Marty [Glickman] left to do the Jets. Channel 4 comes to me to do sports. So that was the impact. That's what made it register. I never thought of it as anything more than, this team is really getting good, and I know there are a lot of people listening. But I didn't realize what it really meant.

Bob Wolff: There wasn't a doubt that cable TV would succeed after they had winning teams. And I remember in the early years, they had such devout fans that we used to advertise that if you couldn't get a ticket to the game, you could watch it in the Felt Forum. Pay your way in for five or ten bucks. And part of my job when I was doing PR was to go over and take the stage in the Felt Forum and entertain until the telecast came on.

Leonard Koppett: They were individuals who were terrific to be with. On that team, there were a lot of people who gave you a lot of good quotes, which made it that much better. But you were not yet in the era where the desk is saying, "Get quotes, get more quotes," which is the way it is now.

John Andariese: They were so big in New York, as individuals and as a team, that there was no way that somebody in my position–a radio analyst–would have the nerve to inflict their presence on them. I just felt, and I've always felt, that I was an athlete who happened to be doing what I do, as opposed to a media person. I've never thought of

myself as a media person; I've always had an athlete's mentality about me. Now, I don't know if that's good or bad, but I just never wanted to intrude into their private lives and try and get something out of them. It took me a long time to understand how to think like a media person. And nobody tells you how to do this job, no one gives you lessons on how to be an analyst, not at that time. I think it was probably two years before I ever spoke to Dave DeBusschere, whom I ultimately ended up in business with for a number of years. I felt that I wasn't good enough to be in the NBA, but maybe if the ball had bounced another way I could have been. I tried to relate to the players in their world, as opposed to getting a scoop for a broadcast.

Phil Pepe: The thing that broke the ice for me [with the other writers] was that I played in their card games. I was accepted right away. I fell in with Frankie [Blauschild], Lenny [Lewin], and Murray [Janoff] because they were cardplayers. We played poker. Maybe I was their foil or their pigeon. And I knew a lot of those guys from baseball, anyway.

Leonard Koppett: The team knew enough to be wary of what the press could do for them and how the press could make trouble for them. But they weren't 100 percent on the defensive, as athletes have been since then.

Phil Pepe: One day in Los Angeles, we're playing cards and there's a knock on the door. Somebody opens the door, and there's this huge figure filling the doorway. It's Wilt Chamberlain. So he comes in, and now we're playing cards with Wilt Chamberlain. Talk about being intimidated! Wilt played cards the way he played the game: very aggressively with a loud, booming voice. Of course, he had all the money in the world. We weren't playing for big stakes, but for a guy making about $150 a week at the time, it was big money. And sometimes I'd lose that in a card game. But Wilt would sit at the table with us mere mortals, and he was so big that he'd just engulf the table.

Bob Wolff: One night we went to a Chinese restaurant when they were closing up shop. And

Frank Blauschild said, "I'll take care of it." So he went in and told us to wait. About 10 minutes later he came out and said they were going to serve us. What happened? It seemed that Frank went into the kitchen and was showing off his magic tricks. And he promised them that if they served us, he'd spend another half hour in the kitchen entertaining them with his magic tricks.

Cal Ramsey: After two years [on the stat crew], I got a call, and they wanted me to audition for a job as a radio analyst. One thing I'll never forget is that the audition for this job was done at Rockefeller Center, with Marv, and we did a game simulation of the Knicks against the Milwaukee Bucks as if there were a game going on. We were in a room with one microphone, and we did a whole half and a halftime wrapup. And there was nothing in front of us, no tape or film or anything. It was entirely off the cuff. And at the conclusion, they said they wanted to hire me but as a TV analyst as opposed to radio. So I said, "Great, I'll do that."

John Andariese: I had enough initial experience to feel that this was something I'd like to do. I remember once talking about it to Eddie Donovan at the Old Garden. It was during a college game, with Kareem playing for UCLA. The action was going on upstairs, and I was talking to him down the stairs, and I could see the guys running up and down. So I finally got his attention, and he basically discouraged me. He said that it's very hard to get in and that I didn't know the league, and all the stuff that you would expect to hear. So I went away quietly.

Marv Albert: I let them know that I'd like to have a partner. I always liked to react off people. John had done some work in broadcasting. We didn't really know each other then, but we hit it off and became great friends right at the start.

John Andariese: I got a call to come in and sit in a studio with Marv at WNBC Radio, and audition. And the audition was sitting there and talking to Marv around one microphone. It wasn't a tense situation, just general stuff. I knew there were some other fellows who were being auditioned. Then I got

the call from Alan Fields that they were going to hire me. It was thrilling.

Bob Wolff: In basketball, I had never really worked with a color man. In baseball, I had worked with Joe Garagiola, who was terrific. But with anyone you're working with, I always felt that you're thought of as a team. When I first got together with Cal, I said, "Cal, I'm gonna do all I can to teach you about broadcasting. We're gonna travel together. Before every game, I'm going to show you what notes I'm going to emphasize. After the game we'll critique each other. We're going to be inseparable guys. If you can stand me, I know I'm gonna like you. We can do this." And after a while, I was proud of the fact that people were saying, "Boy, you're a great team. You seem to love working together." And when you have confidence in that, you can start kidding each other.

Cal Ramsey: Bob took me under his wing, and he pretty much showed me how to prepare for games. He was always overprepared. He did his homework. I mean, he had notes on everything. And some of the things he taught me, I still do to this day. He always told me to get to the arena when the players get there. You be there when they get there, and that's how you do your preparation and talk to the players. And to this day, I come to every game an hour and a half before. It's just a habit.

Bob Wolff: We'd go to the airport together, we'd sit together, eat together, rehearse together. I'd visit his home and his mother, Ruth. It was a genuine, wonderful relationship. We'd get beautiful letters. I remember the minister from the Riverside Church wrote me a long letter saying that Cal and I symbolized what friendship and brotherhood means. I was very proud of that, because it transcended broadcasting.

Cal Ramsey: Bob always said that if you come across as if you're friends, the show goes a lot better. And we did become friends, and the show did go a lot better. We came off as friends on the air. Once he interviewed me at my mother's apartment. Bob came up with a film crew and everything. And at the time I had a cat, and the cat was sitting on

Earl Monroe floats in for a layup during his first game as a Knick, on November 11, 1971, against Golden State. The Pearl originally donned No. 33 before switching to No. 15 later that season.

the couch. Bob came over and sat right on my cat. Despite that, we remained friends. He's just a wonderful guy.

John Andariese: Everything I've ever done with Marv has been spontaneous and unrehearsed. Everything. I've never discussed how we should interact, and he's never discussed it with me. Totally spontaneous from the very beginning, so whatever we do on the air is totally natural. What Marv has always done with his analysts is give them a prominence by acknowledging them as prominent members of the sport or of the broadcast. That creates action; it creates response and generates a humanity toward the analyst.

The Knicks may have been the toast of the town, but their practice facility certainly didn't reflect that status. More than 30 years later, mention the words Lost Battalion Hall *to any member of the early-seventies Knicks and watch their faces scrunch up.*

Originally built in 1939 for the Queens Veterans of Foreign Wars and the American Legion, Lost Battalion Hall still stands on Queens Boulevard in the borough's Rego Park section. Now a city-owned community recreation center, it is used by hundreds of Queens residents who doubtless have little or no knowledge of its role in the Knicks' glory days.

But for those who practiced there, they couldn't forget even if they wanted to. Here, then, are some Tales of the Lost Battalion.

Bill Bradley: Oh, God. The subway ride out there. I would take the subway from Eighth Avenue and 57th all the way out to Queens on the E line, and I'd be freezing. Then we'd practice at Lost Battalion Hall, which had a court that was too small, a locker room the size of a closet, and usually hot water. Or lack thereof. Then I'd always come back with Frazier. We'd drive back in his white Cadillac. To drive from Lost Battalion to the Paramount Hotel where he lived used to be endless. We'd come from the Midtown Tunnel, then go across 46th Street, and no matter what happened we'd get stuck on 46th Street! So we'd just stay on that block, at midday, stuck for an hour.

Mike Saunders: I used to play at Lost Battalion Hall when I was in junior high school. It was a few miles from my house, right on Queens Boulevard. It was a Department of Parks place and one of the few gyms, other than a school, that would be open. I used to go and watch practice, carry Danny Whelan's bag upstairs. I used to rebound for Walt Bellamy and Cazzie Russell.

Walt Frazier: One basket was nine feet tall, the other was eight feet tall. All the kids would cut class just to watch us. But the main thing about Lost Battalion was that there was no hot water after two or three guys took a shower. So the big thing about practice was running into the back to take a shower the minute Red called the end of practice.

Phil Jackson: That was a pain, there's no doubt about it. When we first went there, kids could come in off the street and watch us play. They were cordoned off behind these velvet stanchions like you have in a movie theatre. The court was broken—there was a place where the flooring was broken. The backboards were wooden, and the hoops were loose. But the worst part of it was that there was no hot water. It kind of held a badge of courage aspect, though. I think Red realized that it was a little ridiculous that we were still down there working out. He was able to get us some better facilities to work out of. But for a long time, that was our home away from home, and it wasn't easy.

The Knicks of the early seventies were a product of the times, the Vietnam era that had polarized the nation. In fact, the single greatest week in Knicks history was one of the most divisive the country had ever seen.

On Monday, May 4, 1970, the day of the Game 5 comeback against the Lakers, four students were killed by National Guard troops during an antiwar rally at Kent State University. Then, on the day the Knicks won their first NBA title—Friday, May 8—hard-hatted construction workers violently broke up a student antiwar demonstration on Wall Street, then marched to City Hall and demanded that the American flag, which flew at half-mast in mourning the Kent State deaths, be raised to the top of the flagpole. About 20 minutes after the final buzzer sounded on the Knicks' Game 7 win, President

Richard Nixon addressed the nation and defended the recent troop movement into Cambodia. The next day, a massive antiwar rally drew 100,000 protesters to Washington, D.C.

For several members of the Knicks and their extended family, the echoes from the outside world rang loud and long.

Phil Jackson: I think there was a time in our country where there was an "anti" attitude against people who protested the war. And then there were guys on the team who were weekend warriors like Van Arsdale, Komives, Bradley, Cazzie, and Riordan. These were all guys under 6'6". At that time that was the limit. They had to fulfill a role.

Bill Bradley: Once a month I'd do my Air Force duty. We'd have a Friday game somewhere like Chicago and we'd get back at 1:00 or 2:00. I'd get up at about 5:00 to be down at McGuire Air Force Base for a full day. Then at 5:00 in the afternoon I'd leave the base, come back to the Garden, play the game, then get up the next morning at 5:00 and go back to the base.

Phil Jackson: I remember [Baltimore's] Jack Marin calling Bradley a pinko communist. He liked to mouth off and talk trash at that time, so they trash-talked each other. That's one of the slogans he used with Bradley, calling him a pinko communist. I never thought of Bradley as either a pinko or a communist; he was always pretty middle of the road, although definitely a liberal.

Steve Albert: I was in a classroom taking a child psychology class, adjacent to what was known, and is still known, as the Commons at Kent State, where most of the shooting took place. We were watching a movie in which a child was crying, and it drowned out the gunshots. I knew before that day that something was brewing, that there would be a big demonstration at noon. But the safest place to be was in a classroom. Fortunately for me, Kent State had double classes that ran for two hours, and this class was one of them. Had it not been, the first session would have been over at noon and I would have been out there when it all happened.

I counted nine ambulances go by, and we all ran out, and there was the aftermath of it. Smoke was still rising from the guns. They were blaring on the PA system to just grab everything you can and get out of here, get off campus. I ran back–through the haze and all this craziness–to the dorm, hitchhiked to Akron where one of my roommates lived, and from there got on a plane to Newark. I got to the city, took the subway home to Brooklyn, and was home that night watching Walter Cronkite talk about Kent State.

Marv Albert: We were concerned when we heard the news about the shootings. The blinds were down, and he was watching some film and saw babies crying on the film, as the shots were ringing out. My parents had told him to come home, and he hitchhiked home.

Phil Jackson: In our age group, there was never anything other than the idea that this was a war that didn't make a whole lot of sense for America to get involved in. We were fighting somebody else's war, France's war. We were fighting to save Vietnam from internal rebelling. Then, all of a sudden, it became a fight with the North Vietnamese, an undeclared war. And it just didn't make any sense anymore.

Steve Albert: Nobody knew where I was. Four kids were shot, and one of them was from New York. The details were very sketchy. And the kid from New York turned out to be Jeffrey Miller, from Long Island, who, unfortunately, was the one in the famous [John Filo] photo with the girl [Mary Vecchio] kneeling over him. They didn't know anything beyond that. Marv was scouring the wires at WHN, trying to find out anything he could. We couldn't call because all the lines were tied up. I tried to call my parents all day to tell them I was OK. When I got to the airport in Akron, the lines in front of the pay phones, of people calling out, were immense. So I couldn't call.

Phil Jackson: Until 1970 and Kent State and the construction workers beating up some longhairs on Wall Street, you had to carry yourself with the aspect that you may have to defend yourself a little bit for being a longhair and for being antiwar. And then it turned so rapidly. And now people tell me, "How about those veterans that got spit on when they came back from Vietnam?" I don't remember that. I don't remember people being booed or cursed or yelled at for being soldiers. I remember it the other way around–people being cursed for protesting the war. And then it turned so quickly in this country. Kent State was the thing that turned it, where, all of a sudden, it was like, "How come this country's coming apart about a war that doesn't make any sense to this country?"

Steve Albert: The next day, I got a call from Danny Whelan. He found out what had happened, and he invited me to be a ballboy for what turned out to be the game where Willis hobbled out. It was a very emotional week . . . I was part of this amazing moment, where just a few days earlier I was a part of another historic moment at Kent State. It was like *Forrest Gump.*

Mike Shatzkin: I think the Mets and the Knicks, both [brought people together]. And it's hard to separate one from the other. The Knicks' season started with the Mets' championship. And I particularly felt it, because I was a demonstrator. I don't think I wrote about it in the book, but I was tear-gassed in a demonstration in Washington during that season, in November of '69. So I was very much against the war, and all of my countenance and appearance showed it, and I dealt with hostility about it. And I sat among a bunch of season-ticket holders who I think, mostly, were on the other side of that issue. So there was a feeling of alienation, which went away when you walked into the Garden for a Knicks game. So I think it was something where you put those other things aside. Now, it's very hard for me, looking back, to say how much of that is me and how much of that is real, or how true it is for anybody else. But, for me, I would have been uncomfortable at that time, [being] around a lot of the people I was watching Knicks games with, if there hadn't been Knicks games to be the focus. Because everything was about counterculture and opposing the government and the power structure. And of course, most of the people who could afford season tickets are part of the power structure, even when they were six dollars a game.

Bill Bradley: I remember getting a letter after the championship from someone who recounted all the things that had happened that spring. And for him, the Knicks winning was the one thing that happened that was true and good and positive. I think a lot of people felt like that in those times.

It had taken the Knicks 24 years to win their first championship. It would take them just 346 days to be dethroned.

Pacing the newly formed Atlantic Division with 52 wins, the Knicks opened their title defense by defeating Atlanta in the first round of the 1971 playoffs. But victory came with a price. In the closing seconds of the series finale at the Garden, Reed severely injured his right shoulder. The Captain played on, but this year there would be no happy ending.

Behind Monroe, who averaged a series-high 24.4 points, Baltimore finally exacted revenge for the prior two seasons, stunning a Garden crowd into silence with a two-point triumph in the deciding Game 7 of the Eastern Conference Finals.

Phil Jackson: By March [1970], I was ready to play again. But what I found out was I had a mental kind of a scar, and it took me a year of playing to really break free from that. And that was probably the most difficult time I ever went through. The following year I backed up Willis at center, and suddenly I not only had to be bigger and heavier, but I had to deal with a lot more weight on my back, boxing out and that stuff.

For the most part, it's a struggle. Obviously, there's a big dropoff in personnel, between Willis and myself. And Willis isn't quite himself yet. His injury was more threatening than we knew because now he's starting to limp around a little bit. Eventually his knee gave out and he had to have surgery. So it's an arduous season, to say the least.

Willis Reed: We would have been in the Finals and I think we would have won in '71 if I hadn't gotten my shoulder hurt in the last game against Atlanta. I reached in for a ball against Bellamy and dislocated my right shoulder, and it kills me even

today. As it was, even though I was ineffective for the rest of the playoffs, we still went down to the last shot against Baltimore. Bill had a shot on the baseline that would have tied it. So we don't get in that year; Baltimore gets in and gets swept by Milwaukee.

Earl Monroe: I remember saying to Willis [in 1971] when he limped out again, that this wasn't 1970. "You better forget that stuff," I told him, "because this isn't last year."

Walt Frazier: It was surreal, man. We never thought anyone could beat us at home. We never had any doubt that we would beat them. And I remember when the game was over, the fans were still there and we were all still on the court, mesmerized. We could not believe that it happened.

Willis Reed: If I don't hurt my shoulder, Baltimore doesn't beat us. So we would have been playing for the championship against Milwaukee, who we always dominated. Our forwards always killed their forwards. That was a team we could beat.

More and more, Reed's health was becoming an issue. Throughout his 1970 MVP season, his knee had pained him, until he finally broke down during the Finals. The following year, he missed nine games during the regular season with chronic knee tendinitis and played the bulk of the playoffs with the bum shoulder.

So the search for another capable big man was on. And the responsibility for getting one would fall squarely on Holzman, now serving in the dual role of coach and general manager ever since Donovan departed in 1970 to head the expansion Buffalo Braves. (Eddie would return to the Knicks in 1975.)

In San Francisco, Red found his man, a full-time rebounder and part-time memory expert who had already been a seven-time All-Star but had never come close to an NBA Championship. That was about to change.

Red Holzman: We felt that Willis' situation was not as good as he had hoped it would be. Jerry Lucas had always been a forward [in the pros], but he was a center in college. I had seen him a lot in college and I knew he was a great center. What people didn't realize was that this guy was a great

passer and a great rebounder. Very intelligent, as we all know. He had a great idea about the game, knew how to block out, had very good moves in the pivot. He was a perfect fit for us. Also, the fact that Willis was in a situation where he might not be able to deliver as much as he had been, we knew that the guy was a piece of cake to have on the team. All he wanted to do was play and win. He had never won a championship in the pros, and he really wanted that.

Jerry Lucas: The trade totally surprised me. I had no idea a trade was coming. I hadn't pushed for one; I hadn't heard anything. I was totally surprised and very, very pleased when I heard it. I was excited about going to the Knicks. They were the consummate team, incredibly intelligent. I felt I would be a good addition, so I was very, very excited.

The Lucas trade, made barely two weeks after the Knicks were ousted from the playoffs, sent Cazzie Russell to the Warriors. A champion at the state high school level, in college at Ohio State, and in the Olympics in 1960, Jerry Lucas was more than just an athlete. Much, much more.

Jerry Lucas: It was a pleasure for me. I had been a center my entire life until I joined the NBA. As a boy growing up through grade school, high school, college, and the Olympics, it was my natural and normal position. I could see the floor, pass well, do a lot of things to take advantage of some of the bigger guys by pulling them away from the basket. I felt like I was back home. I was so comfortable. I know that I was there to assist Willis if he had problems, to come in and play the center position when he rested. It worked out well, and it was something I appreciated because I felt I was coming back home.

Bill Bradley: Lucas brought a lot of experience on all levels, and a great intelligence. I always loved playing with Jerry because he was such a smart player.

Bob Wolff: In today's society, Jerry Lucas would be written up in all the papers. Lucas has this fantastic mind, as you know. He was a nut on memorizing everything. One day he said to me, "Bob, don't worry about the statistics when you do a game. All you have to do is call down to the phone next to the bench. I have all this stuff in my mind. You don't have to worry about anything. I have all the stats in my head."

Phil Jackson: Jerry would check into a ballgame, and he'd go over to the scorer's desk and give them all his mental stuff. He'd say to the official scorer, "I have 12 points, 14 rebounds, and three assists, right? You've got them all down, don't you?" Or you'd be climbing the stairs to go into an arena and Jerry would say, "There are 14 stairs on this flight, 12 on the next." And you'd say, "This guy's nuts." He had all these numbers in his head.

Bob Wolff: Jerry lived in Scarsdale, and we would drive him home after games. One day he said, "Three thousand, two hundred and five." I said, "What's that?" He said, "The number of bumps we hit in the road." I said, "What does that prove?" He said, "I don't know, I just did it." He was really different.

Jerry Lucas: I'd count the number of steps in every stairwell in every place I went. Or the number of stripes on the highway per mile. There are 132 white stripes per mile in almost every state in America.

Phil Jackson: Jerry was my roomie. He was always working on a perpetual motion machine that he was going to make work. It was his ultimate thing. I just loved playing with his mind and listening to him talk. In the card games, he kept score. He kept track of the money because everybody trusted him.

Jerry Lucas: The guys loved to play poker, and they began to throw money in the aisles of the planes. We flew standard commercial flights, and Red didn't like us throwing the money around. He felt it didn't look good. So Phil Jackson came to me and said, "Luke, here's what you need to do. Keep track of everybody's bets, all the money that's been bet. So when we land, you tell us who owes how much to who." So they were able to play without throwing the money on the floor. For a couple of reasons, they didn't want me to play. I never forgot what cards had

been played. When I was a boy, my family loved to play games of all kinds, including card games, and I grew up doing those kinds of things.

Bob Wolff: Lucas and I were always talking about memory technique. I used to have to memorize uniform numbers in whatever sport I did. But he memorized the number in association with a picture or an image. And I said, "Jerry, you're going through a needless step, to memorize a picture and a number." But then he got on *The Ed Sullivan Show*, and his gimmick was to stand in the lobby and memorize everybody in the audience—what their name was, what they looked like, and what they did. So he'd get on stage and say, "OK, Joe Smith, from Toronto, and you're an engineer." And he'd go boom-boom-boom, through the audience. Then he went into things like teaching people how to memorize the Bible.

Jerry Lucas: I had an idea that I've never really pursued. It's amazing. I still think the idea will work. I began to invent mental games when I was a boy, which started me on the path to creating my learning systems. My mind has always been going and racing, and it still is today. I had a phenomenal idea for a [perpetual motion] machine, something I believe would generate more power than it took to operate it, but I've never pursued it. I've never had the opportunity to work with somebody in a field that would have all the machinery and equipment to put into effect what my thoughts were. It's something that I thought about quite a lot, but haven't for so many years. Now that you mention this, I realize that thought probably hasn't been in my mind for about 25 years, but it was something that was discussed a lot in those days.

Bill Bradley: We all used to have eye signals to each other, but with Lucas it was funny. We had something called the Unknown Language. There was a play called "BF," where I would go toward the center and then duck back behind the pick set by Lucas. The guy that was guarding me would be on the other side in the lane, and I'd have that little baseline jumper that I made a living on for about five years. And we would talk in the Unknown Language. So the guy would be guarding me and

I'd say to Lucas, "Hawyahowyadoya?" and Lucas would say to me, "Nahyanha, nahyanha!" And the defender would break his concentration, particularly if he was a younger player, and suddenly I'd be behind the pick.

Jerry Lucas: The thing that impresses people more than anything else is my ability to rearrange words and spell them out in alphabetical order. I began to do that as a boy when I had nothing to do on automobile trips. I'd see words along the highway and on billboards and rearrange them. *Cat*, obviously, is spelled C-A-T. But alphabetically it's A-C-T. *Chandelier* is A-C-D-E-E-H-I-L-N-R, *telephone* is E-E-E-H-L-N-O-P-T, *basketball* is A-A-B-B-E-K-L-L-S-T. I could probably do it with any word faster than you can understand it. But that's something that people find so hard to believe, but it's something I've done my whole life with every word I've ever seen. To me it's like breathing.

Earl Monroe: We were going up to the Catskills to do an appearance–this was during the season–and we went up in my Rolls. The heat went out, so we're driving up and we're both freezing in the car. All of a sudden, the cops pull us over. Now we've got to sit in the car for 20 or 30 minutes while they check the car, check out my license, and all that. And Jerry's doing all this figuring on a piece of paper. So when the cop says, "OK, we're sorry. We just needed to check you out," or whatever, Jerry says, "I just calculated how much time and taxpayer money you just wasted for nothing." Jerry was something else.

Jerry Lucas: My time with the Knicks let me have the opportunity to be on television shows like Johnny Carson, Mike Douglas, and Merv Griffin, to demonstrate my memory abilities and show people how easily it could work. My exposure with the Knicks and our success was very important in that regard.

Bill Bradley: Lucas was a team player, too. He didn't care about anything but getting that championship ring, and that's what he did with us. And he played center a lot more games that year than

anyone remembers because Willis was out much of the time.

John Andariese: He [Lucas] was such an asset because he played the role of a center, and then all of a sudden he's 25 feet from the basket and killing teams. You talk about mismatches. What center would want to go out and guard him up high? He had a unique talent where he could shoot the ball from such a distance. One of the game's great rebounders. Consummate team player, despite counting his rebounds and points during a game. Always trying to make a deal with his off-court interests and his memory stuff. I don't think he related to other guys that well, but his skills were such that he played a big part in their success. Very interesting guy.

The Lucas trade filled a specific and well-documented need, which became even more glaring when Reed hobbled through the opening weeks of the 1971–72 season. But the Knicks still struggled, losing 8 of their first 14 games.

So Holzman went to work again. And this time, he shocked the world.

Earl Monroe: I really didn't want to leave Baltimore. That was just something that came up, and being a young guy and egotistical, I always thought that when you negotiate with a team, it's just between you and them. It's not in the media. And things got out of hand in terms of things being said in the media. Once I read some of the things that were being said, I said to myself that I wasn't gonna be back there. That's what really prompted me to pursue the trade even more. We had asked for a trade after the [1970–71] season, and it wasn't until I was in the preseason the following year when I decided to leave. It wasn't that I just wanted to jump out of there, but at the same time, things just didn't work out. But I always loved Baltimore and still do.

Red Holzman: I had scouted Earl a lot. People didn't realize that Earl wasn't just a showman, a guy who wanted to shoot. Earl was the type of basketball player who would do anything you'd ask him to do. If you wanted him to pass the ball, he'd pass the ball. His defense would fit in because we played a helping type of defense. Earl knew the game very well. He was very intelligent about the game. He was a great person. He just looked mean on the floor.

Earl Monroe: They [the Bullets] had a list of teams that they could trade me to: Philadelphia, Chicago, and Los Angeles. So when I stopped playing in Baltimore, I went to visit some ABA teams and such. Then one day Larry [Fleischer] called and said, "I've got a deal on the table. It's not a place where you had wanted to go." His words were, "I'm very prejudiced. I want to see you here [in New York]. I want to see you day in and day out." So I said, "If that's the deal, then that's the deal. I really want to play against the best, and the best are in the NBA. So let's do it."

Announced in the midst of a 1–3 Western trip, the trade that put the Knicks' biggest tormentor in orange and blue sent two of the 1970 Minutemen, Dave Stallworth and Mike Riordan, to the Bullets.

How could the game's greatest showman fit in with a unit that preached teamwork above all? How would the number one Knick killer be received by the city he had tortured for the past three years? And how could he play alongside Frazier, who not only played the same position but was every bit as proficient?

At first, no one had any idea.

Walt Frazier: Shocked. I thought we needed a big man, but . . . That was probably the most tumultuous time in my career as a Knick, because now everyone's saying that Frazier's out, he's gonna get traded, they can't keep both of them, and all that. So it was a tough time for me.

Earl Monroe: I realized coming to New York that this was Clyde's team. It wasn't a big thing because I had always played with other guys; it was just basketball. The ego thing always creeps in there, but at the same time, if you're a good basketball player, you know how to win. I was always a winning basketball player. Even when I wasn't scoring an awful lot of points, guys always wanted to play

with me. So I didn't have any problems with that. I just knew it was Clyde's ball and I'd have to fit my way in there.

Walt Frazier: We had respect for each other. People thought we couldn't play together because they underestimated our mutual respect for each other. I asked no quarter, and he asked no quarter. There was a lot of silent admiration there. I never said anything to him; he never said anything to me.

Earl Monroe: The biggest thing was that I didn't have to go out and do everything, so to speak. I could enjoy looking at Clyde doing his thing on his side, and if need be, I could do my thing on my side. My biggest thing was that I could always get mine whenever I wanted to. It didn't matter how everything else was. It was a just a matter of trying to make sure that everybody was happy and that we were winning games.

Bill Bradley: Earl came to the team as our most feared opponent, and he was a virtuoso one-on-one player. He did things no one else in basketball ever did or has done since. He had the ability that Oscar [Robertson] did to get just close enough to the defender so that the defender would be in Earl's face but just about an inch away from blocking the shot, and it would go in. He had great spin moves as well.

Earl Monroe: I've always had a pretty good relationship with the [New York] fans, even when I was with Baltimore, so I didn't really think of it in terms of how the fans would treat me. The biggest thing that I was thinking about was that here were guys I had been playing against, very hard, for four years. Now I'm gonna be in their locker room, and how are they gonna receive me? By the time I got to New York, I had pretty much come to grips with the fact that all the things I had done individually would be thrown out the window. It was a new day, a new era, and I more or less had to try to get myself to change it up and be a part of it.

Walt Frazier: To his credit, he made the sacrifice. He became a team player, whereas he was the featured player with the Bullets. He had to learn to play defense, similar to what Barnett had to do when

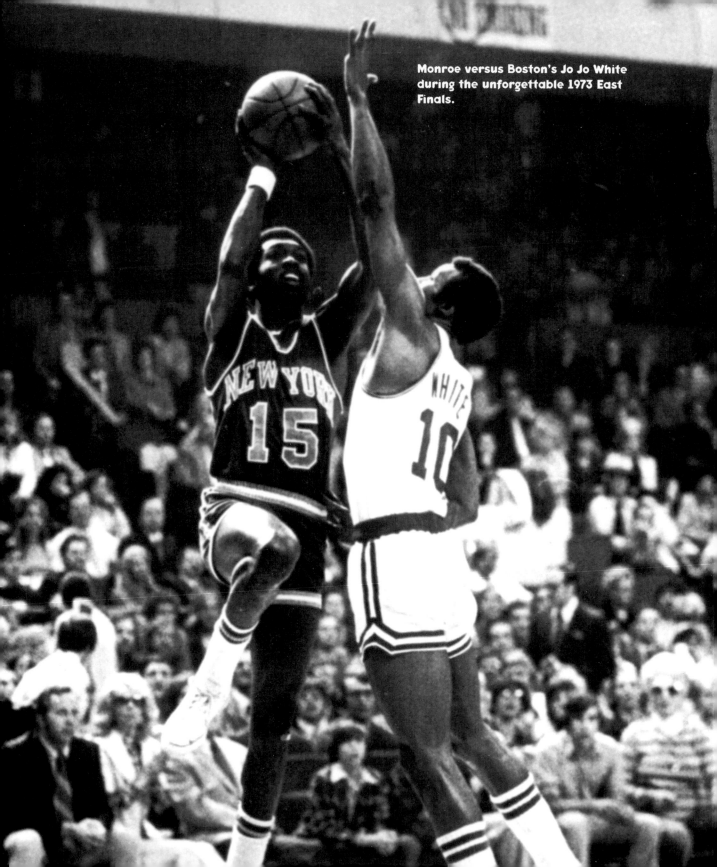

Monroe versus Boston's Jo Jo White during the unforgettable 1973 East Finals.

Red took over. And from that, I gained even more respect for him.

Earl Monroe: I basically came in and tried to make the other guys feel comfortable with me. That's how I approached that whole [first] year. When I got there, I told Red that Dick Barnett's the starter and I didn't want to rock the boat, and that I wanted to earn my way in.

I was hurt coming in. I had developed the bone spurs earlier, and when I came in I told Red that I thought I'd need an operation. He said that I couldn't really get it now because aside from them just trading for me, Willis wasn't playing, and so I should wait until after the season.

Dean Meminger: When I came in the fall of '71, Earl wasn't there yet. I was the heir apparent to Dick Barnett. In fact, I had a great, great exhibition season. But I realized it was a job I'd have to earn. I'd have to earn playing time. And it was somewhat disappointing, after playing well in preseason, coming off the bench and really not getting much playing time. Then we acquired Earl. And then I had to find another niche. But I'd always been the type of player who could adjust. It made me a better all-around player. Although, if I had gone someplace else I could have started. Probably would have played a lot longer, too.

Bob McAdoo: Earl Monroe was a childhood hero of mine. I saw him at Winston-Salem State because I had grown up in Greensboro, North Carolina, about 30 minutes away. I'd go to the CIAA games when Earl was averaging about 41 or 42 points a game, and he'd play against North Carolina A&T. He'd be spinning and twirling and everything, and then we'd go to the park the next day and try to do the same things. So it was an honor to play with Earl.

Walt Frazier: He's nothing like his image on the court. On the court he was very flamboyant, but very quiet off the court. I'm just the opposite.

Mike Glenn: We went up to Harlem to eat one time. We had a nice meal, and afterward, me being a mathematician, I figured out a 15 percent tip to the penny. Earl left a tip that was as much as his lunch. And he said, "Anytime you come here, you know

these are nice people and you should tip well." And that's stayed with me. Lots of times I'll leave a lot more than the 15 percent, because of Earl.

Earl Monroe: When I got there, Red said, "Well, we've got you now, so we won't have any letdowns in our backcourt." He just said to go out and do what you do, and we'll be OK. That's what he always said: "We'll be OK." I told him that one thing I didn't want to do was cause any conflicts. I knew Barnett was the starter, and I wasn't looking to start right away. I said that I'd earn my way. And Red was very straightforward, and I respected him for that.

If I was apprehensive coming to the Knicks, the only apprehension I had was with Red. Because in the [1971] All-Star Game, Red was coaching and Clyde and I started. I hit three baskets, and then Red sat me down and I didn't play again until the second half! So I was very apprehensive in that respect; but as far as anything else, I was cool with it.

Walt Frazier: When Earl came to the Knicks, the big thing I learned from him is that he always had one more dribble, and great footwork. I used to watch him in practice and how he'd maneuver around. That really helped me with the ball, always being able to do something with that last dribble to get a shot off.

Bill Bradley: The point is that Earl understood he was in a different situation. He fit in with the team, and he played team basketball because he knows the game so well and he has such great character. So he was a real stabilizing force in many ways, as well as bringing tremendous ability to the team.

With both knees aflame with tendinitis, Reed played just 11 games in 1971–72, then shut it down for the rest of the season. Lucas excelled as the starting center, while Monroe, plagued all year by bone spurs in his left foot, struggled in a sixth-man role.

After a 48-win regular season, the Knicks defeated Baltimore in six games and a rebuilt Boston team in five to win the Eastern Conference title. In the Finals, they faced a Lakers squad that had blitzed the NBA for a then-record 69 wins, including 33 straight in midseason, an all-time record.

For one game, it didn't matter, as the Knicks routed the Lakers 114–92 in Game 1 behind 29 points from Bradley. But then the Lakers ran off four straight wins, with Chamberlain winning series MVP honors and Gail Goodrich pouring in 25.6 points, much of it against a hobbled Monroe, to finally give Los Angeles its first NBA title.

Willis Reed: My left knee started up, and I had tendinitis in both knees. And we talked about surgery, and then I had the surgery and rehab and all that. I played 11 games, and I just stopped. Because you want to be a part of that. Your life and your career are so short; you're only gonna have it so many days. There are only so many games, and you want to be in as many of them as you can. I went with the team to L.A., and we won the first game and then got swept in the next four. But there was nothing I could do.

Dean Meminger: I started the last game of the championship series in 1972 to stop Goodrich, because he was having his way with Earl. But Gail just went off the deep end. He was killing us, man.

Earl Monroe: I was in a lot of pain, but guys played in pain back in those days. That's just what you did. It was all part of the game. I remember when I was in Baltimore and my ribs were cracked. We were playing against Philadelphia, and their trainer [Al Domenico] said to his team, "Well, if his ribs are really hurting, then go out and hit him in the ribs!" So playing hurt wasn't a big thing. The main thing was how effective you were while playing hurt. And during that [Finals] series, I definitely wasn't effective. That was one of the worst summers I ever had, because I knew I didn't play well. Gail Goodrich ate me up during that whole thing, and my thing was to get back and try to get myself straightened out and try to redeem myself.

Phil Jackson: In that trade, we surprised ourselves. Because Willis goes out, we don't think we have a chance. But we get to the Finals that year. Obviously, it was the Lakers' year; they had won 33 games in a row. They had a great team. We won the first game, [but] lost an overtime game at home that would have changed it for us. We built on some-

thing, and with Willis coming back we really felt we were gonna be good [in 1972–73].

Even as the defending Eastern Conference Champions, the Knicks were not considered favorites to repeat as the 1972–73 season opened. Boston, now completely rebuilt with the likes of Dave Cowens, Jo Jo White, Paul Silas, Don Chaney, and veteran superstar John Havlicek, was coming off a 56-win season and seemed poised to dominate the East.

The Celtics were young and fast, two things the Knicks weren't. When the 1972–73 season started, Lucas and DeBusschere were 32; Reed was 30, with knees that were much older; Barnett was 36 and seeing his playing time diminish; and Monroe was coming off heel surgery.

Unlike the prior year, the Knicks had made no moves regarding frontline players. The reserve unit had changed almost completely from the Minutemen of 1970, and with the exception of Jackson, all were young and untested. The core of the team, of course, was still intact, only now it was three years older, and the rest of the league had caught up. More and more, 1972–73 was looking like their last shot. And, despite what they had done the year before, none of it would mean anything if the Cap'n wasn't healthy.

Willis Reed: Basically, the media had written me off. And I'm not sure if the club hadn't written me off. They were on the fence because they didn't know if I was ever gonna come back. But in my mind, I'm still young enough to play this game. I'm not over the hill. And my decision was to go to Oklahoma City to deal with Dr. Donald O'Donohue, who eventually told me that I had a bad case of tendinitis that would take a long process, a long rehab, to deal with. And he told me that some days I'd wake up and feel great, but [even so] you don't need to run or jump on this leg at all. You need to stay with the rehab until we get to a certain point.

Red Holzman: We knew he would be a contributor, but not as much as in the past, and there were gonna be a lot of blank days without him. When you don't have a guy like Willis Reed, you're really missing a lot. If Willis were able to walk on the court, he'd be a contributor.

Willis Reed: Once you go away from the game, boy, let me tell you something. You don't realize. You stay away from the game for a year or so and it becomes foreign to you. Your reflexes aren't the same. You can see things happening, but you can't react to them. There are a lot of things about the game that change when you're not doing it every day. And that was one of Red's philosophies. He'd say, "I can't give you big guys more than a day off. Two days is too many."

Dean Meminger: We brought in four rookies that [1972–73] season: Harthorne Wingo, Henry Bibby, Tom Riker, and John Gianelli. Those were four new faces that we didn't have the year before.

Red Holzman: Meminger, we felt, was a hell of a defensive player. He was a smart player who knew the game very well, a New York type of guy.

Bibby had just come from a great, great team at UCLA, and he was probably one of the best guys in camp I've ever seen. Nobody gave him a chance to make that team. What was he, 5'11"? Plus, he was a fourth-round pick. But he just played so well and did everything so well, we had to find room for the guy.

Dean Meminger: Bibby added something to the team because he had a great outside shot. Gianelli was another center we could use, another big body. Because we weren't really big, we were relatively small.

Red Holzman: Gianelli was a second-round draft pick from Houston, and they couldn't make a deal with him. Arthur Morse was his agent. We always liked him, and when we had a chance to get him, we got him. And when he came into camp, the first few days, we thought we had another Bill Russell the way he was blocking shots. Of course, he wasn't Bill Russell, but he came in and did a good job.

Cal Ramsey: What I'd say was, "Harthorne Nathaniel Wingo Jr. And Bob, Wingy is doin' it good!"

Dean Meminger: Red liked Harthorne. There was a place on that team for him. He was a young guy who had some talent. Not in the structured

sense, but Red liked him. He thought he showed some potential. He was a project.

Cal Ramsey: Wingy was not a bad ballplayer. He wasn't a very disciplined player, but he was a very talented player. He could jump. He could score. He wasn't a good shooter, but he could run. And he had a very catchy name: Harthorne Nathaniel Wingo Jr. I think his name, and his whole style of play, was unorthodox.

Red Holzman: Wingo was a great kid. Everybody loved him. He went down to the Eastern League, in Allentown, and did well. When we got the chance, we brought him up. This guy appreciated everything that was happening to him. He had been pushing a hand truck in the garment center, you know? And all of a sudden he's making about $50,000. In fact, I think he and Bibby had a little feud. Bibby was gonna get 50, and I think Wingo wanted about 51.

Mel Davis: Wingo was a very introverted guy, a nice guy who worked hard. We both got there early for practice and stayed late. We came from opposite ends of the spectrum, so to speak. He came from the Eastern League, and I came from St. John's. And we were both trying to get some consistent playing time to remain on the team, but it was difficult.

Cal Ramsey: A really, really nice guy. Very humble. Very happy to be where he was. And I think the fans took to him because of his style and his name.

Red Holzman: It was very important to us to have guys do things in practice that pushed these other guys–keep them in shape and make sure they don't get too cocky and all that business.

Phil Jackson: We had a pretty good match of how people were gonna play with each other. Earl's in the backcourt with Walt, Dean Meminger's coming off the bench as a guard, I'm coming off the bench as a forward, and Jerry Lucas and Willis are splitting time. And we've got young players who can help us in critical situations, like Henry Bibby and John Gianelli. It's a team that feels confident that they can win.

Willis Reed: We were a veteran, veteran, veteran, veteran team, that group of guys I played with. And

Reed got the upper hand on Wilt Chamberlain in the 1973 Finals.

the first time we won, it was fun. Because we were all young and grew up together. But on that 1973 team, we had seven guys who were an All-Star at one time or another in their career. You ain't gonna find that ever again in the NBA.

It was just one game, one out of 82 that season, one Saturday night at the Garden. November 18, 1972. But it was a game that symbolized not just a season, but an era.

Trailing Milwaukee by 18 points, 86–68, midway through the fourth quarter, the Knicks ran off the game's last 19 points to defeat the Bucks, 87–86, surviving a last-second close-in miss by Abdul-Jabbar that sent the Garden into a frenzy. It was a game few would forget, least of all a young Milwaukee assistant coach who, 10 years later, would find himself guiding the Knicks.

Hubie Brown: In the last five minutes plus, we never scored. Here we are with the best record in the league, and we could not close with Kareem Abdul-Jabbar, who's in the middle of three MVPs in four years, and Oscar Robertson, on our team. And it was a great lesson. Any NBA basketball fan in New York *swears* he was at that game. The noise was deafening.

Cal Ramsey: Two things stand out from that game: The way Willis was able to move Kareem around, and the fact that Lucius Allen, who shot 72 percent from the free throw line, went to the line during that streak and missed two free throws. That could have broken the run. I saw Lucius recently and told him, and he yelled, "Don't remind me of that!"

Hubie Brown: When Lucius Allen goes to the line and misses the foul shots, Earl Monroe makes the basket to put them in front. But we still have the last shot. We take the ball out on the side, and the noise was such that you couldn't even hear yourself think in the huddle. We went to Kareem, and he missed the shot. It was really a devastating loss.

Red Holzman: There's no pressure on us because we're 18 down with about five-something to go. So we just kept playing, and things started falling into place. Now there's pressure on them. And the thing even went down to the end when Kareem missed the last shot, a shot that was makeable. So everything fell into place as we saw it changing. I

always felt that you've got no place to go anyway. You can't go to the movies until the game's over. You can't go out to dinner until the game's over. So you might as well give it your best shot until it's over. Then you go home, and if you win you're happy, if you lose you're sad. Then you have a couple of drinks and get ready for the next game.

Hubie Brown: I talk about that game a lot, because it was a fantastic finish by New York. The fans were making so much noise that you swore that the basket and backboard were moving every time we shot. It was great execution by the Knicks, and a perfect example of why you never give up in a game. That's why you play. A perfect example of why you never walk out of an NBA game when two great teams are playing one another.

As the season progressed, opposing teams found their Garden visits doubly intimidating. Now they had to contend not only with an increasingly effective Knicks team and the NBA's most rabid fans, but also with a mysterious figure adorned in a variety of outlandish hats, capes, and jumpsuits, who would moonwalk, boogie, and high-step along the baselines before putting his dreaded "Whammy!" on the opposition.

His real name was Marvin Cooper, but no one ever called him that.

Walt Frazier: Dancing Harry came to the team when Earl did. Prior to that, he was the Bullets' guy. I remember we were going to kick his butt because we found him near our locker room at halftime one night. But people accepted him once he came to New York, because of Earl.

Earl Monroe: We first met at Lenny Moore's restaurant in Baltimore. At the restaurant, they used to have a jukebox. Harry would play Sly and the Family Stone tunes on the jukebox, and he would sing to them. He'd lip-synch. That's how we got to know him. At first, he never said he was gonna do anything at the Civic Center or anything like that. See, Baltimore is a small town, and we knew a lot of the folks who used to sit down front.

Dancing Harry: Earl and I would shoot pool in the back room of the club. I was a better player than he was. I used to do a lot of imitating of singers' voices. Sly was very hot back then, and a lot of people would play Sly and Marvin Gaye. Back then, I had the bell-bottoms and the whole Sly outfit, and I would just dance around the bar like Sly. It drew a lot of attention. People used to say, "You should go on stage with that."

Earl Monroe: So then, all of a sudden, Harry started showing up down at the games. Then one night he started dancing and putting hexes on the other team. Back in those days, security wasn't what it is today, so it was a novelty. They had the guy in Detroit who used to dance in the stands all the time, and a couple of other places had people who were somewhat like mascots. So now we had an added attraction in Dancing Harry, and it just built from there.

Dancing Harry: When Earl got traded [to New York], I tried to start dancing again the next year [1971–72]. The Bullets still gave me tickets; that's all they were giving me. The crowd was dead without Earl, so I waited until the Knicks were in the playoffs. I told my mom I was going to the store, and I got in the car and went straight up to New York. I caught Earl before he went into the game. I had my brother-in-law with me, and I asked Earl for a couple of tickets. I thought it was like Baltimore, where it was very easy to get tickets. "Oh, my God!" he says. "Tickets? Why didn't you let me know? The tickets are gone!" So I didn't get in until halftime. I went in, and the Knicks management had already told me they didn't need me. I had been a thorn in their side in the previous year, when the Bullets beat them. So the Knicks weren't too happy with me.

Earl Monroe: It wasn't like I brought him to New York. At first, he'd come up when the Bullets played in New York; he broke out on the floor and had a big audience there. After the trade, he just appeared in New York all the time, and he became the darling of the city. He was being sponsored by clothing companies, and then he started with the cape and the big hats. It was unbelievable.

Dancing Harry: In 1973, I was at most of the home games, especially the big games, with Kareem or

Boston or the Lakers. I always made those big ones. I had a good relationship with the crowds, and I learned how to work a crowd real well and work with the organist. I had little gestures. I'd act like I was telling the players things, but I wasn't telling them anything.

[In 1973–74] they gave me a typewritten letter that said, "Thanks, but no thanks." I was welcome to the games, but they no longer needed my services. Prior to that, there was an article just before the [1973] Celtics series, "Knicks Brass Not Wild About Harry." I took that to Ned Irish, because I felt as though I was a great part of their winning. They weren't the biggest, they weren't the strongest, they weren't the fastest by any means. So there was some magic there that year, and I felt I was a great help to them. So I took that article to Irish, and he told me, "Don't believe what you read, Harry. That's just the reporters writing." Little did I know that the next year, they would give me that letter. I should have believed it then. Walt Frazier used to say, "We win the games, and Harry gets all the press."

Earl Monroe: Harry had a nice little career with that. First he came up from Baltimore to New York, then he was doing stuff in the Catskills. He was in Indiana with the Pacers.

Dancing Harry: The Knicks organization never gave me a penny. The first organization that paid me was the Indiana Pacers.

The Knicks invited me up there for the [2003] reunion [of the 1973 team]. They paid my way. I went there; I had a cape made up with Earl's number on both sides, and a Big Apple. I think it cost me about three bills. I was kind of pissed off that I wasn't formally introduced. They introduced everyone but me.

Earl Monroe: Harry got married about three or four years ago. He called me to invite me to the wedding. I couldn't go, but I sent him a little something. He's still living in Baltimore, so he's kind of come full circle.

Dancing Harry: Every time I go back to New York, I get chills. I went to a Knicks game about six years ago. I had my cape on, and John McEnroe asked me if I was going to perform. I remember so many fans. One time when I was in the Garden, Fred

Dancing Harry does his thing.
Photo courtesy of Gene Kappock/
New York Daily News.

Astaire tapped me and told me, "Go out there! Go out there!" I mean, Fred Astaire! Can you imagine?

The 1972–73 season was about establishing a legacy.

Willis Reed: In the regular season, a young team can go and play and be successful. But when you get to the playoffs, you're gonna win because you're a veteran. You're gonna win because you've got maturity. You're gonna win because you know how to win. You're gonna win because somebody's got the balls to take the last shot and not worry about it. Those are the elements that make a team good, and that's why getting Lucas and Monroe meant so much.

Bill Bradley: For me, the '73 championship was more enjoyable than the one in '70. In '70, it was about, "Can you get to the top?" In '73, it was, "Can you *stay* at the top?" The team had changed and was clearly in a strong position. Jerry Lucas and Earl Monroe had arrived, and they were great complementary personalities and talents. It was just a true joy to play with them. The first championship was intensity and pressure incarnate, and pure success. The second championship was more pure joy, because we had the experience. You knew exactly what to do and how you were going to do it. You still had the physical equipment that allowed you to do it, and you had an extremely meshing team situation both on the court and off the court.

Willis Reed: I don't think I could have come back and played, I don't think we could have won that second championship, if Lucas hadn't come. I really believe that. And I also think, getting Earl . . . Those two guys were the two elements that changed our team because we needed some more veteran players.

Dean Meminger: Jerry Lucas started over the majority of the season when Willis was hurt, and Jerry and I had this chemistry. Backdoor play, "see" play, and all that.

Willis Reed: Lucas and I could play together. Hell, there were a lot of games when I wasn't there. And when I first came back in 1972–73, it was a struggle. That was the hardest year of basketball I've ever played.

Walt Frazier: We were injury-prone. We had guys in and out of the lineup. Ultimately, that helped us because, at the end of the season, we started getting guys back, and we gathered momentum going into the playoffs. Those guys were rested. We knew we were healthy, and we just went on from there.

Willis Reed: I didn't play good basketball. I played inconsistently all year long, and that's why Lucas was such a significant part of it. But by the time we got to the playoffs, I was rolling again. I had the belief that I could get it done. But it was a real struggle.

The Knicks finished the season with a 57–25 mark, the fourth-best record in the league but still 11 games behind the division-winning Celtics, who went a staggering 68–14.

And after beating Baltimore in the first playoff round, the Knicks drew the Celtics in the Eastern Conference Finals.

Willis Reed: I had seen enough playoff games to know that the best team in the regular season isn't always the best team in the playoffs. I knew that we were a very good playoff team. We were playoff-ready; we were a veteran, very mature group of guys. It wasn't the first time we'd been to the big dance.

Don Chaney: That was the best Celtics team I ever played for. That team was unbelievable. We had great balance. We had speed. We had size. We just zoomed past teams and ran them down. We just had an unbelievable confidence level that year. We felt it was going to be our year.

Dean Meminger: Some people thought that was Boston's greatest team. I mean, 68 and 14!

Don Chaney: One thing that set us apart from the rest of the league was that we were required to wear suits and ties to games, and nobody else did. So if you want to compare the Knicks and the Celtics, that's it. I remember John Gianelli walking onto a plane with jeans and a T-shirt with holes in them. And we're sitting there with coats and ties. See, normally what we would do is have a back-to-back deal. We'd play in New York, then right after the game we'd fly to Boston. Now, the good thing about that, and something that really helped our arrogance, is that we always went first class. So when we left New York, win or lose, we'd be in first class. And the Knicks had to pass us to get to the back. So that was really a rewarding thing, even if you had lost.

In Boston, the Celtics routed the Knicks by 26 points in Game 1. Three nights later, in New York, the Knicks returned the favor with a 33-point win.

In Game 3, Frazier scored 23 points in a 98–91 Knicks win that would have far-reaching consequences. In the fourth quarter, Havlicek ran into a DeBusschere pick and suffered a strained right trapezius, or shoulder, muscle, an injury that would sideline him for Game 4 and limit his effectiveness for the rest of the series.

Leading two games to one, the Knicks had their own injury problems, as Monroe would miss a game as well, with a sore hip.

Game 4 was played on a broiling-hot Easter Sunday in New York.

Phil Jackson: I'd had a real good series against Boston. Red left me in for a whole half for a game up in Boston where we beat them. Some people don't realize this, but that's a team that went 68–14 that year. They were really good. And we were angry at Phoenix a little bit for giving them Paul Silas. But we were able to beat them up there, and then Havlicek gets this injury and the series gets into a tit for tat.

Walt Frazier: I just remember it went back and forth. I was exhausted. It was a quintessential game between the Knicks and Celtics in those days.

Phil Jackson: This game is on Easter Sunday and ends up where our whole team, it seems, is drawn out and fatigued. John Gianelli has to play big toward the end of the game and has a couple of blocks. It didn't win the series for us, but it put us in a position where we're up 3–1 with the ability to knock them out.

In a war of attrition in which five players fouled out, the Knicks prevailed in double overtime, 117–110. With Reed and Meminger among those fouled out, Holzman started Frazier, DeBusschere, Jackson, Bibby, and Gianelli in the second overtime. Jackson scored four key points, while Gianelli drew a sixth and final foul on Cowens, the

league's reigning MVP. Frazier finished with 37 points– 30 in the second half and overtimes–while DeBusschere added 22. The game ended with an enraged Boston coach Tom Heinsohn berating officials Jack Madden and Jake O'Donnell all the way into the center court tunnel.

The Knicks led the series, three games to one. Now they had to win just one more game.

Havlicek returned to score 18 points in Game 5 in Boston. Bradley's jumper with 16 seconds left gave New York a one-point lead. But after Jo Jo White missed, Silas grabbed the rebound, drew a foul on DeBusschere, and knocked down two free throws with seven seconds left. The Celtics won, 98–97.

And then, before a stunned Garden crowd, the Knicks collapsed in the fourth quarter of Game 6. Cowens scored 26 points; White added 25. Celtics 110, Knicks 100. The series was tied.

Willis Reed: We had them [Boston]. We had them by the nuts, pardon my French. And you get mad because you know . . .

We lose that game [Game 5] because we got a lead, and Paul [Silas] gets an offensive rebound and then he scores, and we lose the game. DeBusschere was guarding Havlicek, which was not a normal rotation play. Lucas guarded Silas, I had Cowens, and Clyde had Jo Jo. And they had a screen for Jo Jo. Jo Jo comes off the screen; Clyde defends the shot really well. But Silas gets the damn offensive rebound and we lose the game.

Friday [before Game 6], everybody called me and said, "Don't worry. We never lose on Friday night at home." And we get beat by 10! I'm thinking, "Holy shit! At home?" So now we're really fucking pissed off. Because we played this great young team and we had them by the balls.

Now it would come down to Game 7, in Boston, on Sunday afternoon, April 29. And every single member of the Knicks knew that, through their long and storied history, the Celtics had never lost the seventh game of a playoff series. Ever.

Bill Bradley: After we lost the sixth game, Ned Irish came to practice and basically told us we were

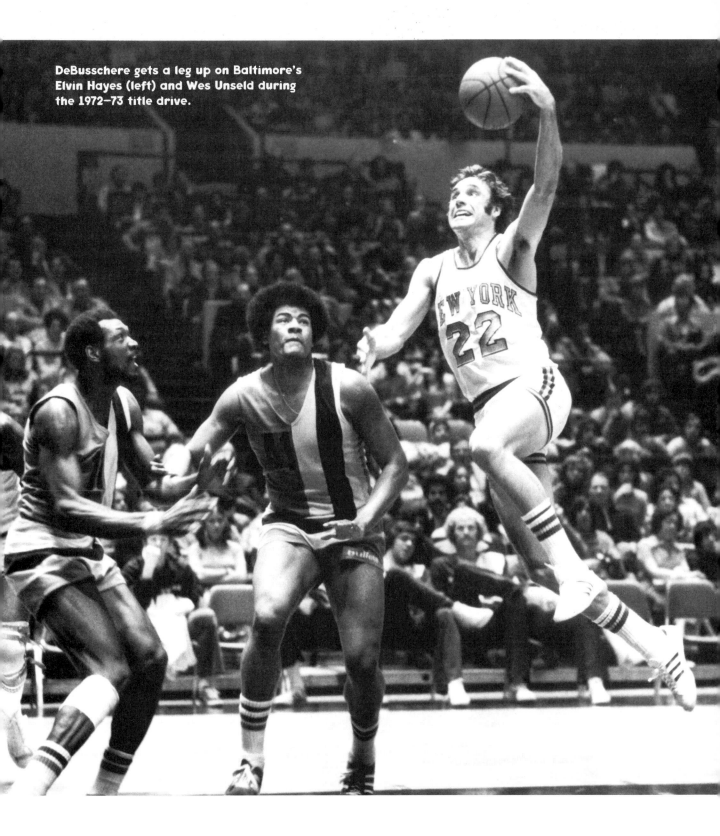

DeBusschere gets a leg up on Baltimore's Elvin Hayes (left) and Wes Unseld during the 1972–73 title drive.

all a bunch of bums. He said he didn't expect us to do anything in the seventh game, and that we had a chance to win it in the Garden and we didn't. Of course, that was all psychological buildup.

Dean Meminger: The consensus was that it was all over for us. No one in the locker room believed that.

Walt Frazier: And everybody said it was over. I couldn't make people believe otherwise. "Nah, you guys blew it."

Phil Jackson: [After Game 6] I had my local rat pack—we called ourselves the Muchachos. We met at a bar after the game. And they all said, "You guys are still gonna win." I said, "Hey, you know Boston's never lost a seventh game." And they said, "Doesn't matter. You guys have the poise."

Red Holzman: There was a feeling of, it's gonna be tough. It wasn't a feeling of, well, we can't go up there and win. It was just a feeling that it was gonna be tough.

Phil Jackson: Now we get up there on Saturday night and we're watching film. And Boston's setting a high screen-and-roll for Jo Jo White, and he's breaking us down. And Dean Meminger's kind of whining, "No one's talking to me about getting help on the screen," and such. So Red said in his acerbic way, "I don't give a damn about the screen. Find a way to get through the screen and stop this guy. Don't bitch about the screen, just get the job done." That night was an impossible night; they pulled the alarm a couple of times at the hotel we were staying at, which was a typical Boston tactic.

Dean Meminger: I had one of those nights where I didn't get any sleep.

Willis Reed: We get there on Sunday, and it's a beautiful day. I'm getting on the elevator to go into the Boston Garden, and who do I get on the elevator with? Mr. Ned Irish. "Mr. Irish! How are you doing today? Beautiful day, isn't it?" And he's all mumbling back. I figured he's not in a very good mood.

Walt Frazier: And whenever you go to Boston Garden, they play these tricks on you. You get there and you can't find the key to get into the locker room. You're in the locker room and you can't

find the guy with tape, or towels. They had these high windows, and you know it's gonna be a hundred degrees or zero, depending on whether or not you can open or close the windows. Well, this particular time they put us in a cubbyhole. They put us in a locker room we'd never been in before. The tall guys had to bend over to walk around. The training table took up the whole room. We really got upset with that, and I think that propelled us to the win.

Don Chaney: John Havlicek really shouldn't have played in the final game, because he had to shoot with his left hand, and he's a right-handed player.

Earl Monroe: I remember Havlicek going left—*finally* going left—because he couldn't go right.

Jerry Lucas: It was a feeling of, we had to do it. There are so many clichés that can be thrown out about things in sports, and you can say all of those things that you want. But there was a collective confidence in our team. We felt good about each other; we felt good about our chances. We felt we could win that game even though we were battling history and everything else you could think of as far as the great Boston Celtics heritage was concerned. We felt good, we felt confident, we felt we could win.

With White scoring six points and drawing two quick fouls on Monroe, the Celtics led 22-19 after the first quarter.

Willis Reed: Jo Jo was kicking our ass. And Red finally made the decision to take Earl out and put Deano on him.

Dean Meminger: We were down by three after the first quarter. The normal rotation was that I'd come in for Earl around the start of the second quarter. Now, Jo Jo was killing us. So Earl and Clyde were having deep trouble with Jo Jo.

I learned to play people's tendencies. And they had hand-checking then. So one of the things I did with Jo Jo was hand-check him on the right and make him go left.

Red Holzman: When we got up there, we did certain things early, like pressing, picking up, and putting pressure on them defensively—constantly,

constantly. And it worked out. Now, you can get buried that way, too. But it worked.

Dean Meminger: During the timeout, in between the first and second quarter, I checked in, came back to the huddle, and said, "Look, we got 'em. We got 'em just where we want 'em. And I got Jo Jo. He's mine." And I knew if we could lock down Jo Jo, we'd win. And my whole focus coming into the game was, "I'm gonna be on you like . . . " I held him, but more than anything else, I clogged up their offense.

Willis Reed: And Deano tied his ass up. I mean, Deano got it done for us. And sure enough, we did something that had never been done before in the history of the Boston Celtics, and that's beat them in a seventh game.

Dean Meminger: See, I played Boston's style. I ran. I played good defense. Boston pressed, and they ran. Jo Jo and Chaney were a little younger than Earl and Clyde, and they'd make them waltz the ball up. Jo Jo and I talked about this later. I'd tell Jo Jo that Chaney can't press me. Sorry. So I would break down the press. It wasn't our game design. The Knicks' game design was a half-court structure, walking it up. But I'm breaking down the press. Because I'd make the intelligent play, Red didn't say anything. I'd break it down, and I'd have Lucas and Bill Bradley on the wings. So without setting up a structured play, I would make a play. And they couldn't figure that out.

Heinsohn then said, "Let's just get back on defense and not press." But their whole success–winning 68 games–was based on pressing people. But it didn't work against us. When I was in the game, my whole attitude was, "These guys can't press me." So going through the season, we matched up very well with Boston. Our record didn't indicate it, but we did.

Meminger played the entire second quarter, scoring nine points to White's two, as the Knicks rallied to take a 45–40 lead at the half. Then they began the second half by outscoring Boston 37–22, with Frazier scoring 13 of the 37 points during the run, to blow the game open. Frazier finished with 25 points and 10 rebounds, while the injured Havlicek went just 1-for-6 from the field for four points. Boston shot just 31 percent in the second half. Knicks 94, Celtics 78.

Red Holzman: They had beaten us on Friday in New York. And before the seventh game, I got [referee supervisor] John Nucatola under the stands, and I called him every name in the book. I bawled the shit out of him and I said, "All I want is a fair shake, blah, blah, blah." Then we got into the game, and it looked like we were getting a fair shake; we were doing very well. And I'm thinking, "Gee, it's great that I got him to understand." I was taking credit for doing all that. Then I find out later that John had his hearing aid turned off and never heard me. Because if he had, he'd probably have thrown me out the window.

Don Chaney: Once Havlicek went down, our confidence was damaged a little bit. I don't think we had the same amount of confidence. But I thought he played extremely well considering that he was playing, basically, with one arm.

Bill Bradley: After the seventh game, I'd never seen Red as happy as he was after that game. He was throwing his fists in the locker room; he was being emotional in a way that he never was before and never was after. So that was clearly the big series.

Jerry Lucas: They had a great team, and we had a great team, and it went right down to the end, right to the wire. It was one of the premier series of my life, and it sticks out in my mind more than the championship series, although winning the championship was sort of the crowning jewel of my career.

Don Chaney: Red Auerbach went out of his way to make sure that everyone in the league knew that we were different. You are a different group of guys, that's why you win. You're different. And that mentality was branded into your brain, so when you walked on the court you walked out thinking, "I'm a different guy. I'm better than you. That's why we win." So when we went back for that final game in Boston, even though we were crippled, the confidence level was there, and we knew that we didn't lose those kinds of games. That's what made it so devastating to come away with the loss.

Phil Jackson: Dean goes out and has this incredible ballgame. There are fights in the stands and everything. But we controlled the game, and it was a sound beating. By this time, we know we can beat L.A.

Marv Albert: The big deal of that season was the Boston series, with the double-overtime game. I think that was the real series, beating that team. Boston was very good.

John Andariese: My heart pounded out of my chest when they won that game. I thought, "Holy smokes, we're going to Los Angeles!"

Willis Reed: When the Lakers finished up in the West, they said that they wanted the Knicks. They didn't want to play the Celtics. And after it was all over someone asked me, "Well, Willis, what do you think of all this?" I said, "Well, I'm happy to know that the Lakers wanted us and they got us."

From 69 wins in their championship season, the Lakers dropped to 60 wins in 1972–73, then defeated Chicago and Golden State to reach the Finals again. But West was weeks away from turning 35, and Chamberlain, playing what turned out to be his final season, was 36. The previous year, the Lakers were untouchable. This year, they could be had.

Dean Meminger: The L.A. series was anticlimactic. Just like it was anticlimactic the year before, when they beat us. But I think the series that defined us that year was the Boston series. By the time we went into L.A., it was, "We're gonna beat these guys."

Earl Monroe: The whole thing in a nutshell was trying to get back to the Finals to try and prove myself. I had a terrible summer, and nobody had to say, "Well, Gail ate you up." I knew that myself. I had never been one to delude myself into not seeing things. I've always been my own worst critic. When we got back to the Finals, it was a matter of making sure I made a statement. And by the end of the series, I thought I did.

Dean Meminger: When we got out to L.A., Wilt came off the court after practice, barefooted,

going to his Bentley parked inside the Forum. And the Big Fella's saying, "Hey, hey, Dream. Hey man, come here. I want to tell you, man, if it wasn't for you, they wouldn't be out here." I said, "Thanks, Big Fella." Then we walked out to the court and he said, "By the way, you see this purple in here [in the key]? You'll be all right if you keep your little ass out of there [the lane]. You can have anything outside, but don't be coming in here getting yourself killed." I said, "OK, Big Fella. . . . I'll be back!"

John Andariese: When we went out to Los Angeles, Marv knew a New York guy who lived out there, and he fixed us up on the off days between the games. So we did what New York guys would do: we found out where there was a basket and we played half-court. Marv, myself, the guy Marv knew, and some other guys that he knew. And this guy just flipped out because the Knicks were in L.A. and he knew Marv and all that stuff.

Red Holzman: I knew after that [the Boston series] that we'd beat the Lakers. I was never the type of guy that figured ahead that we'd beat somebody. And even when we lost the first game, I still figured that we'd beat the hell out of them. And we did.

In five games, it was done.

After the Lakers won the series opener, the Knicks ran off four straight wins, reversing the prior year's scenario. Bradley scored 26 points in Game 2 at the Forum, then the Knicks' defense held the Lakers to 38 percent shooting and 83 points to win Game 3. DeBusschere poured in 33 points with 14 rebounds to halt a furious Lakers rally in Game 4 at the Garden, giving the Knicks a three-games-to-one lead.

With the Knicks leading by 14 points with just eight minutes left in Game 5 at Los Angeles, DeBusschere sprained his ankle on a layup, his only points of the game. The Lakers knocked the lead down to 4, but Monroe capped a 23-point night–and a postseason during which he shot 53 percent–by scoring 8 points in the game's final 2:15.

Around 1:00 A.M. New York time, the Knicks delighted a TV audience of insomniacs by running off the Forum floor with their second NBA Championship, 102–93.

Dean Meminger: It was amazing. They were 69 and 13 the year before, but they were a completely different team the year after. Age caught up with them.

Red Holzman: I just never had any doubts that we'd win, and I'm never that way. I was always very, very cautious. I never wanted the guys to get into saying the wrong thing to give the other team an edge. As much as you can scoff at that, I wanted to set an example of being cautious and saying the right thing. My guys at that time, they knew what they had to say because they were schooled pretty well at it. But, myself, I told my daughter and my wife that we were going to kick their ass.

Jerry Lucas: It really doesn't matter about your age or which level you play. To have the opportunity to be the best and work hard, feel that you've accomplished something nobody else could, is just an amazing feeling. That, really, was the final exclamation point of my career. And I don't think I was more excited over any championship I ever won than at that particular time in my life.

Earl Monroe: I've always said to myself, "I've done it. There's no sense in remembering it; I've already done it." And I've always lived my life like that. Now, you try and remember back to things and such, but that's the attitude I've always had. It was always a feeling that I don't have to tell anybody how good I am; look at what I did. I've always had that kind of attitude.

Dean Meminger: Willis really helped us that series because without him, we'd have nobody holding onto the Big Fella. Willis came back after not being with us the year before. But Clyde also had a great series. And I still think they should have been co-MVPs. Willis deserved it, but Clyde also deserved it.

George Kalinsky: At practice on Wednesday [the day before Game 5], Bradley and DeBusschere started pitching a tennis ball from one end of the gym to the other, trying to see who was the better pitcher. And DeBusschere, of course, had played for the White Sox. They made a little square on the wall, like a strike zone, and started pitching to it. And I'm going back to Phil Jackson playing

volleyball three years earlier [when he was on the injured list] and thinking that if Red was really concerned about guys hurting themselves, here it was.

Dean Meminger: The series didn't dictate that I play a lot. And I think Earl had a message to send to Gail Goodrich. He had a great series. He was healthy, where he hadn't been the year before. And I think he learned to be a better defensive player by then.

Walt Frazier: Earl had a great series on Goodrich. The year before, it had been the other way around. Earl had been hobbling.

George Kalinsky: Before Game 5, Bradley comes over to me and says, "We're gonna win." And I had been concerned that they were so tired from the road trip and all. He said, "Not only are we gonna win tonight, but when we win, watch where the Captain is, because I'm jumping in his arms." And that's what happened.

Earl Monroe: When the final gun went off, I looked at my roommate Dean, and I said, "Dean, this shit's over with, man. Let's go get some room service." One of the things that I'm not is, I'm not the most excitable person. And Dean and I went back to the room, got room service, looked at TV, and went to sleep. Today, when I see all the hoopla and the euphoria of winning, it's kind of funny to me. And everybody does it now; it's the thing to do. Back then, it was great, your first championship and all.

Marv Albert: What sticks out from 1973 was that, winning it in L.A., I think even they were surprised at the ease with which it happened. But there was no real hoopla. I remember being in the dressing room afterward, and there were something like three or four reporters in there. We came back the next day, and there was some attention at the airport with the TV crews. And then it kind of went away. It means more now when you look back.

To this day, the Knicks of the early seventies–the Willis Reed, Clyde Frazier, Bill Bradley, Dave DeBusschere, Earl Monroe, Dick Barnett, Phil Jackson Knicks–remain the standard bearer by which all Knicks teams are measured.

The rainbow's end: game ball in hand, series MVP Reed races to the locker room after the 1973 title clincher in Los Angeles. Lucas is right behind.

Dean Meminger: My life is affected [by that] to the extent that they haven't won since. So that team is bigger than life. Perhaps bigger than the '69 Mets, because they've won since.

Willis Reed: Once you've won a championship and you've been a part of something that never happened before, that makes you different anyway. The other side of the coin is that all of those guys have stayed involved. A lot of them live in the area. Also, the world was smaller then. Anything that happened back then becomes bigger. For example, when we played on Sundays, there weren't six or seven other games. There was one game on television. All of America saw just one game. Now, you can watch 40 basketball games. So the moment was made bigger because the world was smaller. We got to be a team that was loved all over the place.

Dean Meminger: It was time in history. Joe Namath. Clyde. Most of the Knicks were bachelors. We all lived in the city. None of these guys [today] live in the city. People don't touch them. We were part of the city. People knew where we would be after the game. I lived in the city. Clyde lived in a hotel. Earl lived on 88th. We not only played in Madison Square Garden, we were part of the city.

Mel Davis: When we talk now, when I talk to DeBusschere or Willis, Earl, Clyde, or Barnett, we talk about the fact that we were born 20 years too early. With the amount of money the players are making today, with how the league has changed, and what we'd all be worth now. But then I say, "It's all relative. When we were playing, we thought we were on top and making the best money possible." But everything changes.

Red Holzman: When you're working and doing these things, you're busy and you're never satisfied. You never think they're doing anything right. Then you wake up 10 minutes later and 20 years have gone by, and everyone's telling you how great you were.

Jerry Lucas: I loved playing with that group of players. It was the way basketball should be played. I think that Knicks team—and I stress the word *team*— may have been the greatest team ever assembled for many, many, many reasons. From intelligence and knowledge of the game to unselfishness and all the nuances of the game to never putting themselves above the team, all of those things that you talk about in terms of a team, that team possessed it. They displayed it on a daily basis.

The well-traveled Spencer Haywood—here denying the Bullets' Tom Henderson—arrived in New York in late 1975.

THE LINEUP: Willis Reed; Mel Davis; Jerry Lucas; Bill Bradley; Walt Frazier; Marv Albert; Phil Jackson; Sam Goldaper; Dean Meminger; Bob McAdoo; Mike Glenn; Harvey Araton; Mike Saunders; Earl Monroe; Stan Asofsky; Peter Vecsey; Micheal Ray Richardson.

The championship Knicks were unrecognizable after the 1973–74 season. Reed's knee forced him to call it quits. Lucas retired to embark on his career as a lecturer/educator, while DeBusschere was lured away by a 10-year contract to become general manager of the ABA's New York Nets. Barnett, who had come out of retirement briefly, also hung up his sneakers for good. Barely a year after winning their second NBA Championship, four of the Knicks' most important players were gone. The golden era was over.

Willis Reed: At the end of the year, I was in great shape. And I felt that we maybe had a shot to get there one more time, or get close. And going to training camp in 1973–74, I knew that some of those guys were getting ready to retire, and that we'd have to start changing stuff.

Mel Davis: Willis was having some very difficult times with his legs, and we spent a lot of late nights up talking while he was icing down his knees and ankles.

Willis Reed: You know, my whole basketball career, for some reason, has revolved around the Los Angeles Lakers in a lot of ways. Think about it. I had the big fight with the Lakers, with Rudy. The two championships, we played the Lakers. The finals where I don't play, we played the Lakers. And the injury that was the beginning of the end of my career happened at the Forum. I was running down the court, and I felt something snap in my knee. That was in November of '73. We played in L.A., and then when we went to Seattle, I wound up flying home. Had surgery, and that was basically the beginning of the end.

Jerry Lucas: I had published my first book on memory training, *The Memory Book* [with Harry Lorayne]. I had been involved in memory training, developing and creating learning systems. It had just become more and more important to me. I knew that what I wanted to do with my life was to be involved in education, so I decided to retire early. I still had a couple of years left on my Knicks contract, but I wanted to devote my full-time efforts to creating, writing, developing, and teaching. I'm happy I did that. Right now I'm involved heavily in education. I've had the opportunity to teach hundreds of thousands of teachers over the past few years and make a difference, so I really believe that's what I was destined to do. I had a wonderful career with great memories. But to have the opportunity to touch lives and make a difference in other people's lives is unique and something I wanted to do. That was the reason I left early.

Bill Bradley: They [the transition years] were difficult for me, because you have to make a decision. You invest an awful lot in your teammates. You invest in terms of how your abilities mesh, but also how the personalities mesh, and the friendships, and the trust that you give them. So now we get a whole new cast of characters. I'm older at that point. My skills are OK, but they're not quite what they were. And the question is: Are we going to be able to reconstitute the same thing that we had in those five years? It turns out that we're not able to, for a variety of reasons.

Walt Frazier: Once the season started, I realized how much I missed those guys. It was a big adjustment. When you're playing, sometimes you think, "Maybe if these guys weren't around, I would be better." That was not the case. When they were gone, it was very obvious.

Marv Albert: Earl [Monroe] stayed on, as did Bradley. I was amazed Bradley played as many years as he did. He became like a journeyman. He was a guy who was the talk of the sports and political worlds, and he wasn't quite ready to go into politics. That's why he stuck around. Plus, he loved the game.

Bradley would retire in 1977, and during those final Knicks years the future senator would develop a nostalgic and lasting friendship with the future Hall of Fame coach.

Phil Jackson: We spent three years during the demise of the Knicks, and we came together at this point. We could compare what we should be doing and what we hadn't done. Still, we had a look at how lucky we'd been for having been on championship teams. Bill was pursuing things that would later lead him into a political life. He'd written a volume on jail care in America, which is still a problem in our country. He was still flying around for the Air Force, doing banquets and speaking.

Bill Bradley: For me, the last year [1976–77], I realized that I wasn't even going to be starting all the time. Some people said, "You should retire at the top." But I always felt it was important to live through the experience, so that you have the *whole* experience. Retiring at the top is kind of the heroic thing to do. But if you're interested in the full life experience, you have to understand how it's all a cycle and you come back to where you began. Which for me, was on the bench. After having the peak experiences and knowing your ability helped to win championships, and having those memories with

you forever. So the memory wasn't as sweet, but it didn't take away from what had happened before.

Phil Jackson: We'd be at a game, and the next morning Bill would be up at 6:00 in the morning catching a flight [if] we had a day off between games. He'd OK it with Red to fly out to, say, Omaha and speak at an Air Force banquet or whatever. Or he'd be doing somebody a favor somewhere with an appearance. He was just always on the run. I'd always try to cool him down a little. I'd say, "C'mon, let's go out to dinner or a movie," and try to slow him down a little bit. In the process, both of us were just starting families, basically. So we'd moved into a mature role about life, a much more reflective kind of a role.

I was able to go out to the reservation where I'd done some work, and he was able to dig into that and explore that a little bit. We had one great night out in the middle of the prairie, on a starlit night where we just listened to the radio and leaned against the car on this warm summer night. We had these bonding sessions that went beyond basketball and just made our friendship what it was.

Bill Bradley: My interest in the game began to go down, and my interest in public life began to go up. The way I determined this came in the summer [of 1976] before my last year. I'd always practice in the summer. In high school, I wouldn't quit unless I hit 25 shots from five different places, in a row. Then in college, it went to 15 in a row. And then by the time I got to my last year, it was 10 of 13. I knew at that point that my concentration wasn't there for the game.

Phil Jackson: Physically, he was slowing down and hurting more and more. But he was still funny, with a great sense of humor. We still had a lot of fun together on the road, even though we knew that we weren't quite the same kind of team we had been.

Bill Bradley: It's just the nature of how the team evolved. And it reminds you how unique it is when you get a group of human beings who have talent and personalities that come together in such a way that allow you to be the best in the world. So, if anything, the downside of the last year and a half was a reminder of how great the good times were.

Phil Jackson: I think what tied us together was that we both read, we're both intellectual. We both were out of the same class [1967], and we were both heading toward the end of our careers. And Bill's got somewhere to go to, and he's trying to tell me where I should go. He wants me to get a degree and become an Interior Department guy, so I can run in his administration. But I've got my own destiny that's ahead of me, and I know that.

Just before the 1977–78 season came perhaps the greatest shock: Frazier was traded to Cleveland as compensation for the Knicks' signing of free agent Jim Cleamons.

Marv Albert: The fans turned on Clyde at one point, before he went to Cleveland. They wondered if he was really hurt, and that's always unfair because you never really know how much a guy is hurt or not. But as Clyde often says on the broadcasts, "Isn't it funny how guys on losing teams seem to get hurt all the time and don't play?"

Walt Frazier: There had been a lot of rumors. And then there was nothing, so I thought it wouldn't happen. I had a good preseason, and things were quiet. So I thought it had passed. I mentioned the same thing about [the] Sprewell [situation]. I said there was too much talk about a trade. Usually, when you get traded there are no rumors going on. And then it happens.

I was driving home, and my agent, Irwin Weiner, was standing in front of my building with this dreadful look on his face. I said, "Irwin, what are you doing here?" He just kind of hesitated and said, "You've been traded." I asked him where, and he said Cleveland. And I was like, "Oh, man . . . " I was devastated. So I thought of retiring. I was holed up in my apartment for two, three days. But I realized I had to go on. On paper, that was the best team for me at the time. But once you leave the Garden, it's such a downer. Everything else is second-rate.

Less than three weeks after the trade–on October 25, 1977–Frazier would return to the Garden, clad in

Cavalier wine and gold. After a prolonged pregame standing ovation, Frazier would score 28 points in 44 minutes in Cleveland's 117–112 overtime win.

Walt Frazier: I looked at the schedule and I said, "Oh, no." I wasn't ready for that. When I came in off the bus, all the reporters were there. It was like a Hollywood script, though. I couldn't have written it better. The game goes into OT, and I had a superb game, and we wound up winning. It was funny. The crowd was ambivalent. They wanted the Knicks to win, but they also wanted me to win. I'll never forget the ovation, because I really didn't know what kind of reception I'd get coming back. That was overwhelming.

In 1975 the Knicks were eliminated in the first play-off round by the Houston Rockets, ending a nine-year postseason run that included their two championship seasons. The Knicks would see the playoffs only once in the next five years.

In 1975–76 they won only 38 games. Midway through the following season Holzman announced that he would retire and that Reed would succeed him as head coach.

Sam Goldaper: From the Eddie Donovan glory years, they fell apart right after that.

Phil Jackson: We brought in new people, and when you cross-match that with old people and old ways, things happen. The new guys would complain that no one took their laundry or that Danny's tape jobs weren't good enough. The older guys were used to a Knickerbocker way of doing things. *We* took our uniforms out and *we* washed them. There wasn't an equipment man who was doing that. But all these kids had been in these college situations where they'd had everything taken care of for them. They weren't used to the hardships they had to face with the Knicks, which is funny to say. It was just a level of responsibility that was expected of a player. If players could come in and rock the boat like that, it made you wonder about whether they had the responsibility to meet what we had established as a basketball team.

Mel Davis: It was very difficult because the fans expected us to do as well [as the championship teams]. It was a revolving door at one time. It was tough. And I was just trying to sustain myself in the league, because when you don't get a chance to play, you kind of filter out of the league. I was in my fourth year, still looking for a consistent chance to play. And that wasn't happening when, upstairs, the front office was trying to get veteran players to try to put a winning team back on the floor. So I was kind of caught in a catch-22.

Phil Jackson: We had a team that was schizophrenic. We'd go out and get 15-point leads, and then we'd lose. We couldn't finish games out. No one was secure at the end of a game in what we could run. We didn't have that spark. We had some meetings where we said, "What's the matter with us? How come we can't put it together?" Eventually, the person who was held accountable was Red. We all knew he was doing the best job he could. We just needed new blood. The team got stagnant.

Willis Reed: After I retired, I was basically just goofing around. And I got a call from, I guess, Alan Cohen, who was one of the big bosses at the time. Then I guess Eddie got involved, but basically it was Alan Cohen.

Phil Jackson: Red steps back after Bill Bradley retires, and goes into a "retirement." He has an office; he's gonna be a consultant. And Willis comes in and trades Walt Frazier.

Dean Meminger: I was their number one pick, so Red had plans for me. Red was my guy. In fact, after I left Atlanta and was out of ball for a couple of months, Red got me back, in '77. So I knew I was Red's guy. But I couldn't change that chaos in '77.

Bob McAdoo: Willis was basically a disciple of Red, and he did some of the things that Red did. He knew he had a different team. This wasn't going to be the early seventies Knicks, who'd make six or seven passes. It was a totally different team with different talent.

Mike Glenn: We recognized at that time that we were part of a transition. And it seemed like the more success we had, the more people related to the old Knicks instead of us. We felt kind of unappreciated in that respect because everybody still related to Willis Reed, Walt Frazier, DeBusschere, and those guys. We knew we were trying to resurrect that. It seemed like we had to recognize them before we finally got our identity.

Dean Meminger: It was crazy. It was a sad experience because when Willis took over I got cut in training camp. That's when they traded Clyde, and Ray Williams came in. It was all over. The chemistry of that team was gone. McAdoo, Spencer [Haywood], Lonnie Shelton–it was all different. I was used to playing with guys who ran a structured game, who were accountable and responsible. And this group was . . . In fact, they retired Red.

With the championship team all but gone, the Knicks attempted to rebuild in a hurry by acquiring well-known– and available–names. Spencer Haywood–who at 21 was the ABA's MVP and who later became a four-time All-Star with Seattle–arrived in October 1975, and one year later came three-time NBA scoring champion Bob McAdoo.

Mel Davis: I thought I was in the right place at the right time. We were in a rebuilding stage. But then we started making trades for veteran players who were forwards. We brought in Jim McMillian, Howard Porter, Lonnie Shelton [actually a draft choice], Spencer Haywood, then McAdoo and [Tom] McMillen. Eventually my luck ran out.

Bob McAdoo: I hadn't requested a trade [out of Buffalo]. What was coming up was the fifth year of my contract, and since I was a superstar, nobody knew what the compensation was going to be if I decided to bolt. We had new owners in Buffalo. John Y. Brown had come in. He was an ABA guy who didn't want to pay. I was up for a pay raise, because I had been the best player in the league. So the speculation started going around about me getting traded before my contract was up, because nobody knew what the compensation would be if they lost me at the end of the year. It was in the works for me to get traded. Seattle was in the picture and New York, too.

Probably some other teams as well, but those were the two I knew about.

Mel Davis: When we got McAdoo, Buffalo threw Tom McMillen in the deal, and now we've got 13 players. I was having a dinner party at my house and heard on the radio that we just got McAdoo, and with the addition of McMillen someone had to go, and the next thing you know my party's ruined. So I gave Mr. Holzman a call at about 12:30 or 1:00 in the morning and asked him if it was true, and he kind of verified it by telling me not to go to practice, to meet him at the office at noon the next day. So I was the one. But as Willis told me, I'm a professional and there's going to be good times and difficult times. And this was it. I went in there and knew what he was gonna tell me, and he handled it as a professional as well, and I respected him for that.

Bob McAdoo: Randy Smith and I were shopping in Toronto during an off day. And my wife called me—she knew which store I liked to shop in. She found me and told me I'd been traded to New York. Believe me, it was a big shock to me. I thought Buffalo would be the place where I'd probably end my career, because I'd been so successful there and our team had been successful. Randy and I drove back to Buffalo, and we didn't say a word to each other the whole time. He was in shock, and I was in shock. Just couldn't believe it.

Eddie Donovan was the man who had gotten me in Buffalo, and he was probably the first person I spoke to with the Knicks.

McAdoo's Knicks tenure spanned just three seasons, over which he posted 26.7 points per game, still the best figure on the franchise's all-time list.

Bob McAdoo: The first thing I recognized was that when I got rebounds, I was so used to Randy Smith breaking out and running that I'd get rebounds and then get turnovers galore. Because I was throwing it out there, and I was so used to Randy Smith running, but Walt Frazier and Earl Monroe were not running under anything. The ball was usually handed to them and it was basically a walk-up. So that was a shock to me.

With me being the focal point of the offense, guys in Buffalo—Randy Smith, Ernie DiGregorio—were always looking for me. That wasn't happening in New York. I'd go for five- or six-minute stretches and I wouldn't touch the ball. It was a strange deal to me. Walt and Earl were used to having the ball, and the bigs they had before me weren't used to getting the ball. Then, all of a sudden, they get a 30-point scorer, and it was a big change for them. That was the biggest adjustment.

I didn't feel any pressure. I just played. People used to tell me not to read the papers. We didn't have the press in Buffalo that New York had, but you couldn't help it. You'd hear things and see things that were outright ridiculous. It would get me stirred up, and sometimes it would take me to another level. I'd play harder to prove people wrong. I knew that I wasn't even the first choice of the Knicks; I knew that they had been after George McGinnis. Even though I had been the MVP and scoring champion, according to the press I was second on the list behind George McGinnis. I was like, "What is this?"

The Knicks had long coveted McGinnis, a perennial ABA All-Star with the Indiana Pacers. McGinnis' NBA draft rights, however, were held by the Philadelphia 76ers. Following the 1974–75 season, McGinnis invoked an opt-out clause in his Pacer contract. After a proposed trade fell through—one that would have sent Monroe and at least two additional players to Philadelphia for McGinnis' rights—the Knicks signed McGinnis, whom they now determined was a free agent, to a six-year, $12 million contract on May 30, 1975.

The deal had no chance of sticking. NBA Commissioner Larry O'Brien ruled that the 76ers still owned McGinnis' NBA rights, voided the Knicks contract, ordered McGinnis to sign with Philadelphia, and stripped the Knicks of their 1976 first-round draft choice.

The man behind the ill-fated McGinnis signing was Alan Cohen, who had been hired by the parent company Gulf + Western as president and CEO of the Garden Corporation. Cohen found himself in the middle of another controversy when he was quoted in The New York Times *as saying that, given the choice, he would rather see the Garden profitable than have one of its teams win a championship. For the rest of his Garden career, he would be unfortunately dubbed "Bottom Line" Cohen.*

Phil Jackson: He [Alan Cohen] made that reference to the bottom line. Someone mentioned that to me, and I came back and said, "As we know, it's Engulf and Devour and everything's about the bottom line with them." There was some resentment on our team that they just went out and tried to buy players. We had gotten Spencer Haywood, and [then] Bob McAdoo and Tom McMillen from Buffalo, and that was supposed to be a panacea for the team. It didn't seem like it was being done the right way to us, as players. There was something else that could have been done, that was the right way of doing this kind of thing, if we needed an influx of new talent. Then there was George McGinnis, and that was a fiasco. It just seemed like they made some blunders, and it reflected on the sentimental value of the guys who were on the team.

The big-money moves, real and intended, could not lift the Knicks. In the eight seasons from 1974–75 through 1981–82, New York finished over .500 only twice, accounting for the Knicks' only two postseason appearances during this span. McAdoo and Haywood, the team's two most visible players, would be the media lightning rods for everything that went wrong.

Bob McAdoo: It was difficult. I had never experienced anything like that in my life. I was producing; I was doing the maximum of what any player in the league could do at that time. I couldn't understand why things were said the way they were said.

When you look back now, it's like me and Spencer Haywood never even existed in New York Knicks history. It's just unfortunate. While I was with the Knicks, I averaged 27 a game and became the youngest player in NBA history to score 10,000 career points, until Kobe Bryant did it [in 2002–03]. But you look through the Knicks history and see I'm not even mentioned, and that's disappointing to me. I can look back with satisfaction now and say that Lonnie Shelton got a championship ring, and Spencer got one, and I got a couple, after we all left.

So that shows you the talent that was there. They just didn't give it a chance to work itself out. Everybody goes through highs and lows, and New York didn't give it a chance to work.

In 1977 sports and show business impresario David "Sonny" Werblin was named president and CEO of the Garden. Werblin's modus operandi was simple: this was New York, and New York deserved the biggest, most glamorous names out there. It had worked for Werblin during his days as a talent agent with MCA and with the Jets during the Joe Namath era. But at the Garden, the results weren't the same.

While Werblin and Knicks president Mike Burke (who had guided the CBS-era Yankees) continued to commit to veterans, the Knicks of the late seventies would draft and develop a mercurial backcourt tandem: a local product from Mount Vernon named Ray Williams, and a brilliant but troubled performer whose game was sometimes as sweet as his nickname–Sugar Ray.

Micheal Ray Richardson: It was a great feeling [to be drafted by the Knicks]. It was a shock because I went from the smallest place to the biggest. Everybody always dreams about playing in Madison Square Garden, and so that was one of my dreams.

Bob McAdoo: Even though Micheal Ray Richardson and Ray Williams were young, they were coming. Micheal Ray hardly played at all in his rookie year [1978–79], but you could see it in practices. The way he went at people, he was just an aggressive fiend out there.

Mike Glenn: Sugar was a young kid who had tremendous energy. The first thing you noticed about him was that he was hyper. He couldn't sit still. He always was ready to go. He played that way on the court, and he lived that way off the court. He was always in overdrive.

Bob McAdoo: Micheal Ray was a talent. He was ferocious. He would strip balls from people. He was mean and nasty. And so was Ray Williams. They were young guys but, believe me, they weren't afraid of anything. The older guys who were there? They didn't care. They went after them like they were going after anybody on the street. No respect

Bob McAdoo's career scoring average of 26.7 is still the Knicks' all-time best.

at all. They wanted to play, and they came in hungry and ready to play.

Micheal Ray Richardson: I took pride in both ends of the floor. So I was fearless on both ends. I took as much pride in scoring a basket as trying to stop someone. It wasn't really a matter of respect. It was that we were gonna get *our* respect. So the only way Ray [Williams] and I could get our respect was to go out there and earn it. And that's what we did.

Mike Glenn: Driving cars, Sugar Ray made cabs get out of the way. Anytime you rode with him, you'd just clench your fists because he'd say, "That's the only way you get anywhere in this damn city, Stinger. You gotta drive like they do." Cabs would move out when Micheal Ray was driving.

He always had this burning desire to play the entire game. If he could get in and defense a guy up, he wanted to do that. When he got the ball, it was like, "Let's go, Stinger, let's go!" He was just going at such a high speed that he raised up the whole level of intensity for everybody with his hyperactivity.

He was green. He was from Denver, and he was overwhelmed with being in the city without knowing it. But he always tackled things head-on, and sometimes he got in trouble because of that.

Freddie Klein: We loved Micheal Ray. I once said, "Sugar, I have a lot of restaurants here. If you and your lady friend ever want to have dinner, here's my card. Give me a call and I'll take care of everything." So a few games later he came over to me and said, "Freddie, I've been to your restaurant twice and it's closed." He had gone to my office on the second floor.

Mike Glenn: In his rookie year [1978–79], I had a condominium, and Sugar lived with me. I was just a very disciplined person, never had a beer in my life. I always got my rest. But Sugar was a guy who always wanted to hang out. He, Ray [Williams], and I called ourselves The Family. We stuck together. When we got out on the court, we looked for each other. On a fast break, Sugar would see somebody coming at him, then he'd wave the guy on by to get the ball to me. And he'd tell me, "Stinger, when you get the ball, don't dribble it. Just shoot it!" Because he knew he'd lose his assists if I put the ball on the floor.

We had a unity there where nobody messed with us off the court. We would go eat at Ray Williams' mom's house. His mom would ask us what we wanted to eat and Ray would say, "Mom, just make steaks, chicken, and beef." So we'd get everything. We'd go up to Mount Vernon and she'd cook these wonderful meals.

Micheal Ray Richardson: We were the Family. We were really, really close. We would always hang out together and eat together after the game. And if you saw one of us, you saw the other two.

Mike Glenn: We were about as close as any three players could be, on and off the court. When we'd go to parties, we'd always see who was the best dancer. McAdoo and Earl had the accessibility. If you wanted to get into Studio 54, you had to go with McAdoo or Earl because they could get you in.

Sugar had different shoe contracts, and he was always meeting people he could get clothes from. "Stinger, let me introduce you to this guy. Just give him a couple of tickets and you can get some suits . . ." Sugar was always out there hustling. He had street sense, but he had *good* street sense. He was smart; he knew how to work deals. He had two or three shoe contracts at the same time, deals with stereo equipment. But he was a funny guy. Everybody loved him.

Willis just loved Sugar so much. Micheal Ray lived with him for a while. Sugar was his draft choice, and Willis wanted him to do well so much. He just took him in as sort of a little brother and tried to shelter him and bring him along.

Micheal Ray Richardson: Willis was a great guy. He knew basketball talent, he knew the game. He went out of his way to scout me and watch me. One time he came to watch me play in Flagstaff, Arizona–so that was way out of his way. Then after he drafted me, he came to visit me and my mom, so we had already had a special bond.

Bob McAdoo: We had injuries [in 1978–79]. I got injured with a turf toe that kept me out for a month, and you can't lose 28 points a game and expect to keep winning games. We had a young team, but when we were all together and healthy, things were going well for us. But they didn't give it time to work. So Willis was fired and they brought Red back.

There was a big conflict between Micheal Ray and Red. Micheal Ray wanted to play; he was proving himself in practice. And I guess Red was from the old school, and he didn't believe in playing rookies right away.

Within a little more than a year of each other, both Williams and Richardson would be gone. Williams, who became a free agent in 1981, would eventually return to the Knicks. For Richardson, life would take a destructive and tragic turn. Traded to Golden State for Bernard King in 1982, he would wind up in New Jersey just months later and eventually be banned from the NBA for life for violation of the league's substance abuse policy. He would later move to Europe, and, clean and sober at last, would play professionally overseas until well past the age of 40.

Mike Glenn: When Sugar Ray was living with me, he was doing none of those things. I think what really led to his downfall were two things. One, he'd go back to Denver and get into some bad habits in the off-season. And then, the year after we all left was when it really hit bottom for him. I went to Atlanta. Ray Williams was gone. They had brought in veterans like Randy Smith and Mike Newlin. Now The Family was dissolved, and Sugar Ray was all by himself. I don't think he ever felt that unity again. And that's when he was open to other influences, like the drugs. Then I'd hear rumors that Micheal Ray was doing all these horrible things, man. And he'd always lie about anything he was doing. It just hurt me very much. It was just a difficult time for all of us.

Micheal Ray Richardson: What I can give people today is that, no matter who you are, no matter how big you are, you have to be humble. And you have to choose and pick your friends. Because being a professional athlete or entertainer, or in any kind of work, you're gonna meet a lot of false people, and you're gonna meet a lot of people in misery. And misery loves company.

In his first season as coach, Reed led the Knicks to 43 wins and a first-round playoff victory over Cleveland. The signing of 7'1" free agent Marvin Webster would

move McAdoo back to his normal forward slot and, it was hoped, enable the Knicks to challenge the East's elite.

Willis Reed: I thought we had a shot. We had some young talent, and draft picks coming up. And one thing I did in my second year was I had taken McAdoo and made him a power forward, and taken Webster and made him a center. But I still had the flexibility to put McAdoo back at center if I needed to. So that, I think, would have made us a good team. But, alas . . .

Bob McAdoo: I didn't have any problem with that. Whatever Willis wanted was fine with me. No conflict or anything, because I knew I could play both center and power forward. It didn't make any difference to me. I felt in my heart that whoever was in front of me–whether it was at center or power forward–I was gonna beat them. Man on man, I was gonna win that contest.

Sam Goldaper: Sonny [Werblin] had taken a terrible beating from the people at Gulf + Western for having signed Marvin Webster. They thought Larry Fleischer [head of the NBA players' union, 1961–89] talked him into it.

Harvey Araton: Sonny clearly had his own agenda, because he came in with a lot of fanfare as a guy who had his own style, and with the whole Meadowlands thing. The events bear that out. That was my first year on the beat. There was a lot of stuff out there on the grapevine about how good a coach Willis was the previous season. There was all that stuff about how Willis had refused to apprentice as Red's assistant, so there was a sense that maybe Willis had overreached a little bit. Of course, it was a team in transition, sort of a pre–Torre-Steinbrenneresque Knicks team with all these big-money guys and aging veterans.

Willis Reed: If I could have done it over again, I would have changed that. I would have prepared a little more. I didn't get caught up in the basketball part of it; I got caught up in the politics of the game. My first year, we won [43 games]. I got caught up in the fact that when Alan [Cohen] got let go, Sonny came in. And Sonny started firing people. He fired Eddie Donovan, and he fired me.

And we had gone from a team that hadn't made the playoffs in three years to a team that went to the second round [in 1978]. We had some young kids that could play.

Harvey Araton: Apparently, Werblin called Eddie Donovan into his office and he asked him point-blank, "Is Willis Reed a good coach?" And Eddie was in a funny position, because if he said yes, then his neck was on the line. If he said no, then Werblin could have turned around and said, "Then what the hell did you hire him for?" Remember, Werblin was an elderly man who probably had a lot more in common with a guy like Red Holzman than a guy like Willis Reed, who was still perceived to be a player.

Mike Glenn: Willis treated everybody like a big brother. He gave you opportunities to do new things. Willis always encouraged me to develop my own shot, or to challenge bigger players on a fast break by shooting over them. The difficulty where Willis was concerned was that the older guys on the team, particularly Spencer and Bob, saw him as a friend and as a guy they played against. He didn't have that separation that's sometimes necessary between a player and coach.

The 1978–79 season was a nightmare from start to finish. Just 14 games in, the most recognizable figure in Knicks history would fall victim.

Harvey Araton: This all went down early in the [1978–79] season. The newspapers had been on strike at the start of that season, so nobody was really with the team. That was also Nat Gottlieb's first year on the beat [with the *Newark Star-Ledger*]. Earlier that summer, Nat had lunch with Willis. Willis had made some statement to Nat that he had to have a center. This was when they were trying to get Marvin Webster. Willis said that he had to have a true center to win. Nat innocently asked him, "What if you don't get one?" And Willis said, "I don't know. I might quit." Now, I don't know whether he said it half in jest or if he was serious. I don't know. So they finally get Marvin Webster, and give up Lonnie Shelton as part of the compensation.

So there was all this stuff bouncing around. Werblin was aware of all this. Plus, Werblin had Howard Cosell as a confidant, for some reason. Apparently, Cosell was filling his head with, "They fired a legend, William 'Red' Holzman, the only man to win . . . " and all that. So he was being influenced on that end.

The season starts and the papers are on strike throughout the preseason. Then Rupert Murdoch cut his own deal with the unions and got the *Post* back on the stands before the *Daily News* and the *Times*. So I start writing. And Willis is hinting over the first few games that the refusal of Werblin to come out and say that Willis was his coach and to adopt him as his own was circulating down to his young players, and that it was something of a distraction.

Willis Reed: One thing I found out was that once you stop being an athlete, there are a lot of other people who now control what happens in your life, more so than you do.

Harvey Araton: Now we're in Seattle at practice. I asked Willis, "Is all this stuff going on hurting the team, and preventing this team from playing up to its potential?" And Willis basically said, yes it is, and that these guys didn't know what to believe. Then he uttered the phrase, "Am I in or am I out?" I went back to my room and called Werblin. And I made sure to say to him that Willis did not say this as a demand. He said it as almost a plea, because he felt that it was affecting the team. So Werblin gave me a response, and then I wrote the story. I called my office and said the same thing I told Werblin, that this was not a demand. Willis is a proud guy; this was a job he always wanted, and he felt it was distracting and hurting his chances to do the job well. These were the early Murdoch days, and any smell of controversy was going to be completely blown up. And the back page was something like: "Willis to Sonny: In or Out?" and "Willis Reed threw down the gauntlet . . . blah, blah, blah." They rewrote my lead and all.

So now the story is out there, and everyone is buzzing about it. And Willis wasn't happy with the way it was presented, and I tried to explain to him that I made every attempt I could to not blow it up. The next stop was Denver, and then we came home

The seas turned rough for the Cap'n when he became the Coach.

on a Friday afternoon [November 10, 1978]. I remember driving to my parents' house in Brooklyn, and I called my office and said, "Apparently, Willis has been summoned." We had been told that Willis had been summoned to meet with Werblin late that afternoon. I was at my parents' house, probably doing my laundry, then got into my car, drove straight to the city, and went to the Garden.

Willis Reed: I heard from a reporter the summer before the season started that I wasn't going to be the coach much longer. So the word was already out there. It was gonna happen.

Harvey Araton: We waited and waited and then sometime that night, around 7:00 or 8:00, Mike Burke came out first. He came out looking

dapper as ever and said that Willis had been replaced as coach and that Red Holzman would take over the team, and that there would be a press conference the next day. Werblin was not available. Then Nat Gottlieb said, "We've got to find Willis." I ran out into the street and, sure enough, I saw this big, hulking figure walking down 31ˢᵗ Street. I ran up after him, a little wary, and I asked him a question. He said something, but I could see that his lips were trembling. He was devastated. This was the team he had played for and was a hero for, and he got fired. Also, he didn't really get a chance; that was the truth of the matter.

Mike Saunders: Fourteen games into my first season, and what a baptism of fire. I guess it really did prepare me for things to come. I went for a haircut in my old neighborhood in Queens, and then suddenly–boom!–I hear that there was a change.

Harvey Araton: At the press conference the next day, Werblin said, "I don't take ultimatums too well." And I had specifically told him, on the phone, that it was *not* an ultimatum. I had made it clear that this was not an angry coach speaking, that it was a cry for help and for the respect of the team and the confidence of the Garden management.

Willis Reed: And you know what? I tell guys now that what I learned was, I don't know how long I'm going to work, I just know how long I'm going to get paid. When I get a job, I take a contract and I know how long they're going to pay me. I don't know any more than that. That's just the way it is. It was just unfortunate. And it broke my heart.

Three months later, McAdoo would be traded to Boston, a transaction whose origins would be the stuff of Knicks legend.

On Saturday night, February 10, the Knicks met the Celtics at the Garden. In the stands were Celtics owner John Y. Brown and his fiancée, Miss America-turned-sportscaster Phyllis George. George had mentioned to her soon-to-be-husband that she was impressed with McAdoo's performance, and that his moribund Celtics needed someone of that caliber. Not one to disappoint his intended, Brown quickly sought out Werblin and Donovan. And sometime that evening–some say at the Garden's Suite 200 club, others say later at P. J. Clarke's–the two parties agreed on the deal: McAdoo was to be traded to Boston for the Celtics' three first-round picks in the 1979 NBA Draft, along with a player to be named later [Tom Barker].

McAdoo, however, was still in a Knicks uniform when the two teams met again in Boston the next day. Twenty-four hours later, all hell broke loose.

Sam Goldaper: When I was in Boston [on Sunday afternoon, February 11, 1979], I was told about the McAdoo trade, that it was being talked about. When I came back that night, I finished my story, and I got a call from someone whose identity I won't reveal, telling me to come to P. J. Clarke's.

That's where the trade was consummated. I did the story, and the *Times* broke it. Nobody had it or would confirm it until the next day.

Mike Glenn: The trade totally shocked me. I thought that McAdoo was one of those guys who was untouchable. Mac was our heart and soul, a guy who came out and scored every night. When Mac was there, we had confidence. We knew that we had a guy who could score against anybody in the league, and wasn't intimidated by anybody. We had an advantage at that position every night out.

Sam Goldaper: I heard that they were in [the Garden's] Suite 200 talking about it on Saturday, but I don't know if that was true. The place where they called the league from was P. J. Clarke's.

Bob McAdoo: I didn't have a clue. I was in bed sleeping, and somebody rang my doorbell at about 5:30 in the morning. It was Micheal Ray. He'd been up most of the night, and he told me that he'd heard that I'd been traded. I said, "What? Get outta here!" He said, "Yeah, man. I heard you've been traded!" So I'm wiping the sleep out of my eyes and I said, "Man, go out and get me a newspaper." So he runs out and gets *The New York Times,* brings it back, and there's the headline: "Bob McAdoo Traded to Boston." And I sat there and I was almost in tears.

Mike Glenn: When it happened, I think it changed my whole perspective of the NBA for life. From that point on, I knew it was a business. And every NBA player has that experience where he realizes that it's not high school, it's not college. Anything can happen, and anybody can go.

Bob McAdoo: Here I am, playing my heart out for New York. I'd just bought a house in New Jersey and was really feeling comfortable. I thought we had a great team, especially when everybody was healthy. And here I am traded to Boston, of all places. No way I wanted to be part of the Boston Celtics. We were rivals, first with Buffalo and then with New York. And on top of that, I knew John Y. Brown was there, and I didn't want to be any part of any team that he was a part of. He was the one that traded me from Buffalo, and I'm saying to my young self, "Why do you want me in Boston, when you didn't want me in Buffalo?" They had to pay me now, because they assumed my Knicks contract. I mean, why? Why? Why? Why? I was gonna be away from my family and all that. Plus, I never got a call from the Knicks at all. Never got a call. I learned about it in the newspaper. I'm a superstar in the league and I don't get enough respect to even get a phone call from anybody from the Knicks organization.

The trade, made without the knowledge of Celtics president Red Auerbach, stripped Boston of three first-round picks that Auerbach had been hoarding for years. Now, on the whim of the owner's girlfriend, they were gone.

Just six months earlier–in August of 1978–Auerbach, already fed up with Brown's constant meddling, had turned down Werblin's offer of a four-year contract to run the Knicks. Now, in February 1979, he and the rest of the Knicks Nation could only wonder what would have happened had he said yes.

Sam Goldaper: Red Auerbach didn't know about it. Red Holzman didn't know about it. I told Red Holzman.

Bob McAdoo: I went into a bad situation, bad feelings, everything. And I knew that. I knew that Red [Auerbach] wasn't in on the deal, and I knew from the beginning there was gonna be trouble. And there was. I go up there, possibly fighting for my fourth scoring championship, and they have me coming off the bench with three minutes to go in the game. On a team that wasn't any good. It was their way of showing John Y. Brown that, hey, you don't do deals around here without us knowing about it. And I'm the player stuck in the middle of all this garbage.

Mike Glenn: So then we were all saying, "What are we gonna get in return?" And we heard: three draft picks . . . for Bob McAdoo? At the time, it sounded like a very bad deal. We had lost so much. And trades, of course, have a long life and it's tough to evaluate them down the road. Those draft picks turned into Bill Cartwright, Larry Demic, and Sly Williams, three guys who had pretty good careers. And Cartwright, of course, had a *great* career.

Bob McAdoo: I really enjoyed playing there. I just don't think they had the patience to see it

through and see it grow. I was really frustrated because I'd already experienced frustration in Buffalo. And then I said to myself, "What can you possibly do to stay in one place?" At that point in my career, I had averaged almost 30 points a game and 15 rebounds, and I had gotten traded twice. So I kept thinking, What the hell did I have to do? At that point, I was really frustrated about playing professional basketball. And my father had to talk me into going to Boston, because I wasn't going.

In time, the constant losing took an emotional toll on the only Knick who remained from the glory days.

Earl Monroe: It just got to a boiling point. You just hoped that other people cared as much as you did about these things. You can be a losing team, but somewhere along the line you've got to come to grips about why you're losing. Is it my fault, or whose fault is it? And you have to try and sort it out.

Mike Glenn: Earl was always like a big brother to all of us. We kind of depended on Earl. He was a treasure to have around. He gave us leadership on and off the court.

We went through a period where we lost a few. And being young guys, we were all enjoying New York City, the parties and Studio 54 and all that. Then we lost one game at the Garden, and Earl just blasted us out. He started yelling, "You guys think it's *funny*! These teams are coming into the Garden and kicking our butts and you're thinking it's *funny*! I don't think it's funny!" He's taking off his uniform and yelling at us at the same time. That was the first time we'd really seen that side of Earl. And Red was looking on and nodding his head and thinking, "Yeah," and amen-ing to everything he was saying.

Earl Monroe: I remember that. There was also a time in Indiana where we were up by something like 20 points and lost the game. I went into the locker room, and they had the kind of lockers there that just stood up and you could knock them down. I went in there and just tore up the locker room before anyone could come in. I started with the table where we got taped, throwing that. Then I started knocking all the

Ray Williams goes over the Sixers' George McGinnis—the object of the Knicks' misguided affections three years earlier—in the 1978 playoffs.

lockers over, hitting them and hollering. I just went off, because I had always been a winner. Then everything else just culminated here. Losing, losing, losing. It got to be unbearable, and it just came out that way. When I went in there, there was a kid there–Butch Beard's son. He's been afraid of me ever since.

With the luster of winning big gone, everyone who cared about the Knicks made their own mental adjustments to the situation.

Marv Albert: I never had a problem with enthusiasm. You had to deal with it objectively. I still loved doing the games. Obviously, it's easier when the team succeeds. Advertisers are there, and the audience is going to be listening. But you can't let it affect you. You have to treat the game the way it is.

Mike Saunders: It was a different league back then. Very few teams had their own practice facility. A few, like Cleveland when they played in Richfield, had the great luxury of having a practice court right in their building. They were the envy of the league. I was running all over, schlepping stuff back and forth.

At Upsala College, I painted and boarded the windows myself for security reasons. I boarded the windows first, so there was no ventilation and I started getting woozy from the paint. We'd chain the door so no one could get in. Then when I'd get there in the morning I'd kick the door a few times and rattle the chains to scare the mice away.

We get Tom Barker in a [1979] trade, and I'm traveling with a blank jersey. Now, the jersey has to have a number on it. I get a piece of chalk, and every time he goes into the game, I'm writing a big "6" in chalk on the back. Try doing that today.

Stan Asofsky: In the losing years, I felt we had a lot of fun, with the Ray Williamses and the Ken Bannisters. Seriously. It was a lot of fun.

It was during this time of tumult that the Knicks learned the power–and potentially devastating harm–of a single word.

Harvey Araton: Whatever year it was that they had an all-black team [1979–80], there wasn't a huge

buzz about it. But we, at the *Post*, decided to do two columns, and [Peter] Vecsey and I both wrote about it. And my column concerned my talking to Werblin, who told me, you know, "We're color-blind, we don't care, it's nonsense. In this day and age, who cares as long as the players are good?" And Vecsey wrote a column in which he also dismissed the notion that an all-black team would somehow turn off the fans. And he threw out the line, "It's not like anybody is going to call them the New York Niggerbockers." And it got in the paper. It was one of those Friday specials where they ran two columns on the page.

There wasn't a soul who publicly called them the Niggerbockers. It was Vecsey who dropped the line in the column, but *not* to call them that. It was to say that the thought of people going around calling them that was absurd.

Peter Vecsey: I honestly don't remember the context of it. I certainly remember using the phrase–which I won't even repeat here–because I had heard people on the streets use it. I wish I was clever enough to actually come up with all the nicknames that have been attributed to me over the years. I remember using it. I don't remember [Araton and I] writing on the same day. I think I wrote it long before anybody was talking about it. And then people started reacting to it.

It got an unbelievable reaction. I think I used it only once–you probably couldn't even get it in the paper today. I saw Spike Lee's comment about that term being used all the time. And, again, I think we used it only once just to accentuate what some people were saying in the city. But I don't think we ever used it again–not in our paper. I don't think I ever used it in a column again. But obviously there was a huge reaction to it. So here's Spike Lee, who's a lot younger than I am, who's probably one of those guys that's still reacting to it years later. And for good reason–it's a derogatory term.

Harvey Araton: Then that thing slowly took on a life of its own, as the years went by. Because the team didn't draw–they'd draw 11,000 or 12,000 or whatever–there was a notion that it was racist. Then, much, much later, you had people saying, "Well, that was the team they all called the Niggerbockers." But

Micheal Ray Richardson: electrifying, breathtaking, tragic.

nobody ever called them that. That's one of the biggest unfair myths that I've ever seen in the years I've covered the NBA. *Nobody* called them that. It was just Vecsey dismissing the notion that people would judge them by their color, by dropping in a line that probably never should have gotten in the paper.

There would be a brief revival under Holzman: a 50-win season in 1980–81 that led to a playoff berth. Center Bill Cartwright, who came to New York via the first of the three picks acquired in the McAdoo trade, had made the All-Rookie Team the year before and was the team's leading scorer in his first two seasons. But after dropping from 50 wins in 1980–81 to 33 the following season, Holzman permanently retired from coaching. At the same time, Eddie Donovan was succeeded as general manager by his greatest player acquisition, Dave DeBusschere.

Mike Glenn: When he was finding his way around the post [as a rookie], we found that Cartwright had a nice turnaround jumper. And about midseason, Red began to have a lot of confidence in that. He started to call Bill's number more and he wanted the ball to go into the post. Bill would get frustrated sometimes with Ray and Sugar Ray; he thought they'd look for each other too much and would forget to come to the post. But Bill was really developing into a terrific post player.

I think if Bill had played for Red throughout his entire career, he would have been one of the great scorers in the history of the game. What happened afterward was that Bill had new coaches who tried to change his game and told him not to shoot the fadeaway. In the NBA, a player has to do what his skill is. If you're a seven-foot fadeaway jump-shot shooter, that's what you do. After Red left, people started changing Bill's game.

We were always cognizant of our shooting percentages, and we'd have little competitions. Cartwright used to joke that when his shooting percentage got too high, we should get him even more shots so we could shoot him down.

I remember in the [1981] playoffs, Micheal Ray challenged Artis Gilmore one-on-one. And Gilmore must have had five blocks. So we were young and we'd never been in the playoffs before. We didn't know better. And Red's previous teams knew better.

Willis Reed: Eddie [Donovan, who died in 2001 at the age of 78] was a great guy. Eddie died on a Saturday at about 2:00 in the afternoon. I had left him on Friday at about 1:00. I had been to see him at his daughter's house. And it was so funny. We were laughing and talking about when I got drafted–just basketball stuff. And finally when I was leaving out the door he said to say hello to Gail, my wife. I got a call the next afternoon. I was sitting at home watching television, and [his son] Sean called to say that his dad had died at about 2:00. So Eddie played a very important part in my life.

It was a whole new ballgame when Hubie Brown arrived in 1982.

THE LINEUP: Hubie Brown; Ernie Grunfeld; Mike Saunders; Rory Sparrow; Trent Tucker; Bernard King; Marv Albert; Dr. Norman Scott; Patrick Ewing; Harvey Araton.

The dynamic Bernard King, who joined the Knicks in the fall of 1982, would embody the ups and downs of the Knicks through much of the Reagan years. But before the arrival of King, the Knicks coaxed veteran coach Hubie Brown away from the broadcast table to lead the franchise back into contention.

Hubie Brown: The guy who got me the job with the Knicks was Frank McGuire. Frank and Sonny Werblin were very close. Frank was the one who talked to Sonny about me. Then Howard Cosell called me. I had arrived back in Atlanta and was sitting in my lawyer's office; it was a quarter to twelve. And Cosell called to tell me that if I wanted the job, I had to meet Sonny Werblin at the Waldorf-Astoria at 7:00 that night. Now, remember, I'm in Atlanta. I had just done a Boston-Philadelphia playoff game on TV in Boston the night before. So I flew up there and met with Sonny, and he offered me the job. That night I went to dinner, right from there, with Howard Cosell and his wife and Sonny and his wife. We went down to Little Italy to that Italian club that had 125 members–124 Italian guys, and Sonny Werblin. And there they were, charter members listed on the wall.

Ernie Grunfeld: That was a different era. Coach-and-player relationships were a lot different than they are today. And Hubie, of course, had his own style. Hubie had a great basketball mind. He paid attention to detail like nobody else I ever played for. He demanded that everybody compete, that everybody give 110 percent, that everybody under-stand their roles and accept responsibility for them. I enjoyed playing for Hubie because he was the type of coach where, if you gave it your all, he was gonna be happy with you. And there's no question about his knowledge of the game.

Mike Saunders: Hubie had been very close to his trainer in Atlanta, Joe O'Toole. They were like a two-man operation that ran everything, every aspect of the organization, from soup to nuts. Now Hubie comes here, and I have huge shoes to fill. With Hubie, things were kind of tense. That was his style, to create some tension in the air to get the best out of the players. What I found was that I relied more on my sense of humor at the time, to break the tension a bit when it was appropriate. And Hubie encouraged that. Hubie loved to laugh, so that worked very well.

Hubie Brown: I was out that year [1981–82] and had done television for USA Network. Al Albert and I were the Thursday night Eastern game, and the second game–the Western game–was Eddie Doucette and Steve Jones. That year went so well that CBS picked me up, and I did 12 games of theirs along with USA. So my being out that year was really the start, part-time, of my job as a television guy.

But I felt I was still in my prime as a coach. So when the Knicks job opened up, it was a great opportunity in spite of the fact that when we came in with our staff–Mike Fratello and Richie Adubato–we changed eight of the guys from the team the year before. The only guys we kept were [Bill] Cartwright, [Marvin] Webster, Paul Westphal, and Sly Williams. We just made a total changeover. I just thought that it was a great opportunity at that time to go in there and have an effect on basketball in the metropolitan area. Hopefully, we could turn it around. And we did.

Hubie Brown had earned his coaching spurs as a player at Niagara University, as an assistant to Larry Costello in Milwaukee, as a championship coach in the ABA with the Kentucky Colonels, and finally in the NBA with the Atlanta Hawks. Equal parts teacher and drill sergeant, he brought to the Knicks an aggressive, all-consuming, and sometimes abrasive style that was, at all times, uniquely his own. And in 1982, it was exactly what the lethargic Knicks needed.

Ernie Grunfeld: Hubie believed that you play like you practice, and he wanted you to practice with high intensity and high energy, and to execute. He felt that if we could do it in practice, we could do it in a game just as easily. . . . He understood the length of the season. As the season went along, our practices got shorter and shorter. But the intensity level stayed high, and that's what he wanted.

Rory Sparrow: I had some forewarnings about coming to [play for] Hubie Brown from some of the Atlanta Hawks who had played for him. The key was that Mike Fratello coached me at Villanova, and he had a relationship as an assistant with Hubie here in New York. So Mike was here when I got to New York, and he told me, "Just play your role like you did in college. We need somebody to come in, play good defense, and distribute the basketball."

Mike Saunders: Hubie was very organized, and a great preparer, a great organizer. He'd take out his yellow legal pad, divide the page into four boxes, and just start organizing things.

Hubie Brown: It's always interesting how the attacks about our style are never by the best players,

because the best players understand it right away. That's what we were trying to get across. And you never know until you coach a group who the problem people are and who the guys are who will fit your style of play. See, that's the key. That's very, very important.

Ernie Grunfeld: They were making changes, with a new coach in Hubie Brown. I was a free agent, and they wanted to bring in some role players. Hubie liked the way I played; he knew I was a team player. I was versatile; I could play more than one position. Most kids who grew up on the playgrounds of New York dreamed of playing for the Knicks. To get the opportunity, I was thrilled about it. I was upset they didn't hire any private planes. They didn't have a band waiting for me at the airport. In those days, everything was a lot different.

Trent Tucker: Anytime you're a first-round draft pick, they expect you to have an immediate impact. I came to training camp late, so that put me behind right there. I had to slowly work myself into shape. Coming out of college, you think that you're prepared, but you're really not prepared for NBA basketball until you actually play a game or two.

Hubie Brown: When we got there, we realized that with Marvin Webster anchoring the second unit, we wanted to press and trap with that second unit. A lot of the guys who were there didn't fit into that mold. We had drafted Trent Tucker and, unfortunately, Westphal was hurt in camp. Mike Newlin kneed him, and Westphal had a very bad thigh injury. That stopped Paul early. But we put together a pressing second unit, and that's why there was a major turnover of people. We traded for Truck Robinson. We traded for Bernard. At the start, we had Ed Sherod at the point. Then when Westphal came back, Paul and Ernie played in the backcourt down the stretch and in the playoffs.

Before the Knicks even went to training camp in 1982, most of the team that had gone 33–49 the year before was gone. Now, with Brown's first season as Knicks coach just days away, the biggest change of all was starting to take shape.

Hubie Brown: [When Bernard King was in college] I did his banquet, the Ernie and Bernie Banquet at the University of Tennessee. They had 2,500 people there, the largest ever in the history of their banquet. Afterward, [Tennessee coach] Ray Mears and Stew Aberdeen, his assistant, and I all went to Aberdeen's house. And it's like quarter to five in the morning. Now, people forget that Ernie Grunfeld was the leading scorer in the history of Tennessee basketball, and not Bernard King. So I say to them, "What is it with this guy Bernard King?" And they said, "He's the greatest *practice* player both of us have ever coached in our lives. And he's the greatest *game* player. His focus, his energy, and his ability to close." I never forgot that.

So that Monday, when DeBusschere came in and offered Bernard King for Sugar Ray Richardson, I said, "Do it." Then he said, "But . . . ," and he listed all the problems Bernard had in the past. And I said, "True, but the guy that's leaving also has a sheet. So let's take our chances." That's how I felt. And he never disappointed. His years with us were as great as any player has ever had in New York.

Bernard King: Any young person growing up in New York aspires to one day make it to the NBA. Then when you finally fulfill that dream, the ultimate dream at that point is to play for your hometown team, and who else but the Knicks would be that ballclub? I had the memories of watching the great Knicks of the past when I was a young person, in terms of Willis Reed, Cazzie Russell, Dave DeBusschere, Bill Bradley, Earl Monroe, and all those other Knicks greats. To be able to wear the same uniform as those greats was certainly a goal of mine.

Ernie Grunfeld: I had no idea it was in the works. At that time, we had Micheal Ray Richardson, and I don't think anybody realized that it [the trade] was something that was about to happen. It happened early in training camp. Bernard signed an offer sheet with the Knicks, and then the Warriors worked out the trade for Micheal Ray. So we were reunited. I was already there, and we had also drafted Trent Tucker, so it was sort of a new beginning for that team.

Bernard King officially became a Knick on October 22, 1982. The 25-year-old King brought with him a 21.9 career scoring average and a reputation as one of the NBA's most explosive performers during his years with the Nets and Warriors, earning All-Star honors in 1982 with Golden State. He also brought a troubled past, with a string of prior arrests and a well-documented battle with alcoholism. But at Golden State, he rebuilt his life both personally and professionally, and in 1981 he earned the NBA's first-ever Comeback Player of the Year award.

Now the native New Yorker, who had teamed with Grunfeld so successfully at the University of Tennessee, would become a streaking meteor that would flash across the Knicks landscape.

Hubie Brown: I've always said that I was around two assassins in my coaching career: Kareem Abdul-Jabbar and Bernard King. They demanded the ball with their eyes and not with their mouths. They could close any game–double-teamed, triple-teamed, no matter–because they would make the high-percentage shot. If they didn't, they would make the proper pass. If they got fouled, they made the foul shots. They were cold. They were executioners. And they did it within the team game. And I was just proud, as a coach, to have had the time to be around them. Because both guys were all about team. Both guys were incredible workers, and just led by example, not by talk.

Ernie Grunfeld: There were some issues with Bernard at that point, but no one ever doubted his greatness. He was a terrific player from Day One, from the first time he arrived in the NBA. Nobody ever questioned that. But I think, coming home and playing in front of his family, and having dreamed of being a Knick while growing up, it was all a new beginning for him. And he sure took advantage of it.

Rory Sparrow: Bernard was probably just as good in the first year [1982–83], when I got there, as he was in the second year. It wasn't until early into the second season [1983–84] that he emerged as a player whose talent demanded the ball. Prior to that, people were concerned that he didn't play defense, so they didn't play him as much and he didn't get the ball as much, and it limited his effectiveness. But once they began to realize what a potent scoring machine he was, it changed the whole way we played.

Bernard King: There was a long, drawn-out matter with the offer sheet being matched, or not being matched, and ultimately going to arbitration, and my eventual trade to the Knicks. So I had no correspondence with the organization; I wasn't permitted to talk to them. But once the contract was finalized and the trade was actually made, we were really through with training camp at that point. Having missed training camp, it was a little difficult for me. Obviously, you train as much as you can on your own, but you can never simulate what you get in a professional training camp. I came in coming off an All-Star year in Golden State, so there was a respect there from the organization, there was a respect there from my teammates, and there was a respect there from Hubie. But we got off to a very difficult, slow start—myself included, as a result of missing training camp. And I recall sharing with Hubie that I wasn't performing at the level that he would have liked for me to perform at, at that point. But hopefully, when it was all said and done, you're gonna see one of the finest players you've ever coached.

King's brilliance, Brown's intensity, and the revamped Knicks lineup led to a playoff berth in 1982–83. After beating New Jersey in the first round, the Knicks were swept by eventual champion Philadelphia, losing the four games by a total of 22 points.

Hubie Brown: In that first year, we were second only to the Sixers for the best record in the second half. In the playoffs, we beat Jersey and then we lost to Philly. No one played Philly that tough—nobody—after that second round. We lost to them in the Garden on a Saturday-Sunday, by two and by three. Franklin Edwards hit the shot to beat us in the Saturday game, when Truck missed the foul shots. If he would have made them, who knows what would have happened in that series? But they beat us. Moses Malone was the MVP and was spectacular.

When you look at that series and how close we were to them, because they won the championship, we were very optimistic about the next year.

Bernard King: That [the Philadelphia series] was a great barometer for our ballclub. And let's be realistic: that was a great, great Philly team that swept everyone. So we were a part of that group. But, if you look at each of those games that we played against Philly, we played them as difficult as any team they faced in the playoffs in their run to the championship. Every game was close; they weren't blowouts. So we felt that we were poised and in a position to compete the very next year. We were all excited about the upcoming season and the things we were headed for.

Trent Tucker: In Game 2, we had an 18-point lead at halftime, and the Sixers came back to win. I think that was the pivotal game of that series. That got them over the hump. If we had won that game, it would have given us a lot of confidence coming back to the Garden, to see if we could extend the series. But that was a great 76er team. They won the championship that year, while we were just starting to get ourselves together for the first time as a unit. So it was a stepping-stone for us as well.

Bernard King: Great players bring out the best in competitive talent, and I was a competitive guy. There was a play in that series where I went up for a layup and Julius Erving and Moses Malone blocked my shot. I retrieved the ball, went up to the other side of the rim, and dunked. And that was something I had never done in a ballgame, ever, on any level. I was always the sort of player who looked for signs of improvement in my own personal game. And that told me that I had not fulfilled my true potential as a player. So that summer I worked harder than I ever had before. So going into the next season, I felt really good and that I would get off to a great start, and ultimately as a team, we would as well.

In 1983–84, King bumped his scoring average up to 26.3, fifth in the NBA. The highlight of his season was a pair of back-to-back 50-point games on a trip to San Antonio and Dallas, a feat no other Knick has approached, before or since.

Following a 47–35 regular season, the Knicks headed to the playoffs and a thrilling four-week run that, more than anything, defined Bernard King's New York career.

Detroit, featuring an extraordinary third-year man named Isiah Thomas, was up first.

Bernard King: I had come out of the [1984] All-Star Game, whereas my teammates were on their break. Then we went to San Antonio, and I recall sitting next to [assistant coach] Rick Pitino and sharing with him that I thought it was very important that our ballclub get off to a good start in the second half of the season. Having scored 18 points in the All-Star Game, my confidence level was soaring, obviously. But we were also missing some key players [during that time] in Ray Williams and Louis Orr. So more of the offense went through me than it ordinarily would, and I played more minutes than I ordinarily would. Also, we were playing an up-tempo game, which I loved. Whereas with Hubie, it was primarily a set offense. So the game was really tailored to my style of play.

I scored the 50th point on the last play of the [Dallas] game. I wasn't aware of it. One thing I've always done is, I've always looked at the clock in terms of how many minutes were remaining in the game, and I've always been aware of the 24-second clock to insure that we'd get a good shot off. The one thing I wouldn't look at was points, so I had no idea that I was close to 50. When I played, I played with such intensity, in terms of being in a zone, that I'm looking to make things happen for my ballclub and my teammates, that I never thought about the number of points I was scoring.

Rory Sparrow: Going into the Detroit series, we had stumbled and we weren't feeling confident. So we go into that series not playing as well as we can. But going into that series, Hubie did another great job of coaching. He worked the situation where we'd take advantage of Bernard and then let other people on their team win the game instead of Isiah, like Kelly Tripucka or somebody else. Because at the end of the day, Kelly couldn't outscore Bernard.

Bernard King: When you're playing with two dislocated fingers, and you're in severe pain when you just catch the ball, or when you take a dribble, or when you take a shot, or when you get hit, you have to go to another level of intensity in your mind-set. I was going within myself to be able to play, because, realistically speaking, I should not have been playing. That was the only way I managed to play, was to try and block out that pain. So as the end of the season developed and we went into the Detroit series, I felt confident that we were going to be able to play well. And I also felt very confident that I was going to have to do a superb job for us to beat this team on the road.

Rory Sparrow: The last part of the season, Bernard is slowly and surely pushing himself away from the team, putting his game face on. It's nothing personal, but he just liked to concentrate. And he couldn't slap five! When you're a team, everybody slaps five after a basket. But because of these injuries, he couldn't do it.

Trent Tucker: Hubie was thrown out [of Game 1], and Pitino coached and went right to the press-and-trap. Darrell Walker made some key steals with the game on the line to give us a chance to get back into the game. It was a great team effort, on the road with the head coach not around and your assistant coach has to take over and carry on the duties. He had some young players who were able to step up, especially Darrell Walker.

With just nine seconds left, Sparrow's two free throws capped a Knicks comeback from a 12-point fourth-quarter deficit and gave New York a 94–93 Game 1 win.

Rory Sparrow: A lot of pressure. I always remember what Mike Newlin told me when I first came up: Always think that you could possibly miss the shot. Then think past the missing to the making. I was focused on my technique. Not the fans, not Isiah whispering to me that I wasn't gonna make them. And that was at the Silverdome, so I had no backdrop.

As the series progressed, King was unstoppable. He scored 36 points in Game 1, followed by 46, 46, and 41 in the next three. Meanwhile, the Knicks held Thomas to just 18 points per game over the first four games.

Rory Sparrow: I always thought Isiah Thomas was a super, super player. But based on his team, he'd always take off certain times and let other players get into the game. So what I tried to do was minimize his impact early in the game–make him pass, play him extremely hard–and then hope that some of those other players would get hot so he wouldn't shoot the ball and not necessarily be in a rhythm at the end of the game. I had a lot of success with Isiah because one of the greatest things that he did was that he liked to dribble a lot. So that always helped me: I was always able to cover players that dribbled a lot rather than players that made quick moves and had a lot of athletic ability. The fact that Isiah dribbled a lot gave me the opportunity to be a better defender on him.

Hubie Brown: Sparrow played him well. Sparrow was a good matchup against Isiah. We had gotten Sparrow the previous year, and he was the link to that team, because he was such a great defender. When you talk about full-court pressing, man-to-man, the best three guys I ever saw do that were Mo Cheeks, Danny Ainge, and Rory Sparrow. They were the three best guys at wearing down point guards during the course of a season. And I think Rory played Isiah extremely well, and that was the major reason we won that series. Plus, [that was] the reason we were ahead in Game 5, without the home-court advantage, until Isiah went on that incredible finish. That has to be one of the greatest highlights in the history of the NBA.

Deadlocked at two games apiece, the series would be decided in Game 5. Due to a scheduling conflict, the game was moved from the spacious, air-conditioned Silverdome to a stiflingly hot Joe Louis Arena in downtown Detroit.

No matter the locale, the Knicks had other worries. Their best player was hurting. Badly.

Hubie Brown: He had splints on both of his middle fingers, both dislocations. At the shootaround, Bernard is ill and can't come to the shootaround. They're feeding him intravenously. He's averaging over 40 in the series. Now, we can't hit him on the break because he can't dribble, with

the pain in his hands. So we're thinking, How the hell are we going to win without this guy?

Rory Sparrow: Bernard wouldn't shake your hand. During the last part of the year, Bernard had been jamming his fingers, and it became a small bone of contention between Bernard and Truck. In other words, Bernard could sit out with the jammed finger but Truck got hurt on almost a nightly basis, but he had to practice. So now Bernard would come out, and he wouldn't shake your hand. Instead, he'd hit the back of your hand with the back of his hand. But Truck would say, "Yeah? But throw him the ball and see him grab the ball!" That was a little rivalry thing going on.

Ernie Grunfeld: In Game 5, he not only had the problem with his fingers, he also had a fever. He had a 102° temperature. And he came in and played one of the great games in playoff history.

Rory Sparrow: So now everybody's wondering how he was gonna play. But it's a testament to his greatness as a player. When the game was on the line, he could focus in and just do what he did. So if you threw him a bad pass, he still had great hands even though his hands were bandaged up. And that whole series, he was phenomenal because he was hurt the whole time. It's crazy how great he was.

Hubie Brown: Game 5 was on the neutral court, Joe Louis Arena, because the Silverdome wasn't available. And the place was incredibly hot, right in the first quarter. Unbearably warm.

After three quarters, with King scoring 26 points, the Knicks led 85–79. Sparrow held Thomas to just nine points over the first 36 minutes, and all seemed secure.

And then . . .

In mind-blowing fashion, Thomas scored 21 fourth-quarter points–including 16 in the final 1:57–to force overtime.

Ernie Grunfeld: That game was unbelievable. First of all, it was hot, and the humidity level was very high. The way the game went [was], we had good control of the game. Then, all of a sudden, Isiah just did what great players do, and the whole momentum turned. And some of the shots he made were just incredible. Ray Williams was on him and Rory Sparrow was on him, and Darrell Walker. And Darrell was a great defensive player. We tried everything. We tried double-teaming him, but he got a lot of his points in transition. But when a great player gets like that, it's very hard to deny him.

Trent Tucker: We all played Isiah. It was funny because both Ray Williams and Rory Sparrow fouled out in the fourth quarter, so here come Darrell Walker and myself, a rookie and a second-year player, in Game 5 on the road at Joe Louis Arena with everything on the line. I remember Hubie calling us to the sideline and saying, "Hey, hey, hey. Relax. This is what it's all about. This is the fifth game of the playoffs, and you two guys have a chance to do something really special. Just go out and enjoy the moment." And for us to hear that, from him, in a pressure situation, just gave us the sense of confidence we needed as young players to get the job done.

Rory Sparrow: If you watch the tape, I'm doing a good job defensively on him. If you get a player to shoot the shots that he shot, without the fouls, you've done a great job, because he was in positions where most people can't make those shots. I tried to force people into areas where they're not comfortable shooting. If they make it, they make it. If not, you're doing a good job.

I got a couple of looks. I made one and missed two or three. But I'm doing a real good job defensively on Isiah–I stole the ball from him a few times–so I'm thinking that I don't have to have a good night offensively. Just keep him under control. So as it's going along, he's under control, we have a nice little lead, and I'm feeling confident that everything is going well. I have his rhythm down, and he's not as excited and as dominating as he can be.

Then, in the fourth quarter, he makes one tough shot with me right in his face. And that seems to get him going. He makes another tough shot where he might have been aided by an official's call, so now he goes to the line. And now he becomes this beast. He's at the top of his game. He's doing things that he hasn't done all season: dribbling, creating, shoot-

ing, and scoring. He shows why he's a Hall of Famer. I don't know how many points he scored, but my kids always tell me it's too many.

Trent Tucker: I was fouled [at the end of regulation], but time had expired. It was a good call. Walker stole the ball from Isiah, and I leaked out and tried to beat John Long down the floor. And as I was trying to get to the basket, I was fouled. It was a very good call; time had expired. They made the right call. Then we were able to get ourselves together in overtime.

Hubie Brown: We argued that, but we weren't gonna get that call.

Trent Tucker: There wasn't much said. We had a second life. Isiah had gone crazy in the fourth quarter, then Walker made the big defensive play to deny him the chance to win the game in regulation. Once we got our second life, it was like, let's just go out and execute, let's stick together and play it out and see what happens.

In the extra session, the Knicks ripped off nine straight points and held Detroit scoreless for more than three minutes. King capped a 44-point night with 4 points and four rebounds in overtime, and wound up averaging 42.6 points per game in the series. The Knicks won the game and the series, 127–123.

Bernard King: You're enveloped in playing the game. You're not watching Isiah Thomas score points. So you're enveloped in, what do we have to do to shut Isiah down? What do we have to do as a team to ultimately put the Detroit Pistons away? That's what my focus was. My teammates did an exceptional job in that fifth game, considering that I got in early foul trouble, and for the better part of the third quarter they were able to open up a lead for us.

Rory Sparrow: Bernard was phenomenal in that series. But had it not been for Darrell Walker and Trent Tucker, we would never have won that series. Darrell made the big steals in the first game, and he made an even bigger steal in the regulation of the fifth game on Isiah. Darrell was able to come in after I fouled out, play defense, do a great job defensively.

And then he and Trent didn't lose the ball under the pressure going into the overtime. They got the ball to where it had to be, even made a couple of big shots. Sitting on the bench, I knew what they were going through. Not only trying to stop Isiah but getting the ball to Bernard, because everyone knows that we have to get the ball to Bernard. They did an unbelievable job.

Bernard King: Isiah was willing himself to carry his team. He did a great job of that. But I think that, ultimately, we were just a better team in that series.

Hubie Brown: Then you see what Bernard did in Game 5. It was one of the great moments in Knicks history for an individual. What he did, and then what he did in the overtime, were miraculous. He carried us, in spite of the incredible physical condition he was in.

Bernard King: I remember one telling play in that game late in the fourth quarter. Earl Cureton was defending me. We were in a timeout, and the play was designed for Billy Cartwright. I've never questioned the coach's authority; I'd been taught otherwise by all the tremendous coaches I'd had during the early part of my career. You just don't question the coach. The coach is the coach, and you're a player. But Hubie was designing a play for Billy Cartwright, and the game's on the line, and the play's not for me. Well, I had a problem with that. [King laughs.] Here I am playing with two dislocated fingers and I've averaged 40 points a game for five games, so if the game's on the line, give me the ball. That's always been my history as a player, so I couldn't understand in that intense moment that the play could be designed for anyone else.

So, consequently, what I said was this: "Hubie, do I have the right to take the ball myself?" And he didn't answer me. Then I spoke up even louder, "Hubie! Do I have the right to take the ball myself?" I was emphatic. Finally, he looked up at me and said, "Yeah." Because what I was saying, in effect, was, "Hubie, I'm gonna break your play." But I had to ask first; I'm not the type of guy to break a play in my professional career. I always did what was designed for me to do, so I had to ask the question before I could actually do it.

We inbound the ball. And Earl Cureton, I'll never forget, says, "Come on and bring it!" I've never had a player speak to me that way during a moment where the game, lots of careers, and the money are on the line. And he says, "Come on and bring it!" Fortunately, I brought it and scored the basket.

Ernie Grunfeld: After the game, we were all so drained. To do what Bernard did on the big stage, under those circumstances–a deciding game against a player who was incredibly hot. It was a tremendous experience to be a part of.

Rory Sparrow: That was the hottest gym. I lost so much weight, drank so much water. The intensity was such that you couldn't breathe. From the opening tip to the end of the game, you couldn't get a deep breath. When we walked off the court, we were more exhausted from that game than from playing the prior 82 to get to the playoffs. It was unbelievable.

In less than 48 hours, the Knicks would start the next round, against their oldest rivals, in the league's most intimidating arena.

The Celtics not only won the first two games–by 18 and 14 points, respectively–but they virtually shut down the Knicks' most potent weapon. After blitzing the Pistons, King could muster only 26 points in Game 1 and 13 in Game 2.

Hubie Brown: When you play Friday night [in Detroit] and you win, and the game is overtime, there's so much pressure and tension involved. . . . The team was drained. The next morning, we have to fly to Boston. We get there, and we're playing one of the best teams ever, one that's eventually going to win the championship, on their court. And it's an afternoon game. So the preparation was limited, and it's almost like a sacrifice game.

In both 1982–83 and 1983–84, we split the season series with the Celtics. We played them better than anybody. That's why we felt that we would do OK. But they beat us in double figures in Game 1 and in Game 2.

Ernie Grunfeld: I think the quote from Cedric Maxwell was, "That bitch ain't gettin' 40 on us!"

Bernard King: We, as a club, would be aware of any player that was playing that well, and that effective, as I was in the framework of our team. Certainly you want to gear a lot of what you do to stopping that one player. And any challenge that's verbally given to me or put out there by an opposing player is not something I've ever responded to. And I didn't respond to that, whether it was a reply or a response. I've always felt you let your play do the talking.

The series shifted to New York, and at the off-day practice session at Upsala College, every Knick was asked to look deep inside.

Ernie Grunfeld: The Celtics had a great team: Larry Bird, Robert Parish, Kevin McHale, Cedric Maxwell, Dennis Johnson, Danny Ainge. Boston Garden was a tough place to play, and they got us in the first two games. Hubie wanted to send a message that it wasn't over, so he worked us over in practice. I don't know what his intention was, to get us upset or wake us up, or whatever. But whatever he did worked. They had pushed us around a little bit, and the message was that we weren't gonna take it anymore, especially not on our home court.

Bernard King: Obviously, going into that series, we had come out of a very tough and difficult fifth game. I was coming off the flu and still playing with the dislocated fingers. Boston was prepared and ready for us, and we didn't play very effectively against Boston on the road. They did a good job, besides receiving three fouls on every play. [King laughs.] That was one thing they did a little differently than Detroit. One guy would foul you, and the foul's already called, and then two other guys would hit you. And that's a fact.

Hubie Brown: We never practiced. We flew back, went into the locker room, and put all of the staggering statistics on the board. And then we challenged them, because we were confident as a coaching staff that we could beat them. But it would come down to performance, and we weren't getting it, because our three best guys had to match up against Bird, Parish, and McHale. The meeting was long, and we covered every category, because during the

season we were 3–3 with them, as we were the previous year. It was a man's meeting. It was very challenging. And the most important thing coming out of that meeting was that we *had* to feel that we could beat them. And I thought we could do that in Game 3.

Rory Sparrow: We got into some arguments. Everybody got pulled over to the side. Bernard and Hubie got into it. And everyone had this thought that it was all over. But then Truck made this passionate speech to the players, rallying them. "Forget the coach, forget it all," he said. "This is about us. We need to focus on us and pull ourselves together and play." And then Bernard made a speech about how he's risking injury every night because his hands were all messed up. So by the end of the day, the press is down on us, but going into it [Game 3] I felt we had gotten through our petty issues and were more united than ever before.

Trent Tucker: We had a heart-to-heart, and it was time to see if we were ready for the challenge. The Celtics threw two haymakers at us. They weren't just trying to knock us out, they were trying to embarrass us. We had to stand up and prove that we belonged in the same place as the Celtics. [For Game 3] we had a huge home crowd at the Garden. They were rabid and ready to roll. They gave us the energy we needed to win the third game. Once we won that game, we felt that the fourth game was a game that we could win. It was gut-check time for us, but we were able to respond.

Ernie Grunfeld: So it [Game 3] started and Kevin McHale got a rebound, and we wanted to make sure that he wasn't gonna score. I grabbed him and threw him down on the floor. I hadn't thought about doing it at the time; it just happened in the heat of the moment. But I think it sent a message to them and to our players. After that, the Celtics realized they were in for a battle. But that was just a small part of the game, because the biggest part was Bernard's performance, where he got 43 in Game 4 and 44 in Game 6.

Rory Sparrow: So when we win the third game, it gives us the confidence to win the fourth game.

Ernie Grunfeld: Kevin McHale and I talk about that today, and what we realize is that those two teams really hated each other. We had real disdain and we didn't like one another. And it made for a great series. Those types of rivalries don't happen that much anymore.

Rory Sparrow: In the first two games, they dominated us. In Games 3 and 4, we won. Then we went back up there for the fifth game, and they beat us. The reason they beat us, as was stressed in practice the next day, was that they were much more physical than we were. They ran us into screens, they boxed us out, their picks were harder, they fouled harder. So one of the central themes going into Game 6 was that we didn't meet the challenge.

Hubie Brown: We came back and played great to win Games 3 and 4. They beat us again by double figures [in Game 5], but we came back in Game 6 at the Garden to win by two. Bird missed the shot at the end. And if you remember, the people stayed in the arena and were just clapping and cheering. Mike Lupica wrote that for 25 minutes after the game, nobody left the Garden. People were still buzzing and talking because it was such a heated rivalry at the time.

Rory Sparrow: In Game 6 we went out to reestablish ourselves on our court. Gerald Henderson ran me into the backboard, and we had a little argument. So, with the ammunition of not being aggressive enough, two plays later Bird is out on a break. I see him coming, and I see the opportunity to block his shot. So I go up to try for the block, but he protects the ball with his body so I can't block it. I know because of the angle I've taken, I'm gonna foul him. One of the rules that we had was you always foul a guy so he can't get the shot up. That was one of Hubie's pet peeves: wrap him up, wrap him up. But I was already in the air. The only thing to do was foul him really hard so he couldn't make the basket. So I took a swipe at the ball, but because of the angle, I hit him in the head. He goes one way, the ball goes the other, and Earl Strom is running up to me yelling, "You're outta here! You're gone!" It was crazy. So I get thrown out, and I'm sitting in the locker room watching the game, and again I'm won-

dering how Darrell and Trent are going to handle this. And, again, they did well and we won.

The 106–104 Game 6 win at a delirious Madison Square Garden evened the series at three games apiece. After the two opening losses, King had regained his touch and torched the Celtics for 24, 43, 30, and 44 points.

Just as they had 11 years before, the Knicks faced a Game 7 at the Boston Garden.

Rory Sparrow: Every other time we had been to Boston, the locker room was dead cold. Game 7? It was a hundred degrees in that room! So when we get ready to go out, it's so hot that we can't have our meeting in the room. We have to meet in another room. So that was the first thing that went wrong. Hubie's asking us to play a great game. He's saying that this is the game where you've gotta bring all your energy and your focus.

Hubie Brown: They got us in Game 7. Bernard was leveled in the first minute. He took a blow right across his nose and was knocked out. A forearm by Parish, right in front of our bench, and he never recovered.

Bernard King: When you're a scorer and you have possession of the ball a lot, you're gonna get hit. That's part of the game. Any player that's played at that level will tell you that's something you're going to deal with. Under that scenario, there's only two things you can do. You handle the hit and you move on, and you let people know it's not going to affect you. Or you retaliate. And by retaliating, you put yourself in a position to be tossed from the game. So you can't retaliate, in other words. You simply can't retaliate.

Rory Sparrow: So we come out. Truck and I are having good first quarters, but Bernard's not, and Mr. Bill's not, and Ray Williams is struggling. After the first quarter, we're in the game but we're not in the game [trailing, 36–26]. So then Hubie calls this big timeout. He pulls us out to the middle of the floor and says, "Here I am in the effin' seventh game of the Eastern Conference Playoffs. I'm up here playing the effin' Boston Celtics. And they've got Larry Bird. They've got Kevin McHale and Robert Parish.

Goddamn cannons! And here I am. I've got Truck Robinson, Billy Cartwright. Pea-shooters! How am I supposed to win with pea-shooters?" And he walks away! And we're standing there like, "I know he didn't just give up on us." So he takes that little stone that he always rubbed and walks away, and we're standing in the middle of the floor trying to figure it out. And then we just say, "Look, we've just got to play like we've played. Just play through it." But they [Boston] played a great game.

Hubie Brown: The biggest thing in that game was that Larry Bird went from an All-NBA, All-Star selection to a legend. Look at his numbers. The points, the rebounds, and the assists [39, 12, and 10]. Staggering. They needed a great performance from him, and they got it. And unfortunately for us, Bernard just couldn't recover from getting hit.

Trent Tucker: Larry Bird played the greatest game I've ever seen him play. He had a triple double and made sure that his team wouldn't be in a position to lose. When you talk about MVP and Hall of Fame–type players . . . Larry Bird, on that day, played his biggest game of the season. He stood very tall.

Rory Sparrow: Larry Bird was phenomenal. He talked so much noise; he made so many shots. He was good. And Bernard didn't play his best game; they held him to 24. So we were all disappointed, but we were optimistic for the next season.

Ernie Grunfeld: We had Bernard. We had size with Cartwright and Marvin Webster. We had a solid bench. We felt we could play with anybody.

Hubie Brown: We think that we can play with the best. That time was like now: all the dominant teams are in one conference. Now, all the dominant teams are in the West. Back then, it was the East. So how can you get past Philadelphia and Boston? Because that's who you have to get past, to get to the Eastern Finals. We felt that we were one free agent away. We pick up Pat Cummings, and we think everything's going to be fine. We're very positive.

Bernard King: We were extremely close. When you consider the Boston team that we took to seven, after losing the first two, with Bird, one of the greatest players ever, and Robert Parish and Kevin

McHale, Dennis Johnson, Cedric Maxwell, and that tremendous bench they had, we took one of the greatest teams in history to seven games. So we believed in our hearts that we were poised to contend for a title. Going into the following season, that's how everyone prepared. We expected that we would play at that level. Injuries before the season countered that plan, and it never happened.

As the Knicks climbed back into prominence, they were defined by the fierceness and will of two men. From the bench it was Hubie Brown.

Hubie Brown: We only had four rules with the Knicks. Number one, you be on time. If you're not, you're gonna pay a heavy fine. Number two, you play hard. If you don't, you lose your time. We play 10 guys a quarter. Number three, we want you to know your position. You don't know your position, you lose your time. And then the last thing is, we just ask you to know when to pass and when to shoot.

Now, when you write that down on the board, they think it's easy. But then you see that we're gonna *enforce* every one of those four things. And the selfish people never get it, and the selfishness will always make one or more of those four things difficult to do.

Rory Sparrow: He's the most organized coach and one of the best strategists, as far as coming up with a game plan and implementing it. He was really brilliant at that. And you didn't understand a lot of his brilliance until later, after you could reflect on it. I always felt that if the games were close, he would make the correct coaching decisions in the last two or three minutes to win ballgames. He could almost will you to win games. His only drawback was that his people skills at that level, because of his drive, weren't the best in the world. He alienated some of his players because of his constant drive to make players be better and to get players to push the envelope of success. If they were successful, he wanted more. As the players said, he'd get on the horse and just try to ride it and ride it.

Hubie Brown: The preparation of the coaching staff is better because of the inventions of the fax machine, the computer videos, and so on. The practice sessions are exactly the same. Every bit as demanding, every bit as organized, and every bit in regards to the discipline involved. Coaching the games—the preparation and the games themselves—we still run them exactly the same. I don't think there's been a dramatic change at all.

Ernie Grunfeld: In the first part of the season, we'd practice for two hours. Then after the first 20 games we'd practice for an hour and 45, then after 40 [for] an hour and a half. And for the last 20 games we'd probably only practice for an hour and 15 minutes. He'd tell you that going in.

Mike Saunders: Hubie loved to do speaking engagements. We were talking about it one day and he said, "That's my golf." Hubie wasn't a golfer, and I guess he got absorbed in preparing and giving the talks. That got him away from the tensions of being the coach. So "That's my golf" was a line that really captured why he did it.

Rory Sparrow: All of his personality was to get the most out of his players. If you go through Hubie's history, most of his teams overachieved. And he takes great pride in that. But when you have a talented group like we had, you don't want them underachieving, but you don't have to push them as much to overachieve. If they just do what they need to do, they're gonna be good enough to win a lot more games. Some of Hubie's yelling and pushing caused some of the players to drift from the game plan.

Trent Tucker: Once I got to know Hubie as a coach and a person, he was much easier to understand. I understood that he came in with a lot of pressure on him, and he had a lot of young players under him. People don't understand the pressure of the NBA game. Everyone's job was on the line. Once I got to understand the business and nature of the NBA, that's when I began to appreciate Hubie Brown as a basketball coach, and the things he was trying to teach us, trying to make us better players. A lot of things that I know about the game today as I analyze basketball came from Hubie Brown.

And on the court it was the incomparable Bernard King.

Trent Tucker: Anytime you're going into the playoffs and facing heavy competition, you hope there'll be one guy you can rely on who's going to get you 35 or 40 points in a big ballgame. And we knew that Bernard King could do that for us, and by him being able to carry the load offensively and force the double-teams from the defensive end, we were going to get the chance to have other guys be successful in our offense. He was a tremendous low-post offensive player. He ran the court very well. He was very determined to carry us on his back offensively, and he did a fantastic job doing that.

Ernie Grunfeld: He led by example. His work ethic, intensity level, and competitive nature were unparalleled.

Marv Albert: Bernard was unstoppable. If you talk to players of that era, they say he was the guy. I loved the demeanor, the seriousness, the game face, which he did for himself as much as for anyone else, just to get himself ready.

Ernie Grunfeld: People really don't understand. Bernard played the games with such high intensity. Well, that's how he practiced, too. He had the uncanny ability to turn his focus up from being very mellow, say a half hour or 45 minutes before a game, to just turning it on like a light switch. I've never seen anybody with that kind of ability to play with that kind of energy on a nightly basis. Whatever pain he had, he could put it out of his head. He just focused so hard to push any negativity out of his head.

Marv Albert: What impressed me most about him was that when he came to camp following the off-season, he'd always come back with two or three new moves. There are some great players who work on their games all summer long; they don't take off. Larry Bird, Michael Jordan, Kevin McHale. And Bernard would do that. He'd always come back with new stuff, as great as he was.

Ernie Grunfeld: He was a terrific teammate. He was very unselfish. He made the passes when he had to make them. He was unbelievable in transition. People talk about his great low-post game, but he was an amazing transition player who could finish in traffic and go over people.

Rory Sparrow: Night after night, he could do some phenomenal things. The rest of us would just do what we could defensively to stop teams. One of the great things about Hubie Brown's system was that he had a full 10-man rotation. The first group would come in and play solid defense, then the second group would trap them to death and get them tired. It was a system designed to slow people down offensively and then let Bernard score as many points as he could.

Marv Albert: He had a brief career in New York, but he's one of the most underrated players in the history of the game. The series against Isiah . . . They were both playing on a different level. They were playing their own game in another universe.

Ernie Grunfeld: Once he missed six or seven games, and then we had other guys stepping up, like Truck Robinson and Ray Williams. Then Bernard came back and those other guys' production went down. So we had a team meeting led by Hubie, who was saying, "Look, you other guys gotta give us more." But the other guys said that they weren't getting as many touches because Bernard had come back and most of the plays were going for him. Then Bernard stepped up and told Hubie, "Next game, don't call my number at all. I'll get mine. Just don't call my number. But, I want the ball every time in the last two minutes of the game." At first Hubie refused, but Bernard insisted. He said, "Let's try that, because we have to get everybody involved. Don't call my number." Next game he had 42, with *one* play called for him. But it showed that he believed in his teammates as much as we believed in him.

Bernard King, of course, couldn't do it all on his own. And when, during the next season, the injuries started to pile up, the Knicks started to struggle.

Rory Sparrow: Ray Williams was probably the second most talented guy on that team. He could really score, and he sacrificed a lot of what he was as a player to fit into the system. And he had difficulties doing that because he was so talented. It was a challenge for him to be less instead of more, because he's

a guy who needed the ball. And I kept it from him to give it to Bernard. So when Ray got the ball he wouldn't have much time to do things with it. Ray probably made the largest sacrifice of all the players on the team to make us go.

Truck Robinson was a very sensitive guy. He was hard as nails, an ultimate professional who knew how to play and did all the right things. But he was very sensitive and because he was such a big guy, people didn't think he was sensitive. People would say one small thing to Truck and it would rile him for a week. And Hubie never really understood that, and consequently he didn't get as much out of Truck as he could have. Truck was a guy who always kept us together because he gave such good advice.

Bill Cartwright was a good offensive player, and Hubie was trying to transform him into not only an offensive player but a defensive presence as well. He had Marvin Webster there to help him learn. Hubie really got the most out of Cartwright.

Mr. Bill was a very quiet leader. You'd miss a shot and then coming up the floor you'd be running next to Mr. Bill, and he'd whisper in your ear, "Did you see me open on that play?"

Hubie Brown: Our problem is that over the summer, Cartwright gets the stress fracture and has the operation. Truck breaks his ankle. Marvin Webster doesn't play again. So we lost three of our key frontline people, and we never recovered. We were right there as one of the top defensive rebounding teams in the league, and that was our strength. Then came our ability to have Bernard, Cartwright, and Truck score and all be basically post-up guys. And our second unit, our bench, was so good in the second half of '83 and the whole following season, with Darrell Walker and Trent Tucker in the backcourt and Louis Orr, Ernie, and Marvin up front. That was very big with what we were developing. And unfortunately, we lose those key guys, and Billy, for two years.

Ernie Grunfeld: We already had a lot of injuries that season; Cartwright and Webster were already out. Bernard was leading the league in scoring; his numbers were just incredible.

Midway through the 1984–85 season, the optimism generated by the previous year's playoff run had vanished under a wave of injury.

King, however, was enjoying another spectacular season. On Christmas Day, he poured in a franchise-record 60 points in a Garden loss to New Jersey. Bernard would become the first–and only–Knick in club history to lead the NBA in scoring, with a club record 32.9 average.

But after the night of March 23, 1985, at Kemper Arena in Kansas City, all that King had accomplished as a Knick would be a distant and haunting memory.

Trent Tucker: It was a meaningless regular-season game, but that was Bernard. He played with full intensity every time he stepped on the floor, whether the game meant something or not. But every game meant something to him. He didn't have to chase down Reggie Theus, but Bernard made the extra effort, as he always did.

Bernard King: That is, in fact, how I played my entire basketball life on every single level. If you're on the court, you're expected to give 110 percent of your effort. Because the game was basically over and we're not contending and we're not a playoff team, none of that matters to the fans who are sitting there in the arena. They expect to see you at your very best, and that's what I expected to deliver. That's something, I think, that coaches and my teammates respected about me. It's a play I'm supposed to go after. If I can block the shot, I'll block the shot.

Rory Sparrow: I was trailing the play. He went up to block Reggie's shot, and then he just screamed out and lay on the floor. I thought it might have been a hamstring. But then as I got closer and closer, [I saw] he was really in pain. Oh, man. We just thought it was an injury where he'd be out for a little while, but then we got the word about how severe it was. And from then on, it was just a series of injury upon injury upon injury.

Bernard King: Reggie Theus was going in for a layup. I was trailing the play, several steps behind. He elevated for the shot, and if I had taken another step, or two steps, there was no way I could get to the shot. So I attempted to elevate a little more

powerfully than perhaps I ordinarily would on a play like that. I had been in that kind of a play thousands of times in my basketball life, so it wasn't unlike any other play. The results were different, obviously, on the planting of my right foot.

Ernie Grunfeld: As he gathered to explode, the knee just went. It wasn't even in contact. He went up in the air and he knew something serious had happened. And as he landed, he made sure that he didn't land on that leg. He landed on one leg, went right down, and was very still. So he had the presence of mind to know that something very serious was wrong, because he heard it snap. He told me later that he felt the snap, so he landed on the good leg. It was a frightening moment.

Bernard King: My knee just shattered. I just felt the most excruciating pain I ever had in my life. I recall going up in the air saying, "Oh, my God!" The next thing you realize is that you're on the floor in excruciating pain. You don't realize you attempted to block the shot. At that point, in the air, I knew my career was probably over.

Hubie Brown: I can still see it. He was coming from right to left, and our bench was on the left side. Reggie Theus was fast-breaking. In spite of us not having Bill, Truck, and Marvin, we still had an outside chance to make the playoffs. Bernard had been carrying us. Reggie was out in front on the break, and he's chasing Reggie. They were the only two guys in the play. And as Reggie goes to lay it up, Bernard took that last step to elevate and block the shot as he was running him down from behind. You could *hear* the crack. You could *hear* it so loud. And he just went down like he was shot. I'll never forget it.

Mike Saunders: Bernard was in extreme pain. Earlier that season, he had had some ankle injuries, so sometimes you need to make assumptions as you're going out there. I assumed, at first, that it was his ankle. But he was grabbing his knee. After that, when we evaluated him, we suspected an ACL injury, and unfortunately, that was confirmed.

Dr. Norman Scott: In that era, that was the quintessential career-ending injury, because no one at that point had returned in a skilled position with an

anterior cruciate ligament tear. Remember, this was at best the embryonic arthroscopic era. So we were still in the old era of various open surgical techniques. That's why it was pure pessimism that he would ever return at all, and certainly never to All-Star status.

Hubie Brown: It was so sad. It was sad for him because he was out in front in the scoring race and would still win it. It was sad for the team because we still had a chance, and he could have possibly been MVP had we made it. It was just the final blow to a difficult, gut-wrenching season. But the guys never gave up. And the things he had done that year were spectacular. Christmas Day . . . How could you forget Christmas Day?

It would be two years before Bernard King would play again. The road back would be long, tedious, and eventually controversial.

Bernard King: My mind-set was the same as it was regarding my approach to playing basketball: I planned my success. It didn't happen by accident. I made it to the NBA because I planned it, not because it happened by accident. Because my work ethic put me in a position to compete against the top players in the world. So when I was injured, I had to treat my injury the same way I treated my preparation to make it to the NBA, to stay in the NBA, and ultimately to become better as a player within the league. And when you're faced with something in life that's devastating to your career, potentially career-ending, and you're being told that no one had successfully overcome that sort of injury to have a fulfilling career again, then you have to make sure–at least I believed–that you had to control everything that was within your control. Namely, speaking to the right people, reading medical journals, understanding the nature of what I'm facing and the nature of the injury. I wasn't even aware of what the anterior cruciate ligament was until I was injured.

Dr. Norman Scott: He was the best. I've never seen a patient who was a better student. What people forget is that for one week, he had every doctor in the country who did this type of surgery come in, and he would interview them in his room and tape the interviews. So I'd go see him at night in the hospital and he'd tell me, "Doctor X was here and this is what he said . . . " I would interpret it in simpler terms so he understood. Then he'd ask me what I thought, which way I wanted to do it. At that point, there really weren't one or two standard techniques. There were multiple ways of doing it. So he became a real student. He had at least five different doctors from around the country come in.

Bernard King: So I needed information. I needed to understand what I was dealing with, and that allowed me to pose the right questions. Then, based on the answers I received, I was able to make a decision, feeling secure that I made the right decision and asked the right questions.

Dr. Norman Scott: Bernard became an unbelievable student. I mean, he knew everything. The only time we ever had a fight was when I took his cast off and took the stitches out. He said he had an area of numbness on the side of his leg, and I said, "Of course you do. Everybody has that. It goes away," and so forth. So he went home and he called me an hour after he got home and said, "I am really pissed off. You never told me I would have numbness!" Meanwhile, I had told him everything conceivable that he had asked. So I just lost it at that point. I said, "I never told you what size suture material I was gonna use, either!" But that's how much of a student he was.

Bernard King: Norm is my valued friend for life. He'll always be my friend. I know I probably drove him crazy. He said I was the best patient he ever had, because I challenged him. When I had my cast removed, and we discussed everything I was going to feel with my knee reconstructed, with 40 metal staples running down my knee, I knew all of that was going to happen. I knew I was gonna be on morphine; I knew the pain I was gonna deal with. So when my knee was numb in that one area, that *one* area, I felt that was something I should have known about. "Norm!" I said. "You're the ultimate doctor! Tell me, how could you forget?"

Dr. Norman Scott: He was in the midst of negotiating for a long-term contract, and the papers said it was almost a done deal. It was just a question of getting it signed. And then he goes down with this injury. So this was devastating for him in a lot of ways.

Bernard King: What Norm realized was that I was really focused on getting back, and I was not going to allow anything to stand in my way. Without Norm Scott, I never would have returned. Without [therapist] Dania Sweitzer, I never would have returned. I put in a tremendous amount of time, work, and effort, unlike anyone had put in before, to make it back. But without those two individuals, it would not have happened. Today, I can't take a shower without looking at my knee and seeing that huge scar running down it, and I think of Dania and Dr. Scott. They're with me for life.

King's crippling injury was the final, devastating blow. After coming within one victory of the Eastern Conference Finals in 1984, the Knicks fell into oblivion. They would not win more than 24 games in any of the following three seasons.

But King's was not the only injury that devastated the Knicks. Bill Cartwright, just beginning to come into his own, was sidelined for nearly two years with a broken bone in his left foot.

Rory Sparrow: Everybody went down. And we wind up starting Eddie Lee Wilkins, Kenny Bannister, Ronnie Cavenall, and Chris McNealy. We're playing in the NBA with a lot of CBA-caliber players. Night after night, we played hard, but we made mental mistakes. Combined with the lack of talent, we just lost so many games. And that's when I thought Hubie was probably the most frustrated I've ever seen him. It was really hard on him. Regardless of what game plan he drew up, he didn't have the talent and he didn't have the horses.

If that team were together for another year, without the injuries, and then we got, say, a Gerald Wilkins, we'd have been very good. We were right there. But there are certain things in life and fate that you have nothing to do with. All you can do is play your card and play it as hard as you can. We did the best with what we could, and I think that was a tribute to Hubie and his system.

Dr. Norman Scott: Billy was in '84. He had the fracture, and at that point we didn't know medically whether we should push people toward surgery or not. Today, we would push them. At that point, we said, "Look, it's your option." So Billy said, in a nice way, that he didn't want surgery. So we went with the cast, and it didn't work; he refractured. Then he had the operation and the screw broke in the post-op. And we've seen players where that's happened. So everything had to be redone.

Mike Saunders: Bill's injury taught me about the stresses that the game places on the athlete. He practiced with the team, did everything, simulated every move that he would do in a game. Yet, the second game back, it just gave out again. That shows you the difference between practices and games.

Dr. Norman Scott: Billy was the greatest. You could not help but love him. He's just a nice, nice person. Somehow the press created an image as if the fractures were his fault and that he was soft. He was anything but soft. Billy never, ever complained about anything. He was frustrated as hell, but he didn't wear his emotions on his sleeve. But it just killed him. So it was nice to see him do well later on.

The disastrous 24-win 1984–85 season did, however, yield the one prize that would determine the Knicks' course for the next 15 years: they emerged as the winner of the first-ever NBA Draft Lottery on Mother's Day 1985. With general manager DeBusschere pounding the table in front of him in a moment of unbounded joy, the Knicks had a clear path to drafting Georgetown center Patrick Ewing–not only an All-American, not only an NCAA Champion in 1984, not only a game-changing, defense-oriented seven-footer, but a certified franchise maker.

But Ewing's first two Knicks seasons were anything but smooth, as he missed a total of 51 games due to injury. Despite being named NBA Rookie of the Year in 1986, he struggled to find his niche. The injuries were one reason. Another was Brown's early experiment with a "Twin Towers" front line of Ewing and Cartwright, which had one natural center or the other at power forward.

Patrick Ewing: I knew New York was a great place because I played so many games there in the Big East. I knew what kind of atmosphere it was. I was just very happy that the Knicks were the ones who won the lottery.

Rory Sparrow: When he came to the Knicks, he was a great, great defensive player. When we went through all those injuries, he had to transform himself into an offensive player. At Georgetown, he was a phenomenal defensive player.

Hubie Brown: We were trying to win, and as we got used to it, they would be able to alternate who would play power forward and who would play center against different teams.

Patrick Ewing: The guys who took me under their wing were Trent Tucker, Louis Orr, Ken Bannister, and Darrell Walker. They talked to me about what to expect in the NBA. Basically, they were friends before they were teammates.

Hubie Brown: Our four and five positions were interchangeable. It didn't matter which position you played, whether you were a four or a five. You can ask any big guy who ever played for me: both positions were interchangeable. But because on some nights Cartwright played the center and Ewing played the power forward, everybody got bent out of shape. Patrick had a commercial, if you remember, for Voit, where they called him the "center of attention." So his agent, David Falk, wasn't pleased that he wasn't being referred to as a true center. Who really cared? I thought the object was to try and win the games. And I always liked the quote from Kevin McHale: "What's the problem? I'm a center, and Robert Parish is a center, and we both play together along with Larry Bird." What was the problem? There wasn't a problem in Houston, when they played Ralph Sampson and Hakeem Olajuwon together. So what was the problem? It was a media problem, not an execution problem.

Patrick Ewing: It was tough, because as a rookie most of the plays were run through the center position. It was tough, but I did the best I could.

Hubie Brown: We were still waiting for Cartwright to come back; we were still waiting for Bernard to come back. Truck and Marvin were fin-

ished. And that first year [with Patrick], we're playing Gerald Wilkins at small forward, because Louis Orr held out. Bobby Thornton is the starting power forward; he's a fourth-round pick. And Patrick is at center, with Tucker and Sparrow. He played right up to the All-Star Game. Our last game before the break is in Utah, and he's voted to the All-Star Team. And that night, a Thursday in Utah, he gets injured and has to have knee surgery. But they can't do the surgery until Monday in New York, so he goes to Dallas for the All-Star Weekend. Then they operate, and we don't have him for the rest of the year.

I thought that in our exhibition games, we proved that those two guys [Ewing and Cartwright] playing together would be good. But what we needed was time for Cartwright to get back into shape and into game condition. We liked what we saw. And the reason we played the two of them together was that that's who we had. And when Pitino came the following year, if he didn't play the two of them together, they wouldn't make the playoffs. Then what really made Pitino's second year was the trade for Charles Oakley, because now you've got a legitimate power forward.

With the Knicks continuing to plummet, DeBusschere was replaced as general manager by longtime NBA official Scotty Stirling in January 1986. Meanwhile, King's rehabilitation from knee surgery turned into a point of contention. He did not attend most games, and he went for extended periods with little contact with the front office.

Bernard King: As far as my removing myself from the public eye and not talking to the media, that was my intent. I felt that I was facing something that would be quite difficult, and I didn't want any pity from anyone. I didn't want to hear–because this is how the story would have run–"Wow! He was such a tremendous talent, and it's unfortunate he suffered this devastating injury, and his career is over." I didn't want to hear that. What I wanted was positive reinforcement within my own mind to create a mental state that I could do something that hadn't been done before. If I allowed that sort of negative input to invade my own personal spirit, it would have been very difficult to move forward every day.

Dr. Norman Scott: Each time I would go to see Bernard during his rehab, about once a month, he would show me something new. Every time, he'd show me something new that he could do, at the end of the workout. He was like a little kid.

Bernard King: And what I did, literally, and Dania will tell you this, was that every day I worked with Dania, I treated it like it was my own personal game. I treated it like I was trying to make it into the NBA. And when I closed that door, if our workouts were through, I patted myself on the back and said, "Great job, Bernard." I physically took my hand and patted myself on the back and said, "Great job." Because when you're dealing with an obstacle, when you're dealing with a challenge that you deem to be great, you have to motivate yourself to believe that you can make it happen. And when the management came to see me in the hospital, and I'm lying there after the surgery with 40 metal staples down my knee, I said to them, "All I request is two things: put all the equipment in my house and send a therapist to my home, and I guarantee you I'll be back."

Harvey Araton: He had gotten hurt and was away for more than a year, and nobody had seen him or talked to him. The team was losing. They had drafted Kenny Walker with their [1986] first pick. At the press conference, we asked Scotty Stirling about his picking a small forward, and if that meant he didn't expect Bernard to come back. And Scotty said, "We don't know what to expect from Bernard." By this point, Scotty was already generating some skepticism. So we said, "How can you be the general manager of a team and not have access to this guy? Doesn't he have to tell you? Doesn't he have to answer the phone?" And he said, "You know what? He's up at Upsala College. Go see for yourself. And if you can get in to see him, more power to you."

So Filip [Bondy] and I looked at each other, and we decided that the next day we'd go up there early–*really* early–and sneak into the gym, go onto the stage they had in there, hide behind the curtain and watch him work out. If we got tossed, we got

tossed. The next day, we both hit the rush hour traffic and get there late, and he's already in the gym. So we're standing by the bushes in front of the gym, peeking in there. We see this guy who, from a distance, looks like Ernie [Grunfeld] but turns out to be Bernard's personal trainer. We're looking in, and every time we think he's looking at us, we dive into the bushes. This goes on for about 20 minutes. Then, all of a sudden, Bernard, being a very smart guy and sensing that something's going on, sneaks out the back, comes around, and catches us in the act. He's standing behind us saying, "What the fuck do you guys think you're doing?" And we say, "Well, ahhhhh . . . Scotty told us to come up here and watch you work out."

I say, "Hey, they drafted Kenny Walker. We're just wondering if you have any future with this team. You're working out; obviously something's going on. The fans deserve to know something." Bernard starts to walk inside, like he won't talk to us. Then he stops, turns around, and, again, being a very smart guy, he realizes that he has these two guys here and that he can use them for himself. He says, "You guys want to watch me work out? Come on in." We go in and sit in the bleachers, and he's doing all these moves and shots for about a half hour. Then he brings in this guy that he's been working with, and they're playing one-on-one, running full-court. Bernard's looking pretty good, and he was at the point where he was having so much fun, it was probably a relief not to be hiding this stuff anymore. He was an unusual guy, and why he was going to that extent to work out in secret, who knew? Then he was taking requests: "What do you guys want to see? What do you want me to show you?"

After it's over he grants us an interview, sweet as can be. Filip and I leave the gym and we're in heaven. We have the scoop of the year. We got Bernard. We get in our cars and turn on the radio, thinking we're back page for sure. Guess what happened that day? Len Bias. Len Bias [Boston's first-round draft pick] had died the previous night and it broke that morning. So our big scoop did run the next day, and the back page was actually split, something like, "Bias dead" and under that was "We see Bernard." We thought we had this huge scoop, and we got completely overshadowed by the Bias story. And I don't believe Bernard ever let anyone watch him work out again, until he actually came back.

Dr. Norman Scott: Theoretically, for high school– or college–type athletes, depending on the skill level required, most of them are back playing in about six months. However, when you say "they're back playing," it's a solid year before they're really playing at their level. They're there, but they're just not themselves yet. I think even today, for a torn ACL and a player of Bernard's skill, you're talking at least a year.

Ultimately it would never happen, yet it remains one of the great what-ifs of Knicks history: What would have happened had a healthy Bernard King and a healthy Patrick Ewing played together in New York?

Trent Tucker: If you could have put those two guys together at their peak, the Knicks would have won one or more championships. Because you would have had that dynamic duo that all championship teams need. And you do need two, because if you double-team one guy, you know the other guy can carry the load all by himself. But also by having two great players, it makes the job of the role players that much easier.

Bernard King: We would have won a title. The reason I say that is that you have one of the greatest centers in the history of the game, one of the greatest players, and you have someone like myself that had tremendous leadership ability. But more important, I had the ability to adjust my game. When I came back, I came back with a jump shot that I didn't have [at the time] I was injured. I remade my entire game when I was in Washington. That's always been my mental approach. You adjust your game to the style of play that your club is requesting of you, not the other way around. Consequently, the ball would have gone through Patrick, and I would have loved that. I would have loved to have had the ball, and [with my being] a scorer, he wouldn't have had to see as many double-teams. He would have had the ability to oper-

ate a little more freely in the low post, and it would have taken some of the pressure off him.

Trent Tucker: They differed because they played different positions, but their intensity levels were the same. Their approach to games, their aggressiveness, their ability to carry their teams on their backs if they had to, were all the same. They were superstar-type players. They had the same mind-set. If Bernard had stayed healthy, he would probably have rewritten some of the Knicks scoring records. Patrick was a guy who could block and change shots. Bernard was a great slash-and-mover, a low-post small forward who was so good in the open floor and was so much fun to watch. But when it came down to preparation, those two guys were on the same page.

Hubie Brown, whose intensity and drive had led a moribund Knicks team back into contention, would not survive a third straight losing season. After a 4–12 start in 1986–87, he was replaced by assistant Bob Hill on December 1, 1986.

Bernard King: I knew I wasn't going to get re-signed. I saw it happening. And quite frankly, if I was in their position to have to make that decision, I wouldn't have signed me, either. It's professional sports. Regardless of the fact that you've given your limbs and heart and soul to the organization, you recognize that there's a business side of that. And as a result, you [the organization] don't invest that kind of money or take that kind of risk with a player that's only played six games and you're unsure what your return is going to be. Then you factor in that you're creating a new system, a new style. You've got this great player in Patrick Ewing, and with someone like me, they didn't think my skills were going to fit. I didn't have a problem with that. And I would never, ever criticize the Knicks. You won't find, in print, anywhere, when I've ever said anything negative about the Knicks. Because it was my dream. I fulfilled my dream, playing for my hometown team. But it did feel good to come back and get 49 against them a few years later. [King laughs.]

Hubie Brown: In Ewing's first year, the [salary] cap comes in. And you're only allowed three guys on the injured list. We had 4 guys out at one time, so we could only dress 11. So where did the guys have to come from? They came from the CBA. Those guys tried their best, and they played hard. They couldn't have played any better or any harder than they played. That was a very difficult time.

Rory Sparrow: It was coming. He [Brown] got into a serious shouting match with several players, leading up to that. The frustration was very evident; you knew it was reaching that point. At the end of the day, I don't know how much the fact that we weren't winning was his fault. It didn't have much to do with his coaching. He could have been a better people person, but he had a better team on the injured list than he had on the floor. There was nothing he could do about that. But in pro sports, it's easier to get rid of the coach than 12 players. Then they hired Bob Hill, who was exactly the opposite, just a player's dream. Unfortunately, again, we just didn't have the talent.

Hubie Brown: The Friday before Thanksgiving, we're in Chicago and we lose by two. Then the following Saturday we play Cleveland, and we lose by two in the Garden, and Ewing misses some foul shots. So now we're 4–12 but could be 6–10. If we had won both of those games, who knows what would have happened? Unfortunately, we didn't. And you become unemployed.

Marv Albert: At one point, I think the crowds were getting annoyed with them. It reached its worst level following Hubie, when Bob Hill took over and it was a CBA-type team because everybody was hurt. To me, aside from the early sixties, that was the lowest point.

Hubie Brown: I look back at the Knicks years and say, in '83 and '84, we had the best years that the Knicks had since the '73 championship. We got farther than any Knicks team had since then, and it took a while for a Knicks team to go farther than the '83 and '84 teams. And in both of those two years, we got taken out by the championship team: Philadelphia, who had been on the cover of *Sports Illustrated* as the greatest team ever, and then Boston. And in '84, when we lost to the Celtics, we had gone 9–10 against them, including the playoffs, in those two years. So how bad were we? Unfortunately, we couldn't sustain the loss of Cartwright, Robinson, Webster, and then eventually King. Naturally, I would have wanted it to end better. Unfortunately for us, it just didn't. But it did spawn a television career that—little did I know—was the right thing for me after 30 years of coaching. It opened up a whole new world for me.

After two decades of coaching, Al Bianchi returned to his hometown as general manager in 1987.

THE LINEUP: Al Bianchi; Peter Vecsey; Jeff Van Gundy; Mark Jackson; Rory Sparrow; Trent Tucker; Stu Jackson; Charles Oakley; Kiki Vandeweghe; John MacLeod; Phil Jackson; Maurice Cheeks; Ernie Grunfeld; John Starks; Dave Checketts.

Now the Knicks would be shaped by a couple of Big Apple guys, Al Bianchi and Rick Pitino. Both Bianchi and Pitino put their personal stamp on the Knicks: Bianchi with his easygoing manner and decidedly uncorporate style, and Pitino with an intense coaching philosophy that stressed a pressing defense and a near-collegiate atmosphere, which some critics dubbed "Madison Square Garden University."

Al Bianchi: I was just sitting around, watching my p's and q's. I keep reading in the paper where they're interviewing Jack McCloskey, and people are telling me they're doing this and that. At that time, Peter Vecsey used to visit in Phoenix. Peter was always championing the ABA, and I knew him from those days. At that time, we were pretty close. So he called me for something else, and I said, "Hey, you . . . " He said, "What's wrong?" I said, "Why are you pushing all these other guys? Why don't you push me for the job?" A week later, there's a story in the paper and I get a call from Jack Diller. Amazing. Amazing. I have two meetings with Jack Diller, I meet with him and Richard Evans, and the next thing you know we're hiding out in a hotel trying to hire a coach.

Peter Vecsey: Al and I had been tight for years from our relationship with the [Virginia] Squires in the Julius Erving days of the ABA. We used to hang together; he's a Queens guy and I'm a Queens guy. So when we talked about getting his name into print in New York for the GM job, I had no problem doing it. I always felt that he was a great judge of talent. So I think I put his name in there, but I would

hate to think that management reacted to something I wrote and actually hired a guy off seeing his name in the column. I would love to have that kind of power, but I don't think that ever happened.

Al Bianchi was a basketball lifer. The affable Long Island City product enjoyed a decade-long NBA playing career, then embarked on a 20-year coaching tenure in both the NBA and the ABA. Fired in early 1987 after 12 years as an assistant coach with the Phoenix Suns, Bianchi was named Knicks general manager in July 1987, a surprise choice entrusted with the task of resurrecting his hometown team.

Al Bianchi: When we were kids, across the bridge, our parents would say, "Don't you go over there [into Manhattan] unless you go with your brother, or blah, blah, blah." We would be playing on the other side, looking over at the big buildings of Manhattan. And I thought it was hilarious. I remember looking over there as a kid and thinking, "Wow." Now, all of a sudden, I'm the general manager of the Knicks. It cracked me up, just cracked me up. Because you know there's all those people saying,

"What the fuck does *he* know? He was a player; he wasn't a guy in a suit." And I used to just laugh.

In Phoenix, I was always a happy-go-lucky guy, saying what I think and telling people to go fuck themselves if they didn't like it. Now all of a sudden I'm the general manager, and I could just see people saying, "Ex-player? He's gonna get killed there. Who's he? He doesn't know the salary cap and things like that." I was giggling, I was really giggling about it.

Then I got there and I'm talking to all these press people, and they knew less about the salary cap than I did! And in the corporate structure, they had guys like Ken Munoz, Dave Peterson, and Frank Murphy, where that was all they did. So if you wanted to know anything, you just called them up and said, "Look, I've got this deal. How about this?" That's all you had to do. It wasn't calculus. People made the salary cap out like you had to be a Phi Beta Kappa. Well, it wasn't that way at all.

Bianchi's first task was to hire a coach to replace the fired Bob Hill. Since April, Garden president Richard Evans and MSG Sports Group head Jack Diller had been negotiating with Providence College coach Rick Pitino. Pitino, a native New Yorker who had previously served as an assistant under Hubie Brown, had written the college basketball story of the year, taking the unheralded Friars to the 1987 NCAA Final Four.

In June 1987, Pitino signed a new five-year deal with Providence. That quelled the Knicks rumors . . . briefly.

Jeff Van Gundy: When I went to Providence, I was actually taking calls for coach Pitino, on an alias, from Jack Diller. And I didn't find that out until later. I forget Jack's alias. I'd always pick up the phone in non–office hours when [secretary] Barbara Kobak wasn't there. And it was always the same guy, who I'd never heard of. So I'd go in to Rick and say, "Mr. So-and-So is on the phone." Then Rick would pick up. It stopped for a while, because he turned it down. Then the alias started again, and they finally got it done. Rick asked me to go with him in what was a nonpaying, volunteer position; eventually it

went to Ralph Willard. But I decided to stay with Providence and then went to Rutgers.

Al Bianchi: It's between Rick Pitino and Jim Valvano. And Valvano, God rest his soul, scared the shit out of me. So we were left with Pitino, who I didn't have a problem with. I couldn't open it up; I couldn't say, "I want to interview this guy, too." I think that was one of the sticking points with Rick. I think he kind of thought that I didn't want him. I didn't have a choice in the matter. I chose him over Valvano.

Five days after Bianchi was named general manager, Pitino signed on as coach on July 13, 1987. The fact that the new general manager had not been involved from the start in the hiring of the new coach would forever cloud the relationship between the two.

The arrivals of Bianchi and Pitino were predated by that of yet another New York City product. With Scotty Stirling and Bob Hill already gone, head scout Dick McGuire made the selections in the 1987 NBA Draft at the Garden's Felt Forum. With the 18th overall pick, the Knicks nabbed St. John's point guard Mark Jackson, who, with Bianchi, Pitino, and a revitalized Ewing, would spearhead a startling Garden revival.

Mark Jackson: Prior to the draft, I had been promised by a few other teams that I'd be drafted, so I just started thinking it was too good to be true when it got closer to the Knicks' pick. But I didn't want to get my hopes up too high. The thing I'm thinking all along was that I wanted to get picked early. Then, as it got past the 11th or 12th pick, automatically I'm starting to think, "Please don't pick me," from 13 through 17. I realized as it got closer and closer that my dream was getting closer and closer to reality. I can remember Utah picking 15 and Portland picking 17, and I'm sitting there thinking, "I'm a New York City guy. Please don't do it."

I was one of the last guys remaining [in the Green Room]. And the thing that really stands out for me is the way the crowd pretty much started chanting for the Knicks to select me. I remember Kenny Smith, who was my childhood friend, coming down to sit with me and support me. I tried to put on my best acting skills, because I didn't want to set myself up for a disappointment. So I just sat there. But I didn't know what to expect. It was a great, great moment once they did announce my name. It was something I'll never forget.

Rory Sparrow: They drafted Mark Jackson, and I said that first day of practice, "This kid can play." He had an uncanny ability to find people. I knew when he came in that it was just a matter of time for him to get up to speed, and that he would be a player and I wouldn't play as much. But I'm a competitor, and every day in practice I let him know he was a rookie. As it worked out, Rick decided he was going to change the whole philosophy, press and trap all over the place, so any deficiencies they had wouldn't be as glaring.

Mark Jackson: I'd been sitting out, trying to negotiate my contract. I'd go up there and watch practice and just sit there on the sidelines. I was just anxious to get it started. The thing I recall is that early on, after I signed and started practicing, I realized that Coach had a lot of confidence in me and he would allow me to make mistakes. Basically, Rick was a great, great coach, and I think he's been the key to me being able to hang around this league 16 years later. I had somebody who believed in me from the beginning. So I owe a tremendous amount of my success to coach Pitino and Patrick Ewing, two guys who had the ability to shatter me as a youngster but instead instilled a great deal of confidence in me.

Rory Sparrow: They were nervous that Mark really wasn't ready for the pressure of starting. Then Rick called me into the office and said, "I'm gonna start him." I said, "Hey, Coach, you gotta do what you gotta do. I understand." And he said, "I think it's unfair to you," and so on. "What would you think if we traded you?" I said, "Ohhhhhhh, OK." And the next day I was traded to Chicago, a team on the rise with Michael Jordan, so I really couldn't complain.

One of the new regime's first decisions was to decline to re-sign King, who had become a free agent. After being sidelined for more than two years, Bernard had been impressive in a six-game stint at the end of the 1986–87

season. But with his long-term future still in doubt, the Knicks elected to say good-bye.

Al Bianchi: The Bernard King thing was a no-brainer. Rick and I agreed. Rick wasn't happy with him, and I wasn't happy with him and what went on during his injury. Rick didn't want to deal with him, and I didn't want to deal with him. That's a fact. Whether it turned out right or wrong, it just wasn't going to happen. From the first meeting, I knew that.

Rory Sparrow: Sky Walker was just getting there. Gerald Wilkins was an unbelievable player and nobody knew it. I had been playing with him back in Atlanta when he was still in high school. I used to mess around with him as a kid, and then he developed into really a great player.

Trent Tucker: His [Pitino's] style of play was great for me, but I had to get used to it. Going from Hubie Brown to Rick Pitino was like night and day in terms of how you played offensive basketball. Hubie was a half-court, run your sets, execution type of coach. Rick wanted to go up and down the floor and play the open style: take a guy off the dribble, shoot jumpers, shoot threes whenever you had the chance. So to go from one mind-set to the next, it took some time to get used to. It took time for me to understand that if I wanted to take a three-pointer going one-on-four, it was OK under Rick Pitino's system.

Stu Jackson: Patrick had come out of the Georgetown system, so I think he understood the value of defensive pressure right off the bat. At that point in his career, he was still very much a young center and a very agile, athletic center. He understood his role as the last line of defense in the press, and it was a role he could resonate with. And he bought into it full force. And once I thought we had his buy-in, the rest started to fall into place, particularly with Mark Jackson. Even though Mark wasn't a pressing-type player, he bought in as well. They were the two big keys on our team.

Mark Jackson: Early on, I learned from guys like Rory Sparrow and Gerald Henderson. I think today's guys come into the league thinking, "I can kill this guy." But when I looked at those guys, it was like, "Sure, I think I can do things against them. But they've been here long enough where I can learn some things from them." I was able to play, make mistakes, and get better under some tough circumstances: being in New York City, from New York City, and in front of my family and friends. It was a blessing to have coach Pitino as my first coach. He was the greatest coach I ever played for.

Stu Jackson: There was somewhat of a collegiate feel to our team, initially. I really think Rick is a master at relationship building. At that time, he did an excellent job of getting Patrick, Mark Jackson, and [later] Charles Oakley, who you wouldn't think was a full-court pressing player, to buy into the system when he arrived. So from that standpoint, it had a very collegiate feel.

Al Bianchi: When I mentioned that we were gonna have some psychological testing, Louis Orr almost had a heart attack, like, "What?" And I'm laughing. Finally I got them all together at the hotel and I said, "Look, we're not trying to get into your deep, dark past. We want to know certain things so that the coach has some tools. It's just part of it; we did it in Phoenix." I said I would take it and Rick would take it, whatever. So we went through a whole big thing there.

Stu Jackson: I felt very comfortable in knowing what Rick wanted, the style of play he wanted to play, and how he went about teaching that system and getting the players to buy into the system. The shock came in transitioning from college to pros, and actually it was a good shock. Because I came to understand very quickly that NBA players were similar to college players in that they wanted someone to help them get better. So on that level, there was no difference. I understood that professional players needed to be dealt with in a little different way in terms of not embarrassing them consistently in front of the group or not questioning them, and that sometimes more teaching took place before or after practice.

There was another shock, a humorous one, in which I realized I was in a little bit of a different world. After the first practice, I was correcting Gerald Wilkins on how we wanted him to run the

fast break. And he very politely and respectfully pulled me to the side after practice and said, "I don't want you calling me Gerald." And I said, "Isn't that your name?" He said, "Yeah, that's my name. But people call me Doug E." I said, "Is there some reason they call you Doug E.?" He said, "Yeah, like Doug E. Fresh." I had heard the players referring to him as Doug E. in practice but I had no idea why. So he explained to me why he'd prefer me to call him Doug E., and I called him Doug E. ever since. And I can't ever remember a collegiate player asking me to call him by his nickname.

Rory Sparrow: They were all young and on the verge of emerging into really good players. And Rick took them to another level. They had a young energy. Gerald Wilkins catching the ball and flying through the air, Mark being able to find people, Patrick running the floor and flying to the hoop. I remember how many alley-oops that team used to get. It was crazy. You could see they were going to be a much more aggressive team.

Al Bianchi: Whenever somebody said, "Well, this is how we've done it in the past," I would say, "Excuse me, but how many games did you guys win last year?" Twenty-four. I'd say, "Twenty-four, huh? Twenty-four fucking games. We're gonna do better than that." That was our battle cry.

Pitino's initial season, 1987–88, started every bit as dismally as the three that had preceded it. Losing 28 of the first 42 games amid dwindling crowds and increased media pressure, the Pitino era was deemed a failure barely halfway into the season.

Then, suddenly, the Knicks caught fire. Jackson and Ewing assumed leadership roles, Walker and Wilkins emerged as consistent performers, and two key Bianchi acquisitions, Johnny Newman and Sidney Green, delivered nightly. With 22 wins in their final 37 games, the Knicks made the playoffs for the first time since 1984. They nailed down the first of 14 consecutive postseason berths in the season's final game, with a last-second, two-point win at Indiana.

Mark Jackson: That was an incredible time, because nobody expected us to do anything, and probably rightfully so. But when you look at what you can accomplish with just hard work and dedication, it was incredible. We were guys who just let it all hang out, night in and night out, on the floor. We pressured people. It was a fun time and it was a fun style to play. A lot of people don't want to play that style, but it was our best chance, and we enjoyed it. And every day, just looking at guys' faces, knowing that the press was about to come and they had no answer for it . . . We had a blast.

Al Bianchi: When I was scouting for the Suns, I had a line on Johnny Newman. I knew that he was a pretty active player who could shoot the ball a little bit. Hell, we just got lucky there.

Stu Jackson: The pundits felt that our defensive system of play was a collegiate style, and many of them questioned whether or not it would be successful in the NBA. But you have to remember, that was a relatively young team. Young legs, fresh legs. Many of the players who played a lot of minutes were not that far removed from college. That allowed us to instill that style of play. More importantly, the players believed they could play that way. Hence, we had that "Madison Square Garden University" tag. But from our end, that was a real positive. In that first year, it was obvious how we were gonna play. And in the latter part of that year, you could start seeing the first fruits of success on the horizon.

Trent Tucker: The older guys learned and accepted what Rick was trying to accomplish. We got on the game plan and said, Hey, this guy's our coach and this is a new system for all of us, so let's not be critical. Let's jump on the bandwagon. We had a lot of young players who could play in Rick's style. For me, being a three-point shooter, it was a perfect system for me. Once I was able to adjust from one coach to the next, that's when things began to blossom.

Stu Jackson: The skill level of the players made teaching very easy in terms of their ability to execute the system, from defensively covering their area of the floor to full-court pressure and pursuing the basketball. Those things were done very easily and very quickly.

Trent Tucker: I think the reason that team came together over time was our mind-set. Players were open-minded enough to make a change.

Al Bianchi: Knowing that team, in my mind, they could have won more than 24 games. And that's not throwing rocks at the people who were there before, because I don't know what went on. Plus, they had two centers. And centers are rare. You had Cartwright and Ewing, so you had a pretty good base to work with. Also, you had a rookie coach who commanded a certain level of respect because of his college stuff. So I thought we could do some good.

Mark Jackson: It was great overachieving. And especially the last game of the season, going into Indiana with the winner going to the playoffs. Nobody expected much from us, and to go in there and win the game, you would have thought we had won the NCAA Championship the way we acted afterward. Coach included, jumping around and hugging everyone and everything. That's what made the game fun and that's what made us successful.

Trent Tucker: It was do-or-die. It was our biggest game and a chance for us to get back into the playoffs. It was also a test of our fortitude, to see if we could go into a tough situation on the road and win. It was fun because everybody was on the same page.

Stu Jackson: In my years in coaching, I had very few moments as euphoric as the game at Indiana, the last day of the regular season, when Kenny Walker went up and got a finger on [Steve] Stipanovich's shot and saved a potential Indiana victory that would have knocked us out. At that moment, that was just really special. Not necessarily in Knicks history, but to that team and its growth. What that really said was, "We did it. We did it the way we wanted to do it with our style of play. And we proved some people wrong."

Al Bianchi: Mike Lupica, at first, called us an expansion team. And then, all of a sudden, after we make the playoffs he's on the bandwagon. I always gave him shit about that.

Not even a first-round playoff loss at the hands of the Celtics dulled the glow from that season. Jackson was named NBA Rookie of the Year, while Ewing was named All-NBA for the first of seven times. By all accounts, the Knicks were back on the map.

Then, the night before the 1988 NBA Draft, Bianchi made the first of two moves that would help define the franchise for the next decade. The first, sending Bill Cartwright to Chicago for 24-year-old Charles Oakley and an exchange of draft picks, brought the League's premier rebounding forward to New York.

Al Bianchi: The Oakley trade took a long time because [Jerry] Krause is very meticulous. Also, in Jerry's favor, it [trade rumors] doesn't get out. He's very closed-mouthed, very secretive. And on our end, I'm trying to do the same thing, which was much more difficult. It worked out. There were some rumors late, prior to it, that maybe we were gonna do something.

Charles Oakley: I didn't know anything. Me and Michael [Jordan] were at the fight, the Spinks-Tyson fight in New Jersey. And before the fight some fans said to me, "Hey, Oak. You got traded." I said, "Hey, I don't know anything about it." But as the night went on, the news got out.

Al Bianchi: That was a good fit for both people. The best trades are when both teams are happy. Bill helped them win the championship, Oak came in and gave us some toughness and rebounding.

Charles Oakley: I think it was part of my job. When I got to the league, I knew that there were guys better than me, with more height than me, and I just tried to get in and be a major contributor any way I could. Take a charge, dive, rebound, get second shots. And that's what I lived on. At the time, I had just signed a new deal [with Chicago]. Whatever. But it's a business. Being young, I took it real professionally: didn't moan and groan about it, went to New York, tried to start a new home. Stayed there 10 years.

Stu Jackson: The common denominator of all three of those guys [Ewing, Oakley, and Jackson] was that they were really hard workers. They were durable. All three of them loved the game of basketball; they just really loved playing. All three were vocal, and they all had great character on the floor. You could rely on them; all three were trusted by

their teammates. And we were fortunate that they were three of our best players.

With the draft pick obtained from Chicago, the Knicks selected highly regarded DePaul guard Rod Strickland–a move that puzzled some, since the Knicks already had the league's reigning Rookie of the Year at the point position.

Another much-debated move came midway through the following season, when Bianchi sent a first-round pick to Portland for Kiki Vandeweghe, the son of fifties stalwart Ernie Vandeweghe. A two-time All-Star and one of the game's purest shooters, Vandeweghe had been hampered by back problems over the prior two seasons.

Kiki Vandeweghe: That was an interesting time for me because I was hurt for most of it. I had the bad back and was real marginal and didn't really know if I would ever play again, or, if I did, [play] very well. I was really focused on getting back playing with my team, the Portland Trail Blazers. There were always rumors, and that's part of the NBA, but that was a special rumor for me because it was obviously a dream to play there.

Al Bianchi: The Vandeweghe trade went on and on, and it was a headache. I always felt that if he was healthy and if we could get him here, the way he could shoot, he could help us even if he wasn't 100 percent. Plus, I knew Kiki; I knew his family. He handled it pretty well. When I look back on it, I put him in a really difficult situation, with a lot of pressure.

Kiki Vandeweghe: I was very excited. I was just hopeful that I could contribute a little bit with the bad back. That was my biggest worry. And it was a little bit bittersweet for me because I'd said that I always wanted to play there, but I wanted to play there healthy. I was always a little disappointed that maybe my best years as a basketball player were behind me and I couldn't perform as well as I would have liked. Now I was living a dream but I wasn't healthy, so that was a little bittersweet at the time. But I was excited.

I think there were mixed emotions on the team, because at that time the team was going pretty well. I think they all felt very comfortable in their roles,

Rick Pitino with three of his top students at MSGU (from left to right): Kiki Vandeweghe, Patrick Ewing, and Mark Jackson.

and I know coach Pitino did. He was very worried—and told me so several times—that I would disrupt the chemistry. So that was a tough transition. But overall I was extremely excited to be coming there. I knew I was going to have a great time.

For 1988–89, a new wrinkle would be added to the Knicks offense: an increased reliance on the three-point shot. After sinking 179 three-pointers the year before, the Knicks would nail a then–NBA record 386 long-range bombs in the 1988–89 season. Tucker, Jackson, Wilkins, Strickland, and Newman—known collectively as the Bomb Squad—were given the green light to fire at will.

With the Pitino system now firmly in place, the Knicks won 52 games [including 26 straight at home], *sold out the Garden 20 times, and won the Atlantic Division title by six games.*

Mark Jackson: We had matured. We had gone from a team that would walk into an opposing building not expecting to win, and then letting it all hang out to give ourselves a chance to win, to a team that all of a sudden had a little bounce going into every game thinking that we should win. So now we had the mentality of a winning basketball team. That was the difference.

Stu Jackson: Rick had always been a proponent of the three-point shot. Whenever there's a drastic or game-altering rule, either in college or the pros, there are always coaches who are well ahead of the curve. And in terms of the three-point shot, we [at Providence] were way ahead of the curve. Rick just said, "Hey, look. This is the level we have to shoot threes at, to be as productive or more productive than a two-point shooting team." That was his thing, and it didn't change when he came to the NBA. He really believed in the three-point shot.

Kiki Vandeweghe: It was obviously different from how any other pro team played, and any place that I'd ever played. It was interesting because I wasn't used to pressing. We did at UCLA, but it was a different type of press. It wasn't so helter-skelter and wild. It was a much more controlled press. Also, I had never played with a big center, and [being] the type of player I was, I was used to a motion game. We played a motion game in Denver and Portland, so I was a slashing and driving kind of player. When you play with a big center, most of that is eliminated because he's in the post. So that was an adjustment.

Trent Tucker: It was Rick's style and philosophy on how offensive basketball should be played. He took the talents each guy possessed and found a way to make it work in the system. You had point guards like Mark Jackson and Rod Strickland, who were very good off the dribble and could penetrate, pass, and make plays happen. Then he had slashing guys like Gerald Wilkins, Johnny Newman, and Kenny Walker, who were very good in the open court. And Patrick was the stabilizing force of the whole team with his great talent. With me, it was a perfect fit because Rick allowed me to do the thing I did best, and that's shoot from downtown.

Kiki Vandeweghe: I think it was very much a collegiate style, which, in many ways, was different. It caught teams off-guard. He [Pitino] relied on being very emotional for the games, and that was an adjustment because most teams don't do that in the pros. I thought in many ways it was very effective. I enjoyed playing for him. I learned a lot from Rick. It was an adjustment though, I must say.

Stu Jackson: It was a function of getting younger with Charles. Sidney [Green] was, historically, a full-court player at UNLV. We also had a system in place for roughly a hundred games, and we were that much further ahead. The players knew

what was expected of them in certain roles. We added Strickland to that team, who gave us another young talent, and more important, [he] got guys easier shots.

In the playoffs, the Knicks swept Philadelphia in the first round, celebrating the series win when several overexcited players pushed a janitor's broom around the Spectrum floor at game's end.

Trent Tucker: We were down 10 points [in Game 2 against Philadelphia] with two minutes to go. Ron Anderson is on a fast break, and he's cruising in. And from out of nowhere, Mark Jackson makes a hustle play and blocks the shot. So we come down and score, and we go into a full-court press every time down. And over the last two minutes we score 11 straight points and win. Mark's play saved the game for us.

Mark Jackson: I remember sweeping the Spectrum floor, but it wasn't just me. And people didn't realize the trash talking that was going on when you have a guy like Charles Barkley, who's a great, great guy and a character, and who has a mouth on him. So he made it interesting.

Trent Tucker: I remember seeing the young guys pushing the broom. It didn't mean any harm, but it was a bad thing in the end, when you look back on it. But it was just young players being young players.

Mark Jackson: Those guys had beaten us all season long, and we hadn't beaten them. We were pretty much what they wanted. They thought it would be an easy series, and when we had the opportunity to sweep them, we were young and dumb. We took advantage of the moment and grabbed the broom. But that's what it's all about. People blew it out of proportion, but if I had to do it all over again I'd do the same thing. We were young and dumb, and it was all trash talking and having a good time. It was nothing personal.

In the second round, the Knicks fell to Chicago in six games, coming within an eyelash of forcing a seventh game after Tucker completed a four-point play in the final seconds of Game 6. Ultimately, the Knicks were done in by Michael Jordan, who averaged 35.7 points per game and notched three 40-plus scoring efforts. It would not be the last time the Knicks would have their hearts broken by No. 23.

Trent Tucker: We're down four with about 10 seconds left [in Game 6 at Chicago]. As I went up to shoot, I felt [Craig] Hodges bump me, and out of the corner of my eye, I saw Jake O'Donnell with his arm up. I thought Jake was signaling three, but he had his fist closed. That meant a foul. So I let it go and it went in, and then I hit the free throw for the four-point play. But then Michael hit the two free throws and we lost. And to this day I often think about what it would have been like to play the seventh game of that series, against Michael Jordan and the Chicago Bulls, in Madison Square Garden. Can you imagine how loud, how rocking, that place would have been?

But throughout the season, and especially during the playoff run, there were rumblings of discord. Rumors of friction between Bianchi and Pitino had been gaining steam for the better part of two years. Bianchi, it was said, disagreed with Pitino's reliance on the pressing defense and frowned on the collegiate roots of his system. Pitino, it was said, chafed at the fact that his boss was an "NBA guy." An added factor, in the spring of 1989, was that the University of Kentucky was looking for a coach to rescue its scandal-ridden program in much the same way Pitino had resurrected Providence and the Knicks.

On May 30, 1989, just 11 days after his team was eliminated from the playoffs, Pitino reached an agreement to terminate his Knicks contract. After a day-long meeting with Garden officials, he held his last press conference in the small street-level lobby of 4 Penn Plaza. Then, bound for Kentucky, he walked out the door and onto 31ˢᵗ Street.

Stu Jackson: I was pretty surprised, but we saw it coming. In that second year, Rick, [assistant coach] Jim O'Brien, and I are in a car. Sometimes we'd ride in together. The subject somehow came up about Rick potentially leaving. He had brought it up, and he said that he had a meeting scheduled with C. M.

Newton, and in the same breath he's saying that there was no way he was taking the job. And I remember saying, "You're gone," right there in the car. We're all going to Kentucky, I thought. Because you have to know Rick to really appreciate that. So I was pretty surprised, but at the same time, I wasn't.

Al Bianchi: My initial problem with Rick was that he didn't look upon me as someone who had been around and had some knowledge of the game, who knew the NBA, and [he didn't want] to lean on me. He wanted to do what he did in Boston [with the Celtics]: he wanted to do the whole thing, which I knew would be no way. And that's where we got in trouble.

He [Rick] did a good job; I've always said that. You gotta know the nature of the beast, and you had to have some kind of trust factor, and I don't think it was ever there.

Stu Jackson: My position as an assistant with the Knicks was pretty secure. I felt that Al thought I did a good job. And in the pros it's different: you're an asset to the club, and you're not necessarily tied to the head coach. The dilemma I had was that my wife was from Lexington, and if Rick had asked me to go I probably would have gone.

Bianchi sounded out his old Phoenix cohort, John MacLeod, about coming to New York. But MacLeod, having completed his second season as coach of the Dallas Mavericks, declined. Then Bianchi turned to two in-house candidates: assistant coach Stu Jackson and player-turned-announcer Ernie Grunfeld. Six weeks after Pitino departed, Jackson succeeded his former boss as Knicks coach.

John MacLeod: I thought I was secure in Dallas, and Al asked me to come to New York and I thought about it long and hard. And I finally told him I was going to stay in Dallas, I thought I had a good future there. He wanted me to come in, and he said, "This team is a perfect fit for you." And I thought about it long and hard. My wife is a New Yorker. We had all kinds of connections in New York. But we were comfortable in Dallas, and I didn't want to move the kids again. We had just moved them from Phoenix. And that was the primary reason I decided against it. I try not to think about it too much because it's gone, it's over. These are the decisions that you make. Sometimes they turn out well, sometimes they don't turn out so well. So I thought I was in a good position in Dallas, but it didn't turn out that way.

Stu Jackson: The way Al approached me was very Al-like. He had the cigar going and just said, "You know, kiddo, Rick's gonna take the position," and told me that he'd like me to assume the head coaching job. I said great, and away we went. It wasn't formal; it was just a very simple conversation. I knew about that [Bianchi sounding out MacLeod] by keeping my ear close to the track. And that was fine. I like John MacLeod, and I knew he and Al had a relationship. I almost assumed that MacLeod would be the coach, and had my sights set on speaking with John when he was named and trying to sell what I could bring to the Knicks team. And I was fine with that. You gotta remember I was only 33 years old at the time and just starting out my NBA coaching career.

Al Bianchi: It was down to Stu and Ernie. Stu really wanted the job; Ernie thought he wanted the job. Stu kept calling me, and finally I said to Ernie, "Look, you don't want to coach. One thing I know is that this job isn't forever. Somewhere along the line, I'm gonna get my ass fired, and you might be in a position to take over." My first choice was John. When that didn't happen, I was gonna give Stu a shot.

Stu Jackson: I didn't have a chance to even think about it [whether or not I was ready]. I was gonna be the Knicks coach. I didn't stop to think whether or not I was ready. I mean, I *felt* ready. I felt confident. So now let's have at it. That was my attitude.

Pitino's departure and Jackson's promotion created three openings for assistant coaching spots. Grunfeld filled one, while longtime player and coach Paul Silas filled another. The third went to a former assistant to Pitino and Gordon Chiesa at Providence, an unknown 27-year-old with absolutely no pro experience.

Jeff Van Gundy: I still remember flying out to the L.A. Summer League. I flew all night, got there early in the morning, and went right to practice. Besides Stu, I don't know anybody. I don't know Ernie or Paul. Practice started right when I got there. So I just sat there and watched a little bit. And I was amazed at how good these guys were. Stu never introduced me, so they may have thought I was a ballboy or something. Afterward, I said to Stu and the coaches, "Man, all these guys are great." And they said, "All these guys suck. None of them will make it." So it was quite eye-opening, right from the start.

I couldn't believe how good Patrick Ewing was. He's getting beat up, and then he just elevates up, getting hit the whole time, and knocks it in. Just the physical contact. And then there was Charles Oakley. There wasn't *a* flagrant foul; *every* foul was flagrant. People say you can't imagine the next level. It's hard to imagine everybody being that good. Even as a coach, coming from college, you have no idea how good everybody is and how different it is.

Paul and Ernie were with the team every day, and I was to do all the scouting, plus be with the team. I probably missed 10 or 15 games, but I'd be going right out and coming right back. It was a great way to learn the league, when you study all these other great coaches. My first scouting assignment was to fly out to California, right after the big [1989] earthquake.

I've said this about Patrick, Oak, and Mark Jackson, way back when I became an assistant: they gave me respect before I'd ever earned any. That's just how they were brought up with coaches. They didn't know me, but they were terrific to me. And that carried through with Patrick, Oak, and later Starks. They knew me and they overlooked some of my mistakes.

Under Jackson, Ewing authored perhaps the greatest statistical season of his career in 1989–90. Scoring a franchise record 2,347 points, he was the only player ranked in the NBA Top 10 in scoring (28.6), rebounding (10.9), blocks (3.99), and field goal percentage (.551), en route to earning first-team All-NBA honors for the only time in his career.

But the Knicks' inconsistent play and the Mark Jackson–Rod Strickland log jam at the point forced Bianchi to make a startling midseason move, as he sent

Strickland to San Antonio for yet another point guard, four-time NBA All-Star Maurice Cheeks.

Stu Jackson: We made Patrick a real focal point of the offense. He was at the height of his career–his physical conditioning, his disposition to dominate offensively. So we played off him, much the same way Houston played off Hakeem in those years and other teams had played off other great centers.

Al Bianchi: We were in and out that year. He [Patrick] was having a hell of a year, but the rest of the team wasn't doing what maybe I thought they could do.

Charles Oakley: I think New York fans like hardcore, blue-collar [players]. Patrick was quiet and never opened up. Fans pay their money, this and that. And in the press, Patrick always tried to downplay everything. Fans like controversy in New York, and Patrick wasn't a controversial player. He didn't want that. In New York, they're gonna say what's on their minds, whether you like it or not. So, for myself, I tried to say what was on my mind and let them know how I feel. It's a two-way street.

Stu Jackson: Unfortunately for us, Mark Jackson came into camp in not the best condition. And it led me down a road that, today, I probably regret this coaching decision more than any I'd ever made in my career. Because with the advent of Kiki, with Mark coming back in not the greatest condition, I was fearful that I wouldn't be able to press as much. I spent a whole summer prior to that season formulating how we were going to build upon what we'd already had with our style of play. And then, Rod Strickland came back in the best shape of his early career. I made two mistakes there. I didn't press as much as we had in the past. And also Al really didn't subscribe to full-court pressing. But Al had given me my opportunity. So that, factored with the fact that I had these two new guys [Cheeks and Vandeweghe], really gravitated me toward pressing less, and I regret that.

Al Bianchi: I had sat down with Rod Strickland, who was devastated at that time. I said, "Tell you what, Rod. I know what you're feeling and I understand it. There's a certain amount of me that understands it

from the coaches' standpoint, because the other guy [Mark Jackson] was more dependable about showing up and things like that. You do what the coaches tell you to do, and if I can make a deal for you, I'll do it." Well, that's how it turned out. I wanted to get another guy who had been around, in Maurice Cheeks.

The 1989–90 NBA season was the first in which tenths of a second were required to be displayed on the arena clocks. The need for such precision could not have been driven home more soundly than on the afternoon of January 15, at the Martin Luther King Day matinee against Chicago at the Garden.

With the score tied at 106, the Knicks inbounded at center court off a timeout with 4.6 seconds left. With a foul to give, Chicago's Scottie Pippen fouled Mark Jackson. Now the clock read 0:00.1, as the Knicks prepared to inbound again. Overtime seemed a certainty. After all, what could possibly happen in a tenth of a second?

Trent Tucker: They were gonna use me as a decoy to bring Michael Jordan away from the basket. Then Mark would throw a lob to Patrick underneath so he could tap it in. But Michael read the play, so he went back and took the angle away from Patrick. I saw Mark standing out of bounds with the ball and the five-second count was coming up.

Stu Jackson: We were just running one of our sets from sideline out of bounds that we'd run with under three seconds, and take our chances with it.

Trent Tucker: So I just kept coming along the sideline in front of our bench so he could hand it off to me. I knew I didn't have much time, so I turned and gave it a little flick, and the ball just got over the outstretched hand of Scottie Pippen, just enough. And the ball hung in the air for so long. Johnny Newman was standing behind me and said, "Trent, that ball looks pretty good." We had a chance to have a conversation because the ball was so high, and I said, "News, it's on line." Once it went in, we ran off the floor and went into the showers. We wanted to make sure the Bulls had no chance to protest the call.

Stu Jackson: Trent comes off a screen on the baseline and curls to the ball, catches, turns and fires, and Ronnie Nunn calls it good. We didn't do anything special. In retrospect, we probably should have run something toward the basket with a lob play. More times than not, those sets are run today because they know that they've only got three-tenths or whatever on the clock.

Trent Tucker: To this day, people ask me if the shot counted. I say, "Sure it counted. It's in the record books." It was a shot that won the game and redirected how things are viewed now at the end of a game.

Phil Jackson: It [Tucker's shot] changed the game, basically. Now, not only do we have the three-tenths [rule, where any shot taken in less than that time must be a tip-in], we also have the video and the lights on the backboard. Those are games where, if you lose, you've got to learn to live with that as a player and coach. You're gonna lose some of those close games, and there's nothing you can do about it. Sometimes there are circumstantial things you can't always overcome.

Stu Jackson: I keep it to myself, because once in a while in my conversations here internally, the "Trent Tucker Rule" will come up. And I always wonder to myself if people know that it was actually our shot.

By season's end, the veteran Cheeks had replaced Mark Jackson in the starting lineup, a move that would carry long-term ramifications. Third in the Atlantic Division, the Knicks drew Boston in the first playoff round.

History would not be on their side. Coming into the best-of-five series, the Knicks had lost 24 consecutive games at the Boston Garden, a streak that dated back to February 1984 and included four losses in the 1984 playoffs. In the span of about 40 hours, the streak reached 26. Game 1 was a 116–105 loss. Game Two was a 157–128 embarrassment in which the Celtics set an NBA playoff scoring record.

Stu Jackson: The initial plan of attack was to climb the mountain of history. It was in our minds– it was in everybody's mind–that we hadn't won there in a very, very long time. The last third of the season, we sputtered. So we went in there having not played the best we could play, plus we're fighting history.

The first plan of attack was to try to mitigate the historical and make our guys believe that we could win there. We wanted to take advantage of our younger, fresher legs. Run as much as possible. We still felt we had an advantage at the center spot, and we had to take advantage of Patrick offensively. Well, long story short, in the first game we didn't play well at all. And things went from bad to worse in the second game.

Kiki Vandeweghe: Nobody likes to lose two in a row, especially at Boston Garden. That was no fun. That's always been a place where you relish the victories, for lots of reasons, especially if you're a Knicks fan or a Knick. I think everybody took those losses hard but then came with a real determination. If we were gonna go down, we were gonna go down swinging.

Maurice Cheeks: After the first game, I didn't go back on the bus with the team. I walked back to the hotel. I was that frustrated at the way we played. It wasn't a good time. It looked like we had just stopped playing, and Boston looked like they were ready to drill us and get the series over with.

Al Bianchi: Not to slough it off, but those are the games you try to forget. I don't have any recollection of that.

Maurice Cheeks: When you get beat that bad and you have that long a layoff, you've got a lot of thinking to do. It plays on your mind a little bit. I remember that the guys were trying to regroup, and it wasn't easy. You're still playing against Bird, McHale, Parish, and those guys.

Game 1 had been on a Thursday night, Game 2 on Saturday afternoon. Game 3, back in New York, wouldn't be until the following Wednesday night. With the long layoff, the Knicks now had three and a half days to either resign themselves to fate, or find a resolve few thought they had.

Stu Jackson: Huge, huge factor. We get our brains beat in on Saturday. We spend all day Sunday licking our wounds. No practice. Just a horrible day for all of us, personally. We come back on Monday, and the first thing we do is start statistically breaking down the first two games, talking about the two games, then going to practice. It's a terrible practice. Everyone came away from Monday's practice, I felt, feeling not quite as bad as Sunday, but certainly a close second.

Trent Tucker: We get to practice on Monday, and it was bad. The attitude was like, hey, we haven't played well; we're not in the right mind-set. We were feeling sorry for ourselves. On Tuesday, we began to work a little harder and the intensity was there.

Stu Jackson: In between Monday's practice and Tuesday's practice, I and everybody else made a decision that we had to stop mourning here, and [to say], look, we've got a game. Had we had to play Tuesday, we were three and out. Three and gone. But it was that extra day in between, because when everybody came for Tuesday's practice, there was a different feel. We had an unbelievable practice that day. Unbelievable. Competitive, physical, verbal, energetic, enthusiastic. Almost like a training camp practice. So at least, when we left on Tuesday, people felt like, if we play like this, we've got a shot. Our whole focus was to win the next game. Nothing revolutionary. Let's just win the next game.

Kiki Vandeweghe: Stu just called on the competitive spirit in every single player and said, "Look, guys. We're gonna torch it today in practice." And I think everybody kind of rose to the occasion. Every now and then, a couple of times in your career, you go through those types of practices where it's kind of a turning point. Everybody is of one mind, and you really click together. All 12 guys in the practice are just going for broke. And those become very special times where you bond as a team and you feel like you're part of something special.

Jeff Van Gundy: What people forget about that series is that we had started it having Patrick guard Parish, Oak guard McHale, and Newman guard Bird. So we had to double all three of them in the post. Then after Game 2, Stu made the decision to put Pat on McHale and Oak on Parish to body him out, so we didn't double any of them. That turned the series around defensively. We went from giving up 157 points in Game 2 to 99 points in Game 3.

Stu Jackson: We're not gonna double. And it put such a focus, onus, and accountability on each guy. Stupid me, right? It just fit, strategically, what we were trying to do in the series. Our young legs

against their old legs, our ability to do things physically better than them. So let's try to guard them: Bird, Parish, Ainge, D.J. [Dennis Johnson]. There was a reluctance, initially, to do that. You felt like you had to take away one thing from the Celtics– their low-post game–and hope that they shoot the ball poorly from the perimeter. Instead, we just said, "Screw it. Oak, you guard this guy; Patrick, you guard this guy." No more doubles. And it worked. Because in the third game, while we weren't exactly world-beaters, we wore them down, and it set a tone for the rest of the series.

Trent Tucker: I don't think anyone expected us to win Game 3. It was a struggle, but the Celtics didn't put us away. Kenny Walker made some critical baskets down the stretch and gave us a shot in the arm.

With the Knicks clinging to a 102–99 lead, everyone knew where Boston's final play would go.

Stu Jackson: They ran a flare-screen for Larry Bird on an out-of-bounds play. He's wide open, and he missed it. We were lucky. We were fooled, we didn't switch, we had a mixup. He was wide open, and he missed it.

Jeff Van Gundy: Hey, we could have played Monday, and there would have been no chance to bounce back. But you get a chance to regather yourself, heal your mental wounds, and you get your team to believe that all you need to do is win one game. And that's all we did, was win one game. So now, in Game 4, we're hyped and we just blow them out.

Stu Jackson: My sense was that we had a way we could beat 'em. We had just executed a game plan that was successful against them. And the confidence level with younger players took a quantum leap. We went out in the fourth game knowing we were gonna win.

Trent Tucker: Once we got to Game 4, we realized that we could beat them on our court. So we came out with a swagger. We were pressing and trapping; we began to feel very good about ourselves. And we blew them out.

Before a raucous Garden crowd, Ewing scored 44 points as the Knicks evened the series with a 135–108 Game 4 win. Incredibly, they were headed back to Boston for a deciding Game 5, and all they had to do to complete one of the most stunning reversals in playoff history was end a six-year, 26-game dry spell on the parquet floor.

Stu Jackson: Before Game 5, I made the decision that we were having problems with Mark Jackson. We weren't getting along with him; he wasn't getting along with us. He was upset about playing time. Maurice Cheeks was playing the bulk of the minutes and really playing well. We weren't pressing as much, and at that point we were primarily a half-court team. It was a style of play in which Maurice was still very effective. So we made the decision that we were gonna play him as many minutes as we had to to win the game.

Jeff Van Gundy: Mark had struggled all year, and he [Stu] went with Cheeks for 48 [minutes] in Game 5. That was a preset thing, basically. Stu wasn't gonna take him out.

Maurice Cheeks: I don't remember that, but I was OK with it if it happened. I certainly didn't think I'd play that many minutes, 45, 46, and then 48 in the final game. I'm not saying I wasn't prepared for it, but I didn't think it would happen, because Mark was there, and he was pretty good. But I just didn't think I was going to play that many minutes.

Mark Jackson: It did bother me, because I regarded myself as a winner, as a competitor. To be in the playoffs and be sitting on the sidelines without the opportunity to play was frustrating at times, and it bothered me. But I'm a spiritual guy. I put my trust in God, and I believe that ultimately that was something that was given to me to make me stronger, to make me a better basketball player, but more important, to make me a better person. So I was able to handle pretty much anything that came along after that because of times like that. I think it makes you stronger, and it also makes you appreciate the good times even more so—the things that you normally take for granted, like being out there playing for 40 minutes. All of a sudden, you're not playing. And

you look back and you say, "Wow." Those were times you gotta enjoy, because you never know.

Stu Jackson: Before the game, I had a conversation with Hubie Brown, who was doing the telecast. He asked me how I was feeling about the game, and I said something very ordinary like, "I hope we can pull through," or something like that. And I'll never forget: he said, very sincerely, "You're gonna be fine." And I just sensed from him, being one of the great experts of the game, that he knew what was coming. Also, remember he had been victimized in Boston back in '84. Whether it was true or not, I interpreted what he said to mean that this guy sees that the steamroller can't be stopped and that this is finally gonna be the day that the Knicks are gonna prevail over the Celtics in Boston.

In the locker room, the level of intensity was as great as I've ever been around. So much so that I didn't say a whole lot. I think, on the board, I just put the names. I was into stats and this play and that play, but I never really addressed it because they weren't hearing me. I started talking in the pregame, then bagged it and gave an obligatory mention of some things, and then we went out there and played. They were ready to play.

Boston ran off to an early nine-point lead, but the Knicks cut the deficit to 54–50 at the half. With Ewing spearheading the rally with 14 points in the quarter, New York ended the third period with a 21–10 run to take a four-point lead [87–83] into the final quarter.

And now six years' worth of frustration was washed away. Dennis Johnson had his pocket picked at center court by Cheeks and Tucker, leading to an Oakley dunk. A wide-open Bird clanged a dunk attempt off the back rim. On the bench, Jackson addressed his troops at every timeout with "Here's how we're gonna win this game . . ." With two minutes left and the shot clock running out, Ewing chased a loose ball into the corner in front of the Knicks bench, then threw up a blind, three-point prayer that found the bottom of the net.

In front of a score of friends and family, Ewing scored 31 points and added eight rebounds, 10 assists, and four blocks. Oakley had 26 points with 17 boards. Wilkins, who had flown into Boston just hours before the game following the birth of his daughter, had 12 points and eight assists. But, ultimately, the game belonged to Cheeks, who had 21 points and seven assists in going the full 48 minutes.

Knicks 121, Celtics 114.

Stu Jackson: It [the Wilkins situation] played on my mind big-time. This was all legitimate. She [Vita, Wilkins' wife] had gone into labor, and Gerald left, and understandably so. I remember thinking that it was a tough stroke of luck for the team. I was really happy for him [Gerald]; it was his first daughter. So in that respect, it was a happy time. But in the back of my mind, secretly, I was saying, "God, I hope he makes it back." Then he makes a great effort to get back for the afternoon game, and he just shows up at the game.

Al Bianchi: Whenever we played in Boston, I never sat in the stands. I would walk around in the back, over where they sold the hot dogs, looking up at the TV sets. And everybody back there is laughing at me, "Hey, Al! What are you doing here?" Because I knew a lot of those people there.

Trent Tucker: We knew how tough Game 5 would be in the Boston Garden. Maurice Cheeks played the entire game, and he was marvelous. He did everything that a point guard was supposed to do in that situation as far as running the team and executing our offense. He found guys in the right spot at the right time; he shot when he had to. He took the game on his shoulders. Patrick had a big game and hit that big shot from the corner, but Maurice Cheeks orchestrated that game from start to finish.

Stu Jackson: When I was with Jim O'Brien as a coach, we'd talk a lot about Jack Ramsay. Coaches talk about other coaches all the time. I was a huge believer in Jack. Obie would say that Jack, either in practice or in a game, would always emphasize the things that his team was doing well. And he'd always make a point of telling players how they were gonna win a game, and plant in their mind that losing wasn't an option. And more important, instructing them on how they were gonna win. And I felt that day, one message needed to be delivered a thousand times, versus a thousand messages being delivered once.

We're fighting history here. We had to just stay focused on one thing, and that was winning the basketball game and how we were gonna do that. I just wanted to instill a level of confidence in our guys as to how that was gonna happen.

Trent Tucker: That [the steal on Dennis Johnson] was the ballgame right there. I learned that tactic from Rick Pitino and the press-and-trap. Rick would always tell you to chase the guy down from behind. Continue to chase him even though he's past you, because sooner or later he'll have to stop, and when he stops maybe you'll get a deflection. D.J. was in the middle of the floor, and it was very noisy. He couldn't hear anyone telling him to look out from behind because someone was chasing him, so I was able to get a hand on it and knock it to Maurice. That play set the tone for the rest of the game.

Stu Jackson: When Bird missed the dunk, I knew we could win. When Trent [made the key steal], that play showed the different speeds we were playing at. They looked like they were in slow motion. They were going at 33, we were going at 45. Then Patrick hit the three and I knew it was over. It was a completely busted play, and he picks up the loose ball, turns, and . . .

Patrick Ewing: It was great. The Celtics had us down so much, but we fought back. Oak, Maurice Cheeks, and I had big games. I had about 30 tickets out for that game; all my friends and family were there.

Trent Tucker: On that Sunday, for 48 minutes, we played that game one possession at a time.

Ernie Grunfeld: They just ran into a buzzsaw in that game: Patrick Ewing was not to be denied. He had grown up in Boston and had a lot of family and friends there, and he had one of the greatest games I've ever seen him have, in a huge, crucial situation. To be able to win a game like that, up there, was a real confidence boost we had for those young players.

Jeff Van Gundy: Cheeks was great. Years later, Maurice came to New York one time as an assistant coach and asked me for tickets. And he said, "You owe me! You'd be out of the league if it wasn't for that game." And whenever I see him he just says,

"Fifty-one," because that's the side pick-and-roll play we ran. He says that Dennis Johnson still has nightmares about it, and whenever he walks past him today he just says, "Fifty-one."

Maurice Cheeks: Fifty-one was the pick-and-roll. We milked that play coming to the middle of the floor; it was a side pick-and-roll with me coming to the middle. I got to the middle three or four times. We just milked that play, and I got three or four layups. Then Patrick hit the big three from the corner.

I prolonged his [Jeff's] career, let me just say that. [Cheeks laughs.] He may still be in the league now because Allan Houston hit that shot in Miami. I just remind Jeff that I prolonged his career. And he's Mr. Popularity right now. And I worked on his shirts; I worked on his clothes. He's just polished all the way around now.

Al Bianchi: One of the most satisfying days of my life. When Mo Cheeks had that game–I mean, he had the game of his life up there–you never saw a happier guy than me. It goes back to those games against Cousy and those guys. Since that time, we're all friends. But at the time, there was a lot of hatred.

Stu Jackson: Once you're in the New York sports scene, New Yorkers never, ever forget. There are so many fans around, and even to this day, people come up to say to me that it was one of the most memorable moments in New York Knicks history.

Two days after vanquishing their Boston ghosts, the Knicks began the second round against the champion Detroit Pistons. Five games later, their season was over.

Stu Jackson: Remember, I'm a young coach. More important, I'm a young *NBA* coach. I should not have practiced that Monday, the day after we won in Boston. So we went into Detroit– because after winning the Boston series on Sunday, we had to play Detroit on Tuesday–not being fresh. We practiced [Monday], got on the plane, and treated it like it was the regular season. And I shouldn't have done that. I should have given them the day off. Let them enjoy their victory, but more important, get themselves refreshed to go into Detroit.

I should have used the same sort of mentality that Chicago had the year before, when they won the big [first-round] series against Cleveland, when Michael hit the shot at the end. Then they had to play us two days later. And I'll never forget: Doug Collins made a helluva decision. He didn't practice [the day after], and they flew into New York the day of the game. Here they come marching down the hall, hadn't practiced, hadn't done anything, and, boom, just shocked us. I should have used that as an example. Not that we would have beaten Detroit, but I think we would have played better.

The euphoria generated by the Boston comeback would fade during a controversy-riddled 1990–91 season, during which the Knicks tenures of both Bianchi and Stu Jackson would come to an end.

But just prior to training camp, Bianchi made another move that would solidify the Knicks' identity for years to come. He signed a volatile 25-year-old free agent who had bounced around four colleges, the WBL, the CBA, and the NBA, amid a varied résumé that included, of all things, a job as a grocery store bagger in his hometown of Tulsa, Oklahoma.

Al Bianchi: John Starks was a player who had jumped around. I saw him play in the L.A. Summer League, and I realized he was a pretty active kid. He had his problems, some character stuff that people had talked about. I was pretty friendly with his agent, Ron Grinker. Grinker wanted a $35,000 or $40,000 guarantee to come into camp. Now, if you're in Phoenix you don't do that. But in New York, you roll the dice. So I said, "You got it," and we brought him into camp. When you're a scout, one of the keys to a kid being successful is whether the coaches agree with you. And in this case, they loved his toughness. And he was tough, and that kind of saved him.

Stu Jackson: It was the day before we were gonna cut him, and he came down on a fast break in practice. It was one-on-one, because we were pressing in practice. It's him and Patrick, and the son of a gun challenged him. It was bizarre what he did! So he goes up and challenges Patrick, and Patrick blocks the shot and goes completely through him because he's pissed that this guy challenged him. Down John goes in a heap, they cart him off, and that's the last I ever saw of John Starks.

John Starks: It was the last day of practice before the cutdown date. I knew I had to do something very special to make them understand that I wanted to play here. I had a pretty good training camp. Not knowing the situation, or whether I was gonna get cut or kept around, I tried to impress them on the last day of practice. I remember I didn't miss a shot during that whole practice. Then I decided to go up against Patrick on a fast break. I think he was a little angry about how our team was beating his team. I went up to dunk, and he went up and grabbed the ball. I came down and twisted my knee, and I thought I had torn it up. Patrick felt really bad about that, but it turned out to be a blessing in disguise because it gave me the chance to stick around and wait for the opportunity to play.

Stu Jackson: We were gonna cut him. The decision had already been made. He was gone. We liked him. Al was the one who found him, and he loved him. But we had no roster spot. So now he gets hurt and we can't cut him. Then he hangs around—and this is a helluva thing—because he got injured. Then he comes back and as he's rehabbing, the process of building John Starks really began then. Because the John Starks that got hurt that day was not the John Starks you saw a year later. In that time, he really went to work. And I think Jeff was a huge, huge piece in John's development, coupled with the fact that John could be a crazy worker. He'd get out there and work until he's blue in the face. And it all paid off for him. He goes from a 17-foot jump shooter, to a three-point shooter who couldn't go left, to dunking over the greatest player in the world in one of the Knicks' greatest moments.

Following a 7–8 start, Stu Jackson was fired on December 3, 1990. John MacLeod, whom Bianchi had sounded out following Pitino's departure and who had been let go by Dallas the previous season, took over as coach.

John MacLeod: Al and I have always talked. We still talk all the time. Obviously, because he was there, I was interested in how the Knicks were doing. I wanted them to do well because I wanted him to have success there. So we talked maybe once a week. But we've always talked since we started working together in Phoenix. I've always had an interest in the Knicks.

I thought about it [coaching in New York] from time to time, but not a great deal. Like the song says, if you can do it there you can do it anywhere. It's a tremendous challenge.

It [the offer] was made prior to that [Sunday, December 2]. I was in Seattle, and it was like a Wednesday or Thursday. Al flew out to Seattle, and we went out to dinner and talked about it. He asked me if I would be interested, and I said yeah, I would. He wanted to know how soon I could come up with a decision, and I said I wanted to go home and talk it over with my wife. Then I called him the next day and told him I was ready.

Jeff Van Gundy: The guys told me later that I just sat there and crossed my arms the whole first day of practice [without Stu]. In fact, that day, Stu's car had broken down. So I had to travel up to Yorktown to pick him up and drive him to Purchase. When we got there, Stu went in first. Ernie and Paul already knew, so they told me, and I thought I was gonna get it, too. When Stu came out, he had to take my car home. And I said, "Hey, wait a second. I might be going with you." I went in and Al told me. I was mad because I didn't think Stu was being given a fair shot, but I was thankful that I was able to stay on. But I really felt for Stu. When you come from a coaching family, getting fired is so personal. It was hard; it was really hard.

Stu Jackson: Jeff had to take me to practice. I go in and Al wants to see me. Brings me in, basically gives me the common phrase of, "We're going in a different direction, kiddo." Very short conversation. I don't remember asking him why or for an explanation; maybe I was too proud. Then I left.

Jeff Van Gundy: On the way home, Stu stopped at the Purchase Deli. There's a pay phone right outside, and Stu called his wife. And he saw John MacLeod driving by with Ernie.

Stu Jackson: I don't remember how I got to the phone booth right outside the Purchase Deli, but that was the first place I went. I didn't have my cell phone with me. Went to the phone booth, called my wife [Janet] and my mom and dad, and told them what happened.

I remember calling my parents after I called Janet. And Janet's perspective was never on the coaching profession, or business. For her, there have always been other things that were more important. We had young kids at the time, and she would always try to bring me back to that focus, because basketball just wasn't that important, even though she loved the Knicks and all the guys. She just had a different perspective.

I called my parents, and my mom picked up the phone. I'll never forget this; I said, "Mom, I just had a conversation with Al, and I just got fired." And the first thing out of her mouth was, "Oh, wow!" And she asked me what the weather was like up in New York—you know, "Is it cold up there today?" I said, "Yeah, Mom. It's cold. Mom, you know, I'm telling you I just got fired." She said, "I heard you. Let me ask you something. Did you do the best you could?" I said, "Mom, I did the best I could." She said, "Did you work at it? Did you give it your best effort?" I said, "Mom, you know what I did. I sacrificed a lot of things and worked my ass off." So she says, "Well, as long as you worked hard at it and gave it the best you could, there's nothing you can do about it. So you feel good about it and move on." That was my ride back home, holding on to Janet's perspective and the conversation with my mom.

Jeff Van Gundy: I think Stu handled himself really, really well. He made tough decisions, like changing the lineup that first year. He took Mark and Newman out and put Cheeks and Kiki in.

Stu Jackson: Did I feel bad? I felt bad. Did I regret it? I didn't regret it at all. Then you go into a period of anger, where you're angry at everyone, including yourself. Then you're angry at other people and start blaming them. But then you come out of it and focus your sights on the future.

Jackson's firing was difficult for many of the Knicks, who had great admiration for him. MacLeod came in and gave an increased role to a young John Starks, who had returned from his preseason injury.

Kiki Vandeweghe: There were all types of issues on the team, and there were four or five guys struggling. I worked very hard to become healthy again and feel good about things. John MacLeod came in and went to more of a motion type of game, which really fit me better. I really enjoyed playing for him. Stu and I laugh about this all the time, because that was a tough group under very tough circumstances. I really have a lot of respect for Stu as a coach and a person. It was a tough time for him, I know. Very frustrating. By the end of the year, we ran into a buzzsaw in Chicago. No one was going to beat them that year. Having said that, it was tough. It was just very difficult.

John MacLeod: When you come aboard in the middle of the season, it's difficult because it's hard to make a wholesale change, to change everything over. I thought a lot of the stuff they did was good. They were going through periods where they weren't shooting the ball well, they weren't having good luck in the offense. Sometimes that has a tendency to spiral downward and maybe affect how you play from a defensive standpoint. It was a matter of trying to get them back to winning again and getting them on track, to focus on the team and focus on the defensive aspect of it.

Jeff Van Gundy: John MacLeod . . . To this day I've never met a nicer man in coaching. He was very, very positive. I saw a lot of my dad in him in that he was a basketball guy. He was very, very kind to me, and I had been left over from the old staff and [was] the only man that Stu had truly hired. When John was at Notre Dame, he'd see my dad at various camps around the country. Now, he's the big-time Notre Dame coach, and he always made it a point to seek out my dad and visit with him. That just speaks volumes about him and his kindness.

John MacLeod: I knew Oak before I went to New York. I always liked him, respected him, and thought highly of his game. He was an enforcer, a big, strong guy that could play defense and had that physical reputation as being someone who was one hard-nosed, tough customer. He and Patrick were a great pair.

John Starks: John MacLeod believed in me as a young player. He found that I was a very coachable player; that's what he liked most because he's a teacher. I just tried to do the things that he asked me to do. He always called me a tiger. He'd say, "You've got that attitude; you're like a little tiger." That was really a confidence booster, coming from a great coach like that. He gave me the opportunity to play a lot of minutes, because one thing he loved about me was my aggressiveness and my attitude on the defensive side of the ball.

John MacLeod: The thing I liked about John is that he would drive the ball to the basket. He was fearless. I actually liked a lot of things about him: his aggressiveness defensively, too. He would challenge big guys. And that's how he got hurt. He tried to dunk over Patrick and came down and sprained his ankle. But he had juice, and at that time we needed that. He was a little bit on the wild side, where sometimes some of the shots he would take were ill-advised. But he brought an energy to the floor that I liked.

John Starks: Patrick used to get mad at me all the time because coach MacLeod had a certain way he wanted you to deliver the ball in to the post player. He wanted you to deliver it low, to make the post player bend down to get into position to receive the pass. And Patrick used to say to me, "Man, if you keep throwing that ball low, if you don't get it to me high, I'm gonna let it bounce out of bounds." But I kept throwing it low because that was the way Coach wanted it; and if I didn't do what Coach said, I'd be sitting on the bench.

John MacLeod: So I started playing him. Al said, "You need to give this kid a good look." And I did. I remember one time in Atlanta, I started Mark and put John in for the second quarter, and he had

a heck of a quarter. So then I started him in the second half. I was looking for a change, to get us jump-started. And he had that energy and competitiveness that sometimes positively affects other players.

Despite MacLeod's arrival and the emergence of Starks, the Knicks continued to founder under the .500 mark. Bianchi, facing increased media criticism, found his own situation tenuous.

The prior summer, Bianchi had sought a multiyear contract extension but was offered just a one-year deal, which he signed, reluctantly. On January 31, 1991, with the Knicks in the midst of losing 10 of 14 games, Bernard King poured in 49 points against his former team to lead Washington to victory, as chants of "Al must go" rained down from the Garden rafters. Three weeks later, Bianchi and MacLeod were involved in a shouting match at practice with Mark Jackson that resulted in Jackson's suspension.

Finally, on March 1, 1991, Bianchi was fired. Thirty-five-year-old David W. Checketts, who had been the NBA's vice president of development following a successful tenure as president of the Utah Jazz, was named Knicks president, and would guide the franchise's destiny for the next 10 years.

Al Bianchi: When they offered me a one-year contract [extension in 1990], that was the death warrant. Nobody upstairs really came and said, "This is our guy." So it was just a matter of time.

Peter Vecsey: The Mark Jackson thing was huge. I came to Mark's defense, which was very interesting also because I was after Mark for many, many things. The helicopter move, the sweeping of the broom in Philadelphia, a lot of stuff that he was doing. He'd be in your face trying to intimidate you. But then, again, I saw that he was being picked on, and totally wrongfully. I thought that what MacLeod and Bianchi were doing–trying to force him into a fight, actually, at practice–was wrong. So I went after them even more. That was a huge factor. Then Mark and I, ever since then, have been really tight. Because he saw I was fair. I picked on him for a few things, but I thought he was right in this situation. We've been tight ever since. But we were so at each other's throats in those days that Rod Strickland and Pete Myers had to stop him from coming after me in the locker room one time. His parents were mad at me. I mean, it was bad. Now I'm tight with his mother today because, again, she saw I was fair.

Al Bianchi: My feeling at the time was, "Al, you never should have accepted the one-year contract. You should have told them to just go fuck themselves. When you were going good, you should have done like Rick [Pitino] does and ask for a long-term contract."

Peter Vecsey: Here we were, very good friends, and he [Bianchi] thought that because we were good friends, that he owned me. A lot of people throughout my career have felt the same way, that because we're friendly, they own me. And once they think that, it's all over. Al thought that he could say anything about other people—Rick Pitino, for example—and I was just not going to write or not going to react. So we definitely became adversaries after a while. Then it got to the point where he was threatening me, verbally, on the air and in the papers and to my face. OK, that's fine. Now the gloves are off. So I went after him big-time.

John MacLeod: There were a lot of things that were happening. That was a tough time; Al losing his job, and the thing with Mark wasn't pleasant either, because it was somewhat disruptive. But we got through that thing. I hated to see Al leave. He brought me in there, and my goal was to get this thing going so we could really make something out of it. But it was a tough stretch. So Al's gone and Mark is on the bench, and I kept him there for four or six games. But we started winning; we won something like 12 of 14 and really got going.

Peter Vecsey: I remember a line I had on Al, and I really believe this is true. And I'm saying this about a guy I went out to dinner with many times, whose wife and son I knew: he's a guy—and I wrote this at the time—that thinks he's the only one who was ever born in New York City. In other words, he thought he was the slickest guy going and the rest of us were fools. And that was his undoing. You've got to treat people well and with respect. And certainly

someone in my position you've got to treat with respect. But that was his undoing. When he went after me, saying he was gonna get me and stuff like that . . . And I don't think he ever named me, but we all knew who he was talking about. So that was it.

Dave Checketts: I had actually considered coming in 1987, because Evans had offered me the GM job before Pitino and Bianchi came in. The reason I didn't accept it then was that Dick told me he'd already offered Pitino the coaching job and I didn't want to be brought in with the coach already in place. I wanted to hire the coach; that was one very big stipulation. The coach had to work for me, and I had to hire the coach. So I didn't take it in '87 for that reason, and I didn't know whether it would come back to me. Obviously, in '91, it did.

Al Bianchi: Once I left, I never wished them bad luck. I always had fond memories, and I always watched Starks and Oakley. I enjoyed watching them and realizing that they were the guys that I brought in.

The Knicks slipped into the 1991 playoffs with 39 wins but were blitzed in three straight games by Jordan and the Bulls, who were en route to the first of their six NBA Championships.

On the eve of the playoffs, Grunfeld was promoted from assistant coach to director of player personnel, entrusted with the task of rebuilding what had become a patchwork team. Two days after the Knicks were eliminated from the playoffs, MacLeod resigned to accept the head coaching position at Notre Dame.

Ernie Grunfeld: We were going to a youth movement. I was 31 [in 1986] and maybe the oldest guy on the team. They told me they were going young and weren't going to bring me back. I had some other opportunities to play, but the Garden people came to me and told me they wanted me to stay in the organization. Being a New Yorker, I had always stayed very visible in the community. So they came up with a package for me to stay on as a radio color commentator, along with doing some pro and college scouting. I knew that the basketball situation might be changing in another year or two, so this was a way to stay in it and start a life after basketball. And opportunities like that don't come along very often.

John MacLeod: I had known Dave from when he was at Utah, so it wasn't like a stranger I was working with. I got along great with Dave. But he never said anything about the job or my future or anything like that.

I told Dave that I was going to interview with Notre Dame and he said fine. In fact, I interviewed with them the day of the second game in Chicago. They drove up from South Bend. I told Dave exactly what I was doing and told him what my intentions were, so he had no problem in that area.

Jeff Van Gundy: When we were in Cleveland late in the [1990–91] season, Drexel [University] was looking for a new coach. I had applied. They wanted to interview me, and I asked John and Dave, and they let me interview. I didn't get it, but at that same time Dave called me and said, "I'm not telling you what you should do, but you'll have a position with the Knicks at the end of the year regardless." When John left to go to Notre Dame, I was doing administrative work for Ernie. Then I had to make a decision: go to Notre Dame [with John] and stay in coaching, or go with the unknown with the Knicks. I went back and forth, and eventually I chose to stay in New York. I took the train in every day, had an office. Ernie gave me some good things to do. Then they hired [marketing director] Pam Harris, and I got kicked out of the office into the hall. And I found out right away that that's not me. I'm going like, "Oh, man, this could be rough." Some people, that's their thing. For me, it wasn't.

John MacLeod: I absolutely loved it. My regret is that we weren't better, that we couldn't go any farther in the playoffs. But I enjoyed it. I thought the fans were great, the media was great. If you were doing well, the media would say you were doing well. If you weren't doing well, they'd say you were doing horseshit.

In April 1991, not many could have guessed that a neophyte club president from Utah and a player-turned-coach-turned-de facto general manager were about to lead the Knickerbockers to the greatest sustained period of excellence in their history.

And yet, so much would happen to this club over the next 10 years–so many thrills, so many heartaches–that it would be virtually forgotten that their first baby steps into the spotlight of prominence following three horrific seasons were choreographed by the basketball lifer from Long Island City.

Al Bianchi: There were some things that happened that probably shouldn't have happened. There were some things I did that maybe I shouldn't have done. But, overall, it was really fun. It really was. We had a great time in New York. It was a great four years, and I knew it wasn't forever. I was just disappointed that I really didn't get the backup that I thought I deserved, and I didn't get the recognition of the job that was done there from the day we walked in until the day we got fired.

Sometimes my mind wanders and I look around the league and see some of the jobs some of these general managers do that are still working. And I look back at what I did in New York and I say, "Gee, that doesn't make sense." And I giggle again. Then when I watch TV, I'll see where they have the announcer and the "expert commentator." And I laugh, because all these guys got fired! This is backwards here. How does this work? Then I laugh and say that I'm not gonna try to figure it out.

When I got there, I asked Mike [Saunders] how much money we had in the fine kitty. Well, at Christmastime, I made sure that we took care of everybody who worked in the Garden–Sonya the cleaning lady, everybody. We had cases of booze, presents. We went out and spent money. I took care of everybody in the Garden. And when I walked around there, I was like the fucking Pied Piper. And those people loved me. We did the cops, the elevator operator, the cleaning ladies. We gave them all stuff, and no one had ever done that before. The people who worked with us, the ones who worked game nights, the ballboys, the guys up in the press room, we took care of them all. To this day, when I go back there, those people still come up to me and say, "Mr. Bianchi! How are you?"

Ewing was New York's go-to guy
for the duration of the nineties.

THE LINEUP: Herb Williams; Mark Jackson; Ernie Grunfeld; John MacLeod; Dave Checketts; Pat Riley; Derek Harper; John Starks; Rolando Blackman; Allan Houston; Jeff Van Gundy; Kurt Thomas; Mike Saunders; Latrell Sprewell; Steve Mills; Tim Walsh.

In 1985 the Knicks snared the first pick in the draft by winning the first NBA Lottery. That meant Patrick Ewing, the hands-down best college player that year, was destined to be a Knick.

Herb Williams: Before he got there, the Garden was never sold out. Ticket sales were miserable. And then he was the number one pick, the savior of the franchise. Then people started looking back to the championship days, and that's the image people had when we got Patrick, not knowing that it's not always that easy. You need certain pieces to the puzzle and everything's got to fall into place for you to win a championship.

Mark Jackson: He was a dream come true. He made the game so much easier for me and for everybody around him. When you have a true superstar who can get it done, who demands a double-team, who makes plays out of the post, who's a warrior who doesn't take days off . . .

Ernie Grunfeld: He was a rock. He was our stabilizing presence. He set a great example. And with him, the organization always had someone we could sell, a player we could sell as well as a player who produced every single night. He came to work, he competed, he put up big numbers. He had a winning spirit about him.

Mark Jackson: He set the tone for everyone around him, and he made the game so much easier, especially for a point guard who looks to make plays. He was the ideal person for me to play along with.

Herb Williams: Once he came into the league, I think he felt he had something to prove. He had gotten the big contract, and a lot of people were pissed that he had gotten the deal. So night in and night out, he was playing to prove something to somebody, to prove to people that he deserved the numbers that he got. So he was always a little on edge. I used to mess with him all the time; I used to call him Big Money. When I was in Indiana and he was in New York, he'd always come out here with a serious look on his face. I'd say, "Big Fella, it's not all that serious." He'd always be, "Don't talk to me." So I used to mess with him all the time.

John MacLeod: A lot of people aren't aware of this, but he practiced as hard as anybody that I've ever had. I mean, he practiced every day, and he practiced hard, and he wanted to win. We had some hellacious workouts. Normally, you don't remember practices, but I remember two or three–one in Phoenix and one in New York–where it was like we were playing for the world championship. That's how competitive they were. And Patrick was right in the middle of it. He never asked to come out. He was great to work with.

Herb Williams: I played against Patrick when he was on the [1984] Olympic team, and he was sort of off to himself a lot. If he didn't know you, he wouldn't really say a whole lot to you.

Dave Checketts: [Ours] was a relationship forged by difficulty. By the time I got there, Patrick had had three general managers and five coaches, and it was like visiting with an orphan who had had many parents and had been in many homes and didn't trust anybody. I really worked very hard on that because I realized we weren't going to get anywhere without him.

Herb Williams: New York, at times, can be brutal. And the newspapers were brutal to him at times over certain situations. But unless you're in the locker room or in those practices, you really don't know what happened. And if he didn't tell them, they sort of put their own spin on it. And a lot of times, it wasn't right. But he never corrected them. He just said, "Look, those guys have a job to do. They do their job, and I do mine."

Dave Checketts: Just before I joined the team came the [1991] trading deadline, and [Richard] Evans was talking to me about coming to the Knicks. He had a trade he wanted to do with Miami: Rony Seikaly and Sherman Douglas for Patrick. I actually called Riles [Pat Riley] and a few other people I trusted, and we just said, "Why would we do that? It would turn us into the Miami Heat."

Pat Riley: He's your franchise player, and he was above and beyond that. And it's just an absolute shame that in '94, we as a team could not achieve what he worked so very hard for. He was our go-to guy, the anchor in the middle, the spirit of the team.

Derek Harper: When you have a center of Patrick's caliber, the game becomes a little easier for you, if you understand how to play with a guy like that. My biggest challenge was not stepping on his toes. For me, I almost forced the ball to him a little bit too much. I think there were times where I was really adamant about getting the ball in to him. I just really wanted to do right by the rest of the guys. Patrick was obviously the guy. The thing that sticks out is how much we emphasized the ball going in to Patrick.

Herb Williams: The ball was gonna go through Patrick, and coach Riley made no bones about it. He'd tell you in practice; he'd tell you in meetings: the ball is gonna go through Patrick, so if you don't like it, that's just too bad. That's the way it was.

Pat Riley: Defensively, he was always one of the great helpers and shot-blockers. And a real prolific scorer when you got him the ball deep in the low post. I was very fortunate to be able to have him when I came to New York because it made it very easy to turn that thing around. We won 51 games the first year, and everything went right from there. And Patrick was probably the main reason why it all happened.

John Starks: Most people don't understand the work ethic this man had throughout his career, or his commitment to the Knicks organization as well as to his teammates. He was a very, very prideful person. As a player you respected that, because you knew that when he took the court, he was gonna give 110 percent. And when the chips were down, he was gonna be there for you.

Rolando Blackman: The important factor to note is that with all the talent and things that we had assembled, we had a true, true great one in the post, a guy who not only led in games but led in practice, too, regarding what he did and how he influenced everybody to play hard and do those type of things. I think we could have used more of the talent that was there and not just have Patrick be the whole basis of what we did, but he was such a great player that everyone bought into the system of having Pat be the man and go with the Riley system in that way.

Above all, Ewing's teammates respected him and recognized the size of his heart and his desire to win.

Herb Williams: Trust me, he wanted in the worst way to win a championship in New York. As bad as people wanted him to win one, he wanted to win one even worse. When we didn't win in '94, he was hurt. He was hurt. He didn't say a lot about it, but he was really hurt. That was the year, I thought, we should have won the championship.

John Starks: Patrick was a great, great player. More so, he was a great teammate to be around. He was one of those leaders who wasn't really vocal early in his career. He kind of laid back and expected everyone to play at a high level. And if you weren't playing at a high level, he let you know. He wasn't going to persecute you in the papers or anything like that, because he knew that when it all came down to

An era begins: Ewing with NBA commissioner David Stern and Knicks GM DeBusschere at the 1985 NBA Draft.

the end, people were gonna point the finger at him, regardless. So he really didn't get on teammates in the papers. As a teammate you really respected that, respected a guy who kept it all in-house and got on you when he had to in a private setting.

Herb Williams: He was more concerned about his personal life than the people around him were. He didn't want to get them involved in what he was going through. From time to time you'd hear about certain players, like when the reporter [the *Post's* Thomas Hill] talked to Starks' grandmother about him, and he got upset at that. Whatever Patrick was going through, he wanted to go through it himself. He didn't want his kids to go through it; he didn't want his family members to go through it. So when he talked to reporters, he'd always say that he'd talk about basketball and that

was it. He didn't want to talk about anything going on in his personal life, his family. He wanted to keep all that private. And in a way, I can't blame the guy. In New York, you never know what people may try to do. So he always kept it in that perspective. He always would sit down to do interviews–he never backed away from reporters–but he always kept it at that level: he didn't let it get to a personal level where if you wrote something about him it would hurt. He'd sit down to do interviews, but he always wanted to keep his private life private.

Allan Houston: When things weren't going well, he'd always say, "Look, man. We're trying to win a championship." He never said, "Guys, we've got to do better than this . . . blah, blah, blah." He always said, "We're trying to win a championship." That was his standard. That was his goal.

Ewing was the center of attention for the Knicks over 15 seasons.

Tim Walsh: First off was the hanger at the Garden. After about his third or fourth year, he found this wooden hanger that he used to hang his jacket on. From then on, I had to hang on to that wooden hanger; that was his and he used it every day. Then there was the gum. I had to give him two pieces of gum–Carefree sugarless–with two minutes on the clock before the game. The ice bags [for his knees] had to be Ziploc bags, not any other bags. I had to go out to the grocery store and buy Ziplocs at the beginning of the year, right off the shelf, and he would use those ice bags for his knees. And certain Ace bandages that were more elastic than the normal ones–I had to go out and buy those. One year we got bathrobes, and he held on to that one for a long time. After a while, guys stopped using them but he continued wearing it. And the robe would be on the hanger, so he'd take the robe off and put his clothes on the hanger.

Then there were the codes. Everybody knew the codes. He'd yell, "Timmy!" and point with two fingers down. That meant two ice bags. Or "Timmy!" and then squeeze his nose, that meant a tissue. Or "Timmy!" and he'd act like he was drinking water.

Herb Williams: One time we were in a restaurant and a little kid wanted his autograph. At this point, I didn't really know the demands on him. He didn't want to start signing autographs. He took a picture with the kid and shook his hand, but the kid really wanted his autograph. So I was getting on him, "Just give the kid your autograph!" But, again, he didn't want to get started signing, so I said to him, "How bad can it be?" So he did, and before he got finished signing that piece of paper, there must have been 30 people around our table. Now, he's just signed for a kid that's four or five years old, but now you've got 30 grown-ups asking for his autograph, telling him that if you signed for this kid, you had to sign for everybody. These were grown people and they were actually getting pissed. So from then on, I left him alone. I understood why he didn't want to sign in public.

Ernie Grunfeld: I think a lot of times he was misunderstood in a lot of ways. But anybody who knows Patrick Ewing has great respect for him. He's a private person, but everybody wanted a piece of him. And if you were his friend, you were *really* his friend. He had a circle of people that he trusted and

was close to, and if you were in that circle, you really loved the guy because of the type of person he was and the loyalty he showed.

Herb Williams: One time we were in a mall–me, Patrick, and John [Starks]–to get something to eat, and then we went to see a movie. I'll bet at least 20 or 30 people followed us into the theater. I'm thinking, "Man, this is crazy." So now I'm sitting there watching the movie, and *I* don't even feel comfortable. It was things like that, that made you appreciate him even more, and how he dealt with it.

Tim Walsh: After a while, he realized that he was high-maintenance. When he went to Seattle and Orlando, he went around telling people how much he wore me out.

John Starks: Coaches respected him because he was a leader who was gonna do as much as he could for the team. People used to get on him and say that he wasn't a great passer, but through the years I think he learned to trust his teammates a lot more. As the years went by, I think he became even a greater player because of that.

Jeff Van Gundy: Everybody says Patrick was loyal to me, and I was loyal to him. And we were. But they make it sound like we never had a disagreement. What Pat was great at was this: we had so many disagreements, but he never aired them to his teammates and he never aired them to the media. We were always very supportive of each other. Then we got behind closed doors and we went at it. I think that was his greatness. He could be stubborn and disagreeable, but he always did it in the right manner.

Herb Williams: He knew it was his team; he knew everything would go through him. I mean, all you had to do was read the newspapers: he got blamed for everything. Anything that went bad, he got blamed. He didn't mind. He never took it out on his teammates. He never blamed anybody. He never made any excuses for being hurt or anything. He took it all on his shoulders. That's the way he dealt with it.

Kurt Thomas: A lot of people don't know this, but when we traveled, I sat right beside Patrick. He took me under his wing when I came here, and we got along well. I was just inspired by how much he loved the game, and a lot of people took that for granted. All he wanted to do was win. If he had to shoot the ball, if he had to block shots, rebound, score, whatever, he was willing to do it. And just a great person.

Mike Saunders: Ice cream is good; it's pleasant. Patrick liked ice cream. So that was it. He wanted me to say something pleasant, or pleasing, when he shot fouls. So instead of saying, "Let's go, Big Fella," or something like that, I'd yell, "Ice cream, Big Fella!"

Tim Walsh: He always showed compassion and caring. Whenever there was a death in the family, he always was there with the phone call and the flowers. He paid attention to those things; he was very aware of your emotions. He'd greet you with a hug and he showed you he cared, that he was concerned about you.

Allan Houston: On the court, just to have his presence . . . He demanded respect from everybody on the court, even the referees. Just from a defensive perspective, he was a guy that bailed us out a lot. It was Patrick's team.

Latrell Sprewell: Patrick is one of the greatest players ever to play the game, especially at his position. He ultimately had the respect from everybody, and playing with him was definitely an honor. The thing that was a little unfortunate was that I got there as late as I did. Allan had an opportunity to play with him a little earlier. But for me, when I got there he was pretty much banged up. And the deeper we got into the playoffs, the harder it was for him to maintain his health.

Kurt Thomas: A true veteran. A solid leader. A guy who didn't do much talking, he just showed you by his play and what he did on and off the court.

Latrell Sprewell: I still believe that if we had him when we faced San Antonio [in 1999], it would have been a totally different series. We definitely needed his size and his presence inside. We didn't have that, and we missed it. It would have been nice to play with him when he was healthier, because when we got to the playoffs, he was awesome. He just took his game to a new level, even being as banged up as he was. You could see his intensity level and focus rise; it was so much different in a playoff situation.

Steve Mills: I've known Patrick for a long time. We spent a lot of time together with the first Dream Team in '92; I was overseeing events for the NBA and the whole operation of the Dream Team. We developed a relationship over the years. We talked about

this in terms of him understanding that this was a business and that we all have to make decisions, both on his part and our part, to move forward. When Patrick was sort of at the end, the summer after his last season with Orlando, he called me. And that was the most meaningful for me because he was calling me as a friend to say that he was thinking about a lot of things–whether or not to stop playing, how it could ever be possible for him to come back to be part of the Knicks organization. So we had a couple of conversations; we had dinner, just to talk about what he wanted to do with his career moving forward.

Dave Checketts: At his number retirement ceremony, he was so articulate and endearing, and people had never seen him like that. But I saw him like that all the time. We had a lot of laughs and a great friendship. He called me when he needed me, but he was never demanding or ornery or difficult. He was always a real pro. I have enormous regard and respect for him.

Jeff Van Gundy: I always thought that Patrick, in general, thought too much about the very, very small vocal minority and never realized that the silent majority always had great respect and appreciation for him. Sometimes as athletes, the only people you hear are the loud, boisterous ones, and you tend to think that's how [all] people feel. And it's not.

Herb Williams: People like me knew that Patrick was a totally different person, one of the kindest people you're ever going to meet. Very funny guy, likes to laugh, likes to joke around a lot. That was never written. I think his image was created through the media. If you talk to the fans in New York, the people there love him. If you read the newspapers, they'd say that he didn't let the people know him, that he was distant from them. But I've been out with him in New York, I've walked down the streets of New York with him, and I saw how the people reacted to him. They loved him.

Dave Checketts: Nothing that ever happened, even when we had our differences about the team and the direction we were going, ever impacted his play. He was a complete pro. And so kind–very unusual for a player. Very loyal and kind to me and my family, my kids. Just an extraordinarily loyal human being that, unfortunately for him, very few people have had a chance to know.

No. 33 is lifted to the Garden rafters on February 28, 2003.

EWING

33

KNICKS

Pat Riley turned the Knicks around in a New York minute.

THE LINEUP: Dave Checketts; Pat Riley; Patrick Ewing; Herb Williams; Jeff Van Gundy; John Starks; Charles Oakley; Mark Jackson; Fuzzy Levane; Anthony Mason; Ernie Grunfeld; Kiki Vandeweghe; Rolando Blackman; Mike Saunders; Phil Jackson; Marv Albert; Hubert Davis; Derek Harper; Pam Harris; Charles Smith; Bob Salmi.

After working for one year as an NBC commentator, Pat Riley, who guided the Showtime-era Los Angeles Lakers to four NBA titles during the eighties, was named Knicks coach on May 31, 1991. And nothing about the Knickerbockers would ever be the same again.

Dave Checketts: I felt like the Knicks, in the Garden, in the middle of New York, should be the league's flagship. You heard that the Celtics and Lakers were held up as the poster boys, particularly in the late eighties, when they had been so dominant. But my feeling was that the Knicks had a special kind of city quality to them. And the reality of any sports team is that if it doesn't stir people's hearts in the community, if it's not compelling, if it's not interesting, if they can't get involved in it on a daily basis, it really isn't worth very much. It has to be something where people say, "We won," or "We lost." And I recognized that coming in. In Utah, I had the good fortune of running a team in a small community and turning it into something that was widely adopted, that people were passionate about. Community ownership, and seeing that people in the city of New York see the Knicks as *their* franchise and the Garden as the heartbeat of the city, and a place where the Who's Who gathered on those long winter nights, that was the philosophy.

Pat Riley: I've always believed very strongly that in order for you to move on and get to another

place, you've got to sort of imagine yourself there. When I left the Lakers, then took the year off and worked with NBC, I saw myself possibly there, if in fact there was a change. I was very highly motivated during the course of that year to try to see myself there. I can remember, when I would jog or work out, imagining myself giving halftime talks to Patrick, Mark Jackson, and Charles Oakley; or how I would do this or that; or where I'd live. And I think that's very important. If you're gonna pursue something, you have to imagine it. That determines your behavior and fuels your motivation. And when the time came, it inspired me to act on the job. So, yeah, I had thought about the job.

Dave Checketts: In January [1991], I was at the league office, running NBA International. We had a bunch of coaches doing international clinics for us, and one of them was Riles. I called him, and of course we knew each other. When I was running the Jazz, we had some legendary playoff series with him. I called him and said, "Let's have lunch." We had lunch at the Regency Hotel, and then Riles said, "Why don't you do it?" I said, "Why don't I do what?" And he said, "Why don't you go and fix the

Knicks?" And I said, "Well, I haven't had that opportunity offered to me." And he said, "You will." Then I said, "If I do it, will you do it?" And he thought, looked around the room, and said, "I would consider it." That's how Pat is. So that was the first conversation we had about it.

Pat Riley: When I was still at NBC, he approached me to find out my level of interest. We had lunch one day and had a discussion about it, and I said I'd be interested.

Dave Checketts: When I took the job on March 1, he wrote me a note that said congratulations, good luck, and all those things. I sent him back a note and called him and said, "So are you going to live up to your end of the bargain?" And he said, "Once you make a decision on the future of your current coach, we can talk." I said, "Well, I don't want to talk until then, but you should be aware I'm going to call you once that decision is made." That happened in late March. By then, we were squeaking into the playoffs on our way to getting swept by the Bulls.

It [the skepticism] got at its peak shortly after I took over when I—as smoothly as I could—arranged for John MacLeod to make an exit. I respected and liked him, but I wanted someone to come in with a new focus. During May of '91, I was trying to make a deal with Riley and also was headed to arbitration with Ewing. And that's when I got hit in the face, in that we were about to lose Patrick Ewing. During that time, Fred Kerber wrote a piece where he said something to the effect that I wasn't gonna get Riley and I was going to lose Ewing, and the last line of the article was something like, "This guy should have stayed in Utah." So I was feeling a lot of pressure there.

There were a couple of points where I thought it wasn't going to happen with Pat. We had been very careful in letting people know through the media that we were interviewing more than Riles. Paul Silas was a candidate, and so were Tom Penders and Doug Collins. I had already named Ernie as VP of player personnel, so Ernie and I were interviewing these guys. The whole time I'm talking to Riles and his agents. Now, remember,

we're getting close to June 1, when Ewing was going to have his right to exercise whether or not he'd opt out. It was a very tense time. We negotiated back and forth with Riles, particularly that last week. And finally, on Friday morning [May 31, 1991], his representatives told us that he was going to wait and see what happened with Ewing. I knew if we did that, it would impact our ability to keep Patrick. So I stood my ground and gave him an ultimatum. I said, "Look, at 4:00 this afternoon we're going to have a press conference, and we're either going to announce you as the coach or that you're passing on the job. You decide which it is." Then I went into a session with Ewing and David Falk, who were at the same hotel I was. I had been on the phone with Riley and his guys, and in the next room were Ewing and Falk. And at that point, I remember looking out the window and thinking of Kerber's line that I should have stayed in Utah, and I was beginning to agree with him.

Patrick Ewing: [We spoke] right before he took the job. Right before he signed on the dotted line, he called me. He flew to Washington, and we sat down at the Ritz-Carlton. He talked about what to expect, what he wanted out of me. I was going to be the focal point of the team and of the offense. It was the first time any coach—and not to take anything away from any of the others—came to me and told me that I was the focal point and that they were gonna try to build a team around me.

Dave Checketts: I got off the phone with Riley and then went in with Patrick. [Garden senior legal VP] Ken Munoz and I were sitting in there with him, trying to figure out whether there was anything we could do to avoid the arbitration. Then Riley called again about two hours later and said, "I'm coming. I'm gonna take it. I just needed to know how far I could push you. But it's all over, and we're friends, and I'm looking forward to making good things happen." Then I went back in with Ewing and said, "We've got our coach."

Almost from the start, the vision of Checketts and Grunfeld; the intensity and aura of Riley; a tough, defensive-minded team; and the infusion of a young and aggressive front office staff all combined to turn the Knicks into a glittering New York happening. Fresh off a multimillion-dollar renovation, the Garden played host to a front-row galaxy of A-list celebrities, a virtually unbroken string of sellout crowds, and an electrifying group of crowd pleasers called the Knicks City Dancers. Clearly, these weren't your father's Knicks.

Pam Harris: The goal was to make the Knicks the hottest ticket in New York. And I knew they hadn't been during the eighties. I had grown up with my dad being this huge Knicks fan and I remembered the early seventies and what that was like. There was all that passion to be regained.

Part of my [marketing] plan was to start a dance team. And the day I started, I had a stack of letters from people who had written to Dave saying they were interested in starting a dance team. So the first thing I did was start to interview people for it. I think that Petra [Pope], in fact, had already spoken to Dick Evans months before. She was one of the people in the stack that Dave handed me.

I thought a dance team would be really fun and different. I had no idea the wrath that was going to come upon me for starting a dance team. People ask me, "What was one of the biggest mistakes you made?" and that kind of thing. I think it was a mistake that I didn't even know I was making, because I think that if I had known how it was going to be received, I wouldn't have had the courage to be the person behind it. There was so much flak about it. I didn't know how furious New York was going to be. I didn't realize how steeped in tradition it was. People felt, "You cannot tamper with New York Knicks basketball. You cannot have a dance team." But it was really great that we had Petra, because she did such a phenomenal job. And, yeah, we went through some ups and downs, but now they're the best dance team in the NBA.

Forty-one times a season, and then into May and June, the pregame clock would run off the last minute to tip-off, and the Garden sound system would rumble with the opening bars of the Four Tops' "I Can't Help Myself." And out of the 33rd Street tunnel would come the most glamorous, the most respected, the best damn coach in the NBA.

Showtime.

Pat Riley: When you come to a new situation, you bring your persona and philosophy. We pretty much cleaned out everything that was there prior to that, and [had] taken a look at the team. They had won 39 games and made the playoffs the previous year.

Patrick Ewing: He definitely had the respect. He had four rings; none of us had one. His reputation preceded him, with all the things he did in L.A.

Pat Riley: We were gonna become the hardest-working, best-conditioned, most professional, most unselfish, toughest, nastiest team in the league. And those were the very first words out of my mouth when I met with them. But I also said, "I can't just say that. We have to become that by working at it." And we became a work team, in that every time we went to practice we were gonna *work* practices, we were gonna *work* to get better individually. And eventually the long, hard, arduous practices developed the team into a very tough-minded team. The Knicks team that I inherited, the one I basically coached my first couple of years, was really a tough-minded, defensive-oriented ballclub. That began to change a couple of years after that.

Herb Williams: Coach Riley was very demanding, more so than any other coach. He expected certain things from you. He wanted you to act a certain way. He wanted you to project yourself a certain way. Event after event, practice after practice, game after game, he'd always be there pressing you and never letting up. If you weren't mentally strong, it could wear you down.

Pat Riley: When I arrived in New York, one of the first things I had to do was create a staff. There were two people who were there that I did keep on [Paul Silas and Jeff Van Gundy]. They had moved Jeff over into the office, in personnel, for a while. I'd heard a lot about him, and the first thing I wanted to do was bring Jeff back to the bench and keep on Paul Silas to maintain some continuity. Then we hired Dick Harter and Jeff Nix.

Jeff Van Gundy: Paul gave me a great piece of advice that I should have used more, about "Better to be thought a fool than speak and remove all doubt." He was the first one to teach me about Peter Vecsey's column. My first year in the league, he sat me down and said, "All right, now you see this guy? You look at the column. You see these bold-faced names? If you don't see your name in there, you breathe a sigh of relief; then you laugh and read the column. But if you see your name in there, you close the paper and put it down." Paul was unbelievable to me from the first day.

Dick Harter would have been a great coach no matter what the sport. He just had the intangibles of what a great coach is. Tough, demanding, yet charismatic enough so that the players like him and want to play for him. We had the right team for Dick and Pat because they were instinctively tough and nasty.

Pat gets hired, and I'm fortunate in that his staff had remained in L.A. with Mike Dunleavy. So he didn't have a ready-made staff. The first time I met him was at the draft. We were in a room together for about one second; everybody else had left. He just said, "I'll talk to you at some other time."

Pat Riley: The three guys that I really liked were Mark, Oak, and Patrick. To me, that was gonna be the core of the team. John [Starks] had a good second half of the season prior to that and started to play some very good basketball at the end of that season. It wasn't until I saw him in training camp that I realized this guy was gonna be able to play.

John Starks: You have to prove yourself to a new coach, and especially a coach of his caliber, because he's been around great players his whole career. Not knowing what his demands were and what he expected of you, you had to go in and show him that you could play in his style and system. It was perfect for me because that's the way I played basketball: very aggressive on the defensive end as well as the offensive end.

Charles Oakley: He had a game plan. He knew when he got the job what he wanted to do,

how he wanted to run the team and get the players to play in his system. We just fit right into his system.

Pat Riley: There wasn't gonna be any point guard controversy. There wasn't gonna be any of that. Mark was established as the starter just about from Day One. Greg Anthony was a guy we had drafted who we liked off the bench. We knew he was gonna give us energy, enthusiasm, and quickness. But Mark was the guy who was gonna run our offense. He's a very smart, very high-character type of guy. I really liked him. He was vital to our success that first year.

Mark Jackson: It meant so much to me because here I am having the opportunity to play for one of the best coaches ever, and to have the opportunity to win my job back. I didn't want anybody to give me anything. My confidence wasn't shaken. All I wanted was a fair opportunity to win the job back. And if I was gonna leave New York, I wanted to leave the way I came in. I wanted to leave while playing solid basketball and being the guy that I was capable of being. From day one, when Riles took over the job, he presented that opportunity. I was so thankful that I was able to get the job back and have a successful season, individually and collectively, and to leave on a high note.

Fuzzy Levane: I knew about Anthony Mason a long time before he played for us. One of my friends in the garment industry had a woman by the name of Mary Mason working for him, cutting clothes and stuff. And she told my buddy about her son, and then he said to me, "Fuzzy, have you ever heard of a kid named Anthony Mason?" I never heard of him. I was covering the CBA.

Pat Riley: Anthony Mason was a very unique player. The very first minicamp we had, we brought him in. He had this horrible shot, but he could defend, he could run, he was very strong and combative, defensive-minded. Once we saw him play enough, we realized this guy was ready.

Fuzzy Levane: Eventually he goes to the CBA and I see him play one game, up in Albany. I finally got to see him play, and I said, "Holy jeez, this guy can play." The way he handled the ball for a big man, and this and that. Fundamentally, he was sound. But along the way, I guess he was a pain in the ass. So at the end of the season I go to my friend Eddie Krinsky, the head of the USBL, because now he's playing for the Long Island Surf. Now I'm seeing him [Mason] a lot, and he's much better than I thought. He was showing me things like bringing the ball up and passing and whatnot. But he had been bad-mouthed by a couple of scouts in our league, that he was a headache. I spoke to Riley up at Kutsher's at the Summer League. Paul Silas was coaching our team. I said to Paul, "We're gonna bring this kid to camp. Play him a lot tonight." And Paul played him. And after the game he must have called Riley, because they didn't bring him to camp, they signed him right there. Which was very unusual. I think Paul saw what I saw. And Riley loved him.

Anthony Mason: I played in the Summer League up at Kutsher's. Silas was up there coaching, and he said I should come up there and try out for the team, that I had a shot to make it. I had also talked to Fuzzy beforehand. When I went up there, I really didn't think I had a chance. There were a lot of guys there with guaranteed contracts, and I didn't think I had much of a chance to play with the team at that level.

Ernie Grunfeld: I had just gotten the job as vice president of player personnel, and we went up to the Maurice Stokes Game at Kutsher's. We knew Mase because he had played the previous season in the USBL, and we watched him play in the Stokes Game. We liked tough, aggressive, hard-nosed play-ers, and Mase fit that bill. After the Stokes Game, we got him for our Summer League team. And when we watched him in practice and saw the things he did, with his work ethic and the things he brought to the table, I signed him to a two-year deal as soon as we got to Los Angeles for the Summer League. We signed him before the other teams could really see what he could do. We got a nice deal; we got him at the minimum for two years. But he didn't play like a minimum player.

Pat Riley: He had sort of been kicked around two or three different places, and now he was ready to step in. It was one of the more fortunate signings we had, because he really fortified–with Oak and Patrick–one of the toughest front lines in the game.

Jeff Van Gundy: Paul and I got to coach the [1991] Summer League team. Now, Pat ran a lot of the practices, and when we got out to L.A., we had a great team. We had Mase, Starks, Greg Anthony, and some other NBA-type veterans. And after one practice at the Inglewood YMCA, he [Pat] said, "Take a ride back with me." So we're driving in his BMW going back to the hotel. He drops me off, and he says, "All right. You're gonna be the third assis-tant; you're not gonna be on the bench, you're gonna do all the scouting, and you're gonna make $100,000." Well, that's like a $40,000 raise. I was like, "OK." I got out of the car, great, thank you, and that was it.

Pat Riley: Jeff won me over that summer with his work in the Summer League. His suggestions, his ideas, his loyalty, all of those things you could see immediately. And he became, as my four years progressed, the number one confidant after Dick Harter left. I just saw something very unique in Jeff, very special. He's very smart. He really knew basket-ball. Absolutely dedicated to the game. He really helped me immensely.

Jeff Van Gundy: Now we're playing our first preseason game at Nassau Coliseum. We're sitting around before the game, then all the coaches got up to go out to the bench. I'm sitting in the locker room. They're going, I'm staying. Then he says, "What are you doing?" I said, "I'm staying in here." He says, "What the fuck are you talking about? Get out there." That's how I got on the bench.

Pat Riley: We definitely emphasized the defensive end because we had a great shot-blocker in Patrick. We had one of the best team defensive players in Charles Oakley. Anthony Mason and John Starks were sort of upstart players for us. I saw that team as being rock solid defensively. And when we made the move to bring in Xavier McDaniel, that was another tough-minded guy. So we had developed a defensive team, and it was based a lot on the personnel. You run with what you've got. I think if we'd had offensive players who could really shoot the ball, or run or cut, I think you'd probably emphasize that part of it. But we became a defensive-oriented post-up team because we had Patrick posting up. Then when John became a player that rose to another level, we became a very good pick-and-roll team with him and Mark Jackson. So we started to cover the bases that first year.

Kiki Vandeweghe: It was a totally different attitude and mind-set. Pat has a different way of doing things and commands a lot of respect. The players responded to that. It was typified by the first day in practice, with the big fight between Anthony Mason and Xavier McDaniel. You could see it coming from the first minute of practice. I was sitting there, part of the group that pulled the two apart. And I'm just going, "Oh, boy. This is gonna be wild." And it was. It was a wild ride.

Pat Riley: I anticipated that [fight] right from the get-go. The first day of practice is all about drills, and so the first 45 minutes to an hour of practice was simply gonna be individual defensive drills. I don't even think we played five-on-five for at least three or four practices. Everything was individually broken down. And one of the drills we got into early was three-on-three blockout drills that are pretty physical and pretty demanding. X and Mase got tangled up on a couple of the blockouts and one thing led to another and a fight erupted that covered pretty much the whole court. And I think that sort of established their territory with one another, because neither one of them said another word to each other the rest of the year, because there was a respect that was gained. I think our guys realized exactly how much we wanted it and that the environment was serious. It was quite a day.

Charles Oakley: The key was that you had to be a hard worker, then try to fit in and learn the system. I think Riles' system was great. The guys didn't mind working hard. They had the understanding that you had to be mentally tough. You're gonna practice tough; you're gonna do things his way. And his way won a lot of games for us.

Kiki Vandeweghe: I appreciate what Pat Riley did much more today. It was difficult for me [at the time] because I wasn't fully healthy and the practices were difficult. As a player at that point in my career, I was easily broken down; whereas earlier in my career, I could have done it and never missed any practice. But this was difficult. There was definitely a change of attitude. A lot of things were different.

Jeff Van Gundy: That first year, they were thinking of this marketing plan where they'd put the outline of a dead body on the court. They decided against it.

In the first year of the Riley Era, 1991–92, the Knicks increased their win total by 12 to 51–31, and only a late-season fadeout kept them from winning the Atlantic Division title. After beating Detroit in a five-game opening playoff round, they took eventual champion Chicago to seven games in the East semis before falling. Now it was time to take the next step.

Ernie Grunfeld: We had a successful season, the first year under Pat. We just felt like we wanted some more length in the front court, and we also wanted some more defense. Mark had been a great player for us, a great playmaker. But we also had Greg Anthony, who was a great defender, and his minutes were increasing because Pat really emphasized the defensive end. And we felt if we were gonna be the team we wanted to be, a team that could go deep in the playoffs every year and compete for a championship, we felt we needed a real defensive presence on the ball. And it wasn't easy trading Mark; he had been a very valuable part of the team. But we had the opportunity to get a 6'11" player in Charles Smith, who could give us a lot of length and versatility in the front court, as well as a veteran leader like Doc Rivers.

It was a three-way trade, actually, with Orlando. Stanley Roberts was gonna go from Orlando to the Clippers, but the deal was held up for about two and a half weeks because Roberts had a no-trade clause in his contract and he didn't want to go to L.A. He wouldn't waive the no-trade clause. Finally, the Clippers got him out there, and he went to one of those Malibu parties, and he realized that it wasn't gonna be so bad. So then he approved the trade.

Doc was really a great leader; he gave you great toughness and professionalism. He really understood how to run a team and get everybody involved. He and Greg Anthony gave us an outstanding combination of two good defensive players, real good toughness, and size.

Rolando Blackman: I remember the rumors. I had the opportunity to talk to [Dallas GM] Rick Sund, and he told me they were trying to work some different things out. And finally I got a call that said I was a New York Knickerbocker. It was mixed emotions for me at the time, simply because our team was in decline, and really it just gave me the opportunity to go to a team in which I had deep respect for the coach and the program and the things that he had done in L.A. and also in New York. So I felt fantastic coming to New York and back home. I was ecstatic, but also sad at the same time to leave a great franchise like Dallas.

Jeff Van Gundy: When Ro came to us, he got hurt weightlifting that fall. So he didn't come to us damaged, but I don't think he was ever the same. But he handled himself so well. The thing about Ro was that he prepared like it was Game 7 of the playoffs every day. And he wasn't even playing sometimes. Just worked and set a great example.

Rolando Blackman: I came from a team that ran some transition, but we were very powerful and strong in the half-court offense with Dick Motta. We were the best-executing team in the NBA. The important thing in coming to coach Riley's system was a little bit different. It was more of a stationary piece to get Patrick the basketball and to have everybody float and play off Patrick, whether it be in the pick-and-roll or [to] throw the ball in to Pat and stand and wait for him to throw the ball to you. That was a different scope, a different scene. For me, I believed in everything coach Riley was doing. I bought into the system; I bought into what was true about him and what he wanted to do.

Bob Salmi: Riles was watching tape one day, and the way he watched tape was unique. All of the lights were out in the room. Every single light out, and one little tiny light in the whole room that just shone down on his notes. He was playing back his video and looking at plays and drawing on his pad. So I thought, we need a break in the action. I reached around the corner with the remote control and I shut off his TV. Now, he didn't know I was doing this, so he picked up the remote control, whacked it a few times, got it back on, and went about his business. I waited about a minute and a half and I turned it off again. Now he was starting to get a little frustrated, and he was hitting the remote control again, and got it turned on. Then I did it a third time, and he was screaming, "Salmi, get in here and fix this thing!" So I stuck my head in the door and I said, "Coach, I think the problem might be this remote I have in my hand." And as God is my witness, this is the reaction I got: he stared at me, didn't say a word to me, and went right back to work. So my dumb ass was standing in the doorway saying to myself, "Salm, it's really been nice working with the Knicks. Now you need to get your resume out."

Herb Williams: It was always us against everybody else. That was his whole thing. It was the team against the other teams in the league, and the team that was gonna protect you when you were down and be with you when you were up. They weren't going to be on and off. We have to stick together. That was his big thing, that you would always stick together. He'd tell war stories about how you'd be in the trenches and have to depend on each other. He'd always use those scenarios to try and keep us together. Or he'd break up the routine, where we'd think we were going to a hard practice and go watch a movie instead. Just so the guys could be around each other, away from basketball, so you could interact with guys more so than at practice. And he always made sure everything was first class. He never skimped on anything, because he was gonna get it out of you in practice.

Bob Salmi: We had a drill where Pat was really challenging the heart and will of the players. He thought they really weren't putting it on the line. And the drill was that the players had to take a charge from Van Gundy or myself. Now, if I hit some of these guys with everything I had, they ain't going down. So we do the drill the first time and I hit Mason, and Mason kind of flops and falls on the floor. Riley loses it. "You guys are blankety-blanks, you're not tough at all." Now they're really mad. So the next time through, I'm gonna hit Mason with everything I have. So I hit Mason. He stayed up; I went down and I broke two of my ribs. That's how intense Pat was.

In 1992–93, the Knicks tied a club record when they won 60 games. That season they ran away with the Atlantic Division crown. The top-seeded team in the Eastern Conference, they had the league's best defense, with 95.4 points per game allowed. Riley was named NBA Coach of the Year, while Ewing finished fourth in the league's MVP balloting.

Pat Riley: We had a championship team, we really did. And we had a championship team that quickly developed. The only trouble was that–and this was true when I was coaching the Lakers, when I knew there were other championship teams in the Western Conference–we just had the unfortunate experience to come along at a time when Michael Jordan was around. That was our biggest nemesis. At least that year [1992–93], I thought our team was better than anybody else in the league at that time. We just could not get by MJ. We were always right there, battling with them. And they knew it. They knew we were the team that probably was the most dangerous team in the East. Finally, when Michael took the year off, we beat them and got to the Finals and couldn't cap it off. It was just a shame. But that team, for about two years, was really a championship-contending team.

Jeff Van Gundy: That team was a great team. Look at it this way: the 1990 team that beat Boston was a fifth seed. If you brought that same team to today's East, it would dominate it. We had Patrick in his prime, Oakley in his prime, Wilkins in his prime, Newman and Mark Jackson at their prime. And then the bench people: Mo, Kiki, Kenny Walker. That's been the evolution of the team from my time. What was a pretty good team in 1990 would be, I think

without a doubt, the dominant team in the East today. So the 1993 team certainly was the best team that I've ever been a part of. The second-best was the 1997 team.

Charles Smith: That [the 1992–93 team] was the best team I ever played on. We had a very tough defensive team, as well as an explosive offense, at times when we got an opportunity to run up and down and play.

After going 7–2 in the first two rounds to knock off Indiana and Charlotte, the Knicks faced Chicago in their first appearance in the Eastern Conference Finals since 1973. Behind Michael Jordan's 32.2 points per game, including 54 points in Game 4, the Bulls would prevail in a six-game series that produced two of the most memorable plays in Knicks history: John Starks weaving through the Bulls' defense for "the Dunk" in the final minute of Game 2, and Charles Smith missing on four close-in attempts in the last seconds of the Game 5 loss, which snapped a 27-game home winning streak and turned the series in Chicago's favor. Smith would forever bear the burden for the shocking loss, despite the fact that the Knicks went just 20-for-35 from the free throw line.

John Starks: [On "the Dunk"] It was a pick-and-roll play for me to come down and revolve around a pick. I'd get on the right side of the court and come off Patrick's pick and get into the lane. But all game long they'd been pushing me down, especially Bill Cartwright and B. J. Armstrong. B.J. was guarding me at the time, and they had been doing it all game long. So I said to myself, "I'm gonna wait. I'm gonna wait until the right opportunity to do something a little different." And sure enough, I set it up beautifully. I knew Patrick was coming over to set the pick. Cartwright was kind of out of position, and B.J. knew that Cartwright was supposed to be pushing me down. So I kind of glanced at Patrick, and B.J. jumped out because he thought Cartwright was already there. Cartwright looked shocked that B.J. had jumped out, and it opened up the baseline. I just went in. Seeing Horace Grant, I knew I had to go strong, and I just went up and over the top.

Because of the situation and the team that we were playing, people still remember that. That play put me on the map. It's funny: in basketball, one play can make your career. That particular play put me on the map, and to this day people come up to me and tell me that it was the greatest play they'd ever seen. It's funny how that play has kept me in the limelight.

Jeff Van Gundy: The one time Jordan had a bad [playoff] game against us, we didn't take advantage of it because we weren't ready to play. Game 3 in '93, we're up 2–0 going to their place. And the Atlantic City controversy is going on. And he goes 3-for-18. And we got blown out because we weren't ready to play. So we took the one time we could have . . . you know? If we'd come out hard and right and taken advantage of his bad game . . . But we didn't. And the next game he crushed us.

Pat Riley: When you stop and think about it, he [Jordan] is gonna get it anyway. What we didn't want was Chicago to get everything and make their offense real efficient. Our whole concept defensively was you guard your own man. We never double-teamed anybody in the post. You either got exposed, or you stopped somebody. We had a lot of good individual defenders; John Starks, Greg Anthony, and our whole front line could pretty much handle their own guys down there. We were gonna play Chicago pretty much straight up and straight down, and wear on them. So we'd send Gerald Wilkins at him, send John Starks at him, send Greg Anthony at him, and occasionally Anthony Mason. The whole thought was that we were gonna wear him down. It's hard to do with Michael, because he'll wear everybody out. And we did have an impact on defending him that first year. And even though we had good team principles and we always had a lot of help [defense], we didn't pull triggers and come in double-teams. We didn't create some gimmick defense. He was either gonna get 50 on us, which I think he got in one [playoff] game, or he was gonna go 9-for-35. That was our philosophy.

Jeff Van Gundy: We were always tough enough to be competitive with him in the playoffs, but we were never good enough to beat him.

Charles Smith: My focus around it [the critical Game 5 play] was, one, it was a broken play. And I happened to be in the right place at the right time to recover the ball from going out of bounds, and I worked my butt off for a series of plays, which seemed like they took a lifetime, to try to score a bucket that did not transpire. I've always been taught to work hard and give it your best shot. I could not live with that play if I knew that I did not give it my all to try to do the best I can. And I stayed mentally tough and went to Chicago and had a good Game 6 because, despite Game 5, there was still a sixth and seventh game we had to play if we were gonna win it all.

Marv Albert: It's like boxing: you always have to have a partner, like Ali with Frazier. And the Bulls had a lot to do with it; you know you're gonna face that inevitable showdown. Also, through the nineties, because of the added exposure–cable TV, highlight shows, sports talk radio, things like that–there was so much more being talked about and written about the Knicks, and it became even bigger. It's funny: I was just in Chicago and I was talking about the same thing with some guys out there, about how they miss the showdowns with the Knicks. They're going through the same situation, in reverse.

Charles Smith: Through my career playing basketball, I've won games and lost games. That particular play, being in New York, just had a lot of focus around it. It caused so much hype around our two teams. The hurt of failure propelled me to be just as determined, moving forward in life, as I've ever been, because the most successful people in life have experienced some gut-wrenching failures. And now I understand.

The fact that I worked hard and did the best I could–that was most important. We're always dealing with real-life issues, even outside of sports. How could I tell my children and other children to work hard and do the best they can, and if they fail, just give up and throw the towel in? No. I'm gonna stand strong, and others need to do the same. You stand strong and you keep moving. Sports teach you that; they teach you how to deal with life. That was an experience that taught me a life lesson that I'll never

Patrick and Oak.

forget after dealing with people, the fans, everyone surrounding that. It was an experience that a lot of people don't get. Life grants us situations, both good and bad. But at the end of the day, it all depends on how *you* handle it as an individual. That's what I learned from Game 5.

No three players symbolized the emotion and intensity of the Riley era more than Charles Oakley, John Starks, and Anthony Mason.

Herb Williams: Oak was the kind of guy that you never had to worry about, regardless of what was going on around him or what we were doing or what was being said. You knew that when you stepped on the court, whether it be in practice or whether it be in the game, that he was going to lay it on the line. He was gonna make the right rotations. He was gonna play hard night in and night out. He was just gonna do whatever needed to be done to win a basketball game.

Starks was a little more energetic, a little more hyper, a little more emotional. But he was one and the same with Oak in that he just wanted to win basketball games. Mase understood how to play the game. Sometimes he got a little pissed because he thought he should have gotten the ball a little more. But it was Patrick's team, and we all knew that going in.

John Starks: Some guys can't deal with the truth. I could deal with the truth. That's what I loved about it, and that's why they respected me. I never got on the fans. I never said, "Oh, man. Why are they booing us?" I liked that, because when some guys didn't give 100 percent, it needed to be known.

Charles Oakley: I think that in New York, well, playing in New York is like Truth or Dare. I've just gotta speak the truth. I played Truth or Dare a couple of times and always told the truth. That's how I presented myself at all times.

Anthony Mason: It was really the starting point of my career, and I'm definitely thankful for those years. I became a crowd favorite, and I miss those days. Whenever I go back, they're always telling me how much they miss me and all that. I'm very thankful for that.

Dave Checketts: Red Holzman was constantly admonishing me to be patient with Mason and Oakley. He's probably the reason they stayed on the team. And both of them turned out to be pretty important to us.

Jeff Van Gundy: Oakley is one of those guys who, if you have him on your team, you just love him. Because he's loyal, and you can take his honesty. I had to speak to him every once in a while about his view of the world. But he was terrific. He'd put his body on the line every time.

Mike Saunders: I would play a lot of Sinatra in the training room. One day I walked into the room at the Garden, and Oak was lying on the table, his hands behind his head, singing Sinatra's version of "The Way You Look Tonight," the great Jerome Kern song. He's going, "Someday, when I'm awfully low . . . " I raised my fist in the air and kind of declared that I had won, finally. My music was accepted. That was one of my crowning achievements.

John Starks: New Yorkers are very emotional people. I was in the airport the other day, talking to a guy from New York, and he told me, "Man, you took me on an emotional ride that I'll never, ever forget." What they loved about me, I think, was my intensity level and the fact that with me, anything could happen at any time. I was a little bit unpredictable at times, but when I got it going it was very, very exciting.

Herb Williams: Those three guys . . . You knew that when the ball was tossed up, they were gonna put it on the line. And that's what you respect about players. You can look in a guy's eyes and know if he's ready to play or not, or if he's ready to go the extra mile or not. And that team did.

For 1993–94, NBA regulations stated that teams could begin preseason practice on October 8. And that's what the Knicks did–when the day was exactly one minute old.

It would be that kind of season.

Pat Riley: You spend the whole summer thinking about what the theme's going to be and how you're gonna start it. After being with that team for two years already, [instead of] going down there to Charleston and having the same old routine of starting training camp, we just decided to do something different. And we did. We started at 12:01 A.M., got on the court, and had a great scrimmage, a great practice. That was the theme: first on and hopefully last off. We almost got there.

The players were a little perplexed by it. But they said, "Coach, whatever it is, whatever you want, we'll do it." It was sort of fun, to be honest.

Bob Salmi: He [Riley] felt that you had to understand that there was a painful progression, and you had to remember that pain. And then if you were willing to persevere and tee it up one more time, that the ultimate prize would be yours. And he kept hammering on that theme. It wasn't going to be then [in 1991–92], but he appreciated the effort. But don't ever let that pain go away. I think that was his biggest thing. He wanted to remind you of that on a regular basis . . . he wanted you to remember how much it hurt [in 1992–93] to be up 2–0 and all of a sudden we're out of it. He wanted that in the back of your mind. And if you're serious about your craft, like a lot of those guys were–you had Doc Rivers, you had Harper, you had Patrick–they understood keeping it in the back of your head.

Herb Williams: Riles kept his hand in it, because in New York you have to do that. Anything you say can be taken out of context. Or you could say something in the beginning of the year, and they could interview you at the end of the year and put those two things together and make it look like you're saying something totally different. So he was always mindful of that, and he understood the pressure of the media and how it could tear a team up really quick. So Riles pretty much put his hand on it. But our guys, for the most part, would police each other on the court. If I had to make a rotation and somebody didn't cover my back, guys would let each other know. Which you almost have to have. If someone messed a play up, guys would tell other guys that. They wouldn't take it personally. But as far as the media, Riles understood that it wouldn't take much to have a rift.

Pat Riley: After we made the trade–and I didn't want to trade Mark–and brought in Charles Smith and Doc Rivers, and [also] getting Derek Harper and Rolando Blackman, I felt that we had a deep front line, a deep backcourt. We had just about all the bases covered. One of the things that really hurt us was when Doc Rivers went down and had to miss the playoffs. But that team was ready to do something. With Michael [Jordan] on the sidelines, this was the year for us to strike, and I think our guys were primed for that.

Charles Smith: The one thing I took away from coach Riley is his ability and creativity to break down various points where the team struggled offensively and defensively, and then put those plays into a practice form, and drill them until we got better at them. We'd rotate in different positions if we had problems with, say, the pick-and-roll defense. Any problems we had, he was always able to create a play for us to work on to get better. So as the season went on, we got stronger and better with our rotations, with our defense, and with our offense.

Hubert Davis: As a rookie, you really don't accept too much. When I first stepped onto the court and saw Patrick, Oak, and Mase, I was just happy to be out there. I really wasn't nervous, I just wanted to go out there and have fun and play. It really worked out for me. Doc and Rolando Blackman took me under their wing, and then Derek Harper came in. The things I've tried to do since in my career are things that they taught me.

Ernie Grunfeld: Doc got hurt against the Lakers. As he was going up, Vlade Divac bumped him, and Doc came down wrong and landed awkwardly. That was a devastating blow, and we went to work right away on trying to find a replacement.

Derek Harper: It was exciting. I remember going home and talking to my kids and my family. I remember the way I explained to them, being traded. I told my oldest son and my daughter how I compared the records. I showed them Dallas' record and where they were as a team, and then where I was going to in New York. So they got excited, and as long as they were cool with it, I was even more cool with it.

Ernie Grunfeld: Dallas was going in a different direction; they were going with a youth movement at the time, and Derek's minutes were down. So we were fortunate to get him. And after four to six weeks of getting acclimated to our system and our players, he really played outstanding basketball for us.

Derek Harper: One thing about being on a losing team is that you don't come early and you don't stay late. And I was finding it hard to come early and stay late in Dallas, just like everybody else was, because I really wanted out at that point. So I wasn't in condition. I wasn't in the kind of NBA shape that I needed to be in when I got to New York. So, imagine going to a system like New York out of shape a little bit. And then go through all of his practices, go through the mental grind that Pat puts on you. He's very demanding as a coach, makes you accountable for every single thing that happens on the basketball court. That being the case, I was right behind the eight ball as soon as I got there.

Rolando Blackman: I found out about it over the radio like everybody else. I understood that we were after a guard who was tremendous like he was, and it was a perfect fit for the Riley system. Doc had gone down, and they got the perfect guard for the Riley system: a tough-oriented, serious defensive player who could shoot the three, lead a basketball team, and had the razor edge to play in the New York City atmosphere.

Derek Harper: I struggled initially. I remember going to New York, checking into games, checking out of games, and having fans sitting behind me asking me, "Harper, how fucking long is it going to take you?" And then, "Riley, is this what we traded for?" I heard a lot of those comments. So mentally I struggled. And the other thing that forced me to struggle was not having my family with me. I was so accustomed to them breaking the monotony of basketball. Not having them there compounded the situation of not playing well. Instead of coming home to your kids and your family, you bring a stat sheet home and beat yourself up even more. So I was doing that for the first 10 or 15 games.

Jeff Van Gundy: Derek came in midseason, and that's always difficult. He was coming from a losing situation, and you get into such rotten habits when you lose. And if you view it objectively, you'd see that. But he did such a great job. He's such a worker at heart that he got himself out of the bad habits, putting in so much extra time.

After winning 32 of their first 43 games, the Knicks staggered through the month of February. Losers of 4 straight games and 8 of 12, they were headed to Sacramento to continue what had been a miserable road trip. Or so they thought.

Pat Riley: Every now and then [with the Lakers] we would sort of detour, surprise them. But that particular time, we were really struggling as a team, losing games and losing our confidence. I was riding them, yelling, screaming. Sometimes you have to sort of deviate from the norm.

Mike Saunders: We're in Phoenix, and we weren't playing well. We were going hard, hard, hard, and I said to Riles, "Do you think we should ease up?" He said, "What do you do when you have severe bleeding?" And the answer is, direct pressure. See, he thought we needed more pressure, more direct pressure, at that point. But that didn't seem to work.

Now we're flying from Phoenix to Sacramento. On the plane, he calls me back where his suite was. He says, "Go up and ask the pilot if we can fly to Tahoe." So I go up and ask, and they say the airport in Tahoe is too small to accommodate a plane our size. But they said, "How about Reno?" So I said, "Great." I go up and tell Riles that it's Reno. He says, "Do it." From the plane, we get a hotel, the Peppermill Casino. We get the rooms; we get the limos. Eight limos for everybody, and Riles just absolutely loved that. And the way he described it later was, "a crescent of limos"; it was a semicircle at the airport when we landed. And the players didn't know what was going on! They had absolutely no idea.

Pat Riley: Let's just go there for 36 hours, forget about the game, just be together and have some fun. Mike pulled it off; he made the arrangements in flight. And as the plane was pulling into what the players thought was Sacramento, they're all depressed and thinking they have to go to practice the next day and all that stuff. Then some of them said, "Hey, this doesn't look like Sacramento." They started to see all the lights and everything. And as they got off the plane, I was standing at the bottom of the stairs and gave each guy $500. They each got into limousines and went off, and I didn't see them for 36 hours. Then we won 15 in a row.

Mike Saunders: We get to the Peppermill, and Riles gives, out of his own pocket, $500 in chips to everyone. We gambled for a day and a half, reassembled, flew to Sacramento, and then went 14–0 in March. It really brought that team together. It was an adventure.

Derek Harper: Every player was given $500 worth of chips. Me being a saver, I cashed the chips in and put the money in my pocket, and then watched everybody else throwing it down. I cashed my chips in, and knowing I was going to be starting [the next game], I had a different thought process. Jeff leaked it to me that I was probably going to go into the starting lineup, so I wasn't in a partying mood. And we were really struggling as a team. So my mind-set changed. I kind of walked around with Rolando. I watched him gamble. I hung out with John [Starks] a little bit, watched him lose a lot of money, and turned in early. I said, "Enough of this shit." It was smoky down there, like most casinos are. So I went to the room and laid back and relaxed and got myself ready.

Rolando Blackman: I didn't come out of my room too much. I went downstairs a little bit. I saw all the gambling and people losing money and I said, "Well, that's not exactly what I want to do." So I used the time to just stay in my room and cool out and really reassess what was happening during the season. After we came back from that, the team was energized and really focused on being together and how we wanted to get it done. It was a good diversion, a good move by coach Riley. It got the job done.

Pat Riley: I was doing that for a couple of reasons. I knew that, right now, we were gonna have to make some changes in the lineup. It was time. We put Harp in the starting lineup, and Hubert Davis and Anthony Bonner, those three guys. That turned

it around. We went to Sacramento and just took off. Never did get my money back, though.

Jeff Van Gundy: Pat wanted to expense it and they wouldn't give him his money back. But, see, what that whole thing was foreboding was that he was changing the lineup. Then we ripped off 15 in a row. Now, did the winning streak have to do with that? No. But one thing that happened at that time was that we had gotten away from playing defense. So then Pat says, "I'm gonna start paying for charges. A hundred dollars each, but only in wins, and they double if we keep on winning." So now we're up to like 14 in a row, and we're playing Miami at home. Eric Anderson gets in with something like three minutes to go. He ran around and was throwing his body in front of anyone that was moving, drew two charging fouls, and wound up making like four grand. Just the funniest thing. But things like that–taking charges, going to Reno–are what makes him [Pat] so good about thinking of the psychology of a team and what a team needs at that moment.

After winning 21 of their last 27 games, the Knicks easily defeated New Jersey in the first round of the 1994 playoffs. That meant the Bulls–again.

But this year would be different. With Jordan retired–temporarily–the Knicks outlasted Chicago in seven games. In Game 3 in Chicago, Harper earned a two-game suspension after a brawl with Jo Jo English, and the Bulls won the game on Toni Kukoc's last-second jumper. But the turning point of the series came in Game 5, when Hubert Davis nailed two free throws with 2.1 seconds left–following a controversial foul call by referee Hue Hollins on Scottie Pippen–to give the Knicks an 87–86 win at the Garden. In Game 7, Ewing scored all 18 of his points in the second half, as the Knicks ended the Bulls' three-year championship reign with an 87–77 win.

Pat Riley: It was the whole Chicago deal. For two years we'd been in wars with those guys. So finally, we had the opportunity. And it went right down to the wire, and it took our best player to make big plays and make shots. The biggest play was the Hubert Davis foul [in Game 5], right in front of their bench. That was a huge, huge play. Them not having Michael, obviously, was a huge loss.

Derek Harper: I'm not a fighter. I'm a hard-nosed basketball player but not one who plays dirty, picks fights, or any of that stuff. But the heat of that series, I'd never been involved in anything like that. Never that much tension in my career as in that series. We tried to do all we could at Chicago Stadium to win a game, then the guy [Jo Jo English] comes towards me saying some things that I interpreted to mean [he was] getting ready to hit me. I reacted to that and nothing else. I reacted to nothing other than I thought this guy was coming to do something to me. Where I'm from, you hit first. That was my reaction. I regret it, but there's nothing I can do about it now.

Hubert Davis: I wasn't the first option. Obviously, we wanted to get the ball down to Patrick. But we gave John a drive opportunity, an opportunity to make something happen. So he drove into the lane and everyone collapsed. In the huddle beforehand, Greg Anthony said, "Hubert, if you've got the shot, you've gotta take it." So John threw the ball out to me and I was wide open.

Jeff Van Gundy: The play was a post-up for Patrick. We threw it in, the ball came out, and Hubert shot. Was it a foul? No. We got a beneficial call. Now, *should* it be a foul? Yes. Because I don't think you should be able to interrupt a shooter with contact. And there was certainly contact. But the way it was called at that time, I know if you had flipped it, we would have been outraged at the call. But, as [NFL coach] Steve Mariucci so aptly put it, bummer.

Hubert Davis: Scottie hit me on the arm. He hit me a little bit, right after the shot. I can't remember which ref called it, but I'll take it. It was definitely a foul. A lot of people said maybe it was after the fact, but I'm just glad they called it.

When I hit the first one, it's tied. Then they called a timeout. And who really cares now, right? At least it's tied. You know, sometimes they go in and sometimes they don't. And one thing I just wanted to do was shoot my shot and be confident in it. And if it didn't go in, then at least I tried. But I knew that the team needed that. And it's really hard to put into words. When you're in a situation like that, you don't really have time to think about it. But when I got home, I was like, "Oh, my God . . . "

Phil Jackson: No, he didn't [foul him]. Ultimately, Hubert had a leg lift or a leg kick, depending on how you want to term it. It was the follow-through for his shot, which, as Darrell Garretson said the next year, shouldn't have been a foul called. It's usually ignored. Reggie Miller has perfected it, so that a leg drifts where he gets it caught on people's bodies. But in those situations, it's ignored.

Hubert Davis: When I'm in Chicago, they still can't stand me. They think I ruined their season. I'm sorry for the Bulls. But, hey . . .

Jeff Van Gundy: The previous year, everybody talks about Charles Smith missing. Yes, he missed. But, yes, he was fouled, too. So the last team that should ever complain about getting a difficult call late is the Bulls. Because much of their dynasty was built upon a favorable whistle at critical times, or a non-call.

Phil Jackson: We got a win back in Chicago and forced a seventh game. I believe the best team won. I think the Knicks won the series even though we would have liked to think that we could have won had we won that game [Game 5]. I think the Knicks were a better team, overall, than we were that year.

Now came Indiana in the Eastern Conference Finals. The two teams split the first four games, but the Knicks held a 12-point edge entering the fourth quarter of Game 5 at the Garden. Then Reggie Miller silenced the sellout crowd by scoring 25 of his game-high 39 points in the fourth quarter to give the Pacers a stunning 93–86 win.

But two nights later, Starks, who missed the regular season's last six weeks due to knee surgery, scored 26 points to lead the Knicks to a season-saving 98–91 Game 6 win in Indiana. Harper was the fourth-quarter hero, nailing the jumper that gave the Knicks the lead for good with 1:50 left, then stripping the ball from a fast-breaking Vern Fleming to seal the win in the closing seconds.

Pat Riley: When that [Miller's Game 5 explosion] starts to happen, there's nothing you can do.

You sort of deal with it. We were up by 12 and then wound up giving up the game. Then, everybody was counting us out. That's what I remember more than anything else, that this was over with now, that we're gonna go to Indiana and get beat.

Jeff Van Gundy: It was very disappointing because we were basically cruising through that game. We're up by 12 after three, at home. And then we just got crushed in the fourth because Reggie was terrific and we weren't as good as we should have been.

Pat Riley: The biggest game that we ever played in my tenure with the Knicks was that Game 6 in Indiana. We had to win and we did, and I don't think a lot of people expected us to. The guys were tough, and we came right out from the get-go.

Jeff Van Gundy: Pat was really toying with putting in a lot of new stuff [for Game 6]. See, the NBA at that time was just so much more physical than it is now. Everybody was just beating on each other on every possession. Then Pat came up with this thing in his mind, that we were in a fight, basically. And he who hits first usually wins, and that was his theme for that game. So we didn't put anything new in. We just came out and jumped them, stayed on them. Then Harp had the big steal and the big shot toward the end.

Derek Harper: Not until then did I feel like I was a Knick. Just from the way the crowd reacted, from the way the bench reacted, from the way the coaching staff reacted. Not until then did I feel officially a New York Knick. That solidified the deal for me. Because after the game, fans were lying down in front of the bus, not letting you move. I came back out for the postgame show and it was, "Harper! Harper! Harper!" It was very exciting, because that's a tough market to be accepted in, especially by the fans.

Back in New York, the Knicks earned their first trip to the NBA Finals since 1973, winning the East with a 94–90 win in Game 7. Ewing poured in 24 points, added 22 rebounds and seven assists, and authored the play of the season with a two-handed follow-up slam of a Starks miss to put New York in front for good with 26.9 seconds left. Following a much-debated flagrant foul called on Miller by referee Mike Mathis, Starks nailed three of four free throws to send the Knicks into the Finals. The game's enduring image would be that of Ewing jumping on the courtside press table in a moment of unrestrained joy.

Dave Checketts: [Before Game 7 against Indiana] I had asked for the NBA Championship trophy to be put in our locker room as a way to say to the guys, "This will give you a chance to play for this trophy." And Riles said no. I think Riles wanted nothing to do with it, that maybe it would jinx somebody, and then we had to hide it. The league agreed to give us the trophy, but if I remember correctly, we had to hide it because Riles said no.

Pat Riley: It's winner-take-all now, and I don't have time to take the risk of being in a very tight game. I just told him [Patrick] to keep his hands in his pockets and that we couldn't afford to have him on the bench. The great players can make the adjustments at that time without losing their intensity, and he did that.

Patrick Ewing: The play was a pick-and-roll with John and me. I got him free. He drove the lane, shot a flip shot up. I rolled with him to the basket, it came out, and I just put it back in.

John Starks: The play was designed for Oak to set a pick and for Patrick to come up and give me a high pick-and-roll. It worked perfectly because it opened the lane up for me to have a chance to get around and go in. I came around Rik Smits, and all I saw was the rim. So I went in strong and kind of flipped it up there. And sure enough, there was my saving grace: Patrick Ewing, following the play. I was thinking, "Oh, my God. Thank you, Big Fella."

Jeff Van Gundy: What people don't realize is that we were down big in the second half. Then we came back on them, and at that point I don't think I've ever heard the Garden that loud, at that pitch. And I still remember sitting there for their last possession, when he [Reggie] is coming off the screen right in front of our bench, and he throws up the air ball. And people always forget Mike Mathis calling the flagrant foul [on Miller]. And John makes only one of the two free throws, but we get the ball back. That changed the whole way the last few seconds were played. That's how important those small incidents

Series MVP Hakeem Olajuwon, skying over Anthony Mason in Game 7, was the difference in the 1994 Finals.

are. That was a ridiculous flagrant foul call, but it had a huge impact on the strategy of the rest of the game. And you need a little luck along the way.

John Starks: I've been hit a lot harder. But they called it as they saw it. I acted a little on it, made it a little more intense. It's not like he [Reggie] has never done it before, either.

I told him [Reggie], "You're a helluva player." I just felt bad for him in that situation because he had shot an air ball on the last play, with a chance to win the game. Oak had stepped out on him and made him shoot the air ball. I felt bad for him because even though we went against each other as hard as we could, you get a level of respect from your opponent. And I have a lot of respect for Reggie because he was out there trying to win and he was going to do whatever he had to do, whether it was get under people's skin or do his thing on the offensive end.

Hakeem Olajuwon had led the Houston Rockets to 58 wins–one more than the Knicks–during the regular season. That one extra win, the one that determined home court advantage, would loom large in the 1994 NBA Finals.

After a split of the first two games, Houston rookie Sam Cassell drilled a three-point bomb with 32.6 seconds left to give the Rockets a 93–89 Game 3 win at the Garden. Two nights later, the New York Rangers would end 54 years of famine by winning their first Stanley Cup since 1940 with a Game 7 win over Vancouver. With the smell of champagne still wafting through the Garden hallways, the Knicks won Games 4 and 5 to take a 3–2 lead in the series.

They headed for Houston needing one more win. Just one more.

Jeff Van Gundy: Cassell's shot [in Game 3] was the biggest shot of the series. We made a huge mistake, being up two. See, the hardest thing to do in any playoff series is win two in a row, and we were poised to win two in a row. When you're up by two, late, you do not give up the lead. Because if they just score two, we have the last shot. If not, you play overtime and take your shot at home. That was a critical mistake. But you have to give him [Cassell] credit. That was a foreboding of all the big shots he was gonna make in his career.

Derek Harper: Sam was a rookie at the time. And I think it was baffling to everybody how a guy that young could step up the way Sam did. Even with that shot, even losing that game, we still went to Houston in a position where we only needed one win.

Mike Saunders: It was thrilling to watch the Rangers win it. Then the next day, Mark Messier brings the Cup into our locker room. Their room across the hall still smelled of champagne. It was like perfume. It was a very special time.

Dave Checketts: When we were down at City Hall for the Rangers celebration, Ernie and I were walking through the crowd, and everybody was saying to us, "You're next! You're next! We'll be here next week for you!" I really thought it was going to happen.

Pat Riley: I did make a point to tell them that you don't want this to get to a seventh game. I said that our chance to win a championship is now. We've finally gotten to the game that's gonna allow you to win a championship, and I don't want you to think that you've got a gift here. The important thing to do is close this thing out. We got 'em down three games to two, and we've gotta be rock solid and close them out. Don't let it get to a seventh game because anything can happen, and usually the home court does play into some effect there.

Derek Harper: There was no doubt in my mind that we were gonna win a championship, going to Houston. I had had a lot of success, not only in the Finals but against Houston in previous years. So I was confident, almost overconfident, in going there. And I figured we could beat that team one out of two games. I just felt like it was our year. It [the plane ride] wasn't quiet, but it wasn't noisy either. I think everyone understood the importance of what we were trying to do. It was sort of like a business flight. Guys did their typical things, but at the same time I think everyone realized what was at stake.

Herb Williams: I thought it never should have gotten to Game 7. Game 6 was our chance to end it. If you're up 3–2 going to their place for two games, the thing you've got to try to do is win the first game.

Derek Harper: I was more ready to play those two games than I've ever been ready to play any games in my career. There was no doubt that I would play well.

Mike Saunders: The champagne, I think, came from the hotel. I brought it to the arena, but I was told that there was a Texas state law that said that you can't bring alcoholic beverages into an arena. I tried to explain that I wasn't bringing it in so I could drink it during the game, that it was for a celebration afterward, but they were adamant that I couldn't bring it in. Also, I bought some nonalcoholic champagne for the celebration as well. So for the guys on the team who didn't drink, they could partake of the nonalcoholic stuff.

Dave Checketts: The night before Game 6, I had a dream that I was wearing the same lucky Knicks blue sport jacket that I would wear that night, and I was having champagne poured all over me. I mean, in the dream I was just soaked in champagne.

Mike Saunders: What ended up happening was that I had to give the champagne to the arena people and they sold it back to me, to kind of make it official. I had to pay some sort of a fee. So we had the champagne ready. I kept it in two large equipment bags. Unfortunately, we never got a chance to pop it.

Trailing by nine points midway through the fourth quarter, the Knicks closed out Game 6 with a 21–14 run. Starks scored 15 points in the game's final 9:11 to trigger the comeback, but there was one shot he couldn't hit: the last-second three-pointer from the left elbow, the one that Olajuwon got a piece of–the one that would have meant an NBA Championship.

Pat Riley: In the sixth game, we got off to a 15–8 lead, and it looked like our guys were really gonna go. And then we made some mistakes and started missing shots, and we found ourselves behind. It went down to that Starks shot. And it was the same play we ran against Indiana to win Game 7, when John went in, missed the layup, and Patrick dunked. We ran the same play, and Patrick was wide open. John elected to raise and let the thing fly. And Hakeem, who was guarding Patrick, double-teamed him and got a piece of it. And I always wonder, to this day, if John had made the right play, which was probably the pass back to Patrick, what would have happened? He had enough time to shoot the ball, or

maybe he would have put it on the floor and drove to the basket and maybe got a three-point play. Who knows what would have happened? But Hakeem made a great play.

Derek Harper: It was designed for him [Starks] to throw the ball in to Patrick. We ran a play called "Floppy Up," and the play was designed for John to come off a double, come off a screen down by Patrick, then dump the ball inside. Defense was a little late; he takes the shot. I would have taken the shot if I was open. John took a lot of criticism after that series, but I don't think that particular shot rated a lot of criticism because it was a shot that any basketball player would take under those circumstances. If it goes, we're having a different conversation right now.

Jeff Van Gundy: Starks was so rollin', and he came off the pick-and-roll with Pat. Which in the previous series, Patrick had put us ahead with, with the dunk. It was the same play, but Starks was going the other way. It could have been the same scenario: miss, then Patrick follow. But there was less time here. He pulls up, misses, Hakeem tips it. Then everybody says the ball should have gone to Pat. Woulda, shoulda, coulda, you know? If it goes in, nobody's saying that ball should have gone to Ewing. He elevated beautifully, and Olajuwon made a helluva play. Because when Starks got into one of those zones, which he was in, I'm counting that thing as in.

John Starks: I think about it all the time. You go back and revisit things and see what you could have done better. Knowing that if I had made that shot, we wouldn't be having this conversation–you think about those things.

Jeff Van Gundy: Probably the most unbelievable time was from Game 6, which was a Sunday, to Game 7, on Wednesday. There's nothing left to prepare for; you've already done all your preparation. All Monday and Tuesday was, was sitting and waiting and playing different scenarios in your head.

Herb Williams: We didn't win Game 6, and we had to stay there for three days. And now all you're hearing is Houston, Houston, Houston. You couldn't watch TV. I was turning channels like crazy because it was like, look, please let's play tomorrow to get this over with. But we had to sit there three days and think about it. And I think Riles was thinking of coming back to New York after Game 6. I don't know why he didn't.

Derek Harper: My wife was there, and I remember telling her to call the kids and tell them that it was gonna take us one more game and we'll be back home.

Ernie Grunfeld: When we went in there for Game 6, everything was quiet. There was a hush in the arena, and I felt real good that we had a shot to win this. Then Olajuwon blocks Starks' shot at the buzzer, and I don't know how he got out there. But that's what great players do. And then the feeling for Game 7 was completely different. There was a buzz in the building now. And for a Game 7, the home team has an outstanding chance of winning.

Dave Checketts: I was convinced we were gonna win Game 6. I was convinced that Starks' last shot was going to go in. It just wasn't to be, and it almost hurt worse to get that close and not be able to grab the trophy. I truly believed we had more talent on our team. Game 6 was really our opportunity to win it, because it's so difficult to win a Game 7 on another team's floor.

Derek Harper: Getting off the bus, I saw the guys with the big boxes of champagne. And I'm thinking, this is it. It was almost like it was meant to be for me. I saw it before Mike Saunders did, believe it or not. I came through that door into the big hall and I said, "Yo, what is that?" They said, "Hey, it's the champagne." I'm like, "What the fuck?"–excuse my French. So this is for us to win this championship. No one in the world could have told me that we weren't going to win that game.

Ernie Grunfeld: If we had won Game 7, I would think that Derek would have probably been the MVP of the Finals.

Derek Harper: I had prepared, number one, doing my advertising for Nike. That was the shoe I was wearing. And thanking God. That was my speech. First I was going to thank God for putting me in a position to do it. Second, I was going to get into the whole spiel about coach Riley making the trade

to bring me to New York. I had everything mapped out. If we had won the championship, this was what I would be saying. I visualized the Nike stuff, businesswise and everything. And it never happened.

Despite the last-second miss, Starks had gone 5-for-7 from the field en route to 16 fourth-quarter points in Game 6. But he would go 2-for-18 for eight points in Game 7. And a legion of second-guessers would point to the fact that Rolando Blackman, a four-time NBA All-Star, would not get off the bench that night, as had been the case in each of the series' prior six games.

Meanwhile, Olajuwon scored 25 points, and Vernon Maxwell added 21 for Houston. The Knicks went scoreless for four minutes during the third quarter and trailed the rest of the way. Rockets 90, Knicks 84.

Jeff Van Gundy: [In Game 7] Carl Herrera stepped up. He played great. That basket at the end of the third quarter was huge. And Kenny Smith making a clutch jumper after Harper had dominated him for the entire series.

Pat Riley: All the critics and the naysayers that looked hard at that and criticized the fact that John was still in the game don't, and did not, take into account that we would have never gotten to Game 7 if it wasn't for John. In Games 4 and 5, he had double-digit fourth quarter performances. In Game 5, without him getting 11 points in the fourth quarter, we wouldn't have won. In Game 6, he had 16 points in the fourth quarter. He was really, really playing well in fourth quarters, making big shots and big plays.

Rolando Blackman: It was heartbreaking; I can't tell you that it wasn't. Because that year I was healthy. The first year I wasn't healthy, but the second year, I had surgery that summer. But it was a situation where, when coach Riley puts his lineup together, he goes with the people that he's gone with before. And that was John and Hubert at the two guard. There was nothing I could do about that, except to be a good soldier, which I was. I made sure I was a leader even though I didn't get an opportunity to play and to be a part of what was going on. Even though my heart was breaking at every instance where we played against these teams I had destroyed before, especially Houston. [In the past] I had a lot of those guys in my back pocket, and they knew it, too. Can't do anything about that. But I was prepared to play, physically and emotionally ready to play. In practice I was running and doing all the things I needed to do. But, it just wasn't meant to be.

Pat Riley: I had not played Rolando very much throughout the series. I wasn't about to give up on the guy [John], because John is one of those guys like Reggie Miller. He can be ice cold for three quarters and then go off on you. I brought Greg Anthony in for a little while, and we were able to cut into the lead. And that was the only time I said to myself during the course of the game, maybe I should just stay with Greg and Derek, because they were playing pretty well. I elected to go back to John. I don't have any regrets, but from a thought standpoint, because he was so cold, maybe if I had let it go for another minute or two, something might have happened. But John was my guy at the time, and it's just a shame that he came up with a bad game in Game 7.

Rolando Blackman: I thought about it at the time. But I think the main factor is that it's not a personal issue for me. It's a team issue. That's what I was thinking all throughout. I ran suicides with these guys; I did all the things that were necessary in order to get it done. But the important thing is that I was thinking about them, in terms of how I could help. For me, it was just [being able to get] John out for two, three, or four minutes. Just get a couple of Gatorades, sit down on the side, and take a look at the game, calm down, then put him right back in. Because he had such a fantastic game the game before. But just to give the man a break instead of letting him try to ride it out. That was my thought. To be ready to play and just give him the few minutes he needed. Believe me, I wanted to get in there and try to hold down the fort.

John Starks: I think a lot about Game 7 and how I prepared for it and how I would have done it differently. You replay all those things in your mind. But that's always going to be with me. I know that, and I just have to accept it and move on with my life.

Dave Checketts: I thought our '93 team was the better team and should have won a championship, and I thought our '94 team clearly should have.

Pat Riley: It's never good. I've been in that situation a number of times, and it's never good. I don't care what happens, there's no solace. There's none of this, "We got to the Finals, this is OK." Especially in a seventh game. You've lost an opportunity to do something that you very rarely get a chance to do.

Derek Harper: After the game, I remember sitting in the locker room with coach Riley, with a Bud Light in my hand, crying. Tears in his eyes as well. Just heartbroken, just sick.

Herb Williams: I remember after Game 7, just taking a shower and walking back to the hotel. I was that upset. I'm still pretty sore [about it]. We stayed over, and it was a sleepless night.

Jeff Van Gundy: Herb Williams walked all the way from the arena back to the hotel. We literally had to pull Starks out of the shower, because he stood in there for 45 minutes. And part of it is facing the music, you know? Riles had a party in his room afterward, but it was a bittersweet thing.

Rolando Blackman: After the game, I made sure that I used all the thought processes and knowledge that I had to keep my composure, and not to blow up or say anything foolish, and not to be so angry that I would take it anywhere else. I just took 10 to 15 minutes in the shower and let the water run over my head and thought about my career and things of that nature. I knew that that was it for me as a New York Knick. I had one year left on the contract and I wasn't going to be back.

Anthony Mason: We were the better team. I definitely think about it a lot. We were the better team, but that's the way the ball bounces.

Charles Oakley: I really don't try to think about it, but Michael [Jordan] and other guys bring it up every now and then. Fans, too. They always say that we got so close. Shot here, shot there. But I wasn't gonna sit at home and mumble about it and think about it, because we had a chance and it's over with. Life goes on. You wanna win, especially when you're in a position like that.

Patrick Ewing: All I know is that we lost. That was it.

In 1994–95, the Knicks won 55 games and surrendered the division crown to Orlando. Mason won the NBA's Sixth Man of the Year award, but he clashed with Riley and earned a late-season suspension for the second straight year.

After defeating Cleveland in the first playoff round, the Knicks fell behind Indiana three games to one in the East semis. The Game 1 loss at the Garden featured another stunning Reggie Miller moment: eight points, including two three-point bombs, in the game's final 16 seconds. Dogged by a sore calf muscle that forced him to wear a hip-to-ankle sleeve, Ewing hit a short runner in the final seconds to win Game 5, then had 25 points to lead another back-to-the-wall Game 6 win at Indiana. But after scoring 29 points in Game 7, his last-gasp layup went off the back rim, and the Knicks lost the series.

A month later, in shocking fashion, they lost their coach as well.

Pat Riley: You lose the edge. And you lose the edge when you start losing big games, and you don't finish something. In the first year, it was a honeymoon and everything was great. There wasn't anything we could have done that was wrong. Even getting beat by the Chicago Bulls was acceptable, because that was growth, taking the world champs to a seventh game. We said the next year would be better, and it was. We won 60 games and ended up going to the Eastern Conference Finals and getting beaten by Chicago again. Then the third year we get to the NBA Finals and we can't close it down. So as you keep elevating and you keep getting turned back, you do lose an edge. And in the fourth year, while I still felt that we were a very good team, there were things. The injuries that we had and what went on between Mase and me, that always got in the way. But we still had a very good team, and, again, losing in the seventh game to Indiana was not an embarrassment. It could have happened the year before, you know. Patrick could have missed that shot. And this year, he did miss it and they moved on.

Jeff Van Gundy: We're in his [Riley's] room in Denver [in March 1995] talking about the game plan for that night. All of a sudden he gets a call from Dave [Checketts]. I asked if he wanted me to

leave, and he said no, so I'm sitting there. And you could tell that while it was respectful, there was definitely a disagreement about things. I don't even know what those things were. And we never talked about it. But I knew from sitting there that he wasn't happy with some things.

Dave Checketts: I had become president and CEO of the Garden [in March 1995]. He [Riley] had asked me, with me moving up, if that would mean he was going to be president of the Knicks. And he really wanted to be Ernie's boss, and Ernie had done nothing, in my mind, that deserved that. Even though Riles was so valuable to the franchise, I didn't think it was a title that he needed. He didn't want to be in the office every day. He didn't want to be holding staff meetings or figuring out PR strategy or looking at season-ticket numbers. That's not what he wanted. He just wanted a title that gave him some sort of power. I didn't get it at all, and I said to him, "Pat, if that's the only thing standing between you and signing this extension, of course we'll do that." And then that set Ernie off. Ernie was really upset.

Pat Riley: [When asked if he knew that the 1995 playoff finale would be his last game as Knicks coach]: No, never. My head wasn't there. Even though I was in a contract discussion with Dave and the Knicks, I was just very, very disappointed. Just really disappointed that the team had taken a step back from the possibility of winning a championship. No, not at that particular time. It wasn't until a couple of days afterward that things began to come to a head.

Dave Checketts: I knew that something had happened, because his interest had been elsewhere. I knew we were losing him during the '95 playoffs and that something had taken place. I wouldn't know what had taken place until much later, but I knew something had taken place.

Jeff Van Gundy: Then we lost when Patrick missed the layup. And things didn't move superquick after that, but I remember him [Riley] calling me up and saying, "You need to bring my things to my house." I didn't know why. He didn't tell me until I got there that the next day he would announce his resignation. I didn't know what that meant, and I didn't know what that meant for me. And then he left.

Bob Salmi: Riley, on numerous occasions, threatened to fire me because I play golf. "If I had known you play golf, Salmi, I never would have hired you," and comments like that. So this one day I'm sitting in the office and he says to me, "Salm, how do I get a set of golf clubs? Big Berthas?" I said, "Riles, don't bother. That's not funny." He says, "No, I'm serious." So I call a couple of guys, get the Big Bertha rep on the phone, and he hooks Riley up with a new set of clubs. A week later, he left for Miami. I should have known.

Dave Checketts: At that point, Pat was feeling that he may never get a team like the Lakers again, so he may never have a chance to win a championship again, and what he had to do more than anything else was get paid. We offered him an extension that, again, would have made him the highest-paid coach in basketball–we were talking about a three-year extension that would have paid him about 10 million bucks. He was gonna get a new five-year deal with Miami–which, again, I wouldn't know until later–for 40 million dollars. So it wasn't even comparable. And it was really despicable what [Heat owner] Micky Arison did, to negotiate with a coach under contract and to ask Pat for a proposal for what he would accept, and then for Pat to draft it . . . which he handed to Arison three days after the Indiana series.

So that's why we went after the tampering charge and tried to get a price out of it, because we knew he was going; I knew he had an offer. Micky thought he was fooling everybody, and I resented it. So I went very hard after it. I was screaming at lawyers for months, until we got in front of the commissioner and were awarded our picks and a million bucks. Which was a small reward, looking back, but I wanted to make Arison pay for doing something to hurt the Knicks, and that was giving Pat an alternative for which Pat was willing to break his contract.

Pat Riley: Any way that I would have done it, I think, would have been looked on as bad, as a negative. Whether I faxed it, whether I had a press conference, everybody would have known the reason why. So, to me, it had just come to the point where, hey, you know, I'm not going to make a three-ring circus out of this thing. And I did not. It became a three-ring circus via the media, but I'm not gonna be involved in it. And I didn't make a statement about it until after I was given the right to negotiate with the Miami Heat. It went right down to the moment of truth where I finally said, OK, this is the way it's gonna be. Then I just faxed it in and I resigned. That was it.

I felt that it was short-lived. I could have seen myself ending my career in New York, even though I don't know if any coach could ever last that long there. I had great respect for Red Holzman and absolutely admired the job he did in New York, and the fact that he's the only coach up there in the rafters. I used to envision my name next to that one day. But it just didn't work out. It was one of the best four-year runs in my coaching career. Just tremendous excitement with the fans, the city, the players. It was electrifying for me in a lot of ways.

Jeff Van Gundy: There's the public perception of him, and then there's the reality. And the reality was that he was so easy to work for, because he valued hard work and he valued ideas. He never blamed, and he never got upset. I think he got upset with me maybe twice. He had an aura about him, certainly. But he was unbelievable to work for.

Pat Riley: I just hope that whatever is thought of me and my four years there, it's that I came there to change things, and I did. We turned things around, and the Knicks became respected again in the NBA. They became what they should be. And I'll always remember that, and I'll always feel very proud of what I did for the four years. I hated the ending, but sometimes that's what happens, and you move on. But it was really a compelling time for me and my family.

It didn't take Jeff Van Gundy long to get the Knicks pointed in the right direction.

THE LINEUP: Jeff Van Gundy; Don Chaney; Herb Williams; Charles Oakley; Patrick Ewing; Marv Albert; Ernie Grunfeld; Derek Harper; Allan Houston; Kurt Thomas; John Starks; Charlie Ward; Dr. Norman Scott; Mike Saunders; Pat Riley; Phil Jackson; Marcus Camby; Dave Checketts; Latrell Sprewell; Tom Thibodeau.

Following Riley's departure, the Knicks were searching for something different. They thought they found what they were looking for when on July 6, 1995, they hired three-time NBA Coach of the Year Don Nelson as head coach.

Jeff Van Gundy: The first time Nellie came in he said to me, "I don't think I've ever seen you before." And if you don't know Don, you say, "That's a peculiar thing to say to someone." But if you know him, you say, well, he's right.

Don Chaney: Nellie was looking for another assistant, and he called my house. He got in touch with my wife, and she basically served as my agent because she said, "Oh, he wants the job." Because Nellie is saying that he hasn't offered me the job because he didn't think I'd want it; he thought I'd hold out for another head coaching job. But Jackie said, "Oh, no. He wants the job. He's driving me crazy around here." And I was. I drove her nuts because I was bored.

Outgoing, gregarious, and freewheeling, Nelson's style and philosophy represented a big break from Riley's. Instead of the grind-it-out, half-court–oriented game the Knicks had played under Riley, Nelson installed an up-tempo offensive attack that relied less on Ewing and more on Starks and Mason, the latter of whom would be moved into the starting lineup after being named NBA Sixth Man of the Year in 1995.

After four years of having their decidedly patterned offense serve as a by-product of a tenacious defense, it appeared as if the Knicks were ready to loosen things up a little. But no matter what the new coach did, the old coach's imprint couldn't be erased.

Don Chaney: You start to get programmed to doing things a certain way. It's like with the Celtics, if somebody were to come in and say that we're playing a half-court game and not a running game. It's a very difficult adjustment.

Herb Williams: Nellie would come in and we'd have practice, run through plays, and in an hour and a half we'd be out of practice. Normally, we'd be there for two and a half or three hours. It wasn't like a Riley practice, but that was the way Nellie was used to coaching. He was used to coaching up-tempo teams that scored a lot of points, and that's what he was trying to get across to us: that if we scored and kept our defense the same, we'd be a much better team.

Don Chaney: Nellie has a very bright basketball mind. He's very innovative. If something comes up, he'll try something nobody else has tried. These players here were so programmed into Pat Riley's way of doing things, so that even if Nellie came up with something that was just pure genius, they didn't buy into it. It was hard for them to buy into it. And it was a struggle. Nellie had to pull teeth every day to get these guys to change, and it was very difficult. I felt that he was climbing uphill all the way, in the struggle to get these guys to think a different way. And when he was fired, he still had a winning record. That says a lot about him.

Jeff Van Gundy: Nellie was brilliant before he got here, was brilliant during, and still is. He sees the game differently. What went wrong with Nellie was that Charles Oakley got hurt and missed 19 games. And in that span we were just terrible. If Oak isn't hurt, it's different. And if we're gonna give the players all the credit when we win, which we should, they need to take some of the responsibility for losing. Before Oakley got hurt, we were 30–16.

Don Chaney: The toughest thing of all was that the Knicks were programmed to Pat Riley's system, and it was very, very difficult for them to be deprogrammed. And it was a problem.

The Knicks lost 8 out of 11 games after Oakley was sidelined with a fractured thumb on February 16. Included in that span were an 0–4 Western trip and a horrendous 17-point loss to the last-place Clippers at the Garden.

Still nine games over .500 at 34–25, the Knicks trailed first-place Orlando by 10½ games on the morning of March 8, 1996. With a game against the 76ers just hours away, their youngest assistant coach received an unexpected early-morning visitor to his Philadelphia hotel room.

Jeff Van Gundy: I'm in my room watching films of Chicago, because we had them next after Philly. As an assistant, I was always working a game ahead. And Ernie came in, and he said what he said. And I was sort of stunned. Then I went up to see Nellie, and he was unbelievable. He said, "Oh, you'll do great" and all that stuff. He was happier for me than I was.

I called my father. I tried to gather myself, and I said, "Hey, Dad. Coach Nelson got fired." And my dad was thinking about my college coach, who had left Nazareth to go to Johns Hopkins. So he said, "Bill Nelson got fired?" That was his first reaction. I said, "No, I'm gonna be the coach for the rest of the year." I don't think he realized what I was saying.

Don Chaney: When Nellie got fired and Jeff was named, it wasn't a surprise to me at all. A lot of people came up to me later on and asked me why I wasn't in the hunt for the head coaching job. But given the circumstances, I think it was the appropriate move because Jeff had been there as an assistant and had gone through it. He was the man for the job at that time.

Jeff Van Gundy: So it was just shootaround, then the game. And we lose to an awful Sixers team and look awful doing it. And I just remember the bus ride from Philly to New York. There was a Philly cheesesteak on the seat next to me. I couldn't even think of eating it, I was so nauseated. The next day at practice, after not sleeping, the guys were unbelievable. You never say, going into the game, that you're gonna beat the Bulls. But I remember feeling better that we were gonna be ready.

Sitting in that chair in the office, 30 minutes before the Chicago game, I called my parents. I just got so emotional when I was talking to them. Because I'm sitting in Red Holzman's seat, Pat Riley's seat. That's when I started having pangs of guilt: Why is it me here? And for my dad to be able to watch it on TV . . .

Van Gundy, whose father Bill and brother Stan were both longtime college coaches, earned his first victory as Knicks head coach on March 10, a 32-point rout of a Chicago team that would lose only 10 games all season.
From that moment on, it was Jeff's team, Jeff's time.

Jeff Van Gundy: With players, the best players just keep moving up. But it's not that way with coaches. Some of the best coaches I know are high school and small-college coaches that, for whatever reason, didn't get that opportunity. But it doesn't have anything to do with their aptitude as a coach.

Don Nelson succeeded Riley
at the helm, briefly, in 1995.

So I always felt somewhat guilty in that he [my father] sort of paved the way for me and my brother, helped us know people and got us started. We'd been going to practices since we were young. He's always made a point to teaching us the profession: this is how you scout, this is how you do this or that. I always thought about that.

Don Chaney: There were a lot of times when Jeff and I would meet in his office, especially when things weren't going well. Because I had been there before. Everything Jeff was going through as a head coach was a new experience for him that first year. I think it helped him just to sit with me and talk things out. He trusted my opinion, and I think it helped him a great deal. What I had to sell, he believed in, because I had been there.

Charles Oakley: Everybody said he was Riley's protégé, and I think Jeff had that tenacity. He challenged guys by working hard. You wouldn't think he was tough-nosed, being that small. But he was. He didn't take no stuff. He let you know.

Herb Williams: It was totally different. You had gone from Pat Riley, who was a demanding coach, who practiced hard, was very detail-oriented, and was known for his defense. Then you go to Don Nelson, who's known for his offense. The thing Nellie was trying to do was say, look, our defense doesn't need any work. The thing we need to do is score more points. That's what he was trying to relate to the team. For whatever reason, it didn't get across. So they end up firing Nellie, and they bring Jeff in, and he's basically doing the same things Pat Riley did, with a few minor changes. Pat Riley had put his stamp on that team. Jeff understood the things that we had done to be successful, so he would have been crazy to do anything else. He stuck with that pattern.

Patrick Ewing: They were two different people. We ran a lot of the same stuff and a lot of things were the same. But Jeff is Jeff and Riles is Riles.

Don Chaney: Jeff's first year was really interesting because he was a definite disciple of Pat Riley, even when he was under Nellie. Jeff believed in everything Pat Riley did, and when he took over, he did things just like Pat, to a T. Blitz the

pick-and-roll, double the low post, things like that. So our team became sort of a clone of Miami's team. Everything they did, we did. Every play they called was one of our plays. So the systems were almost identical. It was very easy to play Miami because all the calls were the same, all the concepts were the same.

Charlie Ward: He was instrumental in me growing as a basketball player because he took time with me each morning before practice in my rookie year, helping me develop my skills and getting me to a point where I felt comfortable with playing. I was a competitor by nature, and he really built my skills to a level, each and every morning, working on my game to where I could become consistent. I was always going to play hard, but shooting and playing defense were things I needed work on consistently, and just enjoying basketball the way it's supposed to be enjoyed. He really gave me the encouragement to keep going, keep working at it. Then when he got his opportunity to be the head coach, he understood and knew what I was capable of doing because he had worked with me. So that was a blessing.

Marv Albert: It was special. You had Riley, of course. And Jeff, who had that edgy type of way that kept it going. They had a lot of good personalities: Starks, Oakley, Mason. It was a very tough, New York–style basketball team.

Jeff Van Gundy: Many times when you're an assistant and then become the head coach, it's hard because your relationship [with the players] has to change. But I always considered it a benefit because I knew [that] those three guys [Ewing, Oakley, and Starks] believed in me more than they would have had I just come from the outside. I didn't have to change too much with them because I had always been up front with them. I would also throw in Harper and Mase, because they believed in what I believed in. It wasn't a hard sell.

After taking over, Van Gundy won 13 of 23 games, then guided the Knicks to a first-round sweep of Cleveland. But in the second round, Jordan and the Bulls needed just five games to knock New York out of the 1996 playoffs.

Soon after, Van Gundy's contract as head coach was extended. Now, with salary cap room to work with and a bevy of talented free agents available, Grunfeld went to work on a massive roster overhaul.

Jeff Van Gundy: After Game 5 in Chicago, when we lost the series, Dave [Checketts] said that he thought everything was going to work out [with me]. Then one morning I was supposed to have a meeting with Ernie about my situation. The back page of the *Post* is saying that I'm getting a two-year contract, and they had rejected a third year. And I go in, and that's exactly what it was. So I asked Ernie, "What happened to the third year?" That's when I went to McDonald's afterward to get a burger, and went home.

Ernie Grunfeld: What I tried to do was remain very competitive for a championship, and at the same time get younger and rebuild. We traded away some guys who were on the last year of their deals, and we wanted to get cap room. And we did; we had about $10 million in cap room that summer.

Derek Harper: I was disappointed, but I've always understood the business. I've always tried to understand the business part of what I did. And that [getting waived] helped me to understand it even more. It wasn't personal. It was a business decision more than anything. I was angry because when I initially came to New York, I was told by management that if I did my job, I would be taken care of. That's sort of what I expected. And I don't mean this in a vicious way to Ernie or Dave or anybody like that. I have total respect for both those guys. I felt like I had done my job: I did what I was brought there to do. As a result, I expected to be taken care of. But, again, it was a business decision that management made. And I live with that decision. I've talked to Ernie since, and I have no ill feelings. I respect his decision, just a little bit disappointed.

Charlie Ward: Harp showed me a lot about the game. I was young at the time, and he taught me a lot of the tricks of the game: the mentality you should play with, how to be a professional, and how to take care of your body. At that time, I really

wasn't paying attention, but now that I've gotten older I see what he was doing and why he was able to play at such a high level every night: because he took care of his body.

Ernie Grunfeld: When we focused on who we wanted to go after, it was always with the mind-set of Patrick being the focal point of the team and building around him. We already had Starks and Oakley, so those guys were really the three building blocks. But we also wanted to get more size and shooting ability, and Allan Houston fit that bill real well. Then we were able to get another point guard in Chris Childs. And I always loved the way Larry Johnson played. He was such a team player. For him, statistics didn't show the whole story. He could play power forward or small forward; he was a great low-post player, very unselfish.

Allan Houston: At that time, I really wanted to stay in Detroit. I thought we had a nice foundation there with me and Grant [Hill] and Lindsey [Hunter]. I felt like I had started to establish myself there. I looked at Miami seriously. I went down there and sat with Riley; they offered something that was pretty attractive. Then when I met with Detroit, I was surprised because it was sort of a bland offer. It was just something that was great for me, personally, but it wasn't what Miami had offered. I thought that was kind of surprising.

And then, I never really expected New York to be in the picture until the last two weeks. Remember, Reggie Miller and Steve Smith were also free agents then. My agent said that the Knicks had shown a lot of interest, so I came to New York. And it was just amazing, the things they did for me. From Checketts and Ernie driving around with me in a limo, showing me Diana Ross' house, Luther Vandross' house, to the video, to the nice place we stayed. My dad has recruited players in college, so I wasn't blown away by the things they were doing. What meant a lot to me was for them to take the time to say, this is what you mean to us and how we want you to be part of our future. Words mean a lot, but actions mean more to me. Obviously, what they were saying was great. But to put a lot of time and effort into that, it said something.

Ewing and Starks
shouldered much of
the load throughout
the nineties.

They could say that I was the first choice, over Reggie Miller and Steve Smith. They could say that, but to me, the things that they did and the effort they put into the whole thing said a lot more. It was great that I had my father, who had been on the other end of recruiting players, to put it in perspective. And then to have Patrick fly out on the plane. To me, those things said something. Whereas in Detroit, the place where they were saying that they wanted me to be the cornerstone of their foundation, I hadn't even talked to the owner or the president. They hadn't said one word to me. So there was a big contrast.

Ernie Grunfeld: So that summer, we rebuilt on the fly. We got a lot younger, we got more talented, and we didn't miss a beat as far as the playoffs were concerned.

Over the frantic summer of 1996, Grunfeld acquired Houston, a sharp-shooting 25-year-old who had averaged just under 20 points per game with Detroit; two-time All-Star forward Larry Johnson; point guard Chris Childs, who had just authored a standout season with New Jersey; and veteran power forward Buck Williams, now in the twilight of a long and distinguished career. Gone were Mason (traded to Charlotte for Johnson), Harper (waived), and Hubert Davis (traded to Toronto). Starks lost his starting job to Houston, then emerged as the NBA's Sixth Man of the Year.

Jeff Van Gundy: We had so many changes: Houston coming in; Starks going to the bench; Buck Williams, LJ, and Childs coming in. Most of our losses were right off the bat. We started off bad, like 9–6, after losing to Miami at home. But from that point on, we were the best team in basketball. I always thought we had a chance that year to win a championship. You always say that publicly, but that year we were really good. Good offensively, good defensively. We had great bench strength. Everyone fit into their roles well.

Don Chaney: Jeff started to evolve in the second year, when he started to move away from Pat a little bit and develop his own identity. We started creating and doing different things. And I think Jeff gradually, each year from then on, pulled away from the identity of Miami and Pat Riley and started developing his own identity.

Allan Houston: I had a lot of high expectations. The previous year in Detroit, I had my first 19-point season in a system where I pretty much could do whatever I wanted. Now I came into a situation where you had established one of the greatest centers of all time, you had John Starks, who I've always respected, and it's New York. The environment is much more intense and the expectations are so much more. Not just in games, but every day, in work ethic, in practice, and in attitude. My whole mentality was a pretty drastic change and adjustment for me. I never lost faith in my ability, but how was I going to apply that? That was the big adjustment.

Don Chaney: He [Larry Johnson] was a leader on and off the court. He was a quiet leader in a sense, but when it was time to speak up, he spoke up and everybody listened. It was like E. F. Hutton. He didn't have a lot of talk all the time, but you trusted him and what he had to say. He carried himself in a very professional way, and guys respected that. Always the first one on the floor shooting. Always. And you trusted LJ in a game because he always made the right decision.

Kurt Thomas: A leader. A hard worker. A guy who's always there, always the first one in the gym, always the last one out. If he wasn't in the weight room, he was on the court. If he wasn't on the court, he was in the weight room. He watched film, he studied the game, he knew his job, and he knew everyone else's job. And that's what he inspired in me: not to just know what I was supposed to be doing on the floor, but to know what others were supposed to do. He really helped me become a better player because of his work ethic. I always looked up to him because he was older than me and because he was from Dallas. Having the opportunity to play with him, I just saw what a great player he was.

Don Chaney: What I loved about him more than anything was that when a ball went up, he might not get the rebound, but his guy's not gonna get it, either. He was our best blockout guy; he was our best rotating guy, defensively, once Oak left.

Allan Houston: All the adjustments that Larry, Chris, Patrick, John, and I had to make were all made at that point. Everybody knew where they fit in.

John Starks: I dealt with it easily. For me, it wasn't about ego. Some guys have a big ego. They can't deal with things like coming off the bench. I don't have a big ego. I looked at it as, this is a way for us to win. Bringing in Allan Houston, I knew he was the type of player who could help us win. That's what it's all about, and I understood that. I already had the accolades. I had been to the NBA Finals. I had already been an All-Star and All-Defensive. So it wasn't about me, it was about the team and trying to win a championship.

Allan Houston: At the end of that [1996–97] regular season, I said that no matter what happened, it's over with. I remember sitting down with my wife and watching old tapes of me in college and with Detroit and saying, "Look, it's a new season. Start over." And I remember being so focused those first [1997] playoffs that it was like starting the season all over again, and I had something to prove.

Ernie Grunfeld: We were really peaking at the right time. In fact, in the last game of the regular season, we went to Chicago and beat them by two in a great game. So we were going into the playoffs on a high note. Played Charlotte in the first round and beat them three straight. Allan's game was coming around; LJ was playing great. We were starting to roll. And we had Miami down. So I really thought that was our best shot. Then came the fight and all the suspensions. But that was an outstanding team.

In their first full season under Van Gundy, the Knicks won 57 games, then steamrolled past Charlotte in the first playoff round.

That meant a second-round meeting with Pat Riley's Miami Heat. In just two seasons, Riley had taken the Heat from the depths of the NBA to an Atlantic Division Championship.

And they would be the Knicks' partner in what became the most heated and intense rivalry in sports, a spellbinding passion play spread out over four consecutive springtimes.

Here, in their first meeting, the Knicks dominated, winning three of the series' first four games. In Game 5 in Miami, the Heat pulled away in the fourth quarter and were on their way to a 15-point win. But the Knicks knew that two days later they would be back home for Game 6, and the Garden would be primed and ready for a series clincher. But first Game 5 had to be completed, with Miami comfortably ahead. With just under two minutes left, Oakley picked up two quick technicals and was ejected. Seconds later, Charlie Ward and Miami's P. J. Brown lined up alongside the foul lane, and in a matter of moments, everything changed between these two teams.

Charlie Ward: Actually, it was a great moment because it gave me an opportunity to look at who I really was and to grow from it. Some people might say it was bad, but I saw good out of it. It was a situation where it just happened, and it was more of a reaction than anything else.

Allan Houston: That was the boiling point of that rivalry. It happened so fast. That year we felt that it was going to be our year. We really did feel that way. It was so dramatic a change in the series, almost like you had a balloon and somebody threw a dart at it, and it just popped. After that we still had to go out and fight and compete. And we still believed we could win, but that aura we felt about ourselves wasn't the same after the fight.

Jeff Van Gundy: People talk about Patrick Ewing's "lack of discipline" leaving the bench. But if you see how they rule it now, they're using common sense. Like with the big Lakers-Kings brawl [in preseason 2002]. They used common sense there. They used no common sense with us; they just said a rule's a rule. But now—and I give the NBA a lot of credit for this—they say, well, a rule isn't a rule just to be a rule. It's gotta make sense and it's gotta fit the crime.

The Ward-Brown brawl resulted in one-game suspensions for Ward, Ewing, Houston, Johnson and Starks—so many suspensions, in fact, that the NBA had to spread them out alphabetically over two games. Brown was suspended for two games.

Ernie Grunfeld and Jeff Van Gundy in 1997, happier times for both. Except for Eddie Donovan, no general manager in Knicks history was as successful as Grunfeld. Van Gundy would become the third-winningest coach in franchise annals, behind only Holzman and Lapchick.

For the Knicks, Ewing's suspension was the most galling of all, since replays showed he did not take more than three steps away from the bench area. The Knicks also took issue with the fact that Brown was the only Miami player ruled against, especially since a high-angle replay showed several Heat players leaving the bench area before being pushed back (although the brawl occurred in front of the Knicks' bench).

Jeff Van Gundy: Now, P. J. Brown got two games and Charlie Ward got one. So they're saying P. J. Brown was most at fault. We [all] should have stayed on the bench, but Patrick *did* stay on the bench. They just decided that they were gonna make him an example. And we could have lost all those other guys, but with Patrick at home in Game 6, we would have won by 10 points. And it still took Alonzo Mourning making a three to put a dagger in us.

Suiting up the minimum nine players–in a game dubbed "Nine Men, One Mission"–the Ewing-less Knicks led for the better part of three quarters in Game 6. Then Miami silenced the Garden crowd with a 15–5 fourth quarter run, as Alonzo Mourning capped a 28-point night with a game-clinching three-point bomb. Miami won by five. Two days later, Ewing returned to score 37 points in Game 7, but without Starks and Johnson the Knicks did not have enough. Tim Hardaway scored 38 points, and Miami won the game and the series, 101–90.

Jeff Van Gundy: We waited to practice until 6:00 the next night [before Game 6] because we had to find out who was gonna play. And when we found out, we practiced well. We played a great game, and we just ran out of steam. I probably should have tried to rest guys a little more, spot some guys. So we started great and they caught us. Game 7, Patrick played unbelievable. We just turned it over too much.

Charlie Ward: It was very uplifting and discouraging at the same time, because you had to sit out a game for what I considered a good, clean play–nothing to hurt anyone. But it turned out to be good in the sense that I learned from that and how to respond in situations like that. And also to grow

deeper in my relationship with the Lord and my faith. The more I grow over the years the more I see that was a blessing to my whole life. Now, I'm a better person. I'm a stronger person mentally from that whole situation. I understand that getting involved in scuffles and those type of things aren't really worth it, financially or any other way.

For a decade, the Knicks' best player was also their most durable. Over a ten-year span, from 1987–88 through 1996–97, Patrick Ewing never missed more than six games due to injury in any one season. But all of that changed on a cold Saturday night in Milwaukee, December 20, 1997.

Leaping for an errant pass from Ward, Ewing was pushed by Milwaukee's Andrew Lang and fell backward. When he crashed to the floor, most thought the Knicks' season had crashed with him.

Dr. Norman Scott: It's an injury that maybe you'd see in football, because they're all such big bodies and they fall in such crazy ways. Certainly you never see it in basketball. It's a very strange injury where there are a lot of bones around the wrist, and one of them almost popped through the skin. They're like pearls, two rows of pearls, and one of them just popped right through.

Mike Saunders: I knew it was a serious injury. I saw how awkwardly he fell and knew it wasn't going to be good.

Patrick Ewing: They told me that my career might be over. That's what the doctors said. I was very determined to come back. I worked extremely hard to try and get back. And nobody thought I could come back. Just because they said it wasn't gonna happen, didn't mean it wasn't gonna happen.

Mike Saunders: Patrick didn't know how serious it was at the time and insisted on shooting his free throws left-handed, so he wouldn't have to be taken out of the game. But as it turned out, there was no way he was gonna play. Fortunately we got him to the hospital right from the plane when we landed, with no circulation [damage], and the nerve, fortunately, was not compromised.

Dr. Norman Scott: He knew we had to do this right away. If he had been in New York, I'm not sure we could have gotten him into the operating room that quickly. It was amazing that here was a guy flying in from Milwaukee . . . but by the time we got everyone assembled and got the staff in, I'm not sure it would have been done much quicker. In the time he was in the air, we were able to do everything back here [to get ready for surgery].

Basically, Patrick and I spoke on the phone from Milwaukee two or three times; once from the locker room, once from the bus. He was very scared. We just tried to be upbeat. But it's a difficult situation where everyone knows the seriousness of it, but what good does it do to tell him he might not play again? You just try to be positive. We all understood how serious it was, but we all tried to stay positive. And then everything went great in surgery.

Ewing's devastating injury—a right wrist dislocation and torn ligaments—forced him to the sidelines for the remainder of the regular season. With the Knicks' primary weapon lost, Houston responded by increasing his scoring average nearly four points from the year before, to 18.4.

The injury also placed an added spotlight on Ewing's backup, Herb Williams. In seven years in New York—which included two trades away from the Knicks, only to return days later—the veteran Williams provided a steadying influence both on the court and in the locker room.

Allan Houston: Patrick being hurt played a bigger role than me being comfortable. I think if Patrick had played, I don't think I would have averaged 18, just because I probably wouldn't have had in my mind that I had to take over in certain situations. When Patrick was hurt, it was like I had to do that. It kind of forced me to dig deep and do what I've always done. So I think a lot more had to do with Patrick being hurt than with me.

Herb Williams: When I came here, I came here to play. My intention wasn't to be the mouthpiece of the locker room; it just evolved that way. Certain things I saw happening, I knew how to defuse them or to let other guys deal with the situation. I was never the kind of teammate who was worried about the guy in front of me or the guy in back of me. I felt we would go out, we would com-

pete in practice, and whoever started, that's who started. We had one common goal–at least I did–and that was to win games. I really wasn't worried about how many points I was gonna score or anything like that. I was worried about winning basketball games.

When I didn't play, I'd try to help them out from things I would see on the court. Or you'd hear guys talking about certain things in the locker room, and instead of letting it go, I'd tell guys, "Hey, this guy feels this way about you, or that guy feels that way about you. You need to talk it out." And a lot of times, it's really nothing. So when the guys sit down to actually talk about it, you find out it's really nothing and you defuse it rather than letting it carry over.

Jeff Van Gundy: The nine lives of Herb Williams! I tell you, a cat has nothing on Herb.

Herb Williams: [On his 1996 trade to Toronto] I'm lying in bed and the phone rings, and my wife picked it up. She said, "Ernie," and when she said, "Ernie," I knew right away I was traded. It was no big deal. So I rolled back over, and he [Ernie] talked to her for about 5 or 10 minutes.

Going 28–28 following Ewing's injury, the Knicks drew Miami in the first playoff round. Following a brawl-marred Game 4 win, which resulted in the suspensions of Mourning and Johnson, the Knicks went into Miami and held off a furious Heat rally to win the game, 98–81, and the series. Miraculously, Ewing returned to action as the Knicks faced Indiana in the East semis, but Reggie Miller averaged 24.6 points, including 38 in the pivotal Game 4, as the Pacers triumphed in five games.

Unquestionably, the series win over Miami—especially in light of what had happened the previous year—was the season's high point. But the Knicks-Heat saga had only just begun. Over four years, it would involve not only one team and city against another but also teacher (Riley) versus student (Van Gundy) and brother versus brother, as Van Gundy's brother Stan had joined the Heat as Riley's assistant.

Jeff Van Gundy: After the fight the next year [in 1998], we bounced back much better than they did. We had the hangover from Game 6 to Game 7 the year before, and they had the hangover from

Game 4 to Game 5 the following year. And we did a really good job coming back. We had two days off between games and that helped.

They started Mark Strickland in the second half [of Game 5], gave them great energy. We're rolling, but Charlie [Ward] gets his fourth foul in the third quarter. Then Hardaway started doing a Hardaway, and we're struggling. Charlie goes back in, and it was a high pick-and-roll where the ball got swung back to Charlie. Charlie jab-stepped, jumper, good.

Charlie Ward: I actually had T-shirts made up for my camp, with [a picture of] that shot on them. What you consider a big three, there's another big three, Scripturally, that I used for my camp. It was very uplifting to a lot of the kids.

Jeff Van Gundy: Then we got Allan a jumper on a post-up to go up seven. Then we got a steal, and Oak got a fast-break layup from Charlie, flagrant foul. He makes the free throw, we take it out, and Starks gets a three. So it goes from 7 to 13 in one possession, and the game's over. And I thought we just handled ourselves so much better with so much less talent. Buck Williams gets 14 rebounds. They just patched it all together.

Allan Houston: I probably won't go through anything like that or experience that kind of intensity again, even if we win a championship. I don't think it'll be as intense as that rivalry.

Jeff Van Gundy: You can't have drama unless you're meeting a team in the playoffs. And to meet a team in the playoffs four straight years, and have it go to a deciding game all four years, is just unheard of. I don't think it'll ever happen again. You know them; they know you. There's a lot of subplots involved. And the tension for the two weeks it lasted, and how it kept growing. And then having it come down to basically one big shot in each game deciding your whole season and your whole fate . . . Nothing like that.

The first year, my brother and I just tried to act like it was the regular season. But after the first fight [Brown-Ward], he called me before Game 6 and we got into it and wound up slamming the phone down on each other. He was blaming Charlie; I was blaming

P.J. What we learned from that was that the playoffs are no time to try to be rational. The regular season, we'd always see each other and talk. The playoffs, no.

Pat Riley: That was absolutely a match made in NBA heaven. And I don't think there's any doubt that, other than Michael Jordan, that drove the NBA. The Knicks-Heat helped drive the NBA during those four years because it was such a compelling series.

Jeff Van Gundy: In the first year, the teams really didn't know each other. Then it became heated, and hatred, and all that. But then it evolved, by the third year, into respect. Both ways, just mutual respect. Not that there wasn't some dislike, but we never came close to a fight after that, not even in the regular season.

Pat Riley: There were bizarre things that happened the first two years, with the fights and suspensions. But the last two years of the series were born out of absolute respect for one another. These two teams were after each other, and the best basketball was really played during those last two years.

By now, Van Gundy had put his stamp on the personality and character of the Knicks. At the same time, Van Gundy's personality and image were stamped as well–as the driven, baggy-eyed, sleep-deprived Everyman for whom every game was life and death. Whether real or imagined, that image was driven home with the surreal sight of Van Gundy holding onto Mourning's leg during his swing out with Johnson in Game 4 of the 1998 playoffs. It was perhaps the most lasting image of a coach who often found himself in situations that, well, just didn't happen to other coaches.

Jeff Van Gundy: People asked me, "What were you thinking?" And I said, "If I was thinking, I never would have been out there." And that's really true. You know, they talk about memory loss. I have no recollection of anything from the time I saw the swing until way after. I always kid Larry. I tell him that no one knows he hit me. He swung and hit me. That's why I was dazed coming down on Zo's leg and hanging on. I had no idea what was happening. And people said, well, they lost Zo and you lost LJ, so that's a good trade for you. But LJ averaged more

For better or worse, this is perhaps the most enduring image of the Van Gundy years: the coach clings to Alonzo Mourning's leg as Zo tangles with Charles Oakley (No. 34) and Larry Johnson (left) in Game 4 of the 1998 playoffs against Miami.

than Zo in that series [20.8 to 19.3]. Plus, we were still without Patrick with the broken wrist. People always forget that.

Anytime you do something and then you see it, you know instinctively that you'll never live it down. That'll always be one of people's first recollections of you. You have to live with that because you're responsible for your own actions.

The whole Jordan con man thing was in January of '97. These two radio guys in Chicago called me when I was an assistant, so now they called me as a head coach. This is about three weeks before the game. And I just said, you know, he's great, he cons everyone, he gets everyone thinking he cares about them and then he rips their heart out, and blah, blah, blah. Then it came out the day we played them. So he gets 51, and they beat us by one. And as he walked by me he shouted, "Shut up, you little fuck!"

Then we go to Indiana. We're off the next day, so I walk into that big mall that's across from the hotel to go to the food court. And it was one of the few times when all of the players were in one spot together. So I get my food and I'm about to go sit off by myself, and they all came over and started killing me, absolutely killing me, but in a joking manner. And, honestly, it was the best time I ever had, with the whole group of them, off the basketball court. Every one of them was there. It was great. Then we went out and beat Indiana.

Phil Jackson: We always got a kick out of Jeff because he was so energetic. He had run over in the fight with Jo Jo English and Derek Harper and had gotten two black eyes in the fight. So the next game, we on the coaching staff looked over and realized that Jeff had been caught in the melee; he's got these two black eyes. Of course, the record shows that Jeff was always in the fight. He's always close. It [the rivalry] was fun. He, obviously, had a lot of fun with it, too.

Jeff Van Gundy: I knew I had stunned Phil with the "Big Chief Triangle" because he came back with that weak "Gumby" about me, as if I hadn't heard that before. But I do regret getting into it with him, because I think it diminished the level of coaching that went on. And he's a great, great coach. In

retrospect, I made fun of his religion, which is something very dear to him, and I do regret that. So while it may have made good copy, I wish I would have just let it go.

My way was to try to make it humorous. People come up to me now and say, "Boy, you look a lot better now than when you were coaching." And I say, "No, I just looked like shit then."

Grunfeld had been promoted to Knicks team president when Checketts succeeded Bob Gutkowski as Garden president and CEO in late 1994. Now, as he looked at his team's roster during the summer of 1998, the most glaring numbers he saw were the ages of his Big Three. Ewing, 36 and coming off wrist surgery. Oakley, 34. Starks, 33. It was time, he reasoned. Time for the Knicks to get faster, sleeker, more athletic, and, above all, younger.

That is, if he could make any moves at all. With proposed modifications in the Basic Agreement between owners and players not agreed upon, the NBA owners voted to lock out the players on July 1, 1998, putting the upcoming season in jeopardy and halting any and all player transactions. Grunfeld had to move fast. Five days before the lockout hit, he traded the man whose work ethic, more than any other's, had personified the Knicks over the past 10 years.

Charles Oakley: I was shocked because I had just met with Ernie, right after the season, to talk about what happened during the season and what we needed to improve on, this and that. He said, "We got a lot of good input from you." Two weeks later, I was traded.

Marcus Camby: I never envisioned myself playing for the Knicks. Growing up, I was always a Sixers and Lakers fan. When I was in Toronto, I thought I was gonna be there for a while, considering the team that we had.

Ernie Grunfeld: We made a trade for a young, athletic center of the future in Marcus Camby, and traded away another player who had been with us a long time in Charles Oakley. But I just felt that I had to do what I felt was in the best interest of the organization for both the present and the future.

Don Chaney: We had to deal with the fact that we had traded Oak and brought Marcus in. We had tremendous loyalty to Oak. We knew what he meant to the team with his toughness and dedication. There was some sadness when the deal was made. And we had to change Marcus' mentality, from being a certain kind of player to replacing Oak. We were looking for that toughness. Now we had to condition Marcus to play like Oak, to bang and to rebound and be a great defender. That was a growth period for Marcus, and a lot of pressure.

Jeff Van Gundy: The Oakley thing was hard because we knew we were going into the lockout. I thought it was a hard move to make for the success of the team. In retrospect, it was the right move. It didn't happen the right way, but it was the right move. It was the right move for the future. And the one mistake I made with Marcus was that I judged him too early, and I think it did affect our relationship for a while.

Marcus Camby: When I got the call that I was going to New York, I was surprised. Of all the places in the league, I never thought I'd end up there. Ernie called me. I was in Connecticut at the time. They sent a car to pick me up. I came down and met with him and [player personnel VP] Ed Tapscott.

Charles Oakley: I didn't take it personally, but I thought I got lied to a couple of times by management in New York. When you get lied to, anything can happen. For myself, I tried to show them the respect they showed me. Once they lied to me, that made me disrespect them more. But I kept on with Toronto, had three good years. My life and career in the NBA have been great. A little work here and there but everything ironed out.

The season before, with Toronto, Marcus Camby had been the NBA's leader in blocks per game. He was tall (6'11"), lean, long-armed, and athletic . . . and nearly 10 years younger than Charles Oakley.

Speculation on how Camby would contribute was overshadowed when the lockout halted all league business for the next five months. Following a last-minute settlement on January 6, 1999, an abbreviated 50-game season would begin in early February.

Free to deal once again, Grunfeld set his sights on another player: a 28-year-old explosive swingman who could break down a defense or shoot from the outside on one end of the floor and defend like crazy on the other. In other words, exactly the type of player his team needed.

But this player came with a history unlike that of any athlete in America. Early in the previous season, Latrell Sprewell, an All-Star in three of his five full seasons with Golden State, had choked his coach, P. J. Carlesimo, during a practice session, making him the sports world's most notorious figure. He was released by the Warriors, reinstated by an arbitrator, then suspended for the rest of the season. What other team, what other city, would take a chance on The Player Who Choked His Coach?

Ernie Grunfeld: We were getting a little older, and I felt we had to get younger and more athletic. Obviously, it was well documented what happened with Latrell. But we knew he was an outstanding player. It's not very often where you can get a player of that magnitude.

Jeff Van Gundy: The Sprewell move was a no-brainer, because you were taking a very good player coming off a very traumatic thing. You knew he was going to be on his best behavior, and he was in the last year of his contract, so if it didn't work out, you weren't gonna be stuck with him. The difficult decision with Latrell was, what do you do with him at the end of the year? Then you have to make a huge commitment to him, or lose him.

Dave Checketts: The lockout was about to end, and Jeff was really interested in getting Sprewell. He'd convinced Ernie, and between Ernie and Ed Tapscott, they were really working me over. I just kept saying no. Finally, as it appeared the lockout may be over, we heard that Indiana and Miami were in the mix for Sprewell. This was where I decided to try to do two things: one, outfox them, and two, settle my own feelings that this was OK. So, early on a Sunday morning, I called [NBA deputy commissioner] Russ Granik and said, "I know we haven't totally lifted the ban on talking to players, but if we're gonna bring Sprewell to New York I want to go see him." Russ said he would call me right back. He called me back and said, "It has to remain very confidential and it can't be a long meeting, but have at it." And he said it with some trepidation, because I don't know if the league necessarily wanted to bring Latrell to New York, either.

Ernie Grunfeld: I knew where he lived. My wife's family is from Milwaukee, and she had a friend that lived up the street from Spree. We'd always go to visit her, and from that we knew exactly where he lived. So we went out there. We wanted to make sure we were all on the same page with Latrell. When we went there, we met a person who was very easy to talk to, very intelligent, seemed to have everything in order, and understood the situation. When we looked in his eyes, he said he'd welcome the opportunity. He said that people had perceived him in the wrong light. We all felt that this was the kind of guy who deserved a second chance, and we gave it to him. He's been a terrific player ever since.

Jeff Van Gundy: It was Ed, Ernie, Dave, and me. And they asked him a lot of questions about what had happened. Really, none of those things meant anything to me, because I knew how people can bullshit you. But I loved how he came to the door. I knew he was a real person when he came to the door in a tank top and red gym shorts. He didn't dress up to give off this image. He sat there and looked people in the eye. And I realized that this guy was real.

Latrell Sprewell: Obviously I knew Jeff and was familiar with him. I don't quite remember what I had on, though. Most of Jeff's questions were basketball-related. He didn't have any questions about any of the stuff that happened in the past.

Dave Checketts: We took a private plane to Milwaukee–Jeff, Ernie, Ed Tapscott, and I–early on a Sunday morning. A car met us and we went right to his house. Here he was, in a sweatsuit. We went into the back room of his house, and we sat for two and a half hours, and I let all those guys talk to him. Jeff spoke about how he would play him, about our philosophy. Ernie spoke to him about his contract and other players on the team and what kind of organization we were trying to build.

Latrell Sprewell: It was more than those four guys. There were a lot of different people, more like seven or eight guys. They brought the whole staff; I think that's the thing that stuck out, that they had so many people with so many questions.

Dave Checketts: And then it was my turn, and I felt that nobody had asked him the tough questions. So I said to him [that] I had read in the paper some time ago about the situation of your dogs attacking your four-year-old daughter and actually bit her ear off. And I said, "When the writers asked you about it, your response was, 'Well, shit happens.'" I said, "You know, I have six kids, and I don't understand how anyone on the planet Earth could respond like that." I was insulted and offended by it, and I couldn't understand how he could give a response so heartless. His eyes were getting bigger and bigger, and Jeff and Ernie were waving at me like, enough already! But I wanted to go right at him.

Then he said, "Well, let me get something." Then he went up to the mantel and he brought back a picture of this beautiful little girl, and he set it down in front of me. He said, "There she is. It's $160,000 in surgery later. She's pretty much back to normal. And the dog's been put to sleep. And no one felt worse about that than I did, but I didn't think it was anyone else's business. And, frankly, with what the press has done to me, I don't care about them. I don't want to respond to them; I don't want them in my personal life." And that gave us an opportunity to talk about the New York press and what his attitude would be with them. If he was going to pick a fight with them, he was going to have more trouble and it would be a disaster for us. It led us to a very open discussion of P.J., of the lawsuit, and really it turned into an extra hour, after which I felt very positive about a guy who had learned a lot of lessons and was ready to step it up a level and be a part of our organization.

Jeff Van Gundy: Every player says, "All I want is honesty," but they don't. They want you to tell them all the good things they do, without the bad things. But Latrell was truly one who wanted honesty. And if you didn't want honesty in return, don't

Dave Checketts was the man at the top for the Knicks—and eventually for the Garden—through the nineties.

ask him, because he was gonna give it to you. That's what I appreciated about him. Everybody gets second chances in life, but very few people do anything with second chances. And he made the most of a second chance. Now, it's almost as if you can't imagine him behaving like he did. He knows he was wrong. And he and P.J. moved on a lot quicker than other people.

Dave Checketts: We flew home that night. Now it's Sunday dinner and I'm at the table with all six of my kids and Deb. And I said, "Let me tell you why I wasn't at church with you this morning." I told them where I was, and Nathaniel, my 16-year-old, said, "Oh, you can't do this. Everyone knows you can't do this. You've had a much different position

on these kinds of guys. Aren't you the one who said you'd never have him on your team?" I said, "Well, yeah, I did say that. But now we really have to really think about it." I told him the story of visiting with him, and Ben, who was 12, said, "Hey, Dad. Doesn't everybody deserve a second chance?" And I said, "Yep, they do. They really do." I thought about Riles getting a second chance with us and me getting a second chance after the Jazz. Everybody needs a chance to come back, and New York is kind of the city of redemption. So I went in and called Ernie and said, "Let's go. Get him if you can."

John Starks: Dave called me and told me that they were looking to get Sprewell, and they were trying to work it out so that I wouldn't have to get traded. They were trying to put some more players in the deal that Golden State would go for. But Golden State was stuck on getting John Starks. I think it was basically a name player for another name player. Dave explained that while they really wanted Sprewell, they were doing as much as they could not to have to give me up. I even called [Warriors GM] Garry St. Jean and explained that I didn't want to be there. But they were hell-bent on getting me. They had to get a name in return for Sprewell, even though that player may not have wanted to be there, which I didn't want to.

The deal was made on January 21, 1999. Sprewell came to New York in exchange for Terry Cummings, Chris Mills, and the player whose spirit, passion, and unpredictability had fueled the Knicks of the nineties.

Sprewell's first appearance in a Knicks uniform came in a preseason contest against New Jersey at the Garden on January 27, with doubts still lingering over how he would be received.

By the end of that evening, all doubts were gone. When Sprewell checked into the game during the first half, he received a loud ovation. When he scored 17 points in the third quarter, the Garden went crazy. He finished with 27 points and walked off to a standing ovation and the world's greatest basketball city was at his feet.

Ernie Grunfeld: It was a controversial decision because we traded away a very popular player in John Starks, one who meant a lot to our organization. To get two players like that [Camby and Sprewell], with their athleticism and youth, was in the best interest of everybody at the time, although not everybody saw it that way.

Jeff Van Gundy: Starks and I had run-ins all the time. But what I loved about him was when it came game time, he played with heart and energy and passion. He played to win, and he truly cared about being a New York Knick. He loved being a Knick.

Don Chaney: When we got Spree, there was huge doubt because here's a guy coming in with a cloudy past, the guy who'd just choked his coach. We knew he had talent, but we didn't know how

he'd fit in with the team. When he was with Golden State, he played big minutes and shot the ball almost every time. We had guys who could score, and we wanted the ball moved and shared, so we didn't know if he would be able to fit in and make that adjustment. And the big question was, is this the right guy for this team?

Latrell Sprewell: You're just wondering at that point how you're gonna be received. I don't think anyone really knew, so it was kind of wait and see what happens.

Jeff Van Gundy: Starks was probably the most popular Knick when I was there. We trade him for Sprewell, and then we hear, "How can you trade for this guy?" and "John Starks is the heart of the Knicks," and all that. Then in that first exhibition game, he [Sprewell] went bam-bam-bam; he went nuts. From then on, all you heard was "Sprewell." And when Sprewell leaves, it'll be someone else. Because people forget that they cheer for the *team.* They have their favorites, but when they leave they're gonna cheer for the next guy, and the next guy.

Latrell Sprewell: It didn't start out that well. In the first half, I didn't shoot well and got off to a slow start. Once I got going in that third quarter, it just felt good to be on the floor again. It had been so long since I'd played in a game. It was a relief to just be out on the floor doing the things that I had always done in the past. That was a lot of fun because I didn't have to focus on all the talk about coming back and what had happened with P.J. It was just nice to be on the floor again. It was rockin'. For a preseason game, it was pretty exciting.

John Starks: The love is still there. It makes me feel wonderful that I did a service to that city by providing a lot of great moments and entertainment to a city that's so hard-nosed–that shows the respect they have–and that I gave the fans what they wanted to see, night in and night out. It made a huge impact on a lot of people's lives. That's the most gratifying thing, that I was able to do that.

Jeff Van Gundy: Even now, I take great pride in watching Spree and how he's handling a difficult situation. When we first started the rebuilding process, losing Larry and Patrick, he was always saying, "More size, we need more size." Now he says, "This is who we have." He's always upbeat. He's done a great job.

John Starks: The organization caught a lot of flack over it [giving Dennis Scott No. 3 in 1999], including Dennis Scott. I felt bad for him, because he got booed. I don't think he ever felt comfortable wearing that number in New York. I heard people were sending in letters and stuff like that, saying that I wasn't gone 24 hours and already they gave out my number. That was a tough time for Dennis to go through, knowing what that number meant to a lot of people in New York.

It would be a season like no other: 50 games compressed into a little more than three months. With two-thirds of the Big Three gone, the Knicks were looking at a year filled with nothing but uncertainty.

The stage was set for the Wild Ride of '99.

Jeff Van Gundy: We had two trades. Patrick [came in] very heavy [overweight] because of his lockout responsibilities, and that abbreviated training camp.

Don Chaney: You didn't know when you were going back to work. You didn't know if there was going to be a season. So it was really tough to focus on anything at that juncture.

Ernie Grunfeld: What people tend to forget about that year was that we not only got Marcus and Latrell, but we also signed Kurt Thomas, which was unnoticed at the time. But that was a very, very important part of the whole summer plan, because he gave us toughness and rebounding that we had lost with Oak. So with getting Marcus' athleticism and shot-blocking ability and Latrell's ability to defend and score, we added three very significant pieces.

Kurt Thomas: I started with coach Riley in my rookie year [in Miami], and that was basically my foundation, making me into the player I am today, as far as being in great shape, having to prepare for games both on and off the court, and having to be focused on the game. Pat is a great motivator, a great speaker. He really knows how to get you going, how

to motivate you to get you going. They [Riley and Van Gundy] are very similar, especially on the defensive end. Very similar. They do things a little different on different coverages, but basically they have the same methods. Offensively, that's where they're very different, in a sense. They still run some of the same plays, but they're definitely very different in their offensive schemes. But they both believe in hard-nosed defense and low scores.

I just came in with the same mind-set that I did my rookie year in Miami. I just felt I had to be hungry because I'd been away from the game [due to injury]. I was gonna do whatever I could to get into the starting lineup. Jeff liked what I brought to the game; he's always loved my defense. He remembered how I guarded Patrick in my rookie year with the Heat, how I was inspired playing against Patrick, covering him one-on-one. The reason for that was that Patrick was always one of my favorite players growing up. So when I had the opportunity to go against him, I was really pumped up.

Allan Houston: What really made that year good for me was that I was very prepared. The lockout year was almost a blessing for me because I had my knee scoped that year [July 1998], and it gave me an extra two months to get my knee right in rehab. So I worked out with a lot of NBA guys at Manhattan College and Basketball City. That just got us ready.

Latrell Sprewell: I was starting, and then I had the [heel] injury, and then I wasn't starting. At that point, I was trying to get back into the swing of things as far as understanding the system and defending. Things were totally new to me, so I was trying to learn and figure out every little detail about how we play here. So it was a lot of learning at that point.

Allan Houston: I looked at it [Sprewell arriving] both ways. I said that I would have to share a little bit and try to find a way for it not to take away from my game. And I looked at it like, this is gonna be great because we're gonna put a lot of pressure on a lot of people. I was playing in the backcourt a lot, and I was looking at it a lot like Clyde and Earl. Ernie and I talked about it; that's what we envisioned.

Otherwise, sometimes it's great, and sometimes you don't know what to do.

For most of the truncated season, the Knicks struggled. Following a 14–9 start, they lost 8 of their next 12 games and struggled to stay above the .500 mark.

Behind the scenes, there was a growing uneasiness. Rumors of a rift between Grunfeld and Van Gundy were gaining steam. Checketts, prodded by Cablevision president and CEO James Dolan and vice chairman Marc Lustgarten, was forced to step in.

Dave Checketts: Basically, Ernie and Jeff were sniping at each other, and I was getting increased pressure from Dolan and Lustgarten to do something about it. And I used to say to them [that] Phil Jackson and Jerry Krause never spoke to each other for years, and the Bulls won six titles. These guys don't have to be the best of friends. [I told them] Ernie doesn't think Jeff respects him appropriately, Jeff thinks Ernie does things to make him look bad. Jeff's a very stubborn guy. He thought Ernie was poking around behind the scenes trying to make it look like he wasn't playing Marcus to try and undermine Ernie. The whole thing was stupid. And after one bad newspaper day– Cablevision always said they never paid any attention to the papers–Dolan decided that he was going to get these two guys in his office, which I fought and ended up losing.

So we had Ernie and Jeff come in; Jeff was really angry because it was a game day. We went up and sat in a conference room, and Dolan took over the meeting and said, "I want to hear what's going on." Jeff was pretty diplomatic and so was Ernie, but it was clear there were some frustrations built up. So I took Jeff and Ernie into another room by themselves and said, "Look, either you guys resolve this or both of you are going, because I won't put up with this any longer."

Jeff Van Gundy: There's been much said about Ernie and me, and certainly I regret that the picture's been painted that it was either me or him. Because at that time, it was both of us. We disagreed on one thing in my whole time, and that was the procedure

on trading for Camby. Ernie and I got along great. He was a great GM then, as he is now. Certainly, if Ernie, who had accomplished all that he had accomplished, was let go, then if we hadn't won that [Miami] series, I probably would have been let go, too.

Dave Checketts: We dismiss the meeting. Jeff goes down to the locker room and Ernie goes back to his office. That night, I get a call from Lustgarten saying, "Jim wants one of them gone. He'll let you choose, but he wants one of them gone." I said, "Come on. We're just about to get guys back from injuries, starting to play better. Why?" Marc said, "He wants one of them gone."

About three nights later, as I'm agonizing over this, Marc called and said, "He wants *Ernie* gone." I said, "On what basis?" Marc said, "He's failed in his management role. He's failed to relate to and communicate with his coach." Now, Patrick had called me the same day and said, "Is there any truth to the rumor that Jeff is gonna get fired? You'd be nuts to do that. This guy is one of the best coaches we've ever had here. He's a terrific coach. Herb and I were talking about it, and I had to call you and tell you that we can't lose him." So now Dolan had ordered me to get rid of Ernie, and the players were concerned enough about a change in coaches to have the captain call me, so I knew what I had to do. It was just a matter of how I was going to do it.

Since he was named vice president of player personnel in 1991, Grunfeld's teams had averaged 53 wins per season. Promoted to general manager in 1993, he remade the Knicks twice over: acquiring Houston, Johnson, and Childs in 1996 and Sprewell, Camby, and Thomas in 1998–99. Ultimately, the clubs Grunfeld built would make four appearances in the Eastern Conference Finals and win two Conference Championships. No other general manager in Knicks history–save for Eddie Donovan–had been as successful.

But on the night of April 20, 1999, Grunfeld's 17-year Knicks odyssey–as player, broadcaster, coach, and executive–would come to an end over dinner at Gregory's Restaurant in suburban White Plains. Four years later, Grunfeld politely declined to be interviewed on the subject.

Dave Checketts: It so happened that I had this dinner set with Ernie in White Plains. I forget what we were gonna talk about; we were supposed to meet on some things. I said to myself that this guy is one of my best friends in life. I'm not gonna drag him into my office and say, "This is your last day. Pack up your stuff and get out," which is how so many corporations fire people. I said that I was going to do this the right way. So I took two hours over dinner and explained what happened and what Dolan was saying. Ernie was emotional and upset; I mean, the Knicks were the only team he ever wanted to be with. I've taken so much heat for, quote, doing it over dinner, or doing him in over dessert, so to speak. But that was my way of trying to be respectful and not do it in the cold, corporate way of "Go pack your stuff and get out of here in 40 minutes." That's just disgusting. That's how corporate America and corporate New York act. I wasn't going to do that to Ernie. And instead of anybody understanding that, all I got was a lot of heat for doing it that way.

I didn't think either one of them should have been fired or deserved to be fired. Frankly, I was upset that Dolan was starting to move in and take that kind of measure with the team because I had always had control over what happened with the team. But he was starting to take my authority and responsibility away, even though we'd been enormously successful.

I think Ernie should be a little more open about it. He's still very angry with me, and I wish he would just let it go because we had a great friendship for many years.

Immediately following Grunfeld's firing (technically, he had been "reassigned" to special consultant), Checketts would be at the center of another off-the-court controversy, although this one would not become public until weeks later. It involved Red Holzman's former whipping boy, who had spent the years since Camelot coaching the Chicago Bulls to six championships.

Phil Jackson: I called Dave when Red died [in November 1998], the year of the lockout. I called and he was at his [Red's] house. As my memory serves, he called me leaving the house on his mobile phone to my house in Montana. And he said, "Phil, I just left the family. Red was a really important person to me. And it was his wish that you come back and be part of the Knicks. I just want to follow through on that." He said, "Right now I've got a good general manager; I've got a good coach. It's not those positions I'm looking at, at all." He said, "I just want you to come back, and if you're interested in coming back and being part of basketball, you know you have a place to come back to."

I said that was very generous and very nice and that I was going to be living in New York during that winter—I had a home in Woodstock that was being finished—and maybe we can talk to each other later in the year. Fine. So that goes on, and the Knicks have the whole fiasco with the Camby trade and Starks and Oakley leaving, Jeff and Ernie having a dispute, and Ernie getting fired. At that time, the Knicks and Cleveland were fighting for eighth place, and I got a call where I was asked to come, if possible, to talk to Dave. Now, there's a little bit of trouble because I think he hears that the New Jersey Nets are speaking to me, and there's obviously some interest there. It's a good organization, and they're willing to make moves and build a team. They've built a new practice facility, so things are looking up. And I know the owner through Bill Bradley, and so forth.

Dave Checketts: [After Ernie had been fired] we were without a general manager, and I was talking with Lustgarten about it and said, "Look, the Nets are interviewing Phil." Because they were; it was very public that they were interviewing him. And there was some interest from other areas. I said, "Look, we can't let him go across the river without talking to him." Even though he'd been the coach of the Bulls all those years, Phil was a Knick. He was a *Knick*. And he's a very good coach. I said, "Maybe he's decided to hang coaching up. Maybe he doesn't even want to coach anymore. I think I ought to have a conversation with him." Lustgarten was supportive of that, so I called Phil. I knew there was a chance it could get out. I didn't talk with him about coaching, and I didn't talk with him about being a general manager. I had Phil come to my home, and we sat down in Connecticut and I said, "Look, you're a Knick. We have a great organization. Maybe you should play a role with us. I'd like to find out what you'd like to do." We talked about the kind of players you should have, the way you conduct business, communication and working relationships. We had a very positive meeting and he left.

Phil Jackson: So I said [to Dave] that certainly I'd like to talk to him. He said, "I'm not offering you any position. I just want to tell you that we're gonna make some moves. We're gonna have a good basketball team. It's too early to talk about anything this year." And I said, "Before you go on, I'll tell you this: I think you have a chance to win the East, simply because you guys have the key to beating Miami. You've built your team around beating Miami, and if you get them in the playoffs and get their spot, you'll have an opportunity to go right through the East because there's nobody else to beat but Indiana." He said, "Well, that's nice. But we're looking to make changes. We're willing to step up and do some things differently in this organization." Four days later, he called me and basically apologized for the fact that someone inside his office had snitched on him to a reporter. And, obviously, he had somebody who was backstabbing him in the organization that let him down.

Dave Checketts: Then one of his people got it to Mike Wise in the *Times*. I was trying to keep things on an even keel, and that's where I really made a mistake. I told Jeff there were no other candidates for coach, which was true but didn't look that way. Then when confronted with it by Mike, I told a lie, which I've obviously lived to regret. But I apologized and tried to correct it, and moved on with life.

Phil Jackson: I have nothing but good feelings about Dave. I told him that I was interested in the Nets–it was a wonderful offer monetarily. I was [also] keeping an eye on the Lakers. I was going to see how that all boiled out because they were a team with a

future where I thought they could win, and if I went back to coaching I wanted to go back to a winning organization and a winning team. I didn't think I had the patience and the youth to go through a rebuilding program at age 55 or 57. So we left that. My agent left his house with nothing confirmed, nothing offered, except that if I wanted to be a part of the organization, I could be a part of the organization at some point when things could be talked about.

When Checketts and Grunfeld had their fateful dinner, the Knicks had lost 7 of 10 games and were 21–21 on the season. Then, suddenly, they found their stride, winning 6 of their final 8 contests to finish 27–23 and claim the eighth and final playoff slot in the Eastern Conference.

Don Chaney: Somehow, in that short season, that team came together. Marcus found his niche, blocking shots and rebounding. Spree came in and did his job in terms of blending in and giving up some of his game, along with the adjustment of coming off the bench. There were a lot of adjustments and sacrifices that season. And you have to give the credit to the players and their character. Guys started accepting roles, and the chemistry developed from there.

Kurt Thomas: We only played 50 games, and people don't realize that there were a lot of new faces on the team. Myself, Marcus, Sprewell. It took time for all of us to gel together. That year was up and down, up and down. We'd win a few games, we'd lose a few games. For some reason, we couldn't place our finger on what was going on. But then, right before the end of the season, when we were fighting for the eighth spot, we finally started getting it together and played great basketball. And that just comes from the veterans on that team: Patrick Ewing, Chris Dudley, Larry Johnson, and all the other veterans. They just kept us all together, and we played inspired basketball.

Allan Houston: Even though we didn't have a great regular season, guys were still prepared so that when we had to win games at the end, we did. When we got to the playoffs, our mentality was that we forget about everything and that this was a whole new season. We're gonna start fresh. We're gonna start the way we want to start. Forget about everything; it's us against the world. We just wanted to say that this regular season garbage is over with. It wasn't what we wanted. It was all of us: Jeff and the team.

Latrell Sprewell: Coach [Van Gundy] was great. He's definitely a hard-nosed guy, an excellent motivator who emphasizes defense more than anything. Offensively, most of the plays in the NBA are the same. Most coaches just have different calls for them, so that wasn't so bad. It was really learning the defense and what we were doing, the rotations, that was the challenge.

Marcus Camby: It was tough, considering who I was traded for. Oak was the heart and soul of that team. He played all-out every game, and the people of New York really embraced him, really loved his hard work. It was a big challenge for me. He was one of Jeff's favorite players. Coming in, I didn't think I got the time I thought I should have been getting. So it was tough in the beginning, sitting on the bench and not getting those kinds of minutes. I just had to remain patient.

Don Chaney: I made a statement about how Marcus was for us what Bill Russell was for the Celtics, in that he corrected all the mistakes we made on the perimeter. He was a shot-blocker, and if you got beat, he'd still be able to block the shot as Patrick had done in previous years. So he had found himself.

Latrell Sprewell: It was a rough year. We struggled to make the playoffs, and we hadn't been playing well. I think we were in Charlotte, and I ended up playing well. We won that game, and [just before that] we went down to Miami and were down big and ended up coming back to win. And from that point on, we weren't looking back as a team, we were looking forward and trying to get in. Once we got in, anything could happen. And that's exactly what happened. We were an eighth seed and nobody expected us to win.

Charlie Ward: I remember us working very hard to get where we were: the eighth seed. We had a good team that year and a great matchup

with Miami, as the one seed. Having that knowledge and knowing we matched up well with them, we knew it was going to be a great series.

Don Chaney: The biggest thing of all was that I knew that our guys were able to get up for big games, that they'd play well in big games. That was the thing that stood out. I trusted that anytime there was a big game, a seventh game or whatever, those guys were going to step up big and give all they could give. That was the confidence I had in that team, that we had step-up guys, to a man.

Jeff Van Gundy: We were still a 50-win team, if it would have projected out over a normal season. We had to deal with the trades, the injuries to Patrick and Sprewell, and the compact time. It was natural that we weren't playing well until the end. Everyone wanted it sooner, but it wasn't gonna happen. The difference between one and eight that year was very minimal. And they had the misfortune to get us.

As the eighth-seeded team in the East, the Knicks drew the Conference's top team in the first playoff round. That meant Miami, again, for the third straight year.

Miami outscored the Knicks 29–10 in the fourth quarter of Game 4 to even the series with an 87–72 win at the Garden. Game 5, yet another series-deciding game on the Heat's home floor, was on an unforgettable Sunday afternoon, May 16.

The Heat raced to an early 13-point lead, but the Knicks had caught them by the end of the first quarter, and it was touch-and-go thereafter. With just under a minute left, Terry Porter's two free throws put Miami ahead by three, 77–74.

Jeff Van Gundy: We blew them out in Game 1. They came back and won Game 2. Then Game 3 was close, and then we just annihilated them with that 32–2 run. And that thing went on for a long time. Mourning got in foul trouble with his fourth, in the third quarter. Then they brought him back in, but nothing stemmed the tide. And all the time I'm sitting there thinking, "We've got to find a way to win Game 4." In that one [Game 4], we played well, but they just had a great fourth quarter.

Allan Houston shoots, and a city holds its breath.

Allan Houston: I didn't start out well in Game 5, so I might have stopped being as aggressive. Patrick had a good game, so we were going to him a lot. In the fourth quarter, I hit a couple of shots. I didn't have a lot of points. Then it just happened.

Jeff Van Gundy: We posted up Latrell, who turned in the middle against Terry Porter. Spree shoots, misses, Patrick [goes] up on the board [with] bad ribs, bad Achilles, gets fouled. And this is what drives me crazy, when people say that Patrick never hits big shots. I can give you so many instances, like those two free throws [to get the Knicks within one]. Then we get the steal; Sprewell does a great job on Hardaway and knocks it away. And then . . .

The original [final] play was a high pick-and-roll for Sprewell. They defended it, and we really didn't execute very well. Ball gets knocked away and out of bounds, so now we're out of timeouts.

Latrell Sprewell: He [Porter] hit the ball out. I didn't know which way they were gonna call it. You're just hoping you get the ball back and get another shot at it. You're just hoping it goes your way.

Tom Thibodeau: With no timeouts left, we had to go to a set play, which was very similar to some of the plays that Miami runs. They knew us as well as we knew them. The two teams obviously mirrored each other. So it was gonna be a battle of execution.

Jeff Van Gundy: That's when we went to something we ran all the time called "Triangle Down," which was just some action and then Patrick screening for Allan. Allan got it; they didn't defend it very well. Their guys were sort of frozen. So Allan put it on the ground, got fouled by [Dan] Majerle upside the head. The ball hits the rim and the backboard. And what people don't realize is that, if that ball had come out, the one guy up in the air–the *only one* jumping–was Allan Houston. He was right in front of the rim. He had followed it after he had shot it. So he would have been there to get the tip, and he was the only one there. Everybody else was just locked, watching it.

Allan Houston: Triangle Down was a play where two guys go up to the top and two guys go to the corner, and really it's for me to come off a pick

to the high post and either try to get off a shot or try and penetrate and make something happen. When I came off the top of the pick, I felt someone coming behind me, and I didn't want to just stop because that would have given them a passing lane for a steal. So I had to keep coming toward the ball. Fortunately, I was starting to come back toward the ball, and then I started moving toward the basket. I knew we didn't have a lot of time left and I didn't want to use it all up, because there was a lot of traffic. I didn't just want to pump-fake and take a bad shot. The only choice I had was to get it, take one step to get my balance, and I saw some daylight. I felt Majerle behind me. That's why I had to lean forward. I knew that if I stopped and went straight up, he probably would have gotten a piece of the shot. So when I took that one step forward, it gave me some daylight.

Jeff Van Gundy: One thing I'll never forget was [Miami's] Duane Causwell. The whole play, he's on the baseline next to their bench. And walked all the way under the basket in that four seconds, just mesmerized by the play, the bounce, the backboard, and in.

Allan Houston: What was really going through my mind was that I thought it was gonna hit the front rim. I was jumping, and then I jumped again, because I was gonna try and tip it in. I just felt it come off a little short. It hit the front rim. Since I felt that, I just immediately jumped in the air and got ready to tip it. Fortunately, I didn't need to.

Tom Thibodeau: Allan gets the ball high into the air; the ball catches the front of the rim, the backboard, back to the front of the rim, up, and in.

Knicks 78, Heat 77, with 0:00.8 left.

Jeff Van Gundy: When they took it out, they settled for that pass-in and the long shot by Terry Porter. They could have burned a timeout to get a better shot. But Porter caught it with eight-tenths left, dribbled it, and shot. And they were gonna count it. They said it wasn't gonna count, but there was no signal. So if there's no signal, they were gonna count it. There was no wave-off or anything, then Brendan [Malone] had to pull me off [referee] Eddie F. Rush.

Tom Thibodeau: Particularly with the history of the two teams. We had lost a game before with clock stuff, on Easter Sunday [1998], with Allan making a [disallowed last-second] shot. Of course, there was so much meaning to that game. There was so much going on that Jeff wasn't taking any chances. It was hard to let that go, even though we had won the game.

Allan Houston: People told me that they were literally injured from being so excited. The TV fell on their head, or they hit something so hard, or they tripped over something in celebration. People literally got hurt because they got so excited.

We had a lady who helped take care of our kids and looked after our house. She was a Hispanic lady and lived in the Bronx. And she said that right before the shot, the whole neighborhood, the whole block, was completely quiet. After I hit the shot, she went outside and people were going crazy in the streets. And that just gave me chills. I have chills right now thinking about it, just imagining that this was the first round of the playoffs. Can you imagine what a championship would have been like? That shot made so many people feel good that they went out partying and celebrating, in the Bronx or wherever they were.

Two days later, the Knicks were in Atlanta to start the East semis against the Hawks. But the effects of Allan Houston's game-winning shot still lingered, as Van Gundy learned when he walked into his Atlanta hotel room and found a telegram from Miami.

Jeff Van Gundy: The year before was probably our low point, when I went out after Mourning, and he [Riley] ripped me pretty hard in the papers the day of Game 5. So when we won in '99, we hadn't talked or anything. And to get that letter [in Atlanta] showed a sign of him saying, we've been through too much and let's just move on.

Pat Riley: There's proof that sometimes the worst thing that can happen to teams is that you get

to play the ultimate game before the real ultimate game. And that's what happened. We were always in the ultimate game, or the last game with the Knicks, before we got to the last game of the world championship Finals. And we just never had enough clock left, or could get the last shot.

Traditionally, the Knicks did not match up well against the Hawks of Steve Smith, Dikembe Mutombo, and Mookie Blaylock. But this year was different. The Knicks blew the Hawks out in four straight games, their first four-game playoff sweep since 1969, holding Atlanta to just 76.5 points per game.

The emerging Camby punctuated the Knicks' dominance with not one, but two resounding dunks over Mutombo. And as the Knicks were putting the finishing touches on a 13-point, series-clinching Game 4 win, the chant of "Jeff Van Gun-dy" echoed throughout the Garden. It was the final touch to a bizarre night in which, three hours earlier, Checketts held a press conference to admit that he had lied when he denied that he had contacted Phil Jackson about joining the Knicks.

Charlie Ward: The Miami series gave us a toughness that we needed to go through to the next two rounds to get to the Finals. Being an eighth seed, we didn't play up to our capabilities throughout the year. Once we got into the playoffs, anything could happen.

Jeff Van Gundy: We played well. They had the misfortune to be playing in the Georgia Dome, so they really had no home-court advantage. Sprewell and Houston were just so good. And they [Atlanta] were banged up. We just dominated them from start to finish.

Marcus Camby: I was telling the reporters beforehand that I was gonna dunk on him. Back then, he was really into the finger waving and this and that. Earlier that year, he had elbowed Chris Childs and knocked out his false tooth. We remembered all that stuff. I thought that if I got the opportunity, I'd dunk on him. So when we went down there, we were riding an emotional high from the shot Allan hit in the Miami series.

Jeff Van Gundy: I heard 'em, but I didn't know it was for me. Not at first. Then I knew. And the funny thing was, after the game, the players were giving me the business in the locker room, started mock-chanting "Jeff Van Gundy." And I said that what usually comes after that is, "sucks." So it was good that they eliminated the "sucks" part.

That was the same time all the stuff about Dave talking to Phil Jackson came out. I don't think Dave did anything wrong in contacting Phil. That's his job. I think that if he had to do it over again, the one thing he would not have done is mislead people once it came out.

Now it was on to Indiana and the Eastern Conference Finals, where another longtime tormentor–Reggie Miller–awaited.

With Ewing scoring six points in the final two minutes, the Knicks ended Game 1 with an 11–3 run to win, 93–90. But two nights later, Miller nailed two free throws with two seconds left to thwart a fourth-quarter Knicks rally, giving Indiana an 88–86 decision in Game 2.

And the Knicks lost more than just a game. Afterward, it was discovered that Ewing, who barely missed a last-second jumper that would have forced overtime, had played the entire game with a torn Achilles tendon. He would be sidelined for the remainder of the playoffs.

Allan Houston: In the playoffs, Jeff wanted to play a certain way. And what happened was that when we just said, "Look, let it all hang out and whatever happens, happens," there was a different style that evolved. And Jeff had to say, "This is working. I'm gonna go with it." It was playing the same defense but being a little more free on offense. We did a lot more running after getting stops, and it made everybody get in a better flow.

Latrell Sprewell: The whole thing was a learning experience for me because I hadn't been in a playoff series that intense. It was a learning experience, but at the same time I was totally comfortable with my role on the team and what I was to provide for us.

Jeff Van Gundy: Everybody said that we were better off without Patrick. Well, we went 8–3 in the playoffs with Patrick, 4–5 without him. In Game 2, he missed the shot at the end, then found out he'd hurt his Achilles.

Kurt Thomas: We felt we should have won [Game 2] in Indiana. Marcus took a charge on Antonio Davis, and they didn't give it to him. We felt we were robbed. Patrick missed the shot at the end, but we felt it shouldn't have had to come to that.

Back home for Game 3, the Knicks trailed by eight points with under 3:30 left, then ran off seven straight to pull within one. Mark Jackson nailed two free throws to give the Pacers a three-point lead, 91–88, with 11.9 seconds left.

Timeout, New York.

Allan Houston: The play was supposed to be for me to do the same thing as the Miami shot, similar to Triangle Down. I was supposed to come to the top, get the ball, and try to make a play. But I didn't look open. LJ was the guy that, if I wasn't open, had to come back to the ball.

Tom Thibodeau: It's very interesting how that all developed. Patrick, of course, was injured, and Larry was playing in Patrick's position. We're trying to get the ball inbounds, and they overplayed the initial entry. Larry flashed back to the ball, and when the ball was inbounded, it was deflected. When Larry recovered the ball, he was in three-point range. He used a shot-fake to get [Antonio] Davis into the air, then dribble.

Allan Houston: That was big because with LJ playing the Patrick position, you wouldn't want Patrick shooting a three. But since it was LJ, it gave us a different look. He could step out if he had to and shoot a three. I don't know if we were really looking to shoot a three at that time. But when he caught the ball, he didn't have too many options. So he caught it, kind of looked around, took a couple of dribbles, and just let it go.

Tom Thibodeau: He gets the ball up into the air and we're all thinking, "OK, he's fouled and we'll get the chance for the three free throws." Then the

Larry Johnson lets fly . . .

ball goes in and the whole emotion of the building erupted.

Jeff Van Gundy: We could have gone quick because we had another timeout. We wanted to get it to Allan, but they covered him well. Charlie's a great inbounder, but this time it got deflected. That's why LJ eventually caught it at the three-point line. They weren't trying to foul. Larry made it and got fouled. And I think the hardest thing about it was making the free throw. But Childs did a great job making sure LJ knew that it was all about making the free throw.

Allan Houston: He got so excited. I remember he was down at the other end of the court, and he saw us coming after him. You could almost see something click in his head like, "OK, I gotta calm myself down." He knew at that point that it was over with, but it was so hard for him to calm himself down. He just wanted to explode and celebrate more. But he knew he had to calm himself down to get ready for the free throw. He wasn't finished celebrating. People talk about that shot, but the free throw was just as big as the shot. And people don't understand how clutch the free throw was.

Latrell Sprewell: LJ knew the circumstances. It was a huge shot and we were fortunate enough to get the call. We were excited, but we knew he had to make that free throw. So we were just supporting him and showing him love and then [saying], hey, make this free throw and we'll let you go. Go concentrate so you can knock this free throw down.

Jeff Van Gundy: Then we got a great stop on Mark Jackson to finish it off. And we had to do it without fouling because I think they were probably looking for a way to draw a foul.

Said Reggie Miller after the game: "I'm usually on the other end of a shot like that."

Johnson's unforgettable four-point play gave the Knicks a 92–91 Game 3 win, but Indiana rebounded to even the series with a 12-point triumph in Game 4.

Then, in stunning fashion, the Knicks played perhaps their best all-around game of the season before an amazed Indiana crowd in Game 5. Sprewell scored 29 points;

Camby added 21 points, 13 rebounds, and six blocks; and Johnson buried two three-pointers in the fourth quarter. Coming back from an early 14-point deficit, the Knicks held off Miller, who had 30 points, and the Pacers by hitting 10 of 12 free throws in the last two minutes. Knicks 101, Pacers 94.

One win away from the Eastern Conference Championship, the Knicks headed back to the Garden for Game 6.

Jeff Van Gundy: In Game 3, we really got off to a bad start. But Marcus played great. [Larry has] the four-point play. And Camby was great from that point through the rest of the series. He made his living on offensive rebounds, cuts against double teams, and running the floor. Everybody had to play well, but he was something that they didn't have an answer for.

Latrell Sprewell: Marcus and I were in the same situation in that we were both coming off the bench, giving the team a little bit of a spark. We were a totally different team when you put Marcus, myself, and Chris Childs in the game. We went from a half-court team to a team that could suddenly get up and down the court. It was almost like we had two gears. I think a lot of people hadn't been used to seeing the Knicks get up and down so much.

Allan Houston: I had a peace about me during that game. It was just a weird, real peace. My wife was pregnant, and we knew that the next day she would have the baby. It actually made me relax that whole game. It took so much pressure off me. I'm usually focused and intense, and that puts a lot of pressure on you. But that took almost all of the pressure off me, knowing that if we won, we were going to the hospital the next day. I was thinking about that during the game, and I was peaceful and relaxed. That's when you play your best.

Marcus Camby: I just wanted to go out there and play hard, try to make plays, try to bring the energy. Playing with Latrell, we were both high-energy guys. Us playing together at the same time really lifted up the spirits of our teammates and got everyone involved and excited.

Jeff Van Gundy: The greatest part about Game 6 was that, with Patrick already out, LJ goes out in the first half after spraining his knee. So we're playing with Kurt, Marcus, and [Chris] Dudley the whole second half.

Marcus Camby: It was a whole different thing. Unfortunately, Patrick had gotten hurt. If he hadn't gotten hurt, who knows what would have happened? That put me in the position to get more minutes, and I was just able to make the best out of the situation.

Allan Houston: I didn't have a good first half. Once I got to a point where I was starting to get going, you know the defense doesn't know what you're gonna do. That's what I was feeling the whole second half when I got going. Wherever I went, they were just kind of guessing. So when I go to the hole, it throws people off. They know I can shoot, but when I get to the hole and make a couple [and get fouled], it's really confusing. At that point, I felt that I could pretty much do what I wanted to do.

Houston scored 32 points, Sprewell had 20. Camby, dubbed the series MVP by Indiana coach Larry Bird, added 15 points and nine boards. On the same floor where he had dashed so many Knicks hopes in the past, Miller shot 3-for-18.

The game ended at the stroke of midnight: Knicks 90, Pacers 82. In six weeks, the Knicks had gone from the eighth seed to the NBA Finals. And as the final horn sounded, the coach whose job status had been so tenuous a month before ran onto the court flashing a smile as big as the way his team had played.

Allan Houston: I was like, "Man, I had to be the first person he could find to hug." So many times, Jeff and I had talks; he was just trying to pull the best out of me as a player, and really challenge me. I wouldn't be where I am today without him challenging me. He was gonna refuse to let me settle for being an average player, or even a good player. He would say, "I see greatness in you." And I think that moment was like [him saying], "This is what I see." At that point, we could have hugged a total stranger.

Out in the West, the San Antonio Spurs won 31 of their last 36 regular-season games, then went a combined 11–1 in the playoffs to win the Conference title. They did it behind a devastating one-two punch of sophomore sensation Tim Duncan and veteran center David Robinson, both seven-footers. With Ewing out and Johnson and Dudley both hobbling, there was no way the Knicks could match the Spurs' size and inside game.

It took just five games in the Finals for the magic to finally run out. It was a bittersweet end to a season that, for so many reasons, no one would ever forget.

Patrick Ewing: That was the toughest one. That was the toughest, tougher than '94. Because I couldn't play. I was there but I couldn't play.

Charlie Ward: We lost Larry and Patrick. That hurt us a lot in the Finals. We could have used both those guys in the Finals, but we gave the best effort we could with what we had. It was unfortunate that two of our better players weren't able to play.

Allan Houston: It was a feeling of David against Goliath. Every series we played, we had so much confidence. We knew that the other team knew that they were in a fight, that we were a team that was hungry and very dangerous. And we had won the first game of every series, on the road, and that changed the whole series. When we went into San Antonio, we came in with the same mentality and hunger. But when we lost that first game, that really took a lot out of us because we knew we had to win the second game. When you're used to doing something that gives you the edge, you feel good about it. But when it doesn't happen, it takes a turn. We really thought we could win. We felt that if we could win the first game, we'd have a great chance. But when we didn't win the first or second game, we didn't lose hope but we knew it was going to be tough.

Jeff Van Gundy: Patrick's out, Dudley can't straighten his arm, and LJ had sprained his knee. So probably from the outside, there wasn't any hope. But I think the reason we were so competitive in that series was that we thought there was [hope]. So Larry battles, but Duncan is great. We lost the first two, then had a great Game 3 to win. Played well in Game 4 and 5, but we just weren't as good as they were. They were playing great basketball. Sean Elliott said later that we gave them by far the hardest competition of any team they played that postseason.

Allan Houston: And the thing that really hurt us was that LJ was really struggling, and we knew it. You've got LJ having to guard Tim Duncan, and that's tough. And David [Robinson] was playing very well. So it was tough.

Kurt Thomas: It was tough going up against, basically, two seven-footers, one [Duncan] playing the best of his career at that point; he basically could not be touched. The only person who could stop him was himself. We just didn't have the size to match up with them, especially when Patrick went down. We really could have used his size and used those six fouls.

Marcus Camby: LJ's a great defender, and Jeff liked him a lot on Duncan. But it was a seven- or eight-inch height difference right there. He was just shooting right over Larry, going glass and all that. We always thought that if we had an extra big body to put on him, maybe things would have been different. But yet, other guys on their team stepped up as well. It wasn't just Duncan.

Jeff Van Gundy: We were older, and we were less athletic at that time. Patrick was always banged up, as was Larry. Basically, what we were trying to do was get them through the season. Chuck Daly once had a great line; he said, "An NBA coach's job is to land the airplane. There's turbulence in the air, and your job is to fight through it and land the plane, so when playoffs come, you're ready." That's what those teams did. We had some injuries and health issues. But when the playoffs came, in all my years, there wasn't one time when I said, you know, we underachieved in these playoffs. That's the greatness of those guys. They always performed at their best. Now, was their best sometimes not good enough? Certainly. But they performed at their best when their best was needed.

Checketts (right) welcomes
new GM Scott Layden in 1999.

THE LINEUP: Steve Mills; Scott Layden; Jeff Van Gundy; Allan Houston; Patrick Ewing; Mark Jackson; Charlie Ward; Don Chaney; Dave Checketts; Herb Williams; Marcus Camby; Kurt Thomas; Latrell Sprewell.

Checketts filled the vacancy in the general manager's chair by bringing Scott Layden to the Knicks in August 1999. A native New Yorker and the son of popular former coach Frank Layden, Scott came to the Knicks after nearly two decades with the Utah Jazz, building a two-time Western Conference Champion around future Hall of Famers Karl Malone and John Stockton.

A month later, in a clear delineation of the club's basketball and business sides, Steve Mills was named executive vice president of franchise operations. A former Princeton guard, Mills had spent 16 years at the NBA office and had most recently served as the league's senior vice president for basketball and player development.

Steve Mills: One thing about being in sports is the idea of working at the Garden, and working for the Knicks is something that I used to think about and dream about. But I wasn't sure anything like that would actually happen.

Scott Layden: We were huge basketball fans and naturally we were big Knicks fans. And then when we moved up to Niagara, we followed the [Buffalo] Braves, but the Knicks were still our team. Do you ever lose that? Clearly, your allegiances change when you go to work for Utah, but deep down you're always a fan of the Knicks.

Steve Mills: Dave and I had spoken a couple of times before '99 about different positions, and ironically, none of them happened to be with the Knicks. They were entertainment jobs, marketing jobs. But in '99 when Dave and I spoke, he told me that he thought he knew a lot about me and he knew the things that I was looking for in my next job, and he thought he would be able to create a situation that I would be very excited about.

Scott Layden: Deciding to come to New York was a monumental decision and one that you don't take lightly, and it's certainly something that your family participates in. Without my family and their excitement, we don't come here. And we had an unbelievable experience in Utah. But to be involved in something different, to have the opportunity to live and work in New York, was wonderful and one we were very fortunate to have. Growing up in New York . . . It was something that's hard to explain.

Steve Mills: Dave couldn't tell me who he was thinking about as the general manager at the time, but he said he had one guy in mind. And if it worked out, he knew I was going to be the perfect complement for him. Ultimately it worked out with Scott, and I came on board after that. And I think the reason was that Dave always knew that the way the business and the league were changing, you needed a general manager who was going to be a general manager, focusing on the players side. Then you needed someone else to sort of take the load away from him–dealing with the marketing, managing the people, dealing with the legal issues. The good mix for us was that I knew basketball, too, and could give Scott some support and understand what was important to him. I also understood the boundaries, when you're gonna disrupt the basketball side of the operation, when people are disruptive to what the players are trying to get accomplished as athletes.

Scott Layden: Things came together very quickly. We've never looked back as a family; we've never second-guessed. Our focus is that we don't dwell on what could have been. We're always looking forward. Our attention has always been in front of us. So the opportunity to come here, the challenge of working here, was what excited us.

Steve Mills: The thing that I saw right away was that there was an opportunity to do more things with the franchise, and more things with the players, that weren't getting done. This is the best place in the world to play in. It's the best building to play in, from an excitement standpoint, from a historical standpoint. And this is the best city to play in. There were things that the players needed to understand about the people who are sitting and watching them play, and that this is the time where you can develop relationships for whatever they want to do with their lives after basketball. This is the time where you can cement that. And at the same time, by getting players to think about things like that, you're actually building the team's bond with the fans. When Ken Chenault of American Express is sitting there, he's a Knicks fan. But if somehow you can get him a little closer to Allan Houston, he feels even better about the Knicks, and Allan Houston is making a connection that's gonna work for him for a long time after he finishes playing. Those kinds of things were obvious to me.

Scott Layden: The great success, tradition, and history, the fact that players want to play here–that all felt like a great opportunity. Which it is. But it's also a tremendous challenge. If you're in pro sports, you know that there are always big challenges ahead. And that's why we all look forward to getting up in the morning, to be part of this great sport and the challenges it brings.

Steve Mills: There are opportunities for players in this market to be spokespeople, to do whatever they want to do after basketball, that don't present themselves anywhere else. It cannot happen anyplace except in New York, because of the size of the market and a building that's in the middle of the city. We still have a lot to do, but those are the kinds of opportunities I saw when I came here.

There would be one more long postseason run, one more battle with the Heat, one more springtime melodrama that held a city spellbound. In 2000, after sweeping Toronto in the first round, the Knicks would defeat Miami in a seven-game East semifinal, winning the deciding game on the Heat's floor for the third straight year. In their fourth Eastern Conference Final since 1993, however, the Knicks would fall to Indiana in six games, with Reggie Miller scoring 34 points in the clincher at the Garden.

Jeff Van Gundy: Anthony Carter's shot [a behind-the-backboard shot in Game 3 versus Miami] was definitely illegal. Then they make a new rule about it, so you know it was wrong even though they said it wasn't wrong. Whatever.

Game 6 was probably the worst half we played that year. We were down by 15 at the half [45–30], but it was like being down 30 because it was such a low-scoring game [the final score was 93–80]. I told them that we'd picked a bad time to play the worst half of the year and that we were gonna win, and this is how we were gonna do it. We tried to tweak our game plan to become as aggressive as we could on both ends.

We got a great spurt [13–3] to start the third quarter, and we got right back in the game. And, again, Patrick, who, quote, never makes a big shot, makes *every* big shot and gets *every* big rebound. And it got down to where Allan got fouled by Majerle [with 17.6 seconds left] and makes both free throws.

Allan Houston: I don't remember that. That's amazing, I don't remember that!

Jeff Van Gundy: Now we're up two. And now I make a decision that goes against the Cassell Theory of '94, in that, I just felt we were on our last legs because we had expended so much effort. So we double-teamed Mourning even though we could lose [on a three]. And Carter had been making great shots. So we double-team, the ball comes out to Carter, and Childs makes a great play to contest Carter's shot and it bounds long.

Game 7 was on Sunday, but the day before, Malik Sealy died [in a car crash]. I talked to the team about it when we got to Miami; it was a very somber meeting. Sometimes you have to forget about what's at stake and talk about reality. I had recruited Sealy when

I was at Providence, not that he would have remembered. It was just tragic.

Hardaway daggered us again, making a three behind a pick-and-roll to put them up one [with 1:32 left]. Then we came with "43 thumb spread": Spree and Ewing run a high pick-and-roll, kick to Johnson, Johnson enters to Ewing. Mourning made a huge mistake going for the steal, giving Patrick a direct line to the basket, and Patrick dunks it. In their final possession, we were gonna double Mourning. I put Camby in to get bigger, so we had LJ, Camby, and Ewing to rebound and defend. The ball goes in, Mashburn throws over to Clarence [Weatherspoon]. Camby slipped on his recovery, but because he's such a great athlete, he gathers himself and contests right on the shot. Then Sprewell had the rebound of his Knicks career, coming over the top of Mourning. It's what we always called "engaged rebounds": one guy blocking out, one guy coming over the top. Camby had the presence of mind, as Majerle was pulling Sprewell out of bounds, to call timeout.

Then in a drama that was drawn out for weeks during the summer, the 38-year-old Ewing–with one year left on his contract–was traded to Seattle, a gut-wrenching move that ended a 15-year era. Earlier in the summer, an apparent trade had fallen through. Then, on September 20, 2000, Ewing went to the Sonics in a four-team, 12-player deal.

Steve Mills: It was a very difficult time because of the fact that Patrick will always mean so much to this city and this organization. He wanted an opportunity to look at different situations, and we wanted to do what was right for him. And at the same time, we had to try to figure out a way to do what was right for the organization. So it was difficult. In this business, there are always transitions that you have to deal with. One day there's going to be a transition as Allan Houston finishes his career. You're always going to have to deal with transitions.

Jeff Van Gundy: I was the one dissenter in that. Not because of cap room, but because I never thought that Patrick would find it better someplace else, and I knew he would not cause a problem if he had stayed. And Dave really didn't want to trade him either. But Dave felt it was his obligation, because of all that

Patrick had given, that if Patrick really wanted to go, he was gonna help him go. I went to Washington before the [first] trade and tried to talk him [Ewing] out of that. Then that fell through, and I went back down there to try and talk him out of it again. But he was convinced that he wanted to go. I think Dave and Scott really tried to help him get what he wanted, which was a fresh start.

Scott Layden: Coming to New York, one of the things to bear in mind is that I was not here during his great career and tenure. But at the same time, I followed him as a basketball fan and watched the great things he did. So it wasn't like I came in unaware of who he was and what he meant to this franchise. That's important. I don't think it was someone coming in here that had no knowledge of what this guy meant to the game. And that's why he was a participant in the trade. Not only contractually, which he had to be, but also emotionally. The way it worked out was that it came together and the decision was made together to part ways. And that's always tough. No matter what the level of the trade is, it's always hard to make a trade. Especially with the people involved and the emotions of it, it's hard. But this particular trade was very hard because of what he had done for the franchise. And there's no question that it was a very difficult decision, and one that was tough not only for him but for the franchise. As always, we hoped it would work out for everyone. It was a very tough thing to do. Without a doubt, it was the toughest trade I ever had to make, with everything that he had meant to this franchise and the way he conducted himself and [had] given so much to make this franchise better.

Patrick Ewing: I thought it was time to go. I just got tired of all the negative publicity, and I thought it was time to go.

Scott Layden: He was not in the room. I did speak to him on the phone right after the deal was complete. But because he was participating in it, it was a little different than other trades. In other trades, the players really aren't aware of what's going on. In this one, because of the one trade that was turned down, and then the subsequent weeks that followed, it was unique. He was probably more informed than any [other] player would have been.

Houston, the main man for the
new millennium, with Sprewell.

It was not a real long conversation. I called to let him know that the deal had gone through. Typical of how Patrick was, he was very professional, very appreciative of the call. I reiterated to him what I thought of him as a person and as a player and thanked him for everything he'd done.

Steve Mills: What Patrick's departure did for us as an organization was that it forced us to focus on other things. Now we're working on how to rebuild the franchise in terms of the fans and the city, getting new people into the building that maybe weren't here before. It forces us to look at how we operate. One of the things about him being here was there was a certain sense of, no matter what you're gonna do, people will come. Just send the invoices out, people will pay. They'll never give up their tickets. That's obviously not the case, but that's also an opportunity to think about what you do, how you connect with people, how your customers and fans should really be treated, and how to promote your team and your players. And those kinds of things are exciting for us. There were very difficult things that went along with Patrick's departure and a change in direction of the team. But with those things we learn and grow and have things to look forward to.

Allan Houston: The Knicks were now comfortable with saying that they were gonna build around me and Spree, and Marcus at the time, and see what happens now. It told me they were comfortable with making that transition. I still don't know what happened with Patrick and that whole situation, but I do know that it really would have been nice for him to retire with the New York uniform on. But things happen.

Glen Rice, Luc Longley, and Travis Knight arrived in the Ewing trade. Then, in midseason, Mark Jackson returned to the Knicks as Childs was dealt to Toronto. In 2000–01, the Ewing-less Knicks won 48 games and headed for the playoffs for the 14th straight year.

In the hours following a seven-point Game 1 win over Toronto, Camby's sister was abducted by a former boyfriend in a hostage crisis that lasted until the following morning. Ward, meanwhile, was the center of controversy as remarks attributed to him in The New York Times *were interpreted by some as anti-Semitic.*

Losing in the first round for the first time in 10 years, the Knicks fell to the Raptors in five games. Johnson was sidelined for the entire postseason with excruciating back pain. He would never play again.

Jeff Van Gundy: You can't take Ewing and Johnson out, and Childs out, and have that same competitive tough-mindedness. We played hard that year. We played to our strengths. Rice was hurt the whole year, LJ was hurt, Camby was hurt sometimes, Ewing had been traded, and we still found our way to 48 wins. In many ways, that was one of our best regular seasons. But they had given all they had.

Mark Jackson: I believed that everything had come full circle. I believed it was a great opportunity for me to come back to New York. And I realized something that someone had told me when I was very young: you don't burn any bridges. I tried not to do that, and I made a conscious effort not to do that. That, in the long run, gave me the opportunity to come back. It was great because New York is home. It's the place I dreamed about playing in. There's no place like Madison Square Garden; there's no place like New York City. It was great for me to come back, especially because I developed a special relationship with a group of guys that I had only battled with. It was a whole new group, and all of a sudden I was playing alongside these guys that I had battled for a couple of years. Just great people. And then to have the opportunity to play for Jeff, who was someone I admired as much as anybody in this game, was special.

Jeff Van Gundy: Larry is out, Patrick was gone, and we're playing a team that we had swept the year before but who had dominated us in the regular season. Played well and won Game 1. Then Camby's thing happened. I made a mistake in playing Marcus in Game 2, right away. I shouldn't have played him. Even if he said he was ready, I shouldn't have played him.

Charlie Ward: That whole situation was really a miscommunication and misunderstanding of what went on and what was said. But the more and more I study Scripture, the more and more I see that Jesus was misunderstood, the more and more people didn't know what he was talking about at the time. It got me to a point where I wanted to grow deeper in the Scripture and more as a Christian man, a man of God. That was a test of my faith, to see if I was gonna quit or try to continue to move forward in my relationship with the Lord. It gave me the opportunity to grow stronger, because I knew there was a reason for this whole thing. Why He chose me to have this happen to, out of all the guys that were in the Bible study, there's no other reason for me to say that I wasn't going to go through this. As much as you don't want negative publicity, I knew there was a reason and purpose behind it. And the reason and purpose was for Him to be glorified through it all. I've had a lot of people come and help me from all different types of perspectives. The Holy Spirit has guided me in understanding what perspective is His perspective. I've had rabbis, priests, and ministers—all different people—giving me their perspective on the Scriptures. God has given His perspective to me, and I do what He's called me to do, and that's to love people.

In July 2001, Houston opted out of his contract, then re-signed with the Knicks for a multiyear package worth an estimated $100 million. At the opening of training camp, Johnson attended the team's media day, but it would be the last time he would wear a Knicks uniform. LJ, whose back had betrayed him for the last time, retired a month later. His loss would be felt in ways that went beyond the box score.

Allan Houston: I learned from the Detroit experience that you can't take anything for granted. You can't take for granted that, even though they may have been pleased with what I brought in the past . . . You just don't know. It's a business, and you just don't know. But what made it different was that I experienced two different ways of operating a business and a team. The Knicks did it one way, the Pistons at that time did it a different way. So I had to go off that experience. The Knicks said one thing, and they did it, they meant it. The other thing was that there really wasn't too much out there that was attractive, that could compete with the experience I had in New York.

I had experienced a lot in New York and developed a relationship with the city and the fans, even though, yeah, they're gonna kill you sometimes. Put it this way: I would have hated to have to make a seri-

ous decision. I would not have liked that, if L.A. or someone really strong had come up with an offer.

Scott Layden: One of the things you have to look at is the transition. You [have to] transition out of losing a franchise player. Whether Patrick was going to be traded or retire, there's a transitional period. Along with [losing] some very good players who helped this team win, namely Larry Johnson and others.

Don Chaney: We depended on him [LJ] to do the winning things, and that's what I loved about him. He stepped up big in ways that didn't show up on the stat sheet. And that's why the void was so huge when he left.

Allan Houston: He was the glue that kept everything together. LJ was a guy who cared about every single person. He had a relationship with every single person, somehow. He was a strong voice, but a soft voice at the same time. And that's very, very rare. I've never seen that kind of presence or leadership since. The thing that made LJ such a great presence was the fact that he basically took a role player's role, and that was really amazing about him. Something that I've studied in the Bible is that, to be a leader you have to give yourself. And a leadership quality that people really don't understand is, if you're gonna be a leader, you can't always demand that you be at the top. You have to be the least among many, and LJ had that quality.

Jeff Van Gundy: Larry may not have been at his best on February 1 against Vancouver in the second half of a back-to-back. But you put him in a big game, and Larry Johnson was playing at a very high level and had probably as many big shots made as anybody. Time and time and time again, he came up huge. And people ask me what the difference is between losing in the first round [in 2001] and going to the Eastern Conference Finals two straight years, and I tell them, "Larry Johnson." In the end, the guy we couldn't do without was Larry Johnson.

Allan Houston: He didn't have to say anything. It was the way he accepted his role, and it was almost to a fault, almost like he passed too much sometimes. But at the same time, he knew that he wasn't feeling his best. He also knew that he was playing with two hungry swing people [Houston and Sprewell] who were close to their prime. He just accepted it. That was the biggest thing he did and the hardest thing to do. That's

Nine years after he was traded away, Mark Jackson returned to the Knicks in 2001.

why people don't understand how hard it is to win a championship or how hard it is to win, period. You've gotta have a guy like LJ. Or a guy like Robert Horry, who could be a great player but who says, "I don't care [about ego]." That all comes down to humility, to letting your pride go. That's what LJ was all about.

A little more than a decade after bringing to 33rd Street a vision that translated into perhaps the most dramatic and compelling period in the franchise's history, Dave Checketts resigned as Garden president on May 15, 2001.

Dave Checketts: Everything that I did around the Garden was because of my love for the Knicks. I even took the Garden CEO job because, frankly, I didn't want any other person to come in there and try to report to them on what I was doing with the team. And in every case, whether it was [Richard] Evans or [Bob] Gutkowski, the owners were sufficiently interested: [Stanley] Jaffe, [Sumner] Redstone, [Rand] Araskog . . . I was really talking to them, and they were calling me. So when they asked me to take that job, I really didn't want it. I didn't want to go upstairs. While I was running the Garden, I kept my office down with the Knicks for a long time because that's where my heart was.

Scott Layden: Dave and I had worked together in Utah for a number of years, and then we worked together here. He's a good friend. I was sorry to see him leave. But Dave is a guy who will always do well. He has great energy. He's a guy who's very talented. And a lot like what happened in Utah, we worked together for a while, and he left. Here, we worked together for a while, and he left. And everybody was saying, "How are you gonna get along without him?" But we got along very well when he was here, and we got along very well when he left. Both here and in Utah. So I had a history of working both with him and without him.

Dave Checketts: Did we accomplish it with the Knicks? Not quite. I really wanted to give New York a championship parade for the Knicks. That was really what I wanted. We got very close. We should have won in '93, if Charles Smith makes a layup. We should have won in '94, if Rolando Blackman had been given any time off the bench. And I still think one of our

best teams was '97, when we swept Charlotte and got up 3–1 on Miami, and then the brawl happened. That was a very good team, and they were playing very well together. They had a great chance, too. And in '99 Patrick gets hurt in the second game against Indiana. The way Marcus was playing by then, and Latrell, the '99 team with a healthy Patrick Ewing would have given San Antonio a real run.

So it wasn't to be. Did we create some excitement? Yes. Did the celebrities return to the Garden? Was it the place to be? Yes. Were there many great, great memories through all of the difficulty? Absolutely. It's a great time to remember.

An even more shocking departure came seven months later, with the 2001–02 season just 19 games old.

Don Chaney: During the summer, Jeff would sit there and say, "I don't know how we're gonna win next year." This is in the summertime. I had sort of felt eventually that it would get to Jeff where he would eventually walk away, because he kept complaining about his daughter and having no time at home and missing his daughter growing up. To me, that was a sign right there. Sometimes his wife would bring his daughter to the office and he'd light up, so you knew he missed being around her, watching her grow up.

Herb Williams: The way Jeff coached, you can't put that stamp on this team. This isn't that kind of team. You don't have a Patrick Ewing or a Charles Oakley or an Anthony Mason. On this team you've got to be more freewheeling, where you get up and down the court a lot more and get shots up. You have to play defense a little bit differently. You have to adjust your coaching style to your personnel and try to relay that to your team. You have to deal with personalities more so than anything else in this league. You've got to be able to relate to players and have players relate to you. If you only believe in one way, guys will shut down on you, and you don't want that to happen.

Don Chaney: I think Jeff had a hard time adjusting, because Jeff is a very loyal guy. He's very loyal to the team and to the players individually. And those guys had all moved away, and it was hard for him to renew his loyalty to a new group of guys. Because he was with those guys in a certain system for so long, I think it was kind of stamped on his brain, the way those guys had to play. And when you bring a different group of guys in, he had a hard time adjusting, getting comfortable with a new group.

Jeff Van Gundy: It had nothing to do with the team, from my standpoint. Just for me, things had changed. I knew that the time was winding down for me. Rightfully or wrongfully, I sensed that the organization was ready for a change, a different personality, someone not so, maybe, possessed about winning. I was ready for a change, for many different reasons.

Don Chaney: It got to a point where he stopped enjoying the good times. When you win, you've got to stop and enjoy that moment. He didn't allow himself to stop and enjoy the good moments; he immediately focused on the next game and got down again. And I used to tell him all the time, "Jeff, we just won." But he never allowed himself to enjoy the moment, and I think that caught up to him after a while.

Scott Layden: He came into the office and told me that's what he wanted to do. This is late Friday afternoon [December 7, 2001]. We talked for a while, and it was quite clear he had made up his mind to do that. We got some things in order and went on from there.

Jeff Van Gundy: I went down to the office to see Scott. People talk about that [day's] practice, but that had nothing to do with it. I'd been thinking about it and contemplating it, making sure, and in retrospect you never can be [sure]. So I talked to Scott, who had been so good to work with. But I thought the organization was ready for a change. And that's OK. I always said coaching in New York is like coaching in dog years. So I had been the head coach 42 years.

Scott Layden: That was a very tough event for the team, for Jeff. Typical of pro sports, though, in that an event happens—a coach decides to resign—and one of the things that happens is that you have to make decisions quickly, gather yourself, and then move on. We had a game right away, on Saturday night against Indiana. At the time, it's a surprise. You never think anybody's gonna leave. But in hindsight, I think we made the decisions that were best for the team. And in a very short time, we got coach Chaney in place and got him underway, looking forward to what was ahead. I felt badly that it happened with Jeff and the team at

that time. But you can't sit around and feel sorry for him or for the team; you have to move, and move on.

Don Chaney: When he gave me the call, I was surprised but not shocked. I sort of saw it coming a little bit. I didn't know it was going to hit that heavy, where he would just step down. I never thought he would do that. But I knew he was different. I knew it was taking its toll.

I was in disbelief. I paused a minute and said, "What?" Because the timing was terrible. The first thing I thought was that he wouldn't step down and that somebody must have fired him. But he said no, he was just tired and he wanted to spend some time at home. And he told me that I might be considered for the job. I couldn't take all that in. I like Jeff a lot, and to see him walk away from the team–although it meant that I had the chance to advance–I wasn't happy at all. For him to do it at that juncture, I knew he was serious about it.

Jeff Van Gundy: When I made the decision, you never know if you're right. And the more I'm removed from the decision, [the more I know] it was right for them and for me. It would have been better for all of us if I had made it during the summer, but certainly it was right. And while there are many things I miss about the job–everything from the players to the coaches to the camaraderie to the competition–I don't miss missing my daughter grow up, which I was definitely missing. At the same time–and I don't think I've ever said this, but I know I feel this–I still have great regret about it. Because I know I'll never have another job like the New York Knicks. You know there's only one [job] like that. But sometimes the hardest decisions you have in your life are never going to be clear-cut. You just make them to the best of your ability.

Don Chaney: I put the phone down, and I just sat there and stared because I couldn't believe it. My wife was down in Texas, so I was alone. And where a normal person would say, "Here's my chance to be a head coach," that never crossed my mind. I was so concerned about why he did it, the timing, the effect on the team, the whole deal. I wasn't ready for it. And usually, I don't normally overreact to things. I'm usually pretty calm. But I overreacted to that because I just didn't understand it. It took me a while to figure it out.

Houston's classic form earned him All-Star honors in 2000 and 2001.

Scott Layden: One of the things you can say about Jeff is that he had a very good staff. Great experience, very good people who worked well together. So the transition there was as smooth as it could be under the circumstances.

Steve Mills: Jeff was a great coach who connected with the fans. We do research and have focus groups, and people would talk about Jeff Van Gundy as much as they'd talk about Allan Houston or anyone else on the team. So following that is always difficult. And Don came in during a very difficult time, not having a training camp to fall on, not being able to develop a system. But even with those things, he came in with the right kind of attitude, with a confidence in the players. He understood what they were going through. He was able to communicate with them about where he wanted to see the team go. That's the part that I respect most about him. Even given a really difficult transition and being thrown into it, he was able to have a great deal of composure and understand what he wanted to get done.

Don Chaney: The biggest problem was that, in the middle of a season, I knew there was no way you were gonna change the mentality of a player, add new things and change the philosophy. That's impossible. You've had the same players who had been under this system for years and you're not gonna change it. I knew that from the experience with Nellie; they just didn't buy into it because they had been conditioned. I knew it was a very tough situation to be in, for me. So I gradually did some things that I liked, but I had to stay basically within Jeff's system. I was just hoping to, later on, have a training camp and bring some new players in. That's what one of Nellie's problems was: had he brought new players in, the transition wouldn't have been as great.

Steve Mills: What's important in this business is that if you're totally consumed in just basketball, it's actually a detriment. There are so many ups and downs in this business that you need things to fall back on and take you away from it from time to time. Don has so much depth to him that isn't apparent to the casual fan—the things that he's interested in, the hardships he's gone through growing up, the adversity and racism he's had to deal with. All this gives him an opportunity to appreciate what he has but also have an appreciation for other things. So it's not the only thing in the world to be a coach in the NBA. And when you have that approach, I think that can make you a better coach.

Jeff Van Gundy: I truly do hope this, that as time passes, the players I coached and the coaches I coached with felt that I worked as hard and as well as possible, to give them the best chance to be as successful as possible. And if a majority of them think that way, then I would feel very good about my time there.

Following a 10–9 start under Van Gundy, the Knicks went just 30–52 for the year. It was their lowest win total over a full season in 15 years and ended their postseason run at a club record 14 consecutive playoff appearances.

Don Chaney: It was the most difficult year I've ever had, and I'm including my Clippers years.

Two months after the nightmare season ended, the Knicks sent Camby, Jackson, and the rights to Nene Hilario to Denver for 2001 All-Star forward Antonio McDyess and the rights to point guard Frank Williams. The Draft Day deal was designed to bolster the club's undersized front line, but McDyess suffered a fractured kneecap during the preseason and was sidelined for all of 2002–03.

Scott Layden: A lot of people talked about, "Well, did you forgo the future by trading for Antonio McDyess?" The counter to that would be [that] Antonio McDyess is a young veteran who's been on the All-Star Team. So at his age, we didn't feel like we were forgoing the future. Plus, in that trade, we stayed in the draft by getting Frank Williams. And we drafted another young guy in the second round [Milos Vujanic], who had some promise and went on to win a gold medal. It's being able to have some young guys in our system who'll help us win. So I refute the notion that we traded away the future. I don't think that's fair. Had we traded the number seven pick and not gotten a pick back, or traded for an aging veteran, then you could make that argument. But, clearly, [we had] an eye on keeping the team in a winning way and at the same time adding some youth to the program.

Marcus Camby: No one from management called me, and it was definitely frustrating. I loved

New York so much. I still have my home there; I'm there in the summers. Latrell and I are still best buddies. It was hard to leave all that behind, especially playing in the Garden. The fans there had been so terrific toward me. They embraced me with open arms, and I embraced them. It was frustrating even to watch the games sometimes.

My heart's still in New York, no matter how many years go by. And if I had a nickel for everyone who's said to me, "It isn't the same around here without you," I'd have a lot more money than I have now.

Don Chaney: Not having him [McDyess] hurt a lot. What he brings is what this team has always needed since Patrick was traded: a low-post presence. And with the players we have on the perimeter, you've gotta have a guy you can throw the ball to inside and let the shooters play and feed off him. That's why we miss Larry; when Larry was here we did the same thing, and Patrick. Without McDyess, our guards are the guys that have to carry us, and they've been carrying us so far. And what I especially like about McDyess is that, defensively, he can guard guys in the low post. We don't have to double Tim Duncan. With McDyess we can play him one-on-one.

Despite the McDyess injury, the 2002–03 Knicks registered a seven-win increase over the prior season, and their overall quality of play was vastly improved compared to the horrific second half of 2001–02. They were able to stay in the postseason hunt until the final weeks behind the performances of Houston, who produced his best season including two 50-plus scoring games; Sprewell; a vastly improved Kurt Thomas and Howard Eisley; and Ward, who with the trade of Ewing became the senior Knick. Along with the NHL Rangers and the WNBA Liberty, the Knicks moved into a new, 105,000-square-foot, state-of-the-art training facility in suburban Tarrytown, three decades and light-years removed from the wooden backboards of Lost Battalion Hall.

Steve Mills: The training center was really important to us. What we were doing before was just so inconsistent with what you'd think of when you think of the New York Knicks, the New York Rangers, and Madison Square Garden. To think that the Rangers were practicing on a rink that wasn't regulation size and the Knicks were practicing in a facility that didn't have air conditioning and you might not be able to practice at a certain time because there was a circus camp going on . . . Those kinds of things were just inconsistent with the commitment we've made financially to the players and what our objectives as an organization are.

The training center works for us on a lot of levels. It's the right kind of atmosphere for our athletes to train in, and it's going to allow the players to bond better. One of the challenges of playing in New York, unlike other cities, is that all the players are scattered around and none of them really live in the city. In a lot of other cities, all the guys live 15 minutes from downtown. Now with the training center they get a chance to spend more time together. We have a place to eat, so they eat meals together. We have a place where they can hang out and play pool or play video games, get on a computer terminal, or just hang together. And that's a big part of team chemistry.

Don Chaney: I grew up in the system in Boston, and I believe in it. I believe in up-tempo. I believe in easy baskets. I believe in the three-point shot. To me, that was the biggest challenge I had: to get our players to play a little more loose, to get them to run a little bit more. I wanted more movement, and you've got to have certain players who buy into that, and you also have to have players who are comfortable in that style.

Steve Mills: He [Chaney] is a unique guy. He's proven that you can succeed at a lot of different levels: as a player, as Coach of the Year. He's proven he can succeed at this level. He's got a tremendous amount of character and clearly understands the game and understands how players think and how to motivate them.

Don Chaney: We've sort of found our little niche now in that our guys are not afraid to take shots; they're not afraid to do things on the floor. I don't want them looking at me every time down the floor to have a play called. I don't want that. I want them to get down the floor and be into the game mentally. Sometimes that backfires on you, and sometimes it doesn't. The philosophy is not that different in terms of what it takes to win. I think you have to play defense to win.

Steve Mills: This year, again, he was dealt a very difficult hand when Antonio McDyess went down.

Sprewell's ferocity was a Knicks trademark in the post-Ewing years.

But I think the way the team has stayed in there demonstrates their confidence in him and his ability to design a system that works for the team we have.

Don Chaney: The biggest change from Jeff's system to mine is that Jeff liked to pack in the lane, take away the drive, and give them the outside shot. My system is to let the bigs stop the drive in the middle and the smalls get out to cover the three-point shots. I truly believe that with the shooters we have now, we lost a lot of games where we compacted the lane and they kicked it to the perimeter. I saw it happen too often. So I try to let our bigs step out, sort of what [Bill] Russell did when I played. He protected the basket. The smalls gotta protect the perimeter. That, to me, was the biggest defensive change we had.

Jeff Van Gundy: Charlie Ward has always been one of the most underrated Knicks. All he's done, ever since he's been in the rotation, is win and make big plays and big shots. He's a very quiet, religious guy. But on the court he's the toughest competitor you could ever have.

Charlie Ward: I'd been playing football for a long time. Even though I was a quarterback, contact was something I enjoyed. I work on my body during the course of the summer to prepare for those things. I think a lot of it is that you see the sacrifice, trying to do whatever it takes to help the team win. That's what I do. Some other guys may not do it as frequently, but there are things that I don't do as frequently as them. But that's what I do; I haven't changed. Now it's more selective. I used to hit the floor a lot. It's more of a selective-type thing now, because my body's getting a little older. But it's still the same mentality and mind-set.

Don Chaney: Charlie is pound for pound the toughest player on our team. What I admire about Charlie more than anything is that when days get tough and it seems like everything is going against you, Charlie rises to the top. He's the guy that you want in the trenches with you, because he battles. Some guys carry you to that point, but when it gets to the nitty-gritty, you can't find them. Charlie is one of the guys who always surfaces. He hits big shots. He's not a great shooter, but he hits big shots. He'll make a big steal. He'll take a big charge. If he has to foul a bigger guy, he'll make the hardest foul. He's a big-play player late in games. He does something to get you a win.

Charlie Ward: Never thought it [being the senior Knick] would ever happen, but then I never thought I'd be in New York, either. You never know what the Lord has in store for you. You just have to roll with the punches and enjoy the time you have here. It may not ever happen again. But it's been nine great years, with all the trials and tribulations and great times I've had here.

Don Chaney: I admire his sacrifices. This year [2002–03], when he got hurt, he lost his starting job. My philosophy is that you don't lose your starting job because of an injury. I was going to give him his starting job back, but I went to him and said, "Charlie, I like the fact that you're coming out with our second unit. We need your defense and leadership in there, and I'd like to keep Howard [Eisley] in the starting lineup and bring you off the bench." And I said that if he wasn't comfortable with that, I'd start him. He said, "For the sake of the team, I'll do whatever it takes to win." And he didn't step back from that for one moment.

Kurt Thomas: I just finally got the opportunity to shoot the ball. I felt that I always could have put these numbers up, but I've had other guys in front of me who were at the peaks of their careers, and I just, basically, had to wait my turn. That's one thing Bob McAdoo always told me from my rookie year in Miami. He said that whenever that opportunity comes, you have to take advantage of it. So whenever somebody gives me an opportunity, I'm going to take advantage of it.

Don Chaney: Kurt is a guy who came out of college with a definite shooting skill. He was a scorer. What he needed was the confidence of a coach that he was gonna make all the right plays. To me, he's one of our most consistent guys in terms of doing what he does best: he's our best team rotator; he's our best team defender in terms of being in the right spot at the right time, leading the defense, things like that. He finds a way to get involved. And he's playing out of position. He's a four playing at the five.

Kurt Thomas: I really don't know if I would have moved over [to power forward had McDyess been healthy]. He might have been at the four. It would have all depended on the matchups, which vary from game to game. But you have Allan and Sprewell, and then you have a guy like McDyess who can play inside and out, and myself who can also play inside and out. And if I play outside, I can pull the centers away from the goal. It would have been a nice one-two punch with me and McDyess inside and Allan and Spree outside.

Don Chaney: I dream about this all the time. Having both McDyess and Thomas up front changes the whole structure of the team. Now Kurt would be in his natural position, and with McDyess there, both guys can defend. It gives Kurt a lot of flexibility as a big, so that if McDyess is double-teamed we have another shooter who can knock a shot down.

Kurt Thomas: I really thought that I was gonna be here just for a year or two and then probably wind up moving on. That was just my gut instinct from the very beginning. But, coming to New York has been wonderful. Me being from Texas, I really didn't like New York when I first came here. So many people, so fast-paced. It took me a while to get used to, since I'm a country boy from Dallas. But now I love New York.

Latrell Sprewell: [When I was going to leave Golden State] it was either New York, Miami, or Indiana. If you look back, and if you put me on any one of those teams, you never know. If it had been Miami, I don't know if we [New York] would have advanced there. If it had been Indiana, I don't know if we would have done good things in the [East] Finals or not. It's one of those things you just kind of wonder about. For me, I was always comfortable in my decision. Obviously, I love New York. I always wanted to play with a great center like Patrick. For me, it was the right decision. I don't know if things would have been any different, better or worse, if I had gone to Miami or Indiana. It was down to those three teams, and they were one-two-three in the East, when you look at it.

I just give an honest opinion, and sometimes people take that and twist it and manipulate it into something else. I just try to shoot straight, and a lot of times that's probably not always the smart thing to do. When you're in New York and you have 8 or 10 guys competing for a story, sometimes your words get a little twisted around. I've learned to be careful in what I say and at the same time try to be honest with people.

It was up in the air as to how people were going to accept me. They embraced me from the first day. I think that was one reason I was able to come here [to New York] and feel so comfortable and be able to play as well as I've played. A lot of times, even when I wasn't playing well, I fed off the fans' energy and I knew they were gonna be supportive. That's one reason I always say that there's no better place to play, because the fans are so knowledgeable. They understand the game, and when you play hard and play the right way, they definitely show you their appreciation. And when you play the wrong way, they definitely let you know you're not doing your job. It's a tough place to play because of a lot of different things, but when you're winning, there's no better place.

[*Editor's note:* Latrell Sprewell was part of a four-way trade on July 23, 2003, that sent him to the Minnesota Timberwolves. The Knicks received Keith Van Horn from the Philadelphia 76ers.]

Don Chaney: Allan is under a lot of pressure because of his contract. With the numbers that he's getting, financially, people expect him to be Michael Jordan. He's not Michael Jordan. What I admire about Allan more than anything is that, all those negative comments aside, with all the questions about his game and the money, he's been very consistent. He's elevated his average. He's hit big shots for us. He's stepped up in his own way to make this team better. Late in the game, he's the only guy on our team that I feel comfortable taking the last shot in a game and making it.

He has a star's mentality in that he's willing to face the consequences if he doesn't come through. A lot of guys are fearful of that. They don't want to be failures. They don't want to be the goat. It doesn't bother him. And this has been quietly kept, but he's become a much better defender. He's really improved his defense.

Still, in an Eastern Conference that produced only one 50-win team (Detroit), the Knicks failed to make the playoffs for the second straight year. With McDyess' playing status still uncertain, with their 10-year sellout streak ending at 433, and working around a $93 million payroll, the Knicks–now clearly the Don Chaney Knicks–faced the future.

Steve Mills: The challenge that faces us is sticking with a plan. And that's sometimes as hard to do in a market where there's so much media attention and so much revenue that comes in from ticket sales and things like that. But I firmly believe that the fans will support you as you retool your team. The sense that New Yorkers will only support you if you're winning right now, I don't buy that. We have to accept and believe that New Yorkers will stick with us, and we'll give them reasons to stick with us as we sort of retool.

Scott Layden: Our fans are aware. We do season-ticket holder functions, where I'll do a Q&A with 50 or 60 of our season-ticket holders. And the fans are right on top of it. Our season-ticket holders know details about the team that are incredible. They know about the injury exception. They know when it expires and what we can use it for. To me, that's great. That's why this is where you want to be.

Steve Mills: We have to embrace youth. In the old days of a salary cap without a luxury tax, we didn't necessarily have to do that. But in today's NBA, you have to embrace youth, and you have to embrace international players. We haven't been forced to do that in the past, but those are things we have to stick with and make sure they're a part of our plan. Also, to have players we feel good about as people, who have a great deal of character. And if we do those things, we'll be fine and we'll get this team back to the level it should be.

Don Chaney: Any coach who spends time in the league, you get better with each game you coach. I've learned over the years to feed off my players. You read them, know what their strengths are, and gear your offense and defense according to their limitations. As a young coach, I wanted players to do things they weren't capable of doing. I expected too much from them. You have to gear your coaching philosophy according to the talent you have. If you have a lot of good athletes, you run more and play an athletic-type game. If you don't have that, it's hard to do.

Steve Mills: I realize every day how important this team is to this city, because you can't go any-place and not see it. Now that more people know

who I am, I have people asking me if they can play center for us. Or you might go to a press conference and there may be a lot of questions about a lot of different things, but the mayor may have to come back to a question that someone has asked about what the impact of the Knicks not doing well is having on the city. Those kinds of things make you realize how important this team is.

Don Chaney: I've also learned to show a lot of tolerance for players in terms of their faults. You can't overreact to guys making mistakes. I've learned communication with players, and I didn't have that early on. I didn't have the skill. And this is what I didn't get earlier: even when things are going well, that's the time to communicate and talk to guys, and not just your starters but the other guys as well. They have to be happy and accept their roles. That's something I didn't have before. I'd meet with a player when there was trouble, but I never constantly kept that touch.

Steve Mills: We're all competitive, and we all want to be successful. But this is about the Knicks and about how we can continue to build on this tradition and make it better. We're not just looking at getting it back to making the playoffs 15 years in a row. We're hoping to get it to the point where we can win another championship.

Scott Layden: Now, do you have some tough days? Are you under scrutiny? Are there times where it's not pleasant? Certainly. But that's what makes it great. That's why there's a charge [for you] to get up and go to work every day. It's exhilarating, it really is.

Steve Mills: There's a letter in my desk that I'll save for a long time. Someone wrote me and said they had season tickets to the Knicks and Rangers for 20 years. And [it said] that if we didn't fix this thing, if we don't get these two teams right, your name will be associated with the worst decade in the history of the Knicks and Rangers. So I've saved that, because to me that's telling me how important this team and this building is to people in this city, and the obligation that we have to continue a tradition of winning and having a team that New Yorkers feel represents them.

Veteran mentor Don Chaney (left) took
over as head coach following Van Gundy's
resignation, piloting a Knicks squad on
which Charlie Ward (right) was the senior
member after Ewing was traded.